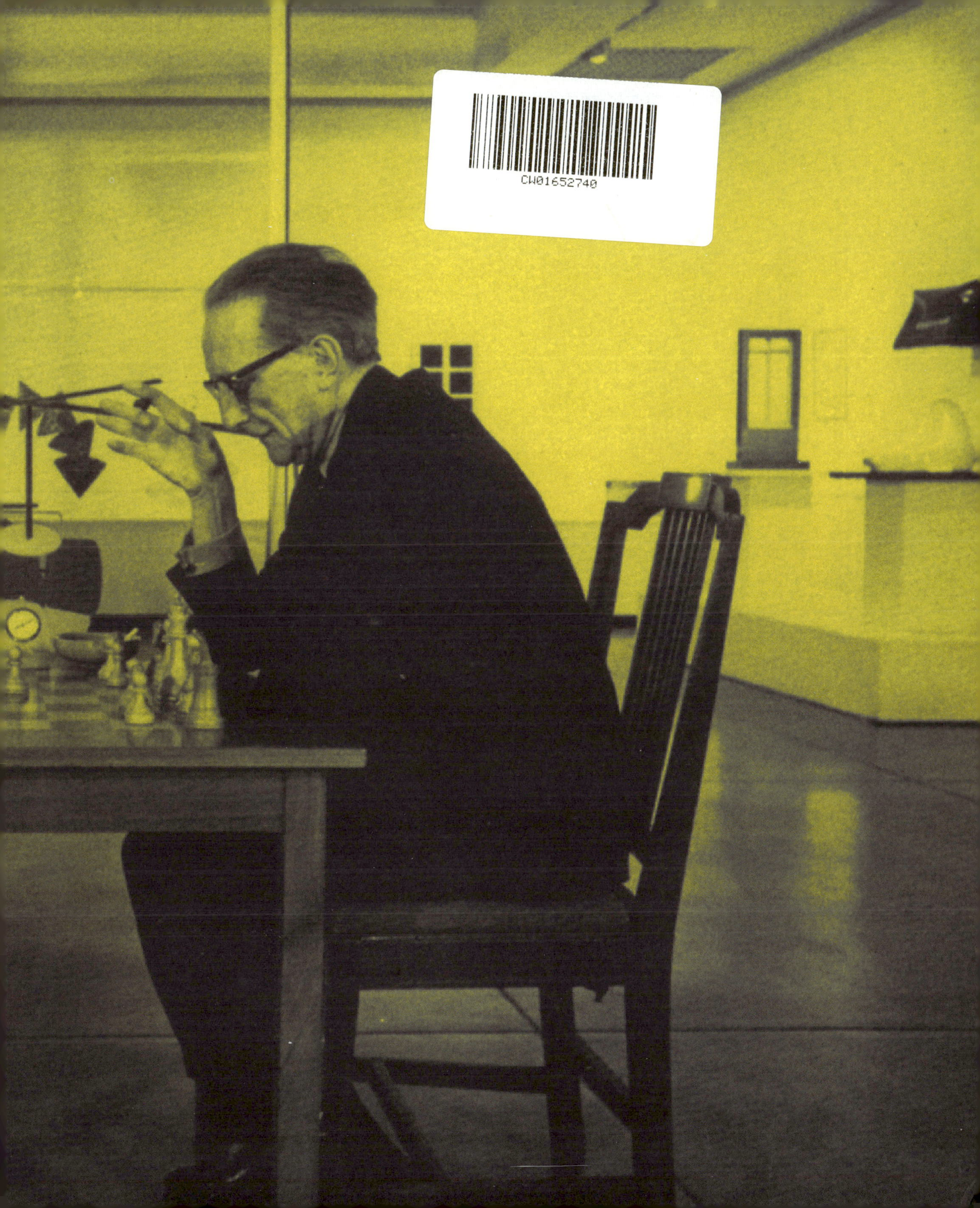

FROM DI
VERSION
TO SUB
VERSION

FROM DIVERSION TO SUBVERSION

Games, Play, and Twentieth-Century Art

Edited by David J. Getsy

The Pennsylvania State University Press
University Park, Pennsylvania

CONTENTS

ILLUSTRATIONS

1 Marcel Duchamp, *Comb,* 1916, steel, $1\frac{1}{4} \times 6\frac{1}{2}$ inches (3.2 × 16.5 cm). Philadelphia Museum of Art, The Louise and Walter Arensberg Collection, 1950. © 2009. Photo: The Philadelphia Museum of Art / Art Resource / Scala, Florence. © Succession Marcel Duchamp / ADAGP, Paris, and DACS, London, 2009.

2 Marcel Duchamp, *The,* 1915. Philadelphia Museum of Art, The Louise and Walter Arensberg Collection, 1950. © Succession Marcel Duchamp / ADAGP, Paris, and DACS, London, 2009.

3 Marcel Duchamp, *Rendez-vous du Dimanche 6 Février 1916,* 1916, typewriter and ink on four postcards, with tape, $11\frac{1}{4} \times 6\frac{1}{2}$ inches. Philadelphia Museum of Art, The Louise and Walter Arensberg Collection, 1950. © Succession Marcel Duchamp / ADAGP, Paris, and DACS, London, 2009.

4 Marcel Duchamp, *With Hidden Noise,* 1916, string, brass, screws, and unknown material, 12.9 × 13 × 11.4 cm. Philadelphia Museum of Art, The Louise and Walter Arensberg Collection, 1950. © Succession Marcel Duchamp / ADAGP, Paris, and DACS, London, 2009.

5 Marcel Duchamp, *Apolinère Enameled,* 1916–17, gouache and pencil on painted tin, mounted on board, 24.4 × 33.9 cm. Philadelphia Museum of Art, The Louise and Walter Arensberg Collection, 1950. © Succession Marcel Duchamp / ADAGP, Paris, and DACS, London, 2009.

6 Marcel Duchamp, *Why Not Sneeze Rose Sélavy?* 1921, painted metal birdcage, marble cubes, porcelain dish, thermometer, and cuttlebone, $4\frac{7}{8} \times 8\frac{3}{4} \times 6\frac{3}{8}$ inches (12.4 × 22.2 × 16.2 cm). Philadelphia Museum of Art, The Louise and Walter Arensberg Collection, 1950. © 2004. Photo: The Philadelphia Museum of Art / Art Resource / Scala, Florence. © Succession Marcel Duchamp / ADAGP, Paris, and DACS, London, 2009.

7 Marcel Duchamp, *The Bride Stripped Bare by Her Bachelors, Even (The Large Glass),* 1915–23, oil varnish, lead foil, lead wire, and dust on two glass panels, $109\frac{1}{4} \times 69\frac{1}{4}$ inches (277.5 × 175.9 cm). Philadelphia Museum of Art, Bequest of Katherine S. Dreier, 1952. © 2004. Photo: The Philadelphia Museum of Art / Art Resource / Scala, Florence. © Succession Marcel Duchamp / ADAGP, Paris, and DACS, London, 2009.

8 László Moholy-Nagy, *Portrait,* c. 1925. Private collection, California. © 2009 Artists Rights Society (ARS), New York / VG Bild-Kunst, Bonn.

9 László Moholy-Nagy, *Negative,* c. 1927. Private collection, Pace / MacGill, New York. © 2009 Artists Rights Society (ARS), New York / VG Bild-Kunst, Bonn.

10 László Moholy-Nagy, *Dessau,* 1926–28. The Museum of Fine Arts, Houston, Gift of the Prospero Foundation. © 2009 Artists Rights Society (ARS), New York / VG Bild-Kunst, Bonn.

11 László Moholy-Nagy, *Bauhaus Balconies,* 1926. Courtesy of George Eastman House, International Museum of Photography and Film. © 2009 Artists Rights Society (ARS), New York / VG Bild-Kunst, Bonn.

12 T. Lux Feininger, *Human Elements in Architecture,* c. 1928. The Metropolitan Museum of Art, Ford Motor Company Collection, Gift of The Ford Motor Company and John C. Waddell, 1987 (1987.1100.413). Copy photograph © The Metropolitan Museum of Art, New York.

13 Edmund Collein, *Extension to the Prellerhaus,* 1928. Bauhaus Archive, Berlin.

14 T. Lux Feininger, *Jump over the Bauhaus,* c. 1927. Bauhaus Archive, Berlin. Courtesy of the artist.

15 "Cartes d'Analogie" (*Cartes d'Analogie*), 1959, from *Le Surréalisme même,* no. 5 (Spring 1959): 21.

16 Joan Miró, Man Ray, Yves Tanguy, and Max Morise, "Exquisite Corpse" *(Cadavre exquis),* 1927. Private collection, Paris. Photo credit: Snark / Art Resource, New York.

17A "Marseille Game" *(Jeu de Marseille),* 1940–41, from *V.V.V.,* nos. 2–3 (March 1943). Court cards by Brauner, Breton, Dominguez, Ernst, Herold, Lam, Lamba, and Masson. Redrawn for publication by Robert Delanglade. Courtesy of Special Collections, Department of Archives and Manuscripts, University Libraries, Arizona State University, Tempe.

17B "Marseille Game" *(Jeu de Marseille),* 1940–41, from *V.V.V.,* nos. 2–3 (March 1943). Court cards by Brauner, Breton, Dominguez, Ernst, Herold, Lam, Lamba, and Masson. Redrawn for publication by Robert Delanglade. Courtesy of Special Collections, Department of Archives and Manuscripts, University Libraries, Arizona State University, Tempe.

18 Marcel Duchamp and Eve Babitz at the Pasadena Art Museum during Duchamp's retrospective exhibition. Photograph © 1963 Julian Wasser. All rights reserved.

19 Joseph Cornell, *Untitled (Forgotten Game),* c. 1949, box construction, $21\frac{1}{8} \times 15\frac{1}{2} \times 3\frac{7}{8}$ inches. Lindy and Edwin Bergman Joseph Cornell Collection, 1982.1852. Reproduction, The Art Institute of Chicago. Art © The Joseph and Robert Cornell Memorial Foundation / Licensed by VAGA, New York.

20 Joseph Cornell, *Untitled (Penny Arcade Portrait of Lauren Bacall),* 1945–46. Bergman Collection. Courtesy Bergman Collection. Art © The Joseph and Robert Cornell Memorial Foundation / Licensed by VAGA, New York.

21 Pablo Picasso, Relief 1: *Bather and Profile* [*Baigneuse et profil*], Juan-les-Pins, August 14, 1930, sand on back of a canvas and stretcher, cardboard and plants, 27 × 35 × 3 cm. Musée Picasso, Paris. Photo: Réunion des Musées Nationaux / Art Resource, New York. © 2011 Estate of Pablo Picasso / Artists Rights Society (ARS), New York.

22 Pablo Picasso, Relief 2: *Face with Two Profiles* [*Visage aux deux profiles*], Juan-les-Pins, August 14, 1930, sand on back of canvas and stretcher, cardboard pasted and sewn onto canvas; sand partially painted, 41 × 33 × 1.5 cm. Musée Picasso, Paris. Photo: Réunion des Musées Nationaux / Art Resource, New York. © 2011 Estate of Pablo Picasso / Artists Rights Society (ARS), New York.

23 Pablo Picasso, Relief 3: *Standing Bather* [*Baigneuse debout*], Juan-les-Pins, August 14, 1930, sand on back of canvas and stretcher, cardboard and plants sewn onto canvas, 33 × 24.5 × 2 cm. Musée Picasso, Paris. Photo: Réunion des Musées Nationaux / Art Resource, New York. © 2011 Estate of Pablo Picasso / Artists Rights Society (ARS), New York.

24 Pablo Picasso, Relief 4: *Reclining bather* [*Baigneuse couchée*], Juan-les-Pins, August 20, 1930, objects, string, and cardboard sewn and glued to back of canvas stretcher and coated with sand, sand partially painted, 24 × 35 × 2 cm. Musée Picasso, Paris. Photo: Réunion des Musées Nationaux / Art Resource, New York. © 2011 Estate of Pablo Picasso / Artists Rights Society (ARS), New York.

25 Pablo Picasso, Relief 5: *Composition* [*Composition*], Juan-les-Pins, August 21, 1930, sand on canvas, wood and plants sewn and glued to canvas, 35 × 27.5 × 3 cm. Musée Picasso, Paris. Photo: Réunion des Musées Nationaux / Art Resource, New York. © 2011 Estate of Pablo Picasso / Artists Rights Society (ARS), New York.

26 Pablo Picasso, Relief 6: *Composition with Glove / Construction with Glove* [*Composition au gant*], Juan-les-Pins, August 22, 1930, glove, cardboard, and plants sewn and glued to back of canvas stretcher and coated with sand, sand partially painted, 27.5 × 35.5 × 8 cm. Musée Picasso, Paris. Photo: Réunion des Musées Nationaux / Art Resource, New York. © 2011 Estate of Pablo Picasso / Artists Rights Society (ARS), New York.

27 Pablo Picasso, Relief 7: *Object with Palm Leaf* [*Objet à la feuille de palmier*], Juan-les-Pins, August 27, 1930, cardboard, plants, nails, and objects sewn and glued to back of canvas stretcher and coated with sand, sand partially painted, 25 × 33 00 4.5 cm. Musée Picasso, Paris. Photo: Réunion des Musées Nationaux / Art Resource, New York. © 2011 Estate of Pablo Picasso / Artists Rights Society (ARS), New York.

28 Pablo Picasso, Relief 8: *Landscape with Boats* [*Paysage aux bateaux*], Juan-les-Pins, August 28, 1930, plants, cardboard, and two toy ships sewn and glued to back of canvas stretcher and coated with sand, sand partially painted, 26.5 × 36 × 7 cm. Musée Picasso, Paris. Photo: Réunion des Musées Nationaux / Art Resource, New York. © 2011 Estate of Pablo Picasso / Artists Rights Society (ARS), New York.

39 Marcel Duchamp, *Etant donnés: 1 La Chute d'eau, 2 Le Gaz d'éclairage,* 1946–66, mixed-media assemblage, 95½ × 70 inches. Philadelphia Museum of Art, Gift of the Cassandra Foundation, 1969. Copyright 2009 Artists Rights Society (ARS), New York / ADAGP, Paris / Succession Marcel Duchamp.

40 Hannah Wilke, *Wedges of . . . ,* 1992, two lead alloy radiation blocks, 3 × 6½ × 6 inches. Courtesy Donald and Helen Goddard and Ronald Feldman Fine Arts, New York. Photo: Dennis Cowley.

41 Hannah Wilke, *Why Not Sneeze?* 1992, wire birdcage, medicine bottles, and syringes, 7 × 9 × 6⅞ inches. Courtesy Donald and Helen Goddard and Ronald Feldman Fine Arts, New York. Photo: Dennis Cowley.

42 *Intra-Venus Series No. 1 June 15, 1992 / January 30, 1992,* 1992, one of two panels, 71½ × 47½ inches, Chromagenic supergloss. Performalist Self-Portrait with Donald Goddard. Courtesy Donald and Helen Goddard and Ronald Feldman Fine Arts, New York.

43 George Maciunas, *Fluxus (Its Historical Development and Relationship to Avant-Garde Movements),* Fluxus Editions, c. 1965. Image courtesy of the Intermedia Collection, University of Maine. Photo: Krista Molnar-Smith.

44 Mieko Shiomi, *Shadow Piece,* 1963, night street performance, Nagoya, Japan, May 2002. Photo courtesy of the author.

45 Fluxus, *Fluxshop / Fluxorchestra Flyer* with *Fluxmanifesto* (detail), designed by George Maciunas, 1965. Image courtesy of the Intermedia Collection, University of Maine. Photo: Krista Molnar-Smith.

46 Dick Higgins, *Piano Sonata #2 (Graphis #192),* 1982. Printed Editions, Barrytown, New York. Courtesy the Estate of Dick Higgins.

47 Dick Higgins, *Five Traditions of Art History,* 1976. Courtesy the Estate of Dick Higgins.

48 *Vaseline sTREEt,* Fluxnewspaper No. 8, May 1966, edited and designed by George Maciunas, 1965. Image courtesy of the Intermedia Collection, University of Maine. Photo: Krista Molnar-Smith.

49 Dick Higgins, *Sonata for Prepared Piano,* third movement, 1982. Printed Editions, Barrytown, New York. Courtesy the Estate of Dick Higgins.

50 Dick Higgins, *Homage à François Villon* (1988), Edition Conz, 1990. Image courtesy of the Intermedia Collection, University of Maine. Photo: Krista Molnar-Smith.

51 Liliana Porter, still from *The Fox in the Mirror, Concert / El zorro en el espejo, concierto,* 2007, video, twenty minutes. Courtesy of the artist.

52 Liliana Porter, *The End of the Journey,* 1980, silkscreen, etching, and chine collé, 25.5 × 38 inches. Courtesy of the artist.

53 Liliana Porter, *The Simulacrum II,* 1992, acrylic, silkscreen, and collage on paper. Collection Yolanda Santos Garza, New York. Courtesy of the artist.

54 Liliana Porter, *Dialogues (with Petrus Christus Postcard),* 1995, silver gelatin prints, 11 × 14 inches each, triptych. Courtesy of the artist.

55 Liliana Porter, *Death Threat,* 1995, Cibachrome print, 16-inch diameter. Courtesy of the artist.

56A Liliana Porter, still from *The Fox in the Mirror, Concert / El zorro en el espejo, concierto,* 2007, video, twenty minutes. Courtesy of the artist.

56B Liliana Porter, still from *The Fox in the Mirror, Concert / El zorro en el espejo, concierto,* 2007, video, twenty minutes. Courtesy of the artist.

57 Blast Theory, *Can You See Me Now?* Collaboration with Mixed Reality Lab, University of Nottingham, first manifestation 2001, Sheffield (detail of play). Copyright: Blast Theory.

58 Rene Hayashi, images from projects in Indonesia.

59 Gazira Babeli, *Grey Goo,* 2006, still from hack of *Second Life.* Image courtesy Gazira Babeli.

60 Anne-Marie Schleiner, *OUT,* New York, still.

61 Anne-Marie Schleiner and Talice Lee, *Riot Gear for Rollartista,* Manchester, 2007.

62 Chris Reilly, screen shot from *Everything I Do is Art, But Nothing I Do Makes Any Difference,* 2005–6.

63 René Magritte, *Key of Dreams,* 1930, oil on canvas, 81 × 60 cm. Private collection. Photo: Banque d'Images, ADAGP / Art Resource, New York.

64 Ellen Brooks, *Untitled (Red Stairs),* 1998, mixed media. Courtesy of the artist.

65 Ellen Brooks, *Untitled (Outside / Cardboard),* 1999, mixed media. Courtesy of the artist.

INTRODUCTION

DAVID J. GETSY

The story of art in the twentieth century has often been told as one of sustained, serious research. Commentators and advocates of modern art have likened its rapid changes and successive innovations to the scientific method and its testing of hypotheses. The analogy to the hard sciences is not accidental, and this rhetorical move aimed to justify modern and contemporary art as a specialized discipline, building evermore upon its own gains. Such narratives of art as research nevertheless rely upon multiple exclusions and scotomata. While there no doubt have been artists who understood their practice as informed by something like the scientific method, there are many more who have willfully pursued less punctilious ways of making art. An often-quoted statement by Pablo Picasso makes just such a case: "I can hardly understand the importance given to the word *research* in connection with modern painting. In my opinion to search means nothing in painting. To find, is the thing.... Among the several sins that I have been accused of committing, none is more false than the one that I have, as the principal objective in my work, the spirit of research. When I paint, my object is to show what I have found and not what I am looking for."[1] Underneath the brashness of Picasso's sweeping comments is a resistance to just such a goal-driven and teleological way of thinking as that which emerged in the narratives of the history of modern art (many of which continue to give Picasso himself a starring role). For Picasso, "research" assumed that one knew what one was looking for and was merely finding the way to get there appropriately—that is, a predetermined hypothesis to be proven valid or invalid. By contrast, Picasso emphasized nondirectedness, chance, and exploration as ways of proceeding.

This collection of essays takes up these very themes in twentieth-century art history: the nonserious, the playful, and the exploratory. It will do this through a focus on games and play, both of which are often sidelined in the narratives of modern art as earnest research.[2] By contrast, the essays in this volume take seriously the supposed non-seriousness of games and play, showing how they contribute to and complicate the narratives of modern art and how they served as sites of creativity and criticality. Games are, at base, representational activities, and artists and critics saw the game as an analogue to art practice, a metaphor for creativity, or a model for art criticism. This collection does not aim to be a comprehensive survey of the many and varied instances in which artists and critics explored games and ludic activities. Rather, it brings together a group of studies of key moments in the history of twentieth-century art as a means of indicating the diversity of issues at play in play. Similarly, the essays have not been organized around singular definitions of either games or play. Rather, their deployments of often divergent ways of characterizing these terms are indicative of the diversity of frameworks for dealing with the ludic, as I discuss below. Collectively, however, the essays in this volume point to the complexity of games and of play, demonstrating some of their central and recurring uses for art in the twentieth century.

The impetus for this collection derived from the burgeoning field of Game Studies, itself fueled by the recent expansion of video, computer, and online games as focal points in contemporary culture.[3] With the growth of the mainstream video-game industry and the simultaneous proliferation of alternate practices that deploy the tactics and technologies of video games for cultural critique or activism, games have emerged as a major topic for scholarly inquiry.[4] The examination of games is of course not itself new, and it has been a long-running site of inquiry for such fields as philosophy, mathematics, psychology, and anthropology. However, when the video-game industry began to outpace the major motion picture industry in revenue and production values, the scholarly foundations of Game Studies in these disciplines were remined and reinvigorated. Drawing on the burgeoning literature and methodology that seek to analyze these developments, the essays discuss the ways in which artists imposed rules of play on their work or sought out games or play as possible means to refine or complicate art theories and practices.

Games are notoriously difficult to define, and much of the literature has focused on questions of taxonomy.[5] This is the case with the foundational text in Game Studies, Johan Huizinga's *Homo Ludens* (1938), and its primary interlocutory text, Roger Caillois's *Man, Play, and Games* (1958).[6] It has become conventional in the literature of Game Studies to rehearse and to refine the ways in which one recognizes and categorizes games, usually with reference to these two texts, which are cited as authoritative justifications for the attention to games or play in the first place. Claudia Mesch's essay in this volume provides a thorough critical overview of the positions of Huizinga and Caillois, discussing in particular the important affinities with Surrealist art practices. In contrast to the historical specificity of Mesch's essay, these two foundational texts and their taxonomies have often been uncritically excerpted and appropriated without reference to the historiographic and (as Mesch urges) political situations of their authors. Accordingly, in this introduction, I will not yet again restate Huizinga's or Caillois's well-worn categories, though their terms are registered at different points in this volume. I demur out of a belief that the taxonomic urge that has underwritten the development of the field of Game Studies often distracts attention from the actual deployment of games and inadvertently shuts down their complexity and polyvalence.[7] That is, the task of taxonomy in many respects is bound to fail with regard to a topic like games, which mutate and morph depending on who plays them, when they are played, where they are played, and why they are played.

Ludwig Wittgenstein, who famously used games as a core concept, proposed a different way forward. However, he argued that there was no essential or single definition of games possible. He wrote:

> **And we can go through the many, many other groups of games in the same way; we can see how similarities crop up and disappear. And the result of this examination is: we see a complicated network of similarities overlapping and criss-crossing: sometimes overall similarities. I can think of no better expression to characterize these similarities than "family resemblances"; for the various resemblances between members of a family: build, features, colour of eyes, gait, temperament, etc. etc. overlap and criss-cross in the same way.—And I shall say: "games" form a family.[8]**

Wittgenstein's concept of "family resemblances" moves beyond the search for an essential definition, pointing to the ways that a definition of a group can be recognized even when there is no single trait shared by all its parts (but providing there is at least a degree of shared traits with others in the same group). This is useful not only in the study of games but also as a warning about relying on stable taxonomies, themselves purporting to be created through scientific methods but, ultimately, relying on subjective distinctions.

A commonly held concept across the divergent accounts of games and their family resemblances, however, is that games are such important cultural and developmental activities because they provide a surrogate arena for interactivity and absorption. Play occurs in the alternate zone established through the parameters of the game, and players identify with and project themselves into this game space, regardless of the degree of verisimilitude of the game or the formality of the rules that make it up. This also holds true in spontaneous, free play outside of traditional games, and Huizinga identifies the play element in multiple facets of human existence. His major contribution was to argue that the centrality of games and play to cultural life derived from the "temporary worlds within the ordinary world, dedicated to the performance of an act apart" created through them.[9] Being "caught up" in a game is the result of the players' psychological immersion in that temporary world apart and of their resultant fueling of identification with its constituents. From a game of chess, to a soccer match, to less formal (but no less engaging) games that sometimes emerge in social interactions (office politics, public flirtation, and so on), participants' heightened engagement becomes possible because of this bracketing within the normal and the everyday of an alternate time and space of game/play in which they can and do act and identify differently and more intensely.

"Play" refers to the participants' immersion in this temporary world, be it a formal game with explicit rules or moments of virtual behavior in the mundane.[10] In this sense, play is a more expansive category—an activity that can interrupt conventional ways of acting.[11] Play can occur spontaneously and outside of clearly defined games. Nonce games, ad hoc contests or collaborations, and performances of virtuality (the "what if?" moment of pretending) are all forms of play that erupt into the everyday. Such ludic behavior is enabled by the ostensible nonseriousness that is bracketed off from the exigencies of the mundane. One is "just playing" when one's activities do not resemble what one would or should normally do. As with games, this is not to say that play does not have real outcomes and repercussions into the mundane. Quite the contrary, play activities such as flirtation, mock fighting, imitation, or parody can at times fundamentally reorder the social relations that they are supposedly apart from. Furthermore, play and games can also provide critical reflection on actual events and situations.[12] It is this potential that has made play a central tool in the critical aims of performance art, for instance. Play's capacity for diversion from the everyday—both in the sense of a light distraction from the mundane as well as a skewed push away from it—also enables its potential for subversion and critique. Accordingly, the liminality of play and its potential for acting and being otherwise, if even temporarily, has made it a powerful metaphor for artistic creation and for the aesthetic encounter. In the first chapter, Susan Laxton provides an overview of play's importance in aesthetics and in conceptions of the avant-garde, and this is a theme that is tracked throughout the book.[13]

Much attention has been given to the importance of play as the foundational creative activity in early child development, and many of the studies of play and games have followed Huizinga in positing play as a central aspect of human relations. The work of Brian Sutton-Smith, in particular, has been central in anthropological and developmental studies of the cultural relevance of play and games.[14] From many quarters, play has been taken up as a core metaphor for the complexity of cultural production.[15] Perhaps the most useful and long-running discussion of the importance of play has been that of the British Object Relations psychoanalyst D. W. Winnicott. Building upon the important work of Melanie Klein's focus on children and her development of the "play technique," Winnicott developed an extensive analysis of the importance of play as a means to understand not just children's experience but also that of adulthood.[16] For Winnicott, play was important because it afforded the opportunity to break down the distinction between self and world for a time. He based his ideas on a revised account of early childhood development, shifting emphasis from Freud's focus on the Oedipal to the development of subject-object relations more generally. The infant, he believed, underwent a process in which the self was differentiated from the world, allowing the slow process of recognizing other subjects.[17] He used the term "transitional space" (sometimes "potential space" with reference to adults) to discuss the position of the infant who still has a porous relation between self and world, between the awareness of itself as a subject in a field of objects and other subjects.

This is significant for play and, Winnicott would go on to argue, cultural and aesthetic experience more generally because it was the position of this "potential space" that the playing child or adult temporarily reinhabited.[18] Children's ability to remake everyday objects into tools of their imagination assumes a lack of distinction between subjective intentionality and the objective environment. In the most direct terms, the cardboard box becomes the spaceship, and so on. For adults, Winnicott argued that it was in the experience of creativity and in the aesthetic encounter through which the "potential space" could be temporarily reaccessed. He used as his example being immersed in the experience of listening to music. The listener will identify with a piece of music and feel that it is somehow speaking to her or his experience, causing a range of emotional and affective responses. Similarly, this example could also be extended to the engagement people feel when watching a movie, looking at a painting, being a spectator at a sports event, or playing a video game.[19] Winnicott's account of play is useful because it offers a description of how and why some artworks are effective on some and not others, how the experience of game-play is meaningful and potentially liberating (think of the massive online communities of adults playing *World of Warcraft*), and why play is a recurring component of social relations and adult life. Furthermore, Winnicott's account privileges artistic creativity as an example of the repositioning of "potential space," drawing an analogy between the child's play and the artist's creation of new images and ideas. As Ellen Handler Spitz argues in her chapter, the equation between child's play and adult art is often overstated. Nevertheless, Winnicott's expanded definition of play and its relation to creativity are useful in thinking about how games can offer both diversion and subversion.

I focus on Winnicott's account of play because of the importance that art and creativity have within it. For Winnicott, the creative act gains not only its individual importance but also its wider relevance for a community through the refusal to accept a gulf between self and world, between subject and object, and between imagination and the particulars of one's objective environment. One need not take on Object Relations Psychoanalysis in its entirety to recognize that this transformative potential and its ability to suspend how we know the world—if even for a time—gives play in its myriad forms its recurring potency. One could see the intellectual roots of such connections in Friedrich Schiller's play-drive, which Laxton discusses in her essay. From different perspectives, this is also the lesson of Huizinga, of Caillois, of Wittgenstein, and of Sutton-Smith: that play offers the capacity to skew the conventional, to treat the commonplace otherwise, and to offer a temporary site from which to revisualize our ways of relating. Games focus and enable play. Their restrictions in the form of rules do limit actions, but in so doing they offer the parameters for creative adaptation and problem-solving. Both games and play became such rich sites of inquiry for artists and critics in the twentieth century because of these abilities to use supposed non-seriousness to view the everyday differently. They incorporated the game as an artistic tool and looked to play as a different model of making and encountering art.

This anthology brings together discussions of some of these moments. It demonstrates how an expansive definition of play allows us to reconsider the history of modern art and shows how games have had a significant presence within it. Games and play, in other words, are not inconsequential or silly. Rather, they offer the suspension of the quotidian as a means of thinking it otherwise. This open-ended exploration is at the core of many modern artists' practice, but it has been inadequately recognized. This book takes the stand that the emergence of the field of Game Studies and its development of methodologies attuned to games, rules, and play allow us to better recognize and discuss the many ludic components that have constituted a fundamental theme in art of the twentieth century.[20] That is, the recent developments of Game Studies can be used productively to discuss the importance of games and play in earlier historical moments. From this perspective, Picasso's playfulness, Surrealist games, Duchamp's affinity for chess, and so on seem less like disconnected threads and more like different ways of addressing the potential of the ludic as artistic practice.

The selection of essays was based upon papers given at the 2006 College Art Association conference with a few additions. The initial idea for this volume came with the overwhelming response to the call for papers from a wide variety of perspectives and historical moments. It was then that I realized that there had already been a greater investigation of games in art history, and the attendance at the resulting two-panel session confirmed that. As one might expect, a central theme was the Surrealist group and its contemporaries, and they have a strong presence here. Beyond that, however, I have attempted to bring in perspectives that use an expanded definition of play in the later twentieth century, focusing on the divergent manifestations this concept can have. Adding to that, the volume also includes essays by two new media artists, Jon Cates and Anne-Marie Schleiner, who assess the historical field to which they have contributed.

Susan Laxton begins the volume with an extensive discussion of the historical sources for discussing play in early twentieth-century thought, showing how it was inextricably linked to aesthetics. Examining Kant, Schiller, Nietzsche, Freud, and Simmel, Laxton charts an intellectual trajectory from the eighteenth to the early twentieth centuries that placed play at the core of debates about art and its evaluation.

Gavin Parkinson uses play as a method to present a challenge to the prevalent interpretations of Marcel Duchamp. Fittingly, this methodological tool unhinges the overly deterministic accounts of Duchamp's body of work and intentions, which seek to find a secret and consistent code through which to explain his divergent actions and works. Duchamp's propositions often have at their core an indeterminate or unknown element that is never revealed nor given secure meaning, and Parkinson himself offers an analogous way of looking at Duchamp. Playfully, Parkinson himself embeds in his chapter such a cryptic element with no interpretative key, saying something at a crucial moment but not in any recoverable or legible way for the reader. Drawing on Jacques Derrida's use of play and on the game-playing that underwrites Duchamp's oeuvre, Parkinson offers a methodological intervention and prompts us to attend to the play of meaning in the work not as a problem to be resolved but as an end in itself. Resisting the classic detective-story mode in which Duchamp's work has been persistently cast, Parkinson instead deploys this method to avoid those interpretations that consistently attempt to put a halt to Duchamp's play.

Moving from the use of play as methodology to its historical role in 1920s in the Bauhaus, Kevin Moore shows how the practice of photography offered an alternative and at times critical way of engaging with the Bauhaus's emphasis on rationalism in design. Play, he argues, manifested itself in the photographic work of professors and students, who explored photography as a subversion of the technological utopia propounded by the Bauhaus. Attending both to the photographs and to their pedagogical context within the Bauhaus, Moore demonstrates how the ostensible purity it aspired to could be subverted through photographic practice. Ultimately, it was photography's liminal role in the curriculum of the Bauhaus that allowed those who used to it explore the ludic and its critical possibilities.

This volume reprints Claudia Mesch's 2005 article on games and early twentieth-century art. Her chapter provides a thorough discussion not just of Huizinga and Caillois but also of the importance of games and play for the Surrealists and for Duchamp. She positions these authors and artists in relation to their historiographic and political contexts, demonstrating the ways in which play was an axis of engagement. In particular, Mesch foregrounds the roles of competition and of collaboration as motivating and enabling factors, arguing that such an approach offers a key to understanding the divergent approaches to games developed by Duchamp and the Surrealists. As such, it offers an important analysis of the historiographic positioning of the foundational texts for Game Studies and for the artists whom we most immediately identify with games in art.

Mary Ann Caws, the distinguished scholar of Surrealism, provides an exploratory and at times personal reflection on the importance of games and chance in Surrealism, gesturing to the ways in which the specific framing of games provided the impetus to reconsider the given world differently. As she contends, the Surrealists saw the freedom of chance as opening the freedom of one's imagination. She discusses how the Surrealist emphasis on the restrictions of rules and of the demands of collective behavior each allowed the possibility of individual personalities to emerge in response. In short, the constraints of the rules provide the opportunity to relate to the world differently. In this way, we can understand the importance of games and their limitations to the Surrealist project.

In my contribution to this volume, I discuss an often-overlooked group of works made by Picasso over the span of two weeks in the summer of 1930. These "sand reliefs," as they are called, engaged with the medium of relief sculpture and used its parameters as rules of a game Picasso played. Across the eight works that make up this set, Picasso toyed with questions of two- and three-dimensional imaging. In particular, I focus on the role of the shadow as a central component of relief sculpture and Picasso's allegorizing of it through the introduction of a silhouette in the early reliefs. By discussing the importance of the silhouette for Picasso in these years, I show how an undirected process of play around it and in the framework provided by relief sculpture generated new ways of thinking about sculpture. Throughout, I attend to the open-endedness of Picasso's play and the back-and-forth testing of rules in the sand reliefs in order to demonstrate how the perspective of Game Studies can bring to light new ways of considering artworks and the artistic process.

In her chapter on Joseph Cornell, Stephanie Taylor draws out the ways in which games and their ostensible nonseriousness often mask deeper and more complex issues. In particular, she shows how Cornell's works can be productively placed within the context of Surrealism's emphasis on sexuality, revealing the very adult concerns beneath the seemingly innocent boxes and assemblages. Taylor examines Cornell's recurring interest in childhood but points to his engagement not just with its idyllic representations but also with its perils. Similarly, she examines his toylike boxes in relation to his obsessions with certain woman, characterizing the works as manifesting his conflicted attitudes toward them. She concludes that play is a central arena of investigation for Cornell, both in his foregrounding of it in his works and their interactivity and in his self-presentation. He used play in both these ways, she argues, to divert the viewer from the disturbing and often deeply personal stories his works told.

In her analysis of Hannah Wilke's use of humor, Debra Wacks looks at the various games Wilke developed and the parodic play through which her work engaged with the reputation of Marcel Duchamp. Through a series of works, Wilke responded to Duchamp's works, using his own preference for wordplay as a tool to subversively mimic his strategies. In particular, Wacks examines Wilke's performances and films that engage with Duchamp in the Philadelphia Museum of Art, showing how the films themselves became games of extended quotation and parody with multiple references to Duchamp's work.

Owen Smith contributes a polemical account of what he calls "amodernism," a term that he uses to describe the destabilizing and open-ended tactics of Dada and Fluxus, in particular. Focusing on the writings of Dick Higgins, Smith discusses the concept of "infinite play" and its usefulness as an interpretative lens to bring out the aims of the Fluxus group and the transformative potential of its tactics. Countering the frequent assumption that Fluxus game-playing is simply unserious, Smith makes a case for their play as a reconsideration of the boundaries between art and life and between artist and viewer. In short, he argues that play functioned as a crucial critical mode for Higgins and for Fluxus.

Florencia Bazzano-Nelson examines the use of toys and play in the artwork of Liliana Porter from the 1960s to her more recent work in film. Showing how the toy can operate to open up possible meanings and to allude to unplayful content, Bazzano-Nelson makes the case that Porter's work has been deeply involved with the use of play as a tactic of subversion.

The next section brings together assessments of recent art practice by two new media artist-critics, Anne-Marie Schleiner and Jon Cates. Schleiner draws upon Situationism as a precedent for new modes of facilitating participation in recent new media art. With an emphasis on public practice, she holds that certain lessons taken from Situationist writings are useful in thinking through current uses of new media to relate to social spaces. Jon Cates outlines the history of video-game modification as art and examines how technologies from mainstream media and popular culture were adapted and exploited by artists to critical ends. He focuses on artworks that modify first-person-shooter games to represent and engage with the museum or gallery space in which they are exhibited. By allowing for an interaction with the space of the art institution, these works offer a new way of considering the role of video games within exhibition contexts. These works have the potential to appropriate and to engage critically with not just these spaces but also with the other works that they take as their targets.

In a fitting close to the volume, Ellen Handler Spitz discusses the frequent elisions between child's play and art. While noting some of the similarities, she argues that both lose when being simplistically equated with the other. She discusses how certain modes of play from childhood are taken up by modern and contemporary artists and draws points of comparison and contrast with children's use of games and toys. In so doing, she maintains the importance of distinguishing between the different personal and public uses of child's art versus that of the contemporary artist, clarifying the need to attend to play in art as a multifaceted and complex topic.

These essays do not settle on a stable history of games or play in twentieth-century art. Games and play themselves resist such easy taxonomies and positivistic accounts. Instead, they exhibit a family resemblance in their investigations of the ludic. Cumulatively, they themselves play with the ineradicable and undeniable presence of modes of gaming and of play as method in our ways of thinking about modern and contemporary art. The conjunction of the capacity for diversion and the potential for subversion links all of these investigations and helps to indicate just some of the ways in which games and play have served such a catalytic function for artists and critics in the twentieth century and beyond.

GAMES AND PLAY IN TWENTIETH-CENTURY ART HISTORY

Part I

1

FROM JUDGMENT TO PROCESS: THE MODERN LUDIC FIELD

SUSAN LAXTON

PLAY AS DISINTEREST

When we judge free beauty (according to mere form) then our judgment of taste is pure. Here we presuppose no concept of any purpose for which the manifold is to serve the given object, and hence no concept [as to] what the object is [meant] to represent; our imagination is playing, as it were, while it contemplates the shape, and such a concept would only restrict its freedom.

—IMMANUEL KANT, *THE CRITIQUE OF JUDGMENT*, 1790, §16, 77

With these words in 1790, Immanuel Kant introduced the criteria against which artistic practices would be measured—in compliance as well as resistance—for more than a century to follow. In the *Critique of Judgment,* the high pleasures of beauty are felt through the contemplation of form alone, disregarding content and free of the pressures of rational concepts; free as well from purpose and consequence in the filling of material needs. Beauty, in art or in nature, was determined to be above all disinterested. The imagination in fact was at *play* in judgments of taste: Kant had coupled the ludic to aesthetics.

Play would remain locked to art throughout the modern period and beyond, weathering the lapidary onslaught of photography, suffering the literalization of autonomy in the art-for-art's sake movement, clinging to the creative process even after the avant-garde finally pried art away from beauty and taste. Labile and inclusive, play persisted, oscillating between indeterminacy and autonomous enclosure depending on the context of its deployment and reception. And while that instability is present even in the supremely rational Kantian system, in the *Critique of Judgment* it was play's disinterest—its strict separation from material reality—that would finally be received as the overriding justification for the ludic alignment with art, and that would ultimately find expression in modernist autonomy.

For if the rise of disinterested form in modernist aesthetics has been attributed to increased commercial pressure on the arts, then it must also be admitted that the ensuing institutionalization of the arts had been rationalized on the basis of Kantian play.[1] Nineteenth-century aestheticist theory received Kantian beauty as "the formal and harmonious arrangement of parts into a whole, [that] has no other end than the pleasure it stirs in the beholder." Form was perceived as autonomous, and the pleasure it afforded due to "the mere play of its elements, [having] no relation to any further end."[2] This collapse of art with a circumscribed ludic field—a play tamed into aesthetics and an art neutralized as play—persists in contemporary criticism, where it functions to make the distinction between art and "reality" explicit: "As it is usually employed, the word *aestheticism* denotes an enclosure within a self-contained realm of aesthetic objects and sensations, hence also denotes a separation from the 'real world' of nonaesthetic objects."[3] In the hierarchy that raises aesthetic objects above the quotidian, Kant's disinterested play continues to be invoked as the transcendent vehicle for art's removal from practical efficacy.[4]

Thus to address the relation of play to art practices in the twentieth century is to address the problem of what exactly constitutes an avant-garde practice. For it is only within this context of autonomous play that the avant-garde project of overturning aesthetic conventions can be understood; likewise, to adopt artistic play as a strategy of resistance, to insist on art as dynamic experience rather than stable and unified harmony, is to tackle the complex implications of deploying play against play itself. The critical ludic practices of Dada and Surrealism, refusing to be dismissed as mere "antic" or "whimsy," established themselves as a counter-narrative not only to modernization's increasingly pervasive means-ends rationality, but against the very notion of stability as an Ideal experience.

The emergence of aesthetics as a philosophical discipline in the eighteenth century has itself been attributed to the historical need to bind off artistic activity in order to define more clearly useful and rational activity.[5] Experiences and objects that could not be categorized as rational or sensual—whose existence could not be justified by the pursuit of knowledge or the satisfaction of carnal needs—but that were pursued entirely for their own sake were relegated to a sphere that, in Kant's *Critique of Judgment,* is consistently parsed through the grammar of play. In fact, Kant's demarcation of a disinterested space for aesthetics is only the most obvious way that judgment-as-play shows itself in the third *Critique;* ludic indeterminacy and illusion also operate to motivate the work of art. The ludic idiom so imbricates the body of the text that it is worthwhile pursuing the various uses of play there—particularly in relation to Kant's idea of freedom—to examine the hierarchical implications that follow from it as well as the contradictions enclosed in it. For at the same time that Kant used the rhetoric of play to enclose art safely away from the rational and practical pursuits of life, play availed itself of its other, unstable gloss, working against its limits from within. And while Kant unwittingly risked the stability of disinterest by invoking play, it is exactly this model of *internal resistance* built into the play signifier that the avant-garde would ultimately seize upon as a contraventive model.

This instability was demonstrated in the third *Critique* even from within the schema of disinterest itself, as an oscillation between freedom and restraint. "The delight which determines the judgment of taste is independent of all interest," wrote Kant, interest being not only "reference to the faculty of desire" but also the "practical interest of reason."[6] Disinterest erects a boundary around aesthetic space, sealing it off from practical reality and sensual satisfactions. It is a restrictive space, yet Kant characterizes it here as liberating, since within the frame of this play-space judgment and art need not conform to natural or conceptual constraints. This led Kant to speak of a freedom that inflects judgment; beauty is experienced as a result of the harmonious "*free play* of the cognitive powers" of imagination and understanding.[7] But by freedom, Kant does not mean a freedom to associate—he is not referring to the gloss on play that implies interaction—but a freedom to be *separate.* In free play, the faculties are free *of* one another, each engaging in its own activity without limitations or compromises, and without one assuming priority over the other.

Thus Kant attempted to keep the indeterminacy of free play in check, much as free will was to be kept in check by the categorical imperative. While judgment exercises itself for its own sake, it is given a middle position without agency: it is attached to both imagination and understanding; it depends on them and cannot operate without them. Free play "has no objective validity" (it proceeds outside of reason and knowledge);[8] it is the sphere of nonsense and fantasy, and in this sense it *is* restricted, confined to a sphere separate from the empirical knowledge and reasonable expectations that are the basis for most human concerns. Kantian play is firmly opposed to notions and to sensuality: "*that is beautiful which pleases in mere estimation* (not in sensation or through a concept)," and as for its products, "they signify nothing, represent nothing...and are free beauties"; that is, fiction, artifice.[9]

This is the "as if" aspect of play, play as pretense and mimetic illusion, a third quality of the ludic (in addition to circumscription and freedom) determining artistic activity in the *Critique of Judgment.*[10] Art must show a "purposive harmony—manifesting itself on its own, contingently and without a purpose," that is, art will appear "as if it had intentionally been arranged for our use, while yet it also seems to belong to the original nature of things, without any concern as to [how] we might use it."[11] Beautiful art is a simulation, but it must be naturalized: a formal organization that maintains its self-conscious illusion for the sheer sake of pleasure. Like play, art in Kant is "just pretending." It mimics meaningful forms and structures, but after all means nothing.

Thus the pleasure derived from aesthetics, as Jacques Derrida has pointed out ("an arid pleasure, without concept and without enjoyment"), is a pleasure that proceeds from "lack"—lack of utility, the detachment from "ends" that is perceived in the sheer play of appearances.[12] Form is cordoned off into the "safety" of play, free from "the constraints of developing bourgeois-capitalist society," with the concomitant expectation that a rationalized material world will also be kept safe from the irrational gratuitousness of play.[13] The three ludic modalities that the Kantian model comprises—disinterest, indeterminacy, and illusion—thus gave rise to three persistent antinomies defining artistic practice: the opposition to work, the opposition to seriousness and meaning, and the opposition to pragmatic reality in the satisfactions of carnal needs.[14]

With art defined in these limited and exclusive terms, the specific grounds on which the avant-garde would challenge aesthetic disinterest are clear: from the Soviet and Weimar Dada perspectives, through radical denaturalization and artwork-as-production; for Marcel Duchamp, through the introduction of concepts; and for the Surrealists, though an activation of desire. What is fascinating is the extent to which these critiques will be made *through play itself.*[15] For while the *Critique of Judgment* manifests a conservative model for play—a unified, harmonious and discrete field with originality and consciousness at its center—modern critical practice will identify an alternative, temporally based and resolutely *interested* play—a play that is already present, if repressed, in Kant, and that shows itself in the form of a fundamental antinomy within the model.[16]

The mistake, Kant's logical lapse, so to speak, was to have underestimated the range of the ludic signifier on which he based the whole of his aesthetics. The play model itself opens the Kantian model onto a whole range of irresolvable contradictions—between disinterest and concepts, certainly, but also between disinterest and desire; as Derrida slyly remarks,

"I take pleasure in what does not interest me."[17] As Mihai Spariosu has pointed out, while play in the *Critique of Judgment* is determined by the rational "truths" from which it is excluded, the entire Kantian model of the mind is haunted by the *irrational,* "in the free, spontaneous and unruly play of the intuition and the imagination, in the disjunctive play between the similar and the dissimilar, in the disparity between the beautiful and the sublime, in the divided moral nature of man, in the cosmic interplay of necessity and chance, in the inscrutable designs of Nature."[18]

Thus even in its Enlightenment form, play takes instability as part of its definition, acknowledging through resistance the term's internal paradox. But Kantian aesthetics sought to resolve that paradox through its ultimate enclosure of judgment within rational concepts. Play, in Kant, is finally a unifying trope; it describes activity undertaken for its own sake, protected within a field bounded in space and time. Philosophically, it is a model that establishes a number of binary oppositions for both play and art: pleasure against work; freedom against utility; formal gestalt made distinct from temporal activity; primal intuition against conceptual knowledge. According to the system set up by this last pair, play and art are aligned with nature rather than with empirical culture, with enduring consequences for artistic play. Whether glossed as a primitivist turn to anarchy or the universal human desire for unity, the persistent notion of art's potential for essential and transcendent meaning was fused with the notion of play as primal from the very inception of aesthetics.

SCHILLER'S PLAY-DRIVE: THE INSTITUTIONALIZATION OF THE LUDIC

Friedrich Schiller's reception and extension of Kantian tropes, including his espousal of play as a foundational condition for art, initiated a series of historical responses to Kantian play and is important for its programmatic clarity. If Kant had described an aesthetics autonomous from empirical truth and sensuous desire, then it was Schiller who assigned a concrete *function* to that autonomy. In *On the Aesthetic Education of Man in a Series of Letters* (1795), Schiller proposed that art and aesthetics operate toward nothing less than the shaping of rational man.[19] His account of aesthetic humanism makes the pivotal role of play in Kant explicit, as beauty's function is grounded in play: "With beauty man shall *only play,* and it is *with beauty only* that he shall play,"[20] but in his characterization of play as a harmonizing force, Schiller aggrandized Kantian free-play by advancing the ludic as the improbable agent of reason. Thus as one critic has observed, Schiller "inaugurates the concept of the cardinal role of art, and of the imaginative faculty…as the reconciling and unifying agencies in a disintegrating mental and social world," a characterization that would persist through Romanticism and well into the modern era, most overtly in the aestheticist movements of the nineteenth century.[21]

The amenability of Schiller's particular interpretation of Kant to modernist aesthetics may have been due to his startling prescience with regard to alienation in modern life. Writing in the wake of the French Revolution, Schiller identified social and cultural difficulties emerging from Enlightenment reformations that would only become exacerbated within the century to follow: "At the present time material needs reign supreme and bend a degraded humanity beneath their tyrannical yoke. Utility is the great idol of our age, to which all powers are in thrall and to which all talent must pay homage."[22] Schiller identified the modern dilemma as one of extreme fragmentation: "Civilization," he contended, through "empirical knowledge," "sharper divisions between the sciences," and the "rigorous separation of ranks and occupations," had had a disintegrating effect, the result being that "the inner unity of human nature was severed too." Famously, he continued: "Everlastingly chained to a single little fragment of the whole, man himself develops into nothing but a fragment; everlastingly in his ear the monotonous sound of the wheel that he turns, he never develops the harmony of his being, and instead of putting the stamp of humanity upon his own nature, he becomes nothing more than the imprint of his occupation or of his specialized knowledge."[23]

The particalization of experience is compounded as individuals are beset with violence from within as well as from without, in terms of an inherent psychological tension between conflicting inner forces that Schiller identified as the "sensuous drive" [*sinnlich Treib*] and the "form drive" [*Formtreib*]. The first of these, "absolute reality," "proceeds from the physical existence of man," and is the realm of materiality, sensation and temporal dynamics; it is a source of instability, and "demands change." Its object is "life," that is, "all material being and all that is immediately present to the senses."[24]

In direct contrast to the sense drive is the "absolute formality" of the form drive, which "proceeds from the absolute existence of man, his rational nature" and is the realm of personal freedom (which Schiller, like Kant, defined as well-demarcated self-determination, as opposed to a deregulated interplay), harmony, stasis, concepts, and law; "it insists on truth and on the right." Its object is "form," figuratively and literally: "a concept which includes all the formal qualities of things and all the relations of these things to our thinking faculties."[25]

So long as these two drives are kept separate and *allowed the freedom to act independently,* they will coexist harmoniously. This watchdog assignment is the task of culture: first, to "preserve the life of Sense against the encroachments of Freedom; and second, to secure the Personality against the forces of Sensation."[26] The dichotomized elements of the individual's "sensuo-rational nature," which in this model anthropomorphize the larger political sphere, are arrayed in a oppositional tension that will be harmonized by a third, equally a priori term functioning to "unite the manifold," an impulse that Schiller called the "play-drive" [*Spieltreib*].[27]

"That drive," Schiller wrote, "in which both the others work in concert," operates to "annul all contingency, annul all constraint, too, and set man free both physically and morally." Its object is "living form": "a concept serving to designate all the aesthetic qualities of phenomena and, in a word, what in the widest sense of the term we call beauty." Play here is the vehicle for a harmonious and *harmonizing* art, the only means by which to regain an original state of balance between the sensual and the rational. Counterintuitively, the play-drive does this by exerting a prohibiting force that preserves the integrity of each of its countervailing partners.[28] Yet Schiller denied the potential for violence implied by play's authority even as he invoked the ludic as the sole term equal to the task of representing the paradoxical idea of a heterogeneous unity. Rather, he held that benign play reconciles the oppositive nature of the human condition, rendering man "whole"—it "unfolds both sides of his nature at once," to the extent that "man only plays when he is in the fullest sense of the word a human being, and *he is only fully a human being when he plays.*"[29]

Yet play itself is not permitted a double nature; ultimately it is overwritten by reason:

Reason, on transcendental grounds, makes the following demand: Let there be a bond of union between the form-drive and the material-drive; that is to say, let there be a play-drive, since only the union of reality with form, contingency with necessity, passivity

with freedom, makes the concept of human nature complete. Reason must make this demand because it is reason—because it is its nature to insist on perfection and on the abolition of all limitation, and because any exclusive activity on the part of either the one drive or the other leaves human nature incomplete and gives rise to some limitation within it.[30]

The notion that the play-drive exists *under* law—specifically a harmonizing and unifying law—would become important to the siphoning of humanist aesthetics into the conventions of Romanticism and the French Symbolist movement. On one hand, rationalized aesthetics would have its critics in anti-idealist thinkers such as Schopenhauer, Nietzsche, and Heidegger, whose theories reverberated in an alternative "poetics of indeterminacy" initiated by Arthur Rimbaud.[31] But on the other hand, a *reconstitutive* role for both art and play with regard to subject/object relations would persist into the modern era in the form of theories of artistic autonomy that can be traced back to Schiller's *Letters.*

Nevertheless, Schiller did fashion the play drive as actively engaged with the sensuous drive, productively revising Kant's passive model of sheer contemplation of the "free play of the cognitive powers," expanding art into the active and practical realm.[32] This would in turn imply an innovation compatible with the avant-garde desire for a return of art to praxis—the breaking down of art's autonomy and the salutary elimination of hierarchy between the noumenal and phenomenal.[33] Likewise, it would seem that Schiller, by stating that reason alone is not adequate to heal the modern dilemma of radical fragmentation, advocated the ludic integration of sensuous desire with art, anticipating advanced art's own carnal interventions in representation. But the embrace of difference in Schiller's play is selective and the prohibitions that the play-drive exerts are self-reflexive and exclusive. Guided by the Kantian withdrawal from sensuous pleasure, Schiller identified a second, destructive strain of play that must be distinguished from "transcendental (aesthetic) play."[34] This is "physical" play, "directed to very material objects"; a manifestation of man's "animal life" and "whose charm resides in a *free association of images.*"[35] Capricious and unstable, this play is characterized by "willful moods and unruly appetite"—attributes that are incompatible with the kind of art Schiller had in mind for the shaping of the Ideal state and its citizens. Furthermore, in spite of his all-inclusive rhetoric of harmony,

Schiller's reconstitutive program for humanity through play has dire economic implications, for "good play" and "bad play" are in fact assigned to class situations, since play emerges from material excess, "good play" being undertaken only in situations of "superfluity in *material things,* an aesthetic surplus."[36] In this model, the underclass would indulge in physical, vulgar play, while the class free of material needs would engage in metaphysical play, "the hard work of thinking for themselves."[37]

Schiller acknowledged the rift internal to play, but he steadfastly insisted on suppressing the paradox by presenting the play-drive as integrated and self-sufficient. His claim that art is not only threatened by "the noisy marketplace of our century" but also by "philosophical inquiry" (concepts) and "science" (empirical truth) concretized the Kantian separation of art from theoretical inquiry, meaning, and practical need.[38] And it is because he advocated this as a prescriptive program of aesthetic education that Schiller has been charged with having fully articulated and institutionalized the autonomy of the aesthetic realm.

Yet for that very reason, the opposition of art to material reality (which affirms the opposition of play to work and utility as well) is not so distinct in Schiller as in the *Critique of Judgment.* Schiller concretized the abstract Kantian concepts "beauty" and "judgment" by conflating them with art and art production in order to render them practically applicable to social reform. Consistent with this, he historicized aesthetic disinterest by specifically opposing it to commerce. Disinterest in Schillerian theory is thus made explicitly political: "If man is ever to solve that problem of politics in practice he will have to approach it through the problem of the aesthetic, because it is only through Beauty that man makes his way to Freedom."[39] Schiller insisted that the agent of reform must be an "instrument not provided by the State," in order that it be safe from "political corruption,"[40] and with this he advanced a model for art that would function as an independent institution to modify social relations toward an ideal state comprised of ideal individuals, each working toward the recovery of a natural perfection that had been radically damaged by modern exigencies.

Thus while art here seems to have been given political agency, it finally mattered to Schiller only because "there is no other way of making sensuous man rational except by first making him aesthetic."[41] This is brought about by the "aesthetic modulation of the psyche" that the play-drive compels when, acting as a corrective, it brings the subject who is either too "tensed" or too "relaxed" back to normative center.[42] This is one of the least satisfying arguments in *Aesthetic Education,* since here Schiller assumes that the "relaxed" subject will not identify with calming aspects of beauty and withdraw into a dangerous passivity, nor, on the other hand, that the energizing aspects of play will aggravate an already tensed subject, producing a state of destructive agitation. But the ideal of an "aesthetically tempered man" who automatically adjusts to center is consistent with Schiller's founding assumption that the original human state as well as the Ideal "absolute condition" is one of equilibrium and naturalizes the fundamentally political and ideological notion of a harmonious state.[43] This sort of order requires an internalization of conformity that can only be accomplished through the cooperation of artistic culture with the ultimate aims of government: a tacit understanding that art would be defined by formal harmony and artists by temperance. Schiller's model entails both absorptions of difference under a transcendent rubric, as well as the active suppression of difference, in terms of the refusal of a vulgar, destructive play. These are the terms that would become anathema to the avant-garde, as their critique of aesthetic play proceeded precisely from their embrace of heterogeneity and extremism.

Technically, since it has reconciliation as its "end," Schiller's play-drive falls outside the ludic as it was philosophically defined in the *Critique of Judgment,* and Kant's play-based gauge for art, "purposiveness without purpose," is conspicuously absent from *Aesthetic Education.* Schiller articulated a *useful* relation between art and politics: the founding of "the State of Aesthetic Semblance," achieved through the "education of mankind."[44] His theory would become "the classical articulation of a traditional bourgeois aesthetic ideology" enclosing "various mediating instrumentalities (schools, especially the *Gymnasium,* the university, literary criticism, and literary histories)."[45] As part of that program, play, now indissociably joined to art, would move along with it into art institutions of the twentieth century, eventually appearing in the form of modernist autonomy. And with play established as the condition of possibility for the production and reception of art, a number of avant-garde movements would seize on the ludic as both the object and the means through which to contest aesthetic conventions.

NIETZSCHEAN PLAY: PROCESS, ILLUSION, AND DESTRUCTION

By the end of the nineteenth century, Schiller's harmonizing aesthetic had become the normative attitude to art, codified as art-for-art's sake, a doctrine of aesthetic*ism.* In the process, the Kantian metaphysic had lost a great deal of its complexity, but the central concept that coupled play to art persisted in the form of disinterest. The ludic/aesthetic at this point organized a self-contained, harmonious realm of objects and sensations separate from the "real world" of nonaesthetic objects; it described a liberatory and ideal sphere of unequivocal goodness. It was Nietzsche who would explode this image of benign art not by separating it from play, but by characterizing play as entirely other to Schiller's Kantian attribution.[46]

Nietzsche's philosophy exposes stasis to process, unity to paradox, truth to illusion, harmony to violence and chaos, singularity to repetition, regulation to chance. In his reformulation of the relations of aesthetics to truth and morality, Nietzsche would not subordinate art to reason or ethics; rather, he reversed the traditional valuation to privilege aesthetics and play as the determinants of existence and experience.[47] Where Kant and Schiller see play as an integral part of culture alone, play in Nietzsche is *cosmic*—encompassing all human activity. Like the surrealists and poststructuralists who were to follow him, Nietzsche refused to separate art from the everyday—not by opening art to the materials and practices of the quotidian, but by insisting that there is no "everyday world" that can claim a privileged reality. Rather, he contended, the entire world as it appears is a mere illusion, a play world commensurate with art.

Nietzsche reveled in play: it permeates his philosophy at the level of form (in, for example, the reversals and fragmentation in the structure of *Thus Spake Zarathustra*) and content (irresolvable contradictions abound across the whole of his work); play's instability grounds not only his conception of art but informs the entirety of his cosmos.[48] Accordingly, for Nietzsche play determined human action as well as the world itself, which he theorized in terms of the purposelessness of Dionysian force and the illusion of Apollonian "appearances." Nihilism, as a condition without ends or purposes, is cast in play terms, as is the means to overcome nihilism: the Will to Power, which creates the ludic illusion of unity, purpose, and harmony. The doctrine of eternal recurrence is characterized as "world play," and the "Overman," in his celebration of the situation, is the most powerful of players.[49] "I know of no other manner of dealing with great tasks," wrote Nietzsche, "than as *play;* this, as a sign of greatness, is the essential prerequisite."[50] This summarization of widely ranging perspectives under one term could only be accomplished under the aegis of what is itself Nietzsche's great precedent in aesthetics: his acknowledgment of play in its full range of signification, that is, as a term that is definitively split and paradoxical, enclosing the notion of a harmonious totality as well as that of destructive indeterminacy.

Nietzsche's appraisal of the world as illusion has been understood as the culmination of a long tradition in Western metaphysics that began with Plato's denigration of representation, and it was upheld by the Cartesian subordination of the object-world to a subjective and internal "reality."[51] Yet Nietzsche's accomplishment, in describing both subject and object in terms of the single rubric, play, was to have collapsed the barrier between art and life, the very revision sought by the interwar avant-gardes. With the object world characterized as "make believe" and the subject playing and *being played by it,* the agonistic and unstable aspects of the ludic as well as play's disinterested and utopian dimension are accounted for. In acknowledging play's duality, Nietzsche could encompass the dynamic process of Becoming as well as the production of Being as a static and illusionary play world. The willful arbitrariness of play—its basis in chance and its antagonistic aspect—come to the fore, overriding a set of self-imposed rules that Nietzsche insisted had been mistaken for necessity.[52] Thus Nietzsche did not exactly deny or negate the Kantian characterization of aesthetic play as a bounded and discrete field. Rather, Nietzsche's play expanded the Kantian realm of static, disinterested form to expose play's other dimension as a *dynamic process*—not the positive liberatory production of beauty, but the mendacious construction of a false harmony, and the repeated destruction of that lovely screen under the rule of eternal return. Dissonance, "dithyrambic madness," and the "bite of displeasure" are drawn into Nietzschean play, as two artistic impulses, the Apollonian and its opposite, the Dionysian, coexist agonistically to account for, respectively, the "image world" and its ecstatic counterpart, an "intoxicated reality."[53]

The Birth of Tragedy lays out the fundamental characteristics of the Dionysian impulse as a "nonimagistic . . . art world of *intoxication,*" emerging from "the truly existent primal unity, eternally suffering and contradictory."[54] Its full expression entails "tremendous terror" as well as "blissful ecstasy," the "rapture" of the "annihilation of the ordinary bounds and limits of existence." In the Dionysian, "everything subjective vanishes into complete self-forgetfulness." All is engulfed in an undifferentiated burst of pure process, in which the artist "is no longer an artist, he has become a work of art."[55] The temporal quality of the Dionysian impulse (its ideal medium, Nietzsche says, is music),[56] as well as its repetitive and purposeless exertions, has led directly to its ludic characterization: "One may call this ceaselessly self-creative, self-destructive, multiple force élan, configurated drive, the Will (as Schopenhauer did) or Will to Power; becoming (*Werden*) or the Heraclitean flux of all things; or, to use the most serene metaphor: ceaseless, purposeless play."[57]

By stark contrast, Nietzsche theorized the Apollonian impulse as commensurate with the idealist tradition of art subordinated to law. Reliant on form and tangibility, the Apollonian sphere, "a visible intermediary world," is the realm of the plastic arts.[58] But unlike the aesthetic models that follow Kant, Apollonian art is not something contained within a privileged "reality," but rather a "veil" of "*illusion*" drawn over reality, "whose influence aims to deliver us from the Dionysian flood and excess."[59]

This soothing illusion—a nominative itself derived from *in ludere,* to play—comprising what we mistake for the empirical world, is, as critics have pointed out, a characterization of the entire object-world as play.[60] The world of appearances is constructed in the manner of the work of art, which in Nietzsche "makes life possible by seducing men to live on through illusion. In this sense art is a game, a form of playing, which makes it possible to live on despite the fundamental pain, terror, and contradiction of existence."[61]

Art for Nietzsche, as the mirror of a lie, was the "mere appearance of mere appearance."[62] "Every artist is an 'imitator,' that is to say, either an Apollonian artist in dreams, or a Dionysian artist in ecstasies, or finally—as for example in Greek tragedy—at once artist in both dreams and ecstasies."[63] Since to grasp this fact is to face nihilism, and the possibility that what we consider truth will reveal itself as merely interpretation, means that most of the world dwells in a fictitious world of "bourgeois security," which Nietzsche aimed to dismantle. Thus Nietzschean play has been identified as an early form of deconstruction, aiming for "the rendering uncertain of all things, the uprooting, the liberation from false certainties and from self-assured mediocrity, the job of destruction, of destructuring"; that is, play at its most critical.[64]

All is play in Nietzsche: the play of indeterminacy and the play of illusion covering it up. And with the opposition between play and reality (art and the everyday) eliminated, the distinction between subject and object in the play world likewise vanishes: "The whole opposition between the subjective and the objective…is altogether irrelevant in aesthetics, since the subject, the willing individual that furthers his own egoistic ends, can be conceived of only as the antagonist, not as the origin of art…in this state he is, in a marvelous manner, like the weird image of a fairy tale which can turn its eyes at will and behold itself; he is at once subject and object, at once poet, actor and spectator."[65]

Likewise the notion that signification is firmly attached to its precedent in a verifiable reality is exploded in the Nietzschean model, and the stability of denotation is replaced by artistic meaning produced through the interplay of subjective desire and its objects: "Willing (the personal interest of the ends) and pure perception of the environment are wonderfully mingled; connections between them are sought and imagined; the subjective mood, the affection of the will, imparts its own hue to the perceived environment, and vice versa. Genuine song is the expression of the whole of this *mingled and divided state of mind.*"[66]

Thus the Apollonian play-world is false but not irrelevant. Paradoxically erected as a shield against the very desire that produces it, it cannot be conceived as disinterested from that desire. The force of desire behind the illusion, which Nietzsche also characterized as play, is the Dionysian impulse: "Again and again it reveals to us the playful construction and destruction of the individual world as the overflow of a primordial delight. Thus the dark Heraclitus compares the world-building force to a playing child that places stones here and there and builds sand hills only to overthrow them again."[67] The Dionysian arts (music and tragic myth) "play with the sting of displeasure, trusting in their exceedingly powerful magic arts, and by means of this play both justify the existence of even the 'worst world.' "[68]

Calling to mind the avant-garde impulse to dismantle conventions and norms, the Dionysian takes satisfaction in the destruction of the Apollonian world; here Nietzsche celebrates the repeated *destruction* of the illusory world as the sign for change augured by advanced art. For when art embodies the Apollonian and Dionysian competition, when the Dionysian as the sphere of displeasure shows itself in the work (as in tragic myth or musical dissonance), the resulting paradox of pleasure in the unpleasant approaches critical self-reflexivity: "Here it becomes necessary to take a bold running start and leap into the metaphysics of art, by repeating... that existence and the world seem justified only as an aesthetic phenomenon. In this sense, it is precisely the tragic myth that has to convince us that even the ugly and disharmonic are part of an artistic game that the will in the eternal amplitude of its pleasure plays with itself. But this primordial phenomenon of Dionysian art is difficult to grasp."[69]

Nietzsche was the first theorist of an anti-aesthetic impulse that would find expression in the Dada movement and would expand and contract in Breton's surrealism finally to explode in the Bataillean theorization of the *informe.* But Nietzsche's early complication of pleasure, expressed through the repeated erection and destruction of a protective screen (later to be fully theorized as the concept of eternal recurrence), most obviously resonates with the Freudian perturbation of pleasure as its opposite in the concept of the death drive and the uncanny. Nietzsche's Dionysian repetition organizes human experience into an a-teleological cycle of self-destruction that prefigured Freud's own—as Freud himself acknowledged—and both are grounded in the ludic.[70]

Play as process and constant flux, inhabiting its definition as engagement (to put into play), is prioritized as action against static norms, implying at once incessant change and constant repetition:

> **This world: a monster of energy, without beginning, without end... enclosed by "nothingness" as by a boundary...set in a definite space as a definite force...as a play of forces and waves of forces, at the same time one and many, increasing here and at the same time decreasing there; a sea of forces flowing and rushing together, eternally changing, eternally flooding back, with tremendous years of recurrence...out of the play of contradictions back to the joy of concord.**[71]

This infinitely repeated cycle is play's distinctive paradox; it reuses the same regulations to produce different outcomes and is repeatedly deployed as an avant-garde strategy. Think, for example, of Surrealism's endless sessions of the game of *cadavre exquis,* each round throwing off an equivalent but distinct variation; or the errant trajectories of "*l'un dans l'autre,*" where the players cast about blindly, but repeatedly root out the one image from "inside" the other. Each fresh result of the game is riddled with internal contradiction—nonsense imagery, schismatic poems, indeterminate forms—presenting the by-products of avant-garde play as a series of nesting paradoxes that mirror the dynamic of their (un)productive medium.

Finally, the invocation of chance as the guarantee of paradox and difference set against the press of conformity and regulation—and the accompanying scenario of a subject temporarily coerced into sustaining the difficult engagement with violence—confirms the link between avant-garde and Dionysian play. In these aleatory models of the ludic, the subject is not so much playing as *being played,* subordinated either to Apollonian delusions or Dionysian chance. Bataille cites Nietzsche's Zarathustra as the prophet "without goals," free of volition: "Incapable of doing anything...I follow a shimmering light that turns me into its plaything...it's hard not to have the feeling of being only an incarnation, a megaphone or medium, for higher powers."[72]

The force Bataille adopted from Nietzsche is not unexpected: "Instead of God, chance,"[73] the antidote to morality, reason, and purpose:

> **"Of Hazard"—that is the oldest nobility in the world; that gave I back to all things; I emancipated them from bondage under purpose....**
>
> **This wantonness and folly did I put in place of that Will, when I taught that "In everything there is one thing impossible—rationality!"...A little wisdom is indeed possible; but this blessed security have I found in all things, that they prefer—to dance on the feet of chance.**[74]

Writing through Nietzsche, Bataille substituted chance for agency: "Committed to the casual stance—I think and express myself in the free play of chance," he wrote. "Possibility in fact is simply chance, chance that cannot be grasped without danger... all that we understand as chance risking itself, disequilibrium, intoxication, dementia."[75] As Bataille acknowledged, Nietzsche's "great dice game of the world's existence" drags along with it the dark side of play, the repetition of pain and destruction that necessarily follows joyful affirmation.[76]

Nietzsche maintained the relevance of play to art, but he remarked on the duality inherent in play and affirmed the suppressed term—that in play which is violent, repetitive, destructive. Instability is shown to permeate "reality"—both at the level of the Dionysian-motivated subject and the illusionary world of objects the subject constructs in order to manage an unreasonable and ultimately intolerable reality. Nietzsche deconstructed normative aesthetics, wielding play (as process) against itself (as illusion) to advance an unstable and groundless art as a critique of identity, of reality itself. His revision of humanist aesthetics represented a radical shift in ludic discourse that was the necessary prerequisite to the subsequent grasp of play as an avant-garde strategy.

THE FREUDIAN LUDIC: FROM SUBLIMATION TO UNPLEASURE

While alternative art practices link to Nietzsche's ludic world at the level of paradox, chance, dynamism, and repetition, as well as through a theorization of a world of conventions masking a profound, inchoate "reality," the Nietzschean ludic-aesthetic has been underaddressed in the literature on the visual arts. More common has been a cloaking of Nietzsche's ideas in the mantle of Freudian psychoanalysis. This at first appears historically counterintuitive—Freud was a great admirer of Schiller, and the poet's influence is obvious in Freud's economic model for mental processes based in conflicting drives. In addition, the desire formulated in *Beyond the Pleasure Principle* for a return to an original unified state recalls Schiller's "nostalgic teleology" toward a state modeled on a harmonious past; and for both these thinkers, the play drive is the medium through which these ideal states are managed.[77]

Yet in spite of the obvious links to Schiller, Freud himself admitted Nietzsche's insight into the psychoanalytic model of the mind. The Dionysian primordial, for instance, the sphere of conflict, pain/pleasure, and paradox, is homologous with Freud's conception of the *id,* and both these spheres occupy an occluded and motivating position underlying manifest reality.[78]

The likeness extends to the deployment of play in its relation to art in both theories, where Freud followed Nietzsche in formulating both a superficial, illusory play in the form of sublimation as well as in identifying a violent ludic counter-impulse identified as repetition compulsion. But Freud's alignment with Nietzschean thought was gradual, expanding over time as he moved away from the Schillerian "Creative Writers and Day-Dreaming" and *Jokes and Their Relation to the Unconscious* to the repetitive cycle of pain and pleasure in *Beyond the Pleasure Principle.*[79] Thus the modern discursive shift from a characterization of play as disinterested judgment to play as dynamic process can actually be traced across Freud's own developing concept of the ludic.

In "Creative Writers and Day-Dreaming," the link between play and art is explicit and conservative: "The creative writer does the same as the child at play. He creates a world of fantasy which he takes very seriously—that is, which he invests with large amounts of emotion—while separating it sharply from reality."[80] Freud was the first to openly state that "the opposite of play is not what is serious but what is real," where reality is pragmatically accepted as the material quotidian (as opposed to the Nietzschean "real" that underlies and constructs an illusory quotidian).

Freud asserted here that play precedes art; that art is an acceptable, sublimated form of play in adults and that further, all "ready-made…constructions" (i.e., traditions) available in inherited models of art are the "distorted vestiges of the wishful fantasies of whole nations." Childhood play is conceived as an "original" state in which art and experience were fully integrated. But unlike Nietzsche's paradoxical play, in this early essay Freud cast play as unconditionally utopian, "a correction of unsatisfying reality" in which the child (and likewise the dreamer and the artist) is the master, and "rearranges the things of his world in a new way which pleases him."[81] At this point, Freud's conjunction of play and art, united by an unequivocally pleasurable "liberation of tensions," is merely Schiller's formulation restated in psychoanalytic terms.

This affirmative view of play is consistent with Freud's deliberate study on the topic, *Jokes and Their Relation to the Unconscious,* which makes the allusion to aesthetics in its first sentence,[82] and where Freud was more specific about the exact cause of dissatisfaction that prompts play: the child "uses games in order to withdraw from the pressure of critical reason," with critical reason described psychoanalytically as a disguised "reality principle."[83] The reference to play as a release from rationality and prohibitions is one of a number of provocative connections Freud made to issues central to the interwar avant-gardes; dreams, eroticism, paradox, automatism, disinterest, and transgression are linked to play as well. "The joke," Freud wrote, "is the contribution made to the comic from the realm of the unconscious."[84]

And the joke centers on play: "the pleasure in jokes exhibits a core of original pleasure in play and a casing of pleasure in lifting inhibitions."[85] Freud's structure of the joke echoes his model for the mind, where the *id* is sheathed in repressive prohibitions secured by the *ego,* invoking what Samuel Weber has identified as the "hierarchical opposition of play and inhibition," although in the case of jokes the corresponding spatial relation between surface and core is peculiarly reversed, with the content of the joke—its "play with thoughts"—readily apparent, and the purposeless "play with words," or form-play, at its core. In a paradoxical instance of the "sense in nonsense" that characterizes both the logic of dreams and the chaotic imagery of the *id,* "the prohibited game returns in and as this smearing of oppositions that are seemingly clear-cut."[86] At their core, jokes share the syntax of primary processes, "giving free-play to modes of thought which are usual in the unconscious." They are structured by condensation and displacement and they indulge in "faulty reasoning" and "indirect representation" as well as "representation by nonsense and the opposite." Jokes depend on unauthorized "connections between elements"—they are involuntary and associative in their formation and emergence, indicating "their origin from the unconscious."[87] And here Freud set up another hierarchy: between play itself and the joke, with the joke as the mere tool by which consciousness is averted in order to access "original" play. Laughter, the sign for pleasure that the joke elicits, "is in fact the product of an automatic process which is made possible by our conscious attention's being kept away from it." The "casing" provided by the joke is merely a ruse to distract consciousness from a release of unconscious thought.[88]

Through this theorization of the joke, Freud allowed a language game into the range of automatist techniques, a development that of course would be of the greatest appeal to Dada and Surrealism. With every word game, every inquiry or spontaneous revision of existing visual or linguistic forms, came the possibility that the outcome, the response, or the perverted product would bear the marks of primary processes so long as play was the only motivation. Yet if they followed Freud's model only up to this point, how far really could avant-garde play strategies be from the very conventions of *aesthetic* play that they were attempting to overthrow?

Because most jokes, Freud insisted, are purposeless. Like beauty, they do nothing and mean nothing. According to Jeffrey Mehlman, this is exactly the great accomplishment of the joke book—to have demonstrated "a new pleasure in 'signs' and their repetition."[89] Like an aesthetic form, whose "enjoyment lies only in itself, which has its aim only in itself and which fulfills none of the other aims in life," innocent joking is an "activity which aims at deriving pleasure from mental processes, whether intellectual or otherwise," that is, pleasure in mental processes for their own sake, outside of meaning.[90]

"Tendentious" or "purposeful" jokes, by contrast, "have sources of pleasure at their disposal to which innocent jokes have no access," that is, they direct themselves to the overcoming of an obstacle to libidinal satisfaction. It is in tendentious jokes that the "rebellion against authority" is most manifest; "the object of the joke's attack may equally well be institutions,...dogmas of morality or religion," in effect, wherever anything commands "so much respect that objections to them can only be made under the mask of a joke."[91] To illustrate, Freud used smutty jokes. The telling of the "dirty joke," he contended, is actually a sexual proposition directed toward a "second person" (who is actually only present in the joker's mind, as an anthropomorphization of an internalized prohibition) who always refuses the offer (otherwise the speaker satisfies the need and the desire is never channeled into a joke). But once the obstacle is encountered and the libidinal energy is redirected into the acceptable form of the joke, neither of these "players" enjoys it. Freud insisted that jokes are the most socially engaged of language play, because they require yet a *third* person—for whom the joke is pleasurable.[92]

Freud devoted an entire chapter to this social dimension of jokes, which, as Weber has pointed out, depends on the hinge between meaning and expectation: "It is this expectation of a meaning that thus becomes one of the negative preconditions of the joke," thus the joke is "socially determined, involving generally held 'inhibitions' or taboos as opposed to purely individual ones," a "collective if temporary transgression of shared prohibitions."[93]

But as if to deliberately withdraw his theories from an overt articulation of a politics of play, the critical efficacy of tendentious jokes was contradicted by Freud's primary characterization of all jokes: that to the extent they result from repressive prohibitions *against* play, they are generated by "law" as a *useful* way to relieve the tensions produced by inhibitions. The dissatisfactions with "selfish regulation laid down by the few who are rich and powerful," to which Freud ascribed the emergence of jokes, concern *material* needs, and the deflection of these dissatisfactions into language games must provide material benefit to regulating agents by suppressing dissent.[94] The pleasure in the play of signs that the joke produces is not then a moment of liberating free-play, but only a substitute—a kind of play-effect that gives the illusion of satisfaction. But importantly, Freud here attached play (that which has been prohibited) to material desire, and allowed a language game at least the power of critique, if not of direct agency. Since jokes replace forms of language that are normally forbidden, even an "innocent" joke can be understood as the result of resistance: it "arises out of the conflict between play and meaning," where the joke is a sign for play's "negation or inhibition, imposed by the demands of meaning and of the critical intellect."[95] This shifts the emphasis from the opposition between reality and utopian play to an opposition between sense and nonsense, and with it Freud draws play (which in its guise as "multiple use" is the basis of language games) even further from aesthetic harmony.[96] As Weber points out, this tension can only be understood in the context of the "game" jokes play with the listener's desire for meaning: the joke "dangles" the expectation of meaning before the listener and then "refuses to provide it," repeatedly denying the ego not just the satisfaction of internal unity, but also the gratifying distinction between subject and object by which that unity could be achieved.[97]

And in the sense that they frustrate the desire for completion, resisting the satisfactions of closure, jokes destabilize that desire, affirming instead the uneasy blurring of distinction between subject and object, an ambivalence that extrapolates to the dimming distinction between art and life, between fiction and reality. In fact, the joke book itself is so engaged with the breakdown of opposites that it verges on being regarded as a play text itself: it advances laughter as the sign for both repression and its lifting; pleasure as both autoerotic and intersubjective; play as sexually motivated yet disinterested. At the start of *Jokes and Their Relation to the Unconscious,* Freud is a disciple of Schiller and Kant, but by its end the irreconcilable conflicts between psychoanalysis and disinterest must have been clear. The pleasures of repetition in the play of signs, the focus on process as opposed to stasis and harmony, and the constant conflict between play and the reality principle point toward the Freudian reformulation of play away from Idealist aesthetics that will become explicit in *Beyond the Pleasure Principle.*

In this crucial text, Freud shifted the ludic model away from pure erotic accounting and reconceived play as mastery acquired through *suppressed* action; that is, the ludic impulse is no longer advanced as an avatar of primordial pleasure in freedom but as a tool of civilization, power, and control. When Freud revised the pleasure principle to account for self-destructive behaviors, retracting play from unequivocal bliss, he could not reconcile this new dimension of child's play with the aesthetic tradition he had inherited from Schiller.[98] Instead, a latent Nietzschean presence informs Freud's account of the destructive pleasures activated by repetition, a connection he would make manifest four years later, in the context of masochism: "The libido has the task of making the destroying instinct innocuous, and it fulfills the task by diverting that instinct to a great extent outwards...toward objects in the external world. The instinct is then called the destructive instinct, the instinct for mastery, or the will to power."[99] Here, then, is a model for play as *unpleasure,* and a distinct shift in the role of the ludic in art from disinterested judgment to a destructive process.

In *Beyond the Pleasure Principle,* Freud severed play from Idealist aesthetics through the ludic alliance with repetition. Drawing on the mimetic aspect of play, he characterized the disagreeable "*fort-da*" game as the child's masochistic reenactment of his mother's departure. Regardless of whether the game is repeated endlessly (as it is in this case) or played only once, the satisfactions of self-torture emerge through the repetitive dimension of representation itself, uncoupling the game from the cult of originality associated with the "free play" of the faculties (Kant) or drives (Schiller). Novelty, "always the condition of enjoyment," is nowhere present in this new formulation of pleasure in pain. In a cycle every bit as hermetic as Nietzsche's eternal recurrence, play beyond the pleasure principle produces *sameness,* "the death of novelty," in marked contrast to the neoteric demands of modern economic self-perpetuation.[100]

Play in this scenario is regressive—not because it signals a return to infantile behavior; in fact, the mastery achieved through this destructive play, Freud informs us, is a sign of dawning maturity[101]—but because of its mechanical redundancy, its dogged determination to reenact past unpleasantness. Freud traced the game to a counter-erotic instinct, one so opposed to the "life-drive" that it is locked in a struggle with *eros* that, again, recalls Nietzsche's agonistic play between Dionysian and Apollonian forces.[102] It is in accounting for this paradoxical pleasure taken in unpleasure—a conundrum Nietzsche had approached through tragedy (and the theater as play's variant)—

that Freud formulated a second paradox, that of life as "a task of ceasing to live."[103] The "death drive" that emerges through play is regressive in that it "*is an urge inherent in organic life to restore an earlier state of things.*"[104]

This characterization of play as regressive is particularly an affront to Schiller, whose program for "education" leaned heavily on the salutary, humanizing effect of an aesthetic play that harked back to the pre-industrial harmony of classical Greece. But the return to a former, pre-civilized state is familiar within the canons of modernism in the form of a primitivist impulse running parallel to modernism's rhetoric of progress. The parallel to the notion of "potlatch," for example, articulated by the sheer wastefulness of a world in pursuit of its own annihilation, is remarkable, although Freud himself seemed intent on repressing the political implications of his theory. Likewise, the mechanical redundancy of a game intent on reducing the subject to an inanimate state, and that scenario's resemblance to the paradigmatic scene of modernist production—the assembly line and its dehumanizing automation—escaped Freud's notice.[105] Yet certain forms of play, from a psychoanalytic perspective, can be understood as a critique of the rhetoric of progress and production commensurate with Georges Bataille's "*nonproductive expenditure.*"[106] The sheer wastefulness of the ludic, the absurdity of its pursuit, places its players in the Bataillean ranks of social dejecta: committed poets and artists.

Like psychoanalytic play, artistic play ultimately provoked a rupture in the field of representation. For along with the rhetoric of progress, the tropes of freedom, agency, and originality—terms that had long provided the link between play and aesthetics—would be contested as well in these destructive models of the ludic. In the cycle of repetition compulsion, the player is *played* in a scenario that requires a hapless agent caught up in play action beyond his control. While mastery through repetition is advanced as a shift from passive to active engagement, the subject has no material efficacy; his substitute satisfaction is precisely the "satisfaction-effect" derived from wordplay in language games. By linking artistic production with the distressing fort-da game, Freud acknowledged an art of unpleasure, turning away from beauty as an aesthetic quality and opening art onto the disturbing, perturbed, and provocatively ugly, sketching an alternative agenda for play as it relates to art: as antiprogress and antipleasure. And as in Nietzsche's game of construction and destruction, Freudian repetition would be characterized as both superficially meaningless and deeply interested, constituting an entirely different model of play—one that critiques the ideal of apparent stability and unity, the foundations of formal autonomy, and the neat closure of meaning. Freud finally arrived at a ludic that operates as a critique of received notions, rather than as a Schillerian tool by which to affirm them.[107]

GEORG SIMMEL: PLAY AS DIFFERENCE AND IMMEDIACY

Play as it is framed in Nietzschean and Freudian texts throws light on the discursive motivations for avant-garde play at the levels of dynamic disruption and the complex power of the unconscious. These theories attest to a shift in play discourse as it relates to representation from a ludic contemplative model to a focus on play as an active and disorderly force. The ambivalent outcome of this change, which can be restated as a shift from stasis and integrity to dynamic flux, is trenchantly measured in yet another ludic theory in circulation in the first part of the twentieth century—that of the sociologist Georg Simmel.

As a neo-Kantian, Simmel understood meaning and experience as grounded in an essential human desire for order and harmony, sought in artistic representation through the apprehension of a visual totality that affirms the self's own agency and inner unity.[108] Yet as he worked through Kant in the modern context the difficulty of maintaining secure ground in the face of a radically fragmented field of experience must have become apparent, and his writings ultimately focus on the rise of cultural "play forms" that have been forced into being in order to preserve individuality and social relations against the encroachments of an increasingly homogenizing quotidian motivated by production. In the modern metropolis, Simmel argued, life has become so rationalized, so overstimulating, and so severely objectified that individuals can cope only by distancing themselves—either through an ultimately damaging blasé attitude or, more positively, by maintaining a kind of constructive reserve. This psychological state brackets off a mental space and time for the exercise of irrational or impulsive thoughts that are not permitted in the "exterior" world.[109] Within this circumscribed "playground," those traits of personal individuality threatened by the leveling effects of the mature money economy could be preserved and indulged. While this scheme thus appeared to posit the ludic as a static and autonomous form of escapism, a close examination of what Simmel called the sociological "play forms" active in these circumstances reveals them as structurally tied to the material and historical conditions from which they emerged. In the modern context, Simmel's play forms signify "difference" itself—from utility, novelty, and a quotidian motivated by means-ends rationality. It is at this level of extreme contingency, where artistic play generates meaning only within its immediate context, that Simmel's play theory will resonate most deeply with advanced art.

The phenomenon that corresponds most closely to Simmel's psychological play state at the level of social relations is "sociability," which Simmel defined as "the associative process as a value"—the "*play-form of association.*"[110] This is pure association as it appears in conversation for its own sake, without pragmatic motivations, in a lively interplay that ultimately means nothing. Like "reserve," sociability withdraws the individual protectively from life's exigencies into a provisional utopian situation: "If we enter into sociability purely as 'human beings,' as that which we really are, lacking all the burdens, the agitations, the inequalities with which real life disturbs the purity of our picture, it is because modern life is overburdened with objective content and material demands."[111]

Because he posited social relations cut off from reference and released into the "pure, abstract play of form," Simmel has been identified with the artistic autonomy associated with the aestheticist movement. Certainly he understood distance from the inchoate complexity of urban life as essential to preserve social relations, a distance that he found in formal abstraction, leading him to equate play forms such as sociability, coquetry, and etiquette with art:

> **Within this constellation called society, or out of it, there develops a special sociological structure corresponding to those of art and play, which draw their form from these realities but nevertheless leave their realities behind them.... And as that which I have called artistic impulse draws its form from the complexes of perceivable things and builds this form into a special structure corresponding to the artistic impulse, so also the impulse to sociability distills, as it were, out of the realities of social life the pure essence of association.**[112]

Clearly Simmel had derived his sociological observations from Kantian aesthetics; his theory of play-as-art preceded and informed his conclusions about association: "Sociability in its pure form has no ulterior end, no content, and no result outside itself"; its "play, obedient to its own laws...represents *aesthetically* that moderation which the seriousness of realities otherwise demands."[113] Furthermore, critics have pointed out that Simmel's model is quintessentially modernist in its hermetic self-referentiality. Yet when he turned away from the direct address of art to examine play forms, Simmel broke from aestheticist preconceptions to permit art a degree of engagement with modern social relations. His sociological project refers constantly to Nietzschean precedents—in his concern with the plight of individuality as threatened by modernism's homogenizing forces and in the articulation of a human condition characterized by constant conflict, as well as in the "pathos of distance," first articulated in Nietzschean aesthetics as the Apollonian play of illusion, and here appearing in "artistic play" as a "complete turnover, from the determination of the forms by the materials of life to the determination of its materials by forms that have become supreme values."[114] That is, the sense that society has permitted its cultural forms to manipulate behavior toward the filling of "pseudo-needs" permeated Simmel's thought. Like Nietzsche, Simmel saw this illusory takeover as an inevitable and unavoidable situation under capital, and like Nietzsche he understood the effective contravention against this illusion as itself ludic. But unlike Nietzsche, Simmel located the destructive dimension of play *within* that veil of pseudo-needs, and not in a counterviolence that is separate and cyclical. For Simmel, recourse is to be found from within the ludic system exactly because the play forms that the system forces into being share the structure, if not the content, of a quotidian made absurd under capital. Simmel grasped the possibility of a dynamic life that can be lived entirely within culture and a material reality that can only ever be understood from within cultural constructs. He agreed with Nietzsche that all is play, but he did not allocate the constructive aspect of the ludic to culture and its destructive dimension to a natural reality that precedes it. Rather, all of culture, for Simmel, was understood as imbricated with a Janus-faced play, and thus riven by conflict, a situation exemplified through the paradoxical nature of artistic play—a form that at once "derealizes experience through self-enclosure and indicates the inner meanings of flowing life."[115]

Simmel described a qualified autonomy for art, making a distinction between empty form and art that retains its attachment to material reality, and it is through this quality that art gains its status as a play form—it is *not* transcendent but deeply contextual because it derives from "the flux of life":

Fully established, art is wholly separated from life. It takes only what it can use, thus creating itself, as it were, a second time. And yet the forms by which it does this, and of which it actually consists, were produced by the exigencies and the very dynamics of life.... Actual forces, needs, impulses of life produce the forms of our behavior that are suitable for play. These forms, however, become independent contents and stimuli within play itself, or, rather, as play. There are, for instance, the hunt; the gain by ruse; the proving of physical and intellectual strength; competition; and the dependence on chance and on the favor of powers that cannot be influenced.... Here lies whatever may justify the analogy between art and play. It is from their origin, which keeps them permeated with life, that they draw their depth and strength. Where they are emptied of life, they become artifice and "empty play" respectively.[116]

Yet even as Simmel went out of his way to lift the Kantian prohibition of sensuous desire as a determinant of aesthetics, he made it clear that the relation of art to life is not one of reconciliation or mirroring. He cited the dramatic actor, who draws on life experience in order to manage gaps in the text of the play, producing an artistic expression that "interweaves those two roles (the personality of the player and that of the portrayed) as organic elements." This relation of art to life is meant to operate reciprocally, as a model for the "replacing of mechanism with life processes" in modern life; a "distinctively modern way of understanding the modern world."[117]

In spite of their autonomy, Simmel's play forms must retain their relation to concrete individuals and social forms or they will cease to have power and will degenerate into empty form. Thus the paradox implied in play situations would be central to their distinctive value: "In them," Simmel wrote, "we are released from life but have it still." "Sociability is a *symbol* of life as life emerges in the flux of a facile and happy play; yet it is also a symbol of *life.* It does not change the image of life beyond the point required by its own distance to it. In like manner, if it is not to strike one as hollow and false, even the freest and most fantastic art, however far it is from any copying of reality, nevertheless feeds on a deep and loyal relation to this reality. Art, too, is *above* life, but it is also above *life.*"[118]

Play forms, then, are constituted exactly through their distinction from life, a difference that is nevertheless perceived through the matrix of life itself. Simmel expressed this difference in the modern context as a unity experienced in play that cannot be found in the fragmented and inchoate flux of the quotidian, and because of this his play forms have been understood as an expression of Idealism.[119] But because play signifies "difference"—difference in general, as well as from the usual course of life—play's inconstancy overrides any historically specific identification of modern play as a totality. As historical circumstances shift, Simmel contended, so does the nature of art-as-play, always pursuing difference for its own sake: "So long as life is instinctive, affective and irrational, aesthetic redemption from it takes on...rationalistic form. Once intelligence, reckoning and balance have penetrated it, the aesthetic need once again changes into its opposite, seeking the irrational and its external form, the asymmetrical."[120]

Simmel's artistic play is contextually bound, but it is emphatically not a reflection theory for art. "Natural" behavior in play is to be avoided, lest the play be understood as a mere mask for objective and subjective motives, "just as a painting becomes a lie when it tries, in panoramic effect, to simulate reality."[121] Rather, art conceived as play in Simmel's model constitutes itself according to and *in opposition to* prevailing life forms and processes. Simmel understood, for example, the attraction to utopian schemes, the stability of autocracy, and the regularity and reliability of machines as reciprocal with the social and cultural disintegration of the nineteenth century: "A time which simultaneously idolizes Böcklin and Impressionism, Naturalism and Symbolism, Socialism and Nietzsche—such a time apparently discovers the most developed stimuli of its life in oscillations between the extreme poles of universal human existence."[122] Simmel's model for artistic play circumscribed an oppositive space for art that, while it offered relief, was theorized not as an escape from reality but an active form of critique: " Art seems to reveal the mystery of life: the fact that we cannot be relieved from life by looking away from it, but only by shaping and experiencing the sense and the forces of its deepest reality in the unreal and seemingly quite autonomous play of its forms."[123]

Simmel effectively posited play's central paradox—a phenomenon apart from reality yet part of reality—as functioning to preserve art's critical dimension. Distance in this model is not meant to substitute for intervention, but to secure a place for the practice of alternative structures. In the modern context, this means that unified forms will be activated against a generalized fragmentation, but the model is labile enough also to account for the emergence of both irrational and nonobjective art in the milieu of a rationalized and objectifying exchange-based economy: for Simmel, so long as play was structured *as* difference, it could not be co-opted.

Simmel illustrated this interactive mode of ludic experience through two figures who are consistently juxtaposed as "other" to their milieu: the adventurer and the stranger. By definition, adventures are departures from the continuity of ordinary life, just as strangers are only constituted as such in extraordinary circumstances. Yet at the same time, they are caught in a paradoxical play situation inside life. Because of its simultaneous distance from and concurrence with life, Simmel classes the adventure with art: "A part of existence, interwoven with the uninterruptedness of that existence, yet nevertheless felt as a whole, as an integrated unit—this is the form common to both the work of art and the adventure." For Simmel, what all these play forms (including art) share is the arrest of meaning and progress brought about by their structural paradoxes. A kind of immediacy characterizes play, most obvious in the extreme contextual dependency of the stranger and the adventurer, whose identity as such depends exclusively on their milieu: "The adventurer... lives in the present. On the one hand, he is not determined by the past...nor, on the other hand, does the future exist for him."[124]

Simmel identified this state of immediacy with madness and with dreaming, most explicitly through their respective suspensions of memory:

a remembered adventure tends to take on the quality of a dream. Everyone knows how quickly we forget dreams because they, too, are placed outside the meaningful context of life-as-a-whole. What we designate as "dreamlike" is nothing but a memory which is bound to the unified, consistent life-processes by fewer threads than are ordinary experiences.... The more "adventurous" an adventure, that is, the more fully it realizes its idea, the more "dreamlike" it becomes in our memory.[125]

The resulting associative chain, play/art/dream/madness, brings to mind Walter Benjamin's critique of the urban dream world of commodities—a world of objectified forms we both create and turn against, even as we allow those objects to determine our behavior.[126] When play's immediacy is read as it is here, in relation to alienation and an economy of exchange, it emerges as a general critique of progress and of the role of novelty in shaping modern experience. For in Simmel's formulation, nothing less than the very link from reality to play and art is based in obsolescence: all play forms hang on the skeletal remains of once-useful activity. As such, they have a kind of historical memory built into them in the form of a subversive reminder of the past that works against the incessant rhetoric of progress. Artistic representation is no exception: "The interpretation of realities, concrete or abstract, in terms of spatial systems or of rhythms or sounds, or of significance and organization, certainly had its origins in practical needs. Yet these interpretations have become purposes in themselves, effective on their own strength and in their own right, selective and creative quite independently of their entanglement with practical life, and not because of it. This is the origin of art."[127]

Simmel argued that play forms such as the hunt, once necessary for survival, and etiquette, which had its roots in the practical purposes of knighthood, gradually pulled away from "the service of life that originally produced and employed them." Likewise coquetry, the play form of eroticism, is a sexual relation released from its original goal of procreation to "exclusively serve its own operation or realization." More globally, and in direct reference to philosophical Idealism, he extended his assessment of outmoded forms into the realms of truth and morality, asserting that cognition as a whole originally had to do with the "struggle for existence," but that now "science has become a value in itself." "The same dialectic," Simmel argued, "determines the nature of law." We tend to follow the letter of the law, forgetting its origin: "It determines, through its own right…how the contents of life should be shaped." Simmel claimed that the only difference between a play form like coquetry and the play forms of science and law is that coquetry openly admits to its artificiality, whereas the arbitrariness of cognition and enforced morality routinely masquerade as natural and universal truths.

This is perhaps Simmel at his most Nietzschean—articulating the paradoxical twofold nature of play as both illusion and the means of exposing illusion. Activities that have been rendered obsolescent in modern life are positioned as the very play forms that run counter to the means-ends homogenization of modern experience. Read this way, play is deployed in the modern cultural field as just so much commodity detritus, engaged with the norms of utility and novelty through its very difference from them. While Simmel's firm distinction between art and utility had its origin in Kantian disinterest, "purposelessness," reinvoked here, in the modern context of productivity and exchange, shifts in value and takes on political significance. This significance shows at one level in the sheer juxtaposition of obsolescence to novelty, as the very presence of outmoded forms serves to unmask novelty as the instrument of commerce. In concrete terms, it is the same revolutionary energy of the destitute that Walter Benjamin, reading Simmel for the notes that would become his *Passagen-Werk,* recognized as central to avant-garde resistance.

Simmel never used the words "use-value" or "ritual" in relation to play forms. Yet he characterized the play-state as historically indeterminate, much in the manner of ritual's liminality. As an experience, it exists in an unpredictable state of immediacy with no effect on the future and no memory of the past, as in sociable conversation, where the topic is allowed to shift associatively without regard for having argued a point or completed a story. Play enjoys a temporal suspension commensurate with its deferral of meaning—as in gambling, where, according to Benjamin, each new game "forgets" the losses that came before it and plays out independently of the next round, or internally, as in the game of chess, where the players proceed from moment to moment in the game, strategy and status (as winner or loser) shifting according to the opponent's unpredictable move.[128] Similarly, Simmel recognized immediacy in the extreme contextuality of play forms—there is the figure of the stranger who is named as such exclusively in relation to his milieu, as well as the constant flux of the adventure, a state that is constituted only in its difference to the slippery notion of normal life.[129] Other of his play forms achieve a state of suspension through juxtaposed actions, as in the stalemate of flirtation, a form poised between consent and refusal and enjoyed perversely for its deferral of erotic satisfaction. Every one of these instances values means over ends, prolonging the play in a demonstration of the pleasures of process over product. So while the fleeting ephemerality of play marks it as emphatically modernist, play resists modernization in that its self-referential dynamism will produce nothing that can be objectified in the service of institutional exchange and exhibition. Rather, Simmelian play forms are pure active experience exempt from exchange value: they play themselves out and then everyone goes home.

The exception to this of course is the art object, which stubbornly clings to its material support. Even Simmel conceded that in their materiality, art objects tend to be caught up in the euphoria of exchange and exhibition, rendering them as subject to "passive *consumption.*"[130] Play forms that spool out as dynamic process, by contrast, resist objectification; sociability and adventuring display a "freedom from firm content and residual reality." Play is grounded, absurdly, in an immediacy that resists grounding. As such, it has the unique potential to turn against a commercially driven status quo, a potential that Simmel assured when he calculated play's very difference from commodities in terms of its distance from the norms of utility and novelty.

It is in this calculation that we find a discursive motivation for an avant-garde turn away from art toward play as part of the desire to reengage art with life. Play as it is aesthetically conceived—as a fixed, hermetic world that refers to nothing outside it—would seem to cut off any possibility of the player engaging with material reality. But when play is understood in its dimension of immediacy, it claims a relation to life that seeks to escape representation: a *presentation* that in its *unforseeability* could be understood as relatively raw and direct.

For Simmel, play is engaged for its own sake, but as such it signifies as resistance to a pervasive means/ends rationality; it is a form that fosters the irrational flow of experience for its own sake. Process in play suspends progress as well as product, the rhetorical and objective staples of the modern culture of commerce. Refusing utility and meaning, ludic practices form themselves in constant opposition to the status quo; thus play serves to *pronounce* the state of reality through the acknowledgment of structural difference. Its focus is on the conflict rather than the reconciliation of life and art, and while Simmel is generally thought to be neo-Kantian, in this respect his theories resonate with a Nietzschean rather than Kantian ludic. Like Nietzsche's, his play is pervasive and has the power to determine behavior. To the extent that play forms exist as necessary adjustments to modern life, Simmel's subject is constructed—played—by his culture, and never regains the individual freedom lost to rationalized culture. In the final analysis, Simmel unwittingly deconstructed Kant, finding in Kantian theory the basis for his investigations of play forms, which in turn demonstrate their inability to stabilize meaning and achieve the unity of Kantian Idealism.

Too often play has been identified with a liberation of desire that is characterized as an unconflicted impulse toward pleasure, a popular attribution that ignores the complexity and elusiveness of pleasure itself. In this short account of the ludic field, I have pointed out a collapse of categories that had already been discursively identified with play by the time the interwar avant-gardes came on the scene: the imbrication of pain with pleasure; of destruction with affirmation; and dynamism with stasis. Play in modernism is marked by displeasure, and by this I mean not only affective unpleasure, but a conscious dissatisfaction with the exigencies of modern life. Dissonance as critique inflected manifestations of avant-garde play as well, withdrawing them from any simple characterization of the ludic as sheer liberation.

Certainly the avant-garde had this idea in common with Simmel: that the pervasive rationality of modern life had a leveling effect on individuality, forcing individuals into a system of exchange that reduced subject, object, and social relations to a single currency for ease of manipulation—itself a system that can be thought of as a kind of play, an endlessly repeatable interchange in which value is disengaged from pragmatic reference to the material world. Play itself would be one mode of resistance to this, deploying obsolescent forms as a critique of the myths of novelty and progress, and intensifying the ephemerality already present in modern life to the pitch of the utterly temporal: experience for its own sake. Dynamic process, the leitmotif of play, never places an object into circulation. Rather, it is enjoyed in the moment, for its own recalcitrant sake, abstracted from and grounded in the very life/play situation it critiques.

THE DUCHAMP CODE

2

GAVIN PARKINSON

Any interpretation comes along and hollows out its object from the inside, comes along and substitutes what the object is supposed to hide for what it's assumed to manifest.

—JEAN-FRANÇOIS LYOTARD

Following his relocation from Paris to New York in June 1915, Marcel Duchamp put work on *The Large Glass* project on hold, producing a few pieces conspicuously informed by his heightened awareness of the imperious faculty of language both to nurture and to block communication. There are halting letters written by Duchamp in English dating from November 1915, and during that period the tyranny of language was a pressing concern for him. Knowing little English, he was confronted by the organizing office of what Michel de Certeau has termed "the scriptural economy"; that is, in de Certeau's words, language as a "scriptural system," which "transforms the subjects that controlled it into operators of the writing machine that orders and uses them."[1] But alongside this feeling of helplessness caused by the everyday difficulties presented by a new language, Duchamp also came to understand the creative freedom provided by language when it is experienced with a certain alienated detachment. Faced with this and eager to exploit it, he began to append script in English or French to the earliest readymades at that time, opening up a gap of nonmeaning by creating a breach between the object and its given phrase, and sometimes by evacuating descriptive or utilitarian sense from the inscription. For instance, the lifeless, blank simplicity of *Comb* of 1916 (fig. 1) is infracted by its capitalized inscription in French, which can translate as "two or three drops of height have nothing to do with savagery," a phrase that itself fends off definitive signification.

Additionally, among his earliest works completed in New York were *The* (1915, fig. 2) and *Rendez-vous du Dimanche 6 Février 1916* (fig. 3), exercises that free language from its descriptive function. Duchamp used script in both of these works, arranging words into sentences so that the general constructions read rationally while sense is evacuated. So, a part of the *Rendez-vous* text translates as follows: "From tomorrow at last I'll have put exactly there the batteries where several melt, they accept though draft their bearings. First, was pricking their leagues on bottles, despite their importance in a hundred serenities?" Similarly, in the cryptic approach Duchamp takes in *The,* each mention of the word "the" is replaced by a star, along with an invitation to fill in the gaps. However, when the reader does this, the hoped-for

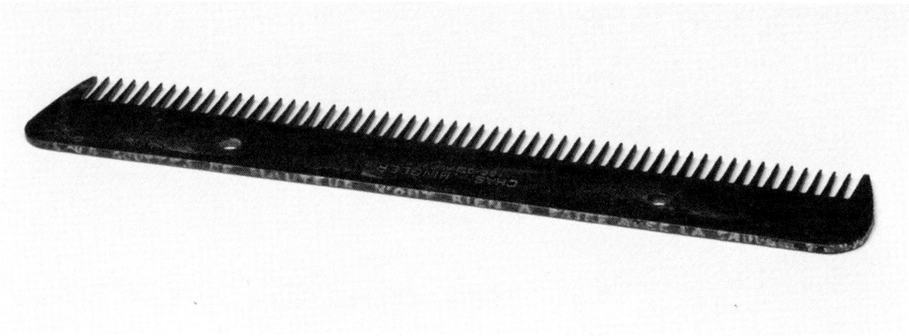

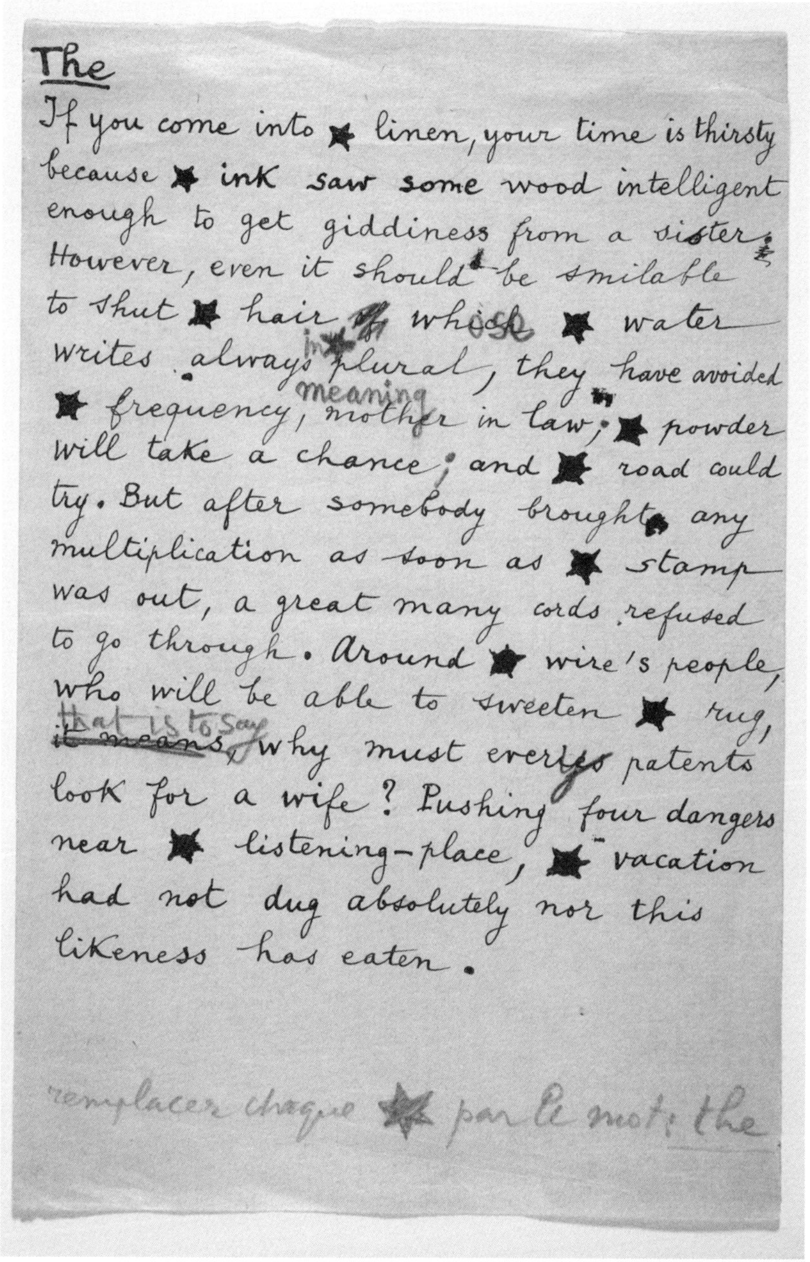

The

If you come into * linen, your time is thirsty because * ink saw some wood intelligent enough to get giddiness from a sister. However, even it should be smilable to shut * hair whose * water writes always plural, they have avoided * frequency, mother in law; * powder will take a chance; and * road could try. But after somebody brought any multiplication as soon as * stamp was out, a great many cords refused to go through. Around * wire's people, who will be able to sweeten * rug, that is to say why must every patents look for a wife? Pushing four dangers near * listening-place, * vacation had not dug absolutely nor this likeness has eaten.

remplacer chaque * par le mot: the

FIG. 1
Marcel Duchamp, *Comb,* 1916, steel, 1¼ × 6½ inches (3.2 × 16.5 cm). Philadelphia Museum of Art, The Louise and Walter Arensberg Collection, 1950.

FIG. 2
Marcel Duchamp, *The,* 1915. Philadelphia Museum of Art, The Louise and Walter Arensberg Collection, 1950.

FIG. 3
Marcel Duchamp, *Rendez-vous du Dimanche 6 Février 1916,* 1916, typewriter and ink on four postcards, with tape, 11¼ × 6½ inches. Philadelphia Museum of Art, The Louise and Walter Arensberg Collection, 1950.

-toir. On manquera, à la fois, de
moins qu'avant cinq élections et
aussi quelque accointance avec q-
-uatre petites bêtes; il faut oc-
-cuper ce délice afin d'en décli-
-ner toute responsabilité. Après
douze photos, notre hésitation de-
-vant vingt fibres était compréh-
-ensible; même le pire accrochage
demande coins porte-bonheur sans
compter interdiction aux lins: C-
-omment ne pas épouser son moind-
-re opticien plutôt que supporter
leurs mèches? Non, décidément, der-
-rière ta canne se cachent marbr-
-ures puis tire-bouchon. "Cepend-
-ant, avouèrent-ils, pourquoi viss-
-er, indisposer? Les autres ont p-
-ris démangeaisons pour construi-
-re, par douzaines, ses lacements.
Dieu sait si nous avons besoin, q-
-uoique nombreux mangeurs, dans un
défalquage." Défense donc au tri-
-ple, quand j'ourlerai, dis je, or-

-onent, après avoir fini votre gê-
-ne. N'empêche que le fait d'éte-
-indre six boutons l'un ses autr-
-es paraît (sauf si, lui, tourne a-
-utour) faire culbuter les bouto-
-nnières. Reste à choisir: de lo-
-ngues, fortes, extensibles défect-
-ions trouées par trois filets u-
-sés, ou bien, la seule enveloppe
pour éteindre Avez vous accepté
des manches? Pouvais tu prendre
sa file? Peut-être devons nous a-
-ttendre mon pilotis, en même tem-
-ps ma difficulté; avec ces chos-
-es là, impossible ajouter une hu-
-itième laisse. Sur trente misé-
-rables postes deux actuels veul-
-ent errer, remboursés civiquement,
refusent toute compensation hors
leur sphère. Pendant combien, pou-
-rquoi comment, limitera-t-on min-
-ce étiage? autrement dit: clous
refroidissent lorsque beaucoup p-
-lissent enfin derrière, contenant

reste pour les profits, devant le-
-squels et, par précaution à prop-
-os, elle défonce desserts, même c-
-eux qu'il est défendu de nouer.
Ensuite, sept ou huit poteaux boi-
-vent quelques conséquences main-
-tenant appointées; ne pas oubli-
-er, entre parenthèses, que sans l'
-économat, puis avec mainte sembl-
-able occasion, reviennent quatre
fois leurs énormes limes; quoi!
alors, si la férocité débouche de-
-rrière son propre tapis. Dès dem-
-ain j'aurai enfin mis exactemen-
-t des piles là où plusieurs fen-
-dent, acceptent quoique mandant
le pourtour. D'abord, piquait on
ligues sur bouteilles, malgré le-
-ur importance dans cent séréni-
-tés? Une liquide algarade, après
semaines dénonciatrices, va en y
détester ta valise car un bord
suffit. Nous sommes actuellement
assez essuyés, voyez quel désarroi

porte, dès maintenant par grande
quantité, pourront faire valoir l-
-e clan oblong qui, sans ôter auc-
-un traversin ni contourner moin-
-s de grelots, va remettre. Deux
fois seulement, tout élève voudra-
-it traire, quand il facilite la
bascule disséminée; mais, comme q-
-uelqu'un démonte puis avale des
déchirements nains nombreux, soi
compris, on est obligé d'entamer
plusieurs grandes horloges pour
obtenir un tiroir à bas âge. Co-
-nclusion: après maints efforts
en vue du peigne, quel dommage!
tous les fourreurs sont partis e-
-t signifient riz. Aucune deman-
-de ne nettoie l'ignorant ou sc-
-ié teneur; toutefois, étant don-
-nées quelques cages, c'eut une
profonde émotion qu'éxécutent t-
-outes colles alitées. Tenues, v-
-ous auriez manqué si s'était t-
-rouvée là quelque prononciation

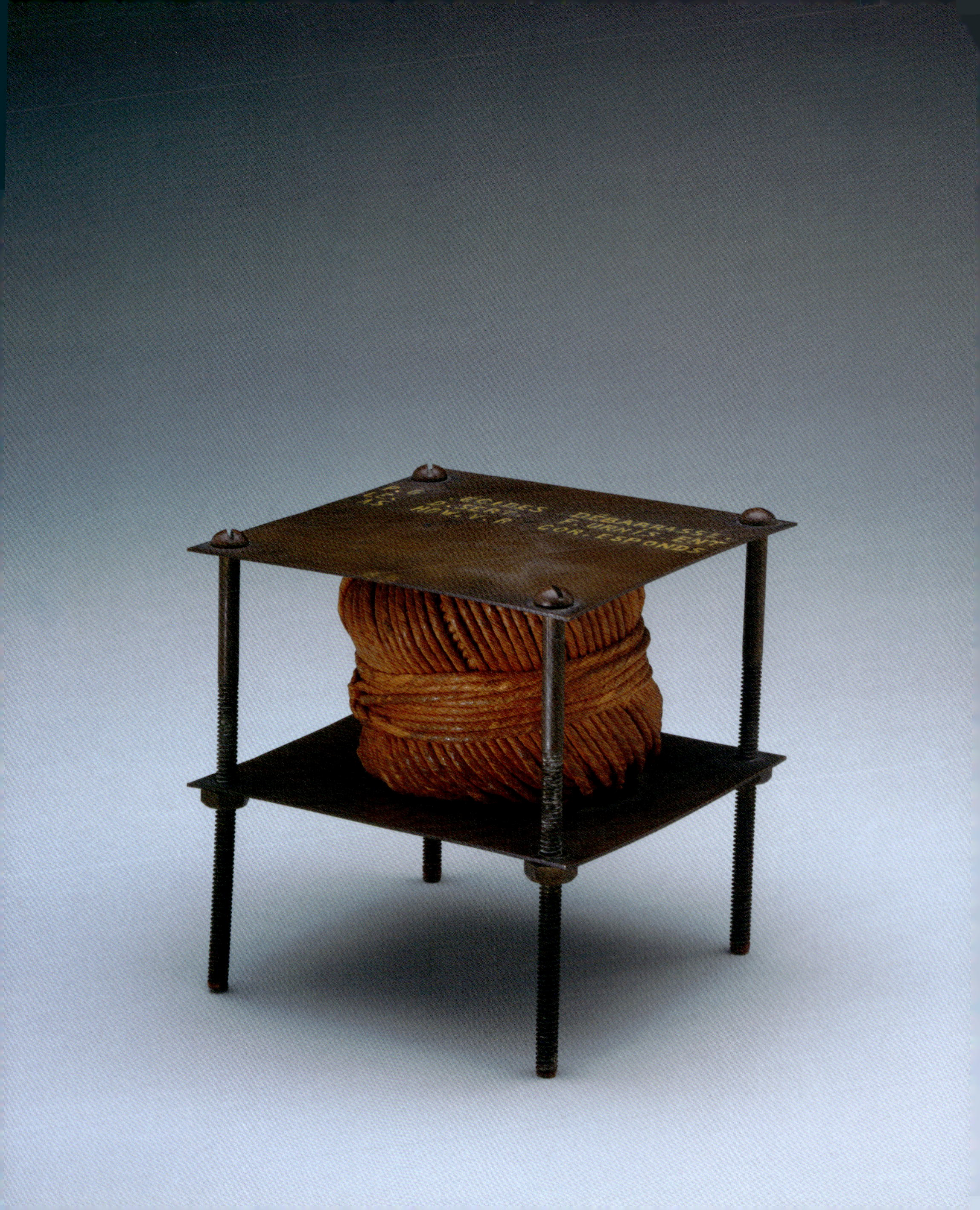
P.G. .ECIDES DEBARRASSE.
LE. D.SERT. F.URNIS.ENT
.AS HOW.V.R COR.ESPONDS

fullness and plenitude of meaning is further delayed, as the text continues to baffle, reading at one point: "If you come into the linen, your time is thirsty because the ink saw some wood intelligent enough to get giddiness from a sister." Full signification seems about to happen, just before us but always beyond our reach, inviting us to speculate further so that we can erase our feeling of a lack or shortfall in our knowledge.

The predominant practices of analysis and interpretation in our culture and society generally, in the service of the pursuit of meaning and value, encourage us to create a pattern, to resolve "problems" by discovering concealed order behind apparent disorder. These "incomplete" works by Duchamp play on our expectation of a future resolution-to-be-found, prodding us back and forth between their endless points of reference until we inevitably discover potential connections within the universal Duchampian iconography.[2] Perhaps the "sister" mentioned in *The* is Duchamp's sister, Suzanne? Might "pricking their leagues on bottles" in the *Rendez-vous* refer somehow to the Readymade *Bottle Rack* (1914)? Could "league" as a measure of distance be linked with *3 Standard Stoppages* (1913–14)? Playing upon our feeling that there is something lacking, Duchamp's objects draw us into an anticipative rejoinder, which is a response ingrained in us by the tradition of inquiry to which we are subject. They captivate our established, critical tendency toward deduction through questions and answers, and academic art history is nothing if not a problem-raising and -solving discipline, fascinated by the problem of Marcel Duchamp.

FIG. 4
Marcel Duchamp,
With Hidden Noise, 1916,
string, brass, screws, and unknown material,
12.9 × 13 × 11.4 cm.
Philadelphia Museum of Art,
The Louise and Walter Arensberg Collection, 1950.

Two other pieces of 1916, *With Hidden Noise* (fig. 4) and *Apolinère Enameled,* bear on their audience in the same way. In the case of the first, Duchamp secured a ball of string between two brass plates with four long screws, then requested his friend and patron Walter Arensberg to open it, place an object inside, and secure the plates again, keeping the identity of the object a secret, even from Duchamp himself. Arensberg died in 1954, taking the identity of the concealed object with him to the grave. Subsequently, at the time of his first solo retrospective exhibition in Pasadena in 1963, Duchamp gave another friend, the curator Walter Hopps, permission to look inside the ball of string, again asking that the hidden component be kept from him. Duchamp's atypical way of thinking is brought to the fore by *With Hidden Noise,* as the requirement *not* to know goes squarely against the prototypical social, philosophical, and pedagogical grain of Western custom and habit. The shortfall he wantonly created in his own knowledge of a work of which he was the author—his incorporation of "incompletion" into *With Hidden Noise* as an element of its composition—is quite at odds not just with the desire for mastery and the universalizing thirst for wisdom and search for truth that have historically characterized inquiry in the arts, humanities, and sciences, but also with basic human curiosity.[3]

Ideas of secrecy and exclusion, broached by the mysterious component, are furthered by three lines of script in a combination of French and English on the upper and lower surfaces of *With Hidden Noise.* As with *The,* there are discontinuities in the text but, again, when we fill in the gaps as invited, we are confronted with an enticing defiance of intelligibility:

P.G ECIDES DÉBARRASSE.
LE. D.SERT. F.URNIS ENT
AS HOW.V.R COR.ESPONDS

.IR. .CAR.É LONGSEA
F.NE, HEA., .O.SQUE
.TE.U S.ARP BAR.AIN

The secrets carried by, and characterizing, *With Hidden Noise* open a space in the future, inviting speculation from we problem-solvers as to its anticipated resolution and "completion." As with Duchamp's work in glass, *With Hidden Noise* cannot be seized and considered only in a past or in the present. For just as the fragility of the works on glass seems to announce an uncertain future in their very material, so *With Hidden Noise* is designed in such a way that it is not fully present to the mind yet has the potential, imminently, to be so.[4]

An "assisted readymade" that he produced a little later, the rectified advertisement *Apolinère Enameled* (fig. 5), conceals letters of the original script to give the work its title, and to include another incomplete message to its bottom right, reading "ANY ACT RED BY HER TEN OR EPERGNE, NEW YORK, U.S.A." Rather than attempting to decode this message, Dalia Judovitz opts for a manifestly subjective interpretation based on an irritating mixture of iconography and punning, contending that the reflected girl's hair that Duchamp drew onto the mirror of *Apolinère Enameled* is meant to designate her as an "heir" to painting; that "heir" is a pun on the French pronunciation of the letter *r* (*air*); which when pronounced in English is a pun on the French word *"art";* about which Judovitz then writes, "This pun on art is a reference to another Readymade, *Paris Air.*"[5] She might have found some meaning here, but, clearly, this cannot be true. Duchamp could not have been referring to *Paris Air* in *Apolinère Enameled* as the former was made at least two years *after* the latter. Given the obviousness of this historical fact, we can assume Judovitz is playing along with Duchamp and hopping from one point to another in the field of interrelatable elements that make up his work; otherwise we would have to assume that such is the programmatic will to deduce that it can occlude a fundamental, documented, irreducible fact: namely, that one event preceded another chronologically.

Another work that has accrued immense interest over the years is the 1921 birdcage containing cubes of marble, a thermometer, and a cuttlebone, *Why Not Sneeze Rose Sélavy?* (fig. 6), accumulating endless meanings courtesy of a scholarly approach to art rooted in a particular history and tradition of interpretation. We are readers, interpreters, pattern makers, and "behindologists," with a remit to read out the rational in the face of the unfathomable. Gestures such as *The, With Hidden Noise,* and *Why Not Sneeze?* are folded into rational explanations as demanded by the confrontation of art history with the shortfall in sense, which, as a rational, logocentric discipline, it abhors. Among the most mesmerizing analyses of *Why Not Sneeze?* are those by Hubert Damisch (it is "about" chess) and Jon Wood (it is "about" Brancusi's studio).[6] These discerning and sensitive interpretations depend heavily on iconographic unpacking, which has long played a significant role in art history—that is, the identification, description, and interpretation of individual elements within

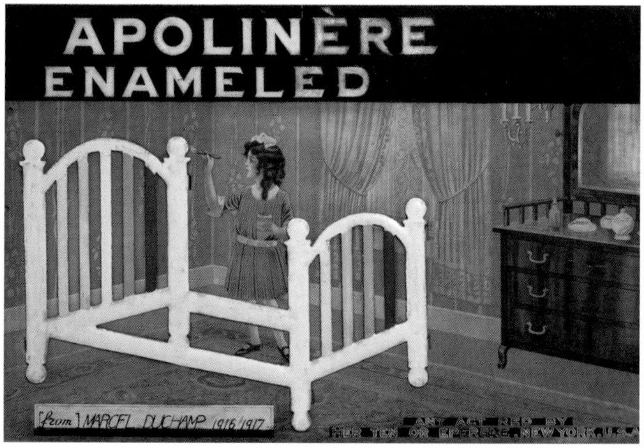

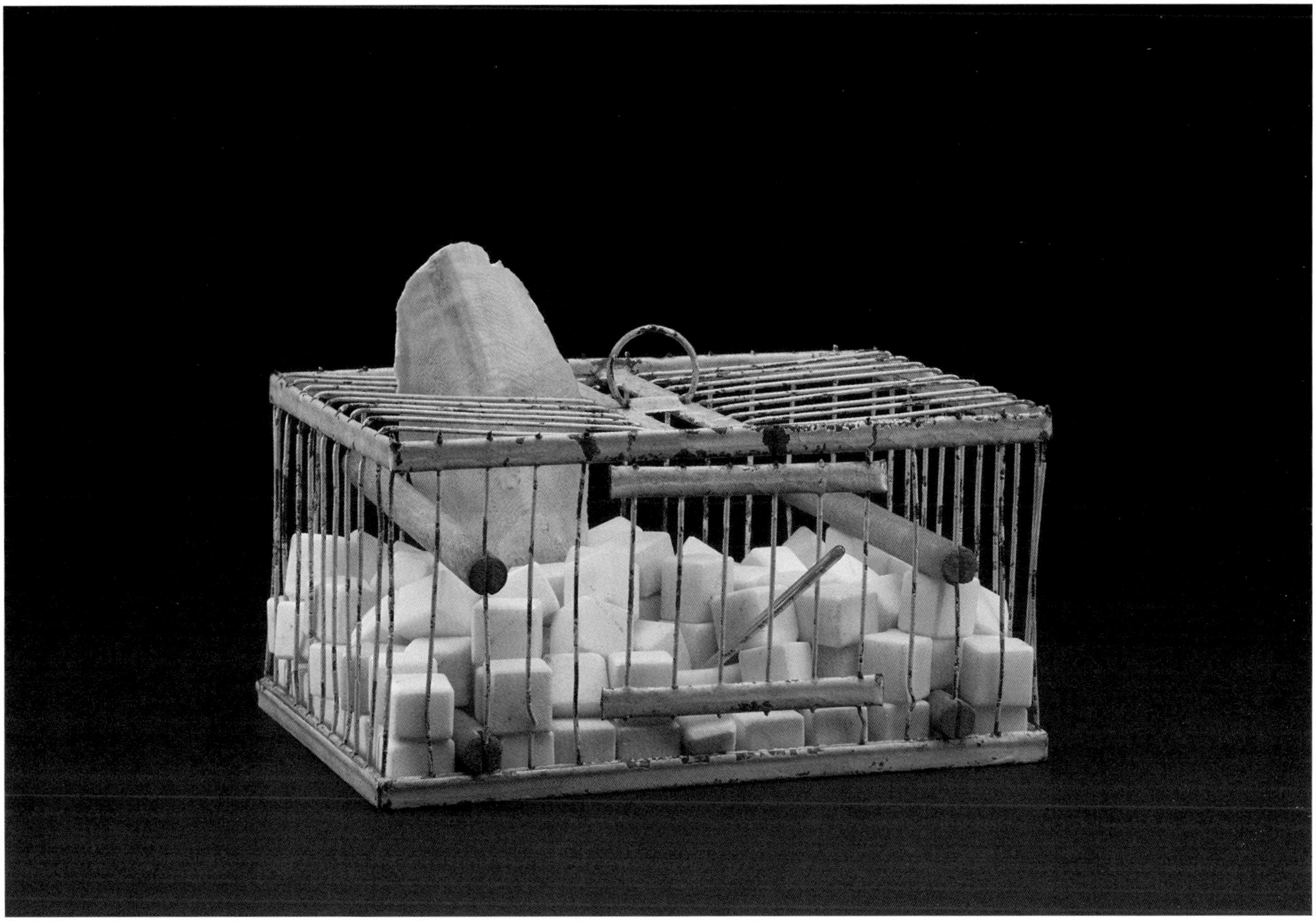

FIG. 5

Marcel Duchamp,
Apolinère Enameled, 1916–17,
gouache and pencil on painted tin, mounted
on board, 24.4 × 33.9 cm.
Philadelphia Museum of Art, The Louise
and Walter Arensberg Collection, 1950.

FIG. 6

Marcel Duchamp, *Why Not Sneeze*
Rose Sélavy? 1921,
painted metal birdcage, marble cubes,
porcelain dish, thermometer, and cuttlebone,
$4\frac{7}{8} \times 8\frac{3}{4} \times 6\frac{3}{8}$ inches (12.4 × 22.2 × 16.2 cm).
Philadelphia Museum of Art,
The Louise and Walter Arensberg Collection, 1950.

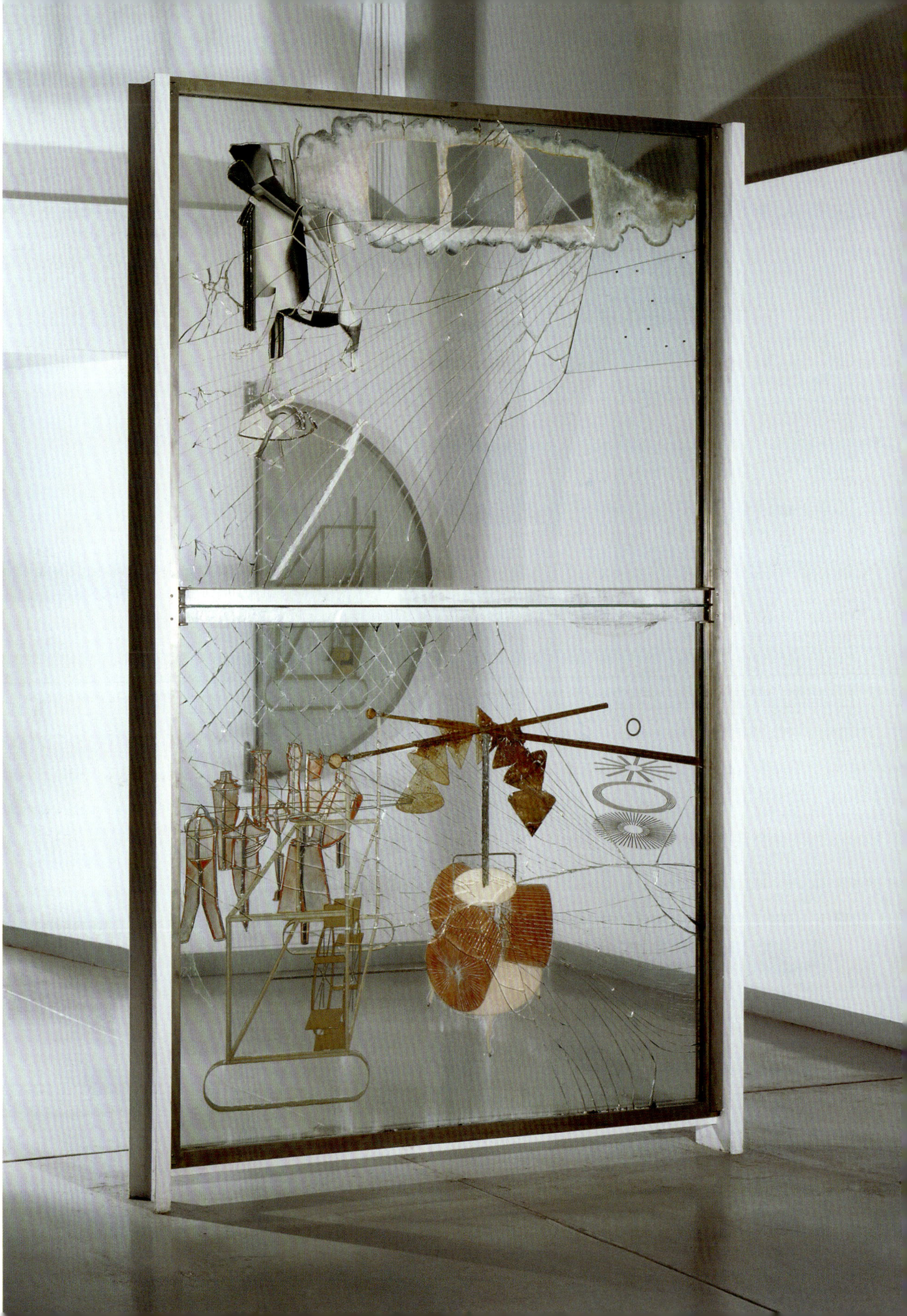

a work of art, which add up to its meaning. However, as John Cage pointed out, Duchamp's multifarious oeuvre encompasses the world ("Say it's not a Duchamp. Turn it over and it is"), and therefore iconographic readings allow anything to be linked to it, and claimed for and about individual works within it.[7] Stubbornly refusing on first showing to yield its "secret," *Why Not Sneeze?* prompts us to anxious inquiry: What does it symbolize? What lies behind it? What was Duchamp up to?

When such questions are put to the "definitively unfinished" *Large Glass* (1915–23, fig. 7), excessively elaborate and ingenious interpretive maneuvers ensue. Although its notes demonstrate that the *Glass* was created over a long period in a fragmentary, multilayered way, and imply it lacks a consistently readable metaphorical, mythological, or theological symbolism while eschewing a straightforward linear narrative in what it purports to represent, Duchamp's commentators tend to see a readable itinerary in the *Glass*, which they subsequently attempt to "resolve" within authorial intentionality. This almost imperceptible shift from the inference of pattern to the assertion of authorial intentionality—from the discovery of meaning to the affirmation of truth—is demanded by empiricist methods of art history inherited from or influenced by those of science and history. To terminate a reading at the level of inference is to remain at the level of poetry, myth, or fiction, whereas to extend that reading into the author's own true meaning (conscious or unconscious) is to assume the deterministic rigor and authority reserved by science and by disciplines like history, which share certain of the truth-telling claims of science. Even though the jumble of the *Green Box* (1934) was the best Duchamp could do as an explanation for *The Large Glass*, writers from Arturo Schwarz and Ulf Linde to Juan Antonio Ramírez have interrogated it and its notes as an oracle, by means of which the dots of Duchamp's disjointed oeuvre can be connected. Notwithstanding its brevity, Duchamp's work, including his writings, possesses a remarkable iconographic richness, and when this is combined with the profuse heterogeneity and multiplicity of the *Glass*, established upon its elliptical linguistic accompaniment in the *Green Box* notes, its audience is allowed a colossal field of interpretation. So, the "enameling" of *Apolinère Enameled* can be related to the prehistoric practice of painting dead bodies, and from there to the red paint used for the *Nine Malic Moulds* of the *Glass*,[8] the galvanized *Bottle Rack* can be linked to the electric current galvanizing the Bride and Bachelors;[9] and *Bicycle Wheel* (1913) can be said to resemble "another copulating machine" like

FIG. 7

Marcel Duchamp,
The Bride Stripped Bare by Her Bachelors, Even (The Large Glass), 1915–23,
oil varnish, lead foil, lead wire, and dust on two glass panels, 109¼ × 69¼ inches (277.5 × 175.9 cm).
Philadelphia Museum of Art,
Bequest of Katherine S. Dreier, 1952.

The Large Glass, while snow might spiral off the snow shovel titled *In Advance of the Broken Arm* (1916) like the Splash of sperm from the Bachelors, and the young girl in *Apolinère Enameled* can be said to be analogous with the Bride of *The Large Glass,* and so on.[10]

It is only shallow people who do not judge by appearances. The true mystery of the world is the visible, not the invisible.

—OSCAR WILDE

As I present them here, then, Duchamp's objects are "anticipative" gestures, seeming to require our assistance for their "satisfactory," "necessary" passage from incompleteness to completeness, uncertainty to certainty, indetermination to determination, obscurity to clarity. They confirm and confound art-historical methodologies in the sense that they are susceptible to its interpretive procedures to such an excessive degree that interpretation ends up seeming futile: if every approach "works" perfectly well, what kind of critical leverage can any approach be said to have at all? Alchemical and psychoanalytic methodologies are too obvious to analyze as case studies to demonstrate this, so I shall look at a sample piece of writing central to the literature on Duchamp, the dexterous 1986 article by Thierry de Duve, "The Readymade and the Tube of Paint."[11] In this, de Duve boldly reframes Duchamp's readymades as "belonging to the history of painting, and not, for example...to that of sculpture,"[12] by clarifying the "historical context common to the readymade and abstract painting."[13] Where it has been generally believed that the use of wallpaper, newspaper, and so on in Picasso's and Braque's collages of 1912 and 1913 was the bridge that allowed Duchamp to cross from painting to the readymade in 1913 (with *Bicycle Wheel* of that year), de Duve jigsaws together a handful of fragments that have appeared under the heading "Duchamp" from 1912 to 1963 (paintings, readymades, passing remarks, puns, scribbled notes), making a case for the readymade as a complex, melancholy assessment of the impossibility of painting in the age of abstraction. Put in the "right" order, Duchamp's obscure objects and aphoristic notes can be made to mean anything you like, and de Duve's ingenuity and elegant connectivity take full advantage of this to produce a classic Duchamp conspiracy theory as the pivot for his essay.

As so often, the story he tells of the readymade's commentary on and critique of painting in the midst of the move to abstraction finds origin and source in Duchamp's own authorship. For Duchamp joked about paintings being readymades in four casual asides between 1961 and 1963—about half a century after the first readymade, and in a different cultural context, that is—remarking that since all paintings were created from already made, manufactured tubes of paint, they were all "readymades aided."[14] De Duve takes this as a late confession by Duchamp finally coming clean about what readymades *really* mean: "The hint is that the Readymade is a sort of abnormal painting."[15] Duchamp does not actually define this as their meaning in these late remarks (even though he said on plenty of other occasions what he himself thought they meant), so invoking Edgar Allan Poe, de Duve argues that within Duchamp's statements, "the clue was certainly there to be picked up."[16]

The plot thickens from this point, with combs in Duchamp's *œuvre* acting collectively as a kind of grassy knoll. The title of the readymade *Comb* or *Peigne* (the subjunctive sense of the French verb *peindre,* to paint) becomes Exhibit A—a pun of "genius," bent to the curve of de Duve's argument and embellished as Duchamp's expression of his abandonment of painting under industrialization and simultaneous retention of the potential to paint.[17] The same message is found by de Duve among the nonsense of Duchamp's *Rendez-vous du Dimanche 6 Février 1916,* in the sentence "after many efforts toward the comb, what a pity," and inferred again from two more of Duchamp's notes, including an innocuous and amusing one from the *Green Box,* reading, "classify combs by the number of their teeth" (while de Duve's footnote links all these combs to the Cubists' use of combs to make fake wood graining in their paintings).[18] There is even a message to us by Duchamp from beyond the grave, like a piece of paper clasped in the hand of a murder victim, which is characterized as "an invitation handed over to us posthumous readers...to reinvigorate the history of modern painting as if it still had its future."[19] De Duve sees this in the note by Duchamp reading, "The possible is an *infra-mince.* The possibility of several tubes of paint becoming a Seurat is the concrete explanation of the possible as *infra-mince.*"[20] Like the other clues that de Duve sought, selected, and connected from an array of flotsam and jetsam covering fifty years, a fragment like this could be trimmed to suit any theory reliant on such ambiguous evidence.

If de Duve's attempt to crack the Duchamp code sounds a bit like a Dan Brown novel in miniature, then there has been at least one comparable attempt (probably not serious) to implicate Duchamp in a *Da Vinci Code*–type conspiracy. This is recorded in the book by Philippe Duboy on the eccentric late eighteenth-/early nineteenth-century French architect Jean-Jacques Lequeu, which states that Duchamp was part of a "secret society, or rather a 'conspiratorial society,' underlying the falsification of Lequeu's work inside the Bibliothèque Nationale."[21] Duboy maintains that among his fellow conspirators might have been Apollinaire, or Georges Bataille, or Jacques Lacan. His evidence is entirely circumstantial, though this is never a barrier to the true conspiracy theorist for whom *tout se tient:* everything is connected.

The danger is in the neatness of identifications.

—SAMUEL BECKETT

Deductive methodologies in the field of literary theory were being parodied as de Duve mapped his constellation onto the Duchampian edifice. Umberto Eco uses the phrase *tout se tient* throughout his 1989 novel satirizing paranoid interpretation, *Foucault's Pendulum,* and crops up in his critical writings of the same period, too, where he assesses the adjacency of academic method and conspiracy in the wider world.[22] In the latter, Eco compares contemporary theories of textual interpretation with, on the one hand, Hermeticism, the belief system distinct from Greek and Latin rationalism, which grew up in the first and second centuries of the Christian era and was revitalized in Renaissance Neoplatonism and Christian Kabbalism in the sixteenth century; and, on the other hand, with Gnosticism, born around the same time. Both Hermeticism and Gnosticism emerged from a crisis in rationalism, seeking truth from books yet finding it "possible for many things to be true at the same time, even if they contradict each other."[23] The conflicting truths contained in books, then, must point to a deeper hidden Truth, through allusion and allegory, discoverable through shards of truth, which would confirm each other by means of "a revelation beyond human utterances."[24] Rejecting noncontradiction, Hermeticism "embraces ideas of universal sympathy (the connection between all things) and similarity."[25] Eco regards language and secrecy as intertwined as much in the contemporary mode of textual interpretation as in the Hermetic and Gnostic quest:

Every object, be it earthly or heavenly, hides a secret. Every time a secret has been discovered, it will refer to another secret in a progressive movement toward a final secret. Nevertheless, there can be no final secret. The ultimate secret of Hermetic initiation is that everything is secret. Hence the hermetic secret must be an empty one, because anyone who pretends to reveal any sort of secret is not himself initiated and has stopped at a superficial level of the knowledge of cosmic mystery. Hermetic thought transforms the whole world theatre into a linguistic phenomenon and at the same time denies language any power of communication.[26]

Eco goes on to quote the German sociologist and theorist of modernism Georg Simmel on the psychosocial significance of secrecy: "From secrecy, which shades all that is profound and significant, grows the typical error according to which everything mysterious is something important and essential. Before the unknown, man's natural impulse to idealize and his natural fearfulness cooperate toward the same goal: to intensify the unknown through imagination, and to pay attention to it with an emphasis that is not usually accorded to patent reality."[27] In other words, the black veil of secrecy, in art and life, frightens us with its threat of otherness—of something different to us so threatening—and we project familiarity in some form onto or behind it to regain our equilibrium and tame what lies beyond our understanding. We drag Duchamp's work out of the darkness of nonmeaning into the light of familiar ground (the chess board; Brancusi's studio) because in its magnetic strangeness it resembles nothing we have seen before, and that is disquieting.

Secrecy and conspiracy also play a key role in *Foucault's Pendulum.* Amused by the preposterous concoctions brought to them by prospective authors of conspiracy theories and the unexplained, Eco's three young publishers decide to create their own super-conspiracy by feeding random bits of information into an advanced computer program. They are then captivated by the interconnectedness it fabricates. "'Any fact becomes important when it's connected to another,'" insists one of Eco's characters: "The connection changes the perspective; it leads you to think that every detail of the world, every voice, every word written or spoken has more than its literal meaning, that it tells us of a Secret. The rule is simple: Suspect, only suspect. You can read subtexts even in a traffic sign that says 'No littering.'"[28] The links forged by writers seeking the "secret cause" that will ultimately unveil Duchamp's work recalls Eco's parody of the reasoning of the paranoid reader by means of a game he suggests, in which the words "peg" and "Plato" can be connected in any way, "metaphorical, metonymical, phonetic, or other."[29] Peter Bondanella elaborates:

Thus we connect *peg* to *pig* by sound; *pig* to *bristle*, because pigs have bristles; *bristle* to *brush*, because Italian masters used pig bristles to make paint brushes; *brush* to *Mannerism*, because bristles used for paint brushes suggest an artistic movement made famous by great Italian painters; *Mannerism* to *Idea*, because Mannerism employed a notion of *concetti* or abstract concepts and ideas in its artistic theory; and finally *Idea* to *Plato*, since Plato is an idealist philosopher.[30]

This is what Eco calls "hermetic drift": uneconomical interpretation that dispenses with the most obvious interpretive route because of its fascination with the play of signs.[31] From one to another the interpreter moves, convinced that a solution lies close at hand in some future formulation lying, for now, just beyond reach. Eco sees such delayed reading as a major tendency in academic literary criticism. Along the same lines, his paranoid theorists in *Foucault's Pendulum* pursue a network of inferred links between Freemasonry, Rosicrucianism, the kaballah, and all manner of esoteric and Hermetic lore, a pursuit that requires the assumption of a secret in the first instance. To deny that there is a secret with the promise that holds of a future disclosure would remove the basis for these activities.

Duchamp was fairly discreet and sometimes contradicted himself when speaking about his work, but that was because he made things that are not reducible to the straightforwardness, clarity, and certainty assumed and demanded by practical written or spoken language, toward which he expressed seemingly limitless reservations.[32] For him to speak or write descriptively about his work would have been beside the point, since the object *is* the statement and should therefore "speak" for itself. Nevertheless his circumspection and minimal, often irrational explanations have been translated as secrecy about something specific; an interpretation reinforced by the fact that he had, indeed, a genuine interest in secrecy and concealment. This informs works such as *With Hidden Noise* and is manifested in secrets meant to disclose themselves in the future perhaps, as in *Paysage fautif* of 1946 (discovered after Duchamp's death to include seminal fluid among its materials), as well as in secrets certainly meant for future unveiling, such as the delayed posthumous revelation that was *Etant donnés* (1946–66). But Duchamp's concern with secrecy in these works has helped promote the belief in some sort of deception and underlying message, creating a kind of rumor industry determined to discover the Big Secret that explains the readymades, *The Large Glass,* or, preferably, the whole oeuvre. Given its diverse allusions to secrecy, it is not surprising that Duchamp's work should encourage interpretation on such a colossal scale; as I have pointed out, for we readers, indeterminism requires some determining gesture, and as all commentators agree, no individual's work is so imbued with indeterminism, uncertainty, and undecidability as Marcel Duchamp's. But I am arguing that these are less problems requiring resolution than manifestations of his practice to be observed. In this light, secrecy is the *purloined letter* of his work, directing our attention not to what is supposedly behind, hidden, or secret, but to that which has disappeared because it is on show; not to *what* is purportedly concealed, but to the *act* of concealment; not to what the work *means,* but to what it *does* (how it suggests meanings).[33]

This is less an argument "against interpretation" (interpretation is essential and unavoidable and the opening of this essay is meant to make that point) than one that tries to comprehend how Duchamp's work acts upon its audience (myself included, of course), though there is a history of useful critical writing under that rubric. Reflecting on the state of literary criticism in 1964, Susan Sontag already saw the malign effects of certain kinds of interpretive approach, rooted, as she saw it, in anxiety:

The modern style of interpretation excavates, and as it excavates, destroys; it digs "behind" the text, to find a sub-text which is the true one. The most celebrated and influential modern doctrines, those of Marx and Freud, actually amount to elaborate systems of hermeneutics, aggressive and impious theories of interpretation.[34]

In most modern instances, interpretation amounts to the philistine refusal to leave the work of art alone. Real art has the capacity to make us nervous. By reducing the work of art to its content and then interpreting *that*, one tames the work of art. Interpretation makes art manageable, conformable [*sic*].[35]

Doubtless, Sontag would have lamented the interpretation industry just sprouting up around Duchamp's work in the early sixties, but at that time she could probably not have anticipated its intensification. For she was writing at the historical juncture that saw a social and cultural turn take place, beginning with the proliferation of conspiracy theories about the assassination of John F. Kennedy, which has continued, accelerated, and spread to our own time, where we are swamped in conspiracy theories, mirroring today's interpretation industry in the humanities and social sciences.

There is no reason to assume that even the most extravagant series of unveilings would ever reach anything but another veil.

—J. HILLIS MILLER

Literature on conspiracy theories has begun to emerge in sociology and media studies over the last few years, which can help shed light on the attraction held by Duchamp.[36] Sociologist Martin Parker writes, "The role of the seemingly ubiquitous conspiracy 'theorist' is to connect things which were previously unconnected—to posit causes, motives, plans and plots."[37] He might almost be referring to the endless adaptability of alchemy and psychoanalysis to the Duchamp corpus when he adds that "conspiracy theories are never falsifiable, but they are never verifiable either," calling them "entirely self-confirming belief systems."[38] Parker does not regard the pursuit of truth by the conspiracy theorist as one that is unhinged from reason, however, but one lodged in established models of investigation and inquiry, and keen to declare itself as such: "Importantly, the grammar of these theories is not insane speculation—or a romantic poetic wildness—but a form of detective work which uses the tools of the hypothetico-deductive method. Photographs, documents, eye witness accounts and so on are used to demonstrate that a particular explanation successfully draws together a series of events and causes."[39] Details of conspiracies are framed as events that must have substantiated "causes," and "like a detective looking for evidence—a stray hair, a missing minute, a footprint—everything is a clue," Parker writes.[40] "Once Sherlock Holmes has us trapped within the web of causes," he continues, "there can be no uncaused event."[41] Accordingly, publications like *UFO Magazine* are, Parker claims, "decidedly rationalist," at least in the way they collate and present their findings.[42]

Parker goes on to point out, too, the close structural relationship between "respectable" theory and conspiracy theory, arguing that "much of sociology, psychology, economics, geography and so on shares the same project and narrative structure" with conspiracy theory.[43] For instance, as an "elevated" theory claiming that "economic decisions are not 'ours' but caused by the hidden hand of markets,"[44] Marxism, for Parker, "has functioned as a pervasive conspiracy theory for most of this century."[45] By an "elevated" theory, Parker means to refer to a certain way of representing and explaining events, shared by conspiracy and the human sciences, which I am arguing extends to theories of Duchamp, of course:

> **Representation is architectural, in that sense of constructing a perspective from which to look towards the earth. Correspondingly, if you cannot see the plan then the plot will not be clear. A comprehension of the past and the construction of the future will be beyond your understanding. Importantly then, in order to see the plan, you must be elevated, lifted, from the terrain....**
>
> **It seems that elevation from the "here and now" allows for time to be thought. Once time can be thought, then so can lineages of explanation which require separate "events" and "causes," "pre-cedents" and "ante-cedents." Plots, plans and conspiracies share this grammar of a series of "events," and some "causes" to tie them together, but they also share the sense of an elevated place for the observer.**[46]

Art history and theory claim with history, social theory, and conspiracy theory (not to mention theories about art theory and conspiracy theory) a privileged position from which to view the causes lying behind events—the Bigger Picture.[47] Like them, it comes under the heading of "dietrology" ("behindology"), because it searches for a "hidden" reality, indicated by and secreted beneath the surface code.[48] Duchamp's work has a peculiar tendency to attract a particularly tenacious kind of dietrologist and to generate a remarkable determination to be seen as a "problem" in need of resolution. This happens in spite of Duchamp's own view that his work provides an ill fit with the grammar of cultural explanation (the requirement to turn things into problems and the subsequent search for explanations), and his indication that language offers a poor translation of his work, both of which are encapsulated in his endlessly quoted Wittgensteinian statement: "There is no solution because there is no problem."[49]

The discipline of art history continues to present itself as one arguing toward a position of, let us say, "soft objectivity," aiming to construct a version of the way things were or are; yet in its practices, it frequently offers speculative "poetic" readings, without declaring them as such. Formally speaking, these are often beautiful baroque structures, and it is undoubtedly legitimate to make things up about works of art with the aid of, say, psychoanalysis, so long as the author of the text acknowledges this as part of the methodology. However, the acknowledgment of lyrical or imaginative invention cannot take place in art history and theory for the reasons outlined above, with the result that certain approaches ultimately become implausible because of their reluctance to relinquish their claims to objective truth and insistence on authorial intentionality. Yet the writings I am discussing might concede that they are ironic or fictional and actually gain from it, since irony is a mode regulated to Duchamp's own playful spirit, and as recent writings in historiography have argued, avowedly subjective, fictional accounts of historical figures and events can carry at least as much weight as conventional historical narratives.[50]

Duchamp's assent to missing links of various kinds—vagueness, lack, irresolution; blind spots, absences, secrets—intrigues his readers versed in traditional and orthodox techniques of interpretation and explication; *intrigues* in the fullest sense of that word: intricating, entangling, trapping. Far from encouraging scholars to observe and comment on its *disconnectedness,* the heterogeneity and obscurity of his oeuvre act as a cue for rampant *connectivity.* Yet even if it were agreed that his work demonstrates a kind of inconsistent wandering, which has led many of his critics deeply into the wilderness of hermetic drift, it could easily be countered that this habit of linking carried out by writers is essential nevertheless, as it is identical with the processes of argument and even thinking itself. To link cognitively, psychologically, historically, or theoretically is to rationalize and coordinate a disorderly field in the service of narrative mastery. In fact, in this chapter, I have done the same thing, making a series of linked maneuvers to give a kind of theory of art theory, tautologically implicated in its own critical appraisal. Play offers an alternative to this, as I will show now.

I mean Negative Capability, that is when man is capable of being in uncertainties, Mysteries, doubts, without any irritable reaching after fact & reason.

—JOHN KEATS

A kind of undeclared game, rather like "Six Degrees of Kevin Bacon," the alluring links in the magic chain of hermetic drift mirror history, method, and theory as some of us have come to recognize them in their various guises in art history. From its beginnings in the Renaissance up to our own day, the connections forged and plots hatched in academic art history are constrained by a will to determine, resembling a game demanding obedience to a strict set of rules. Notwithstanding his love of chess, Duchamp was a gifted game-player himself, evident in his passivity in the face of self-contradiction and interest in chance and indeterminism, which can be viewed as his consent to a kind of game without rules: "I don't want to be pinned down to any position. My position is the lack of a position, but, of course, you can't even talk about it; the minute you talk you spoil the whole game. I also mean that words are absolutely a pest as far as getting anywhere. You cannot express anything through words."[51] Insofar as the standard practices and conventions of art history grasp the object of their inquiry through description, demarcation, categorization, classification, circumscription, and determination, the discipline can never attain its much-sought-after contact with Duchamp's work, because it misrepresents it through the very act of attempting to get in touch with it. Through that response, the work's play is stilled; the object is altered; the game is spoiled.

Humor and play contributed significantly to the atmosphere of Duchamp's work and its exhibition: "Humour and laughter—not necessarily derogatory derision—are my pet tools. This may come from my general philosophy of never taking the world too seriously—for fear of dying of boredom."[52] This "philosophy" is confirmed in one of the notes collected in the *Green Box,* in which Duchamp writes, "Ironism of affirmation: differences from negative ironism dependent solely on Laughter."[53] If humor and laughter were a way of life for Duchamp, as recorded in countless anecdotes by admirers,[54] then they themselves were also subject to the play of everyday inconsistency, for in one place he could speak of humor as indispensable "because seriousness is a very dangerous thing,"[55] then in another could say of the idea behind readymades: "It was a humour that wasn't only intended to make people laugh…it wasn't even black humour. It was really a humour that added a note of—dare I say?—seriousness."[56] Blinded in the headlights of Duchamp's nonchalant self-contradiction, we scramble for the theoretical means by which coherency and order in noncontradiction can be reestablished; our discipline demands that we assign him a fixed spot in the play of differences.

One could maintain, then, that the manner of response to his work discussed here, of drifting hermetically from one vibrant fragment to the next in an endless paper chase in pursuit of Duchamp's own true meaning, is appropriate to its subject.

Duchamp is playing, and his commentators are simply playing along. However, those who have written on his work have taken themselves and Duchamp very seriously indeed, anxious to encompass his amusement, humor, and play within the serious business of "high theory." We should, then, concern ourselves with different kinds of play and their roles in Duchamp's practice and in its interpretation, for the internal contradictions of the practice, noticed by one and all, might be profitably met by a similarly reflexive response in the interpretation. That is to say, in the same way that Duchamp infiltrated art to point to its limitations, responses to it might do something comparable to art history, less to delimit Duchamp's work than to point to the limitations of writing about it through the "high seriousness" demanded by academic art history; a playful, reflexive art history for a playful, reflexive art.

Does the world really present itself to perception in the form of well-made stories, with central subjects, proper beginnings, middles, and ends, and a coherence that permits us to see "the end" in every beginning?

—HAYDEN WHITE

Given the consistent drollery of many of Duchamp's creations, it was to be expected that art historians would elect to determine his work entirely through humor, ironic or otherwise. Jeffrey Weiss attempts to articulate meaning and truth in Duchamp through bluff, mystification, and irony, specifically through the philosophy of *blague*.[57] Rejecting the mountain of interpretation built over the years on Duchamp's slim output, Weiss seeks to present us with a "simpler Duchamp," whose "agenda belongs with specificity to the debates of the period" (late nineteenth, early twentieth century) in the popular spirit of hoax, which Weiss reduces to "ironic *blague* and mystification."[58] Noting that "the dynamics of mistrust are peculiar to the avant-garde debates," he claims, "Duchamp's proximity to hoax shows him to have been transposing the experience in precise ways,"[59] and "his secession from painting is a prank that was almost overdetermined by the situation at hand."[60] Although writing under cultural conditions that most would agree have long since privileged irony—with the art to prove it, from Andy Warhol to Jeff Koons—Weiss foregrounds historical context to insist Duchamp's "decision to stop painting is startling in retrospect, not because it represents a wholly original or improbable gesture, but because, as a joke, it was fully organic to the conditions of the moment."[61] In this way, Weiss stabilizes Duchamp's still-extraordinary decision by means of the historicist and anachronistic rhetoric of "inevitability."[62]

Tracing its arc from the Goncourt brothers' praise for *blague* in 1865 through its adjustments under the Third Republic—the starring role it plays in the pamphlet of sarcastic anecdotes, *La Blagueur fin-de siècle* (1894), its definition as a nihilistic pose in Jules Wogue's 1902 article "La Philosophie de la 'Blague,'" its presence in Joseph Conrad's *Nostromo* (1904), and prominent references to *blague* during the Cubist period—Weiss narrates his admirable historiography of *blague* toward the heart of Duchamp's work with the 1917 scandal of *Fountain,* discovering Louise Norton's use of the term in her essay "Buddah of the Bathroom," which defended and justified "Mr. Mutt's" submission of *Fountain* to the first exhibition of the Society of Independent Artists.[63] Observing the "Readymade's basic allegiance to the joke,"[64] Weiss shifts gears and extends the domain of *blague* to *The Large Glass,* the *Green Box,* the *3 Standard Stoppages,* and Duchamp's word games, asserting that "*blague* asks us to note that the indifferent deadpan conforms to an extant comic strategy of 1912."[65] As a good historian, Weiss rolls irony, parody, absurdity, the comic, and the hoax into the logic of the *blague,* then unites Duchamp's work under its banner, thus determining his indeterminism and giving meaning to his nonmeaning, on the familiar bedrock of artistic intentionality.[66]

Like many writers on Duchamp, Weiss recognizes him as a joker and player of games.[67] But his reading is unusual because, at first anyway, it takes this joking and game-playing largely at face value rather than looking "behind" the surface to step away from such a reading—that Duchamp is joking—as is usually the case once the conspiratorial magnetism of the work and the "secrecy" shrouding it take hold, requiring remedy in an elaborate, hidden cause. Ultimately, however, Weiss steers clear of the unpleasant task of confronting the potential meaninglessness of the readymades, opting instead for their classification through the logic of *blague.* By the time he tells us that Duchamp's work "reveal[s] hoax to be a universal joint which couples the history of the avant-garde to the experience of avant-gardism, a single unit of multiple parts," Weiss's search for origin and meaning for Duchamp's play has settled firmly and dramatically into a groove appropriate to one of Jacques Derrida's definitions of play, as permitted yet circumscribed.[68]

☺∞£♂♠♪́♂☼♪♀@↑∆♪♠☺@≠♂@♀♠♪@£♠♀@☻♂☼£♂☼♀∞́%♀@£% ∞↑☺♠£≠♠♀♠́&@@♪́≠☼?@£&☼≠☼€∞@%∆≠♂%♀@☻♂%?@♀☼>£ @&@♠☺@?@&<≠♂☼>!$<♂☼♪♠♀♠́∞>☻♂@>♂@♀́%♥@%∆♠&@>♀$ @&!♀£&<́≠%!&♠́♂<≠%́☼@&&@£♠$♠>>@☼>√↔∂∂♀♠<☼>!‘♠&@>♀$@ &!≠☻☼♀≠@☺☻%&☺♀≠%♪♠♥@≠♂@♪♀♠<☻♂♠≠♂@☻♠>≠@☺↑☼ ♥@@?@&<%>@☻♂%☺%@♀≠♂♠≠♥☼>☺%∆☻%&♥’[69] ☼↑@♠?@≠♂ ☼♀£%>£@♠↑@☺∞>☺@&♪<%☻>☺∞£♂♠♪́£%☺@≠%♠?%☼☺≠♂ @&@☺∞£ ≠☼%>%∆♪<&@♠☺☼>!≠%♠∞≠♂%&☼♠↑☼>≠@>≠☼%>♠↑ ☼≠<≠%☺@↑♠<≠♂@‘&@♀@>£@’%∆≠♂☼♀́&@♀@>≠♠≠☼%>≠%♪☼♪☼ £☻☼≠♂♂☼☺☺@>>%☼♀@☼>≠♂@∆%&♪%∆≠♂☼♀!♠♪@♠>☺≠%́↑♠ <☻☼≠♂♪<♠∞☺☼@>£@♪☼↑☺↑<>%≠♪♠↑☼£☼%∞♀↑<.

I refer here of course to Derrida's widely read essay on structuralism and Claude Lévi-Strauss, "Structure, Sign, and Play in the Discourse of the Human Sciences."[70] Although Derrida's play is the object of one of Eco's complaints—specifically his book *Limited Inc* (1977), which Eco described as "the *jeu de massacre* performed by Derrida upon a text signed by John Searle"—his theory of radical play and his performative writing strategies conjure up the possibility of an alternative response to Duchamp's work, a kind of *jeu de vivre,* that is beyond interpretation.[71] For Derrida, Plato's play "takes on meaning and works in the service of seriousness, truth, and ontology," where play is subsumed by reason, "supervised and contained within the safeguards of ethics and politics."[72] According to Tilman Küchler, for Schiller, too, "play that does not yield to the demands of transcendental reason is dismissed as 'mere play.'"[73] Play becomes "good" for Schiller "when it becomes an integral part of a metaphysical framework governed by the presence of a final meaning."[74] This anxious play, which is contingent upon "a fundamental immobility and a reassuring certitude" on the basis of which "anxiety can be mastered,"[75] is for Derrida the first of two alternatives:

There are thus two interpretations of interpretation, of structure, of sign, of play. The one seeks to decipher, dreams of deciphering a truth or an origin which escapes play and the order of the sign, and which lives the necessity of interpretation as an exile. The other, which is no longer turned toward the origin, affirms play and tries to pass beyond man and humanism, the name of man being the name of that being who, throughout the history of metaphysics or of ontotheology—in other words, throughout his entire history—has dreamed of full presence, the reassuring foundation, the origin and the end of play.[76]

Their discovery of origin, presence, truth, and full meaning place de Duve's and Weiss's interpretations in the first category, a "saddened, negative, nostalgic, guilty, Rousseauistic side of the thinking of play," circumscribing play in what Derrida calls after Georges Bataille a "restricted economy."[77]

So important to Derrida, Bataille's thought might be employed to extract Duchamp studies from the deterministic straitjacket of what could loosely be termed "Hegelian art history." Beyond mastery, Bataille's notions of "general economy" and, especially, "sovereignty" had major significance for Derrida and others from the sixties and seventies on, as Susan Rubin Suleiman indicates:

[Bataille's] theoretical texts provided a set of concepts or "key words" whose applicability extended from the realm of cultural and individual experience to the realm of writing: expenditure, transgression, boundary, excess, heterogeneity, sovereignty—this last being a key term in Bataille's vocabulary, whose implications, as Derrida brilliantly demonstrated, are the very opposite of Hegel's term "mastery." Mastery is linked to work, and above all to the affirmation and preservation of meaning; sovereignty, on the other hand, is precisely that which enables an individual to expose himself to play, to risk, to the destruction or "waste" of meaning.[78]

I am invoking Bataille not to grid general economy or sovereignty onto Duchamp's work, any more than I want to read it rigorously through deconstruction or a Derridean theory of play or even offer a coherent theory of the readymade. What I am arguing makes little sense in the logocentric fields of art history or theory (which share the task of making sense of art by translating it into written and spoken language). But that is the point. In its insistence on the right of art to incoherence and limitless play, it is an argument that yields some of the obscurity, dissonance, and self-contradiction of Duchamp's work, exposing its scattered heterogeneity without reducing it. The irony is that *all* Duchamp scholars agree on the plurivalency and unruliness of Duchamp's oeuvre in the first instance, though they are then compelled into a second step, which aims to quell this play through the application of yet further meaning-as-truth. That is what I am refusing to do here. Emancipated from their servitude to some theoretical end, readymades (for instance) are returned to some of their digressive facility as souvenirs of a game lacking a single, carefully plotted origin or end, manifesting only absurdity beyond any context that can bestow "healthy" reason on them such as art history demands. Indeed, in later life Duchamp stated his own bemusement at the seemingly limitless play of the readymade—magnetizing interpretation to such a caricatural extent that it denies mastery, unitary classification, or ultimate meaning—when he confessed in an interview that "the curious thing about the readymade is that I've never been able to arrive at a definition or explanation that fully satisfies me."[79]

"There was no plot," William said, "and I discovered it by mistake."

—UMBERTO ECO

In the context of play, the following account of the attributes of Hermes takes on amplified significance for we Duchampians:

[Hermes] has to do with oracles, including a dubious sort known as *klēdōn*, which at the moment of its announcement may seem trivial or irrelevant, the secret sense declaring itself only after long delay, and in circumstances not originally foreseeable. Hermes is cunning, and occasionally violent: a trickster, a robber. So it is not surprising that he is also the patron of interpreters. Sometimes they proclaim an evident sense, like a herald; but they also use cunning, and may claim the right to be violent, and glory in it.[80]

In the shade of Hermes, the seemingly cryptic, apparently inexhaustible paper chase of ambiguity Duchamp left behind takes on the aura of a hermetic text, lending him the mask of a *pharmakeus* or magician. Linking through this term the Egyptian god Thoth, Hermes, Eros, and Socrates, Derrida lists their attributes, to define their resistance to limit and meaning:

[T]he figure of Thoth…takes its shape from the very thing it resists and substitutes for. But it thereby opposes *itself*, passes into its other, and this messenger-god is truly a god of the absolute passage between opposites. If he had any identity—but he is precisely the god of non-identity—he would be that *coincidentia oppositorum*…. He cannot be assigned a fixed spot in the play of differences. Sly, slippery and masked, an intriguer and a card, like Hermes, he is neither king nor jack, but rather a sort of *joker*, a floating signifier, a wild card, one who puts play into play….

Every act of his is marked by this unstable ambivalence. This god of calculation, arithmetic, and rational science also presides over the occult sciences, astrology and alchemy. He is the god of magic formulas that calm the sea, of secret accounts, of hidden texts: an archetype of Hermes, god of cryptography no less than of every other –graphy.[81]

Socrates in the dialogues of Plato often has the face of a *pharmakeus*. That is the name given by Diotima to Eros.... Eros... is a fearsome sorcerer (*deinos goēs*), magician (*pharmakeus*), and sophist (*sophistēs*). A being that no "logic" can confine within a noncontradictory definition.[82]

The mask of Thoth-Hermes as delineated here by Derrida in "Plato's Pharmacy" fits just about perfectly the Duchamp I have been describing. In fact, Hermes—patron of interpreters, *jouer*, god of secrecy and messengers, *pharmakeus*—is even made available as a point of reference to Duchamp's audience (perhaps in relation to the readymade *Pharmacy*?) through the "horned" portrait of *Monte Carlo Bond* (1924).[83] However, it is a *coincidence*, and I would not argue for a moment that Duchamp consciously or unconsciously identified with Thoth-Hermes/Mercury.[84] Instead, the identification I am pretending to make through Derrida here should be regarded parodically, as a kind of anti-interpretation.

Even though there are such connections made within Duchamp's oeuvre by Duchamp himself, we cannot allow them to be *"merely"* playful (pleasurable, solipsistic expansions of the semiotic field constituted by his work), but must locate their deeper meaning. Art history, even more than is usual in scholarship, is a sober business dealing with a serious subject. Although humor has never enjoyed a comparable role in art to that it has held historically in literature or theater, for instance, this is changing, yet art history is still wedded to high seriousness and unpracticed in levity, and its discourse therefore naturally and insistently lifts Duchamp's playful, pointless, idle gestures out of the playpen to an esteemed and supposedly more substantial level of inquiry. Hence its recourse to holistic explanation through alchemy, hermeticism, psychoanalysis, and so on, to sustain the transcendence and seriousness of Duchamp's work, even in the face of the comical deflation of those categories by *Fountain* (1917), *The Large Glass, Paris Air* (1919), and *Box in a Suitcase* (1941–71).

To combat this interpretative ethic of "elevation," integration, and identification, rather than positing a theory or interpretation of Duchamp through play, this chapter openly plays in the context of his work, avoiding giving it origin and presence in meaning (let alone truth) as facilitated by the game of hermetic drift, and allowing Duchamp's work to retain its frivolity and incomprehensibility while writing around it anyway. This option has a precedent in philosophy. Future interpretations of Friedrich Nietzsche's rootless sentence, "'I have forgotten my umbrella,'" found in quotation marks among his unpublished manuscripts, have been derided in these terms by Derrida:

psychoanalysis, familiar as it is with forgetting and phallic objects, might yet aspire to a hermeneutic mastery of these remains. And if not, the psychoanalysts, who are otherwise not so naïve as one might have an interest in thinking them, can still continue to suspect that, if these generalities were to be articulated and narrowed and the context itself thus prudently completed, they would one day be able to satisfy their interpretative expectations. In this respect the analyst, albeit somewhat less naïve, he or she rejoins in principle the impulsive reader or hermeneut ontologist in their common belief that this unpublished piece is an aphorism of some significance. Assured that it must mean something, they look for it to come from the most intimate reaches of this author's thought.[85]

There is no end to its parodying play with meaning, grafted here and there, beyond any contextual body or finite code. It is quite possible that that unpublished piece, precisely because it is readable as a piece of writing, should remain forever secret. But not because it withholds some secret. Its secret is rather the possibility that indeed it might have no secret, that it might only be pretending to be simulating some hidden truth within its folds. Its limit is not only stipulated by its structure but is in fact intimately confused with it. The hermeneut cannot but be provoked and disconcerted by its play.[86]

Neither this umbrella nor Nietzsche's sentence are ready-mades, but Derrida's remarks on the relentless will to interpret such fragments act as a cautionary word for those who seek and find (*because* they seek) all manner of Freudian and other categories in the readymades. It is less the readymades that should be interpreted than theories presuming to interpret them.

With Derrida's writings in mind, Richard Rorty outlined twenty years ago the liberation of late twentieth-century philosophy from "ideological, institutional, and disciplinary constraints," arguing that "this development has made possible a more playful, more cosmopolitan, less professional tone in which to philosophize."[87] Although Gregory Ulmer wrote similarly of something called "post-criticism" in the age of postmodernism around the same time, art history remains on its perch of high seriousness.[88] For the most part, it advocates the collapse of high and low, yet it refuses to recognize the postmetaphysical turn and come down to play. Worse, the ideas developed by theorists of this turn—Bataille's *informe,* Derrida's *différance,* for example—were appropriated by determinist art historians in the 1980s and 1990s to ground bothersome art in origin, presence, truth, and fullness of meaning! By giving an argument "grounded" in an absence—called "The Duchamp Code" or "With Hidden Paragraph"—this chapter is presented without being entirely present. It aims to play off Duchamp's play rather than give it form and meaning, and to push art history more toward art than history. It would be boring to take it too seriously.

3

MY UTOPIA: PLAY IN BAUHAUS PHOTOGRAPHY

KEVIN MOORE

Walter Gropius's Bauhaus building in Dessau is an icon of the artistic rationalism that the school propounded during its heyday in the 1920s. With its frank clarity of design and function, the building projects an aura of supreme rationalism, organization, and technological know-how. Photographs of the Bauhaus building by professors and students, however, tell a different story. Taken from unusual angles, juxtaposing human figures and architectural vignettes, isolating elements in abstract, often Surrealist fashion, photographs of the Bauhaus convey a disorienting sense of subjective vitalism, fragmentation, and irreverent humor.

The apparent contradiction between the Bauhaus style embodied in Gropius's architecture and the playful experimentation of the Bauhaus photographers manifests a tension inherent in Bauhaus philosophy—one between invention and application. What role would creativity play in the technological utopia? Negotiating the terms of this relationship took on some urgency at the Bauhaus during the 1920s, a time of radical economic and social change. Outside the institution, a struggle over two visions of Germany was taking place, one side asserting a return to prewar traditions and the other pushing for modernization. Officially identified with the latter impulse by the mid-1920s, the Bauhaus had conjoined the ideology and aesthetics of Russian Constructivism and the pragmatism of American industry. And yet fissures of "romantic anticapitalism" continued to pervade the institution until it folded in 1933.[1] Such ambivalence is nowhere more evident than in the school's photographic output, which exhibited qualities at once boldly modern and insistently humanistic.

If the playfulness of Bauhaus photography strikes one as anachronistic given the turbulent context of its production, it is perhaps even more so considering the strict guidelines imposed within the institution itself. In an environment committed to the production of industrial design, photography occupied an amorphous position as a sideline activity. Yet this peripheral position was in fact the starting point for photography's liberation. Not obliged to the theories, conventions, or standards of a formal discipline, photography offered a means of personal expression and artistic exploration. If in workshops students constructed environments of rational, functional design, photography deconstructed those environments and reconfigured them, using the instrument of the camera to express subjective human perception.

More than one historian has described Bauhaus photography as "playful" and the term is appropriate in more ways than one.[2] In his writings on photography, László Moholy-Nagy, master of the introductory course at the Bauhaus, frequently referred to children and primitive peoples as examples of human vitality uncorrupted by the restrictions of modern civilization. In *The New Vision* (1938), he wrote of children: "Their spontaneous expressions spring from an inner sense of what is right, as yet unshaken by outside pressure. They are examples of a life governed by inner necessities."[3] Moholy's campaign for the preservation and development of creativity stands in anxious opposition to the increasing mechanization of Weimar society. While he accepted and supported Gropius's proclamation that the future of art lay in its utility and capacity to conform to the principles of mass production, Moholy continued to promote and protect what he saw as the most vital aspect of humanity: the will to create for the sake of creation as a natural expression of one's biological existence. Essentially, this was the will to play.

MOHOLIAN FORM

In Bauhaus lore, 1923 was a pivotal year. In an address titled "Art and Technology: A New Unity," Gropius announced a change of direction from craft to industry, noting that the Bauhaus would now "combine the creative activity of the individual with the broad practical work of the world," thus avoiding an ill-perceived fate for the modern artist, isolated on the "romantic island."[4] The shift was implemented most emphatically in the *Vorkurs,* or preliminary course, where the quasi-mystical Johannes Itten was replaced by the constructivist Moholy-Nagy. The shift marked more than a change of taste from Expressionist *Innerlichkeit* to Constructivism. It more adequately described a shift in the conception of art making as an act of individual expression to the channeling of creativity toward a utilitarian social end. In pedagogical terms, this meant less emphasis on nurturing inner creativity and more emphasis on design production.[5]

Gropius had advocated a program of collective, socially conscious art production since 1919. The key difference in 1923 was the voiced allegiance to technology and industry. In the vocabulary coined by sociologist Georg Simmel twenty years earlier, Gropius aligned the school more squarely with the laws of the "money economy," mandating that art should no longer be appraised in terms of connoisseurship and subjective judgment but according to certain empirical tangibles, such as expense of materials, functionalism, cost of distribution, etc. As Simmel put it, the rationality of the money economy engendered "an unrelenting hardness," a matter-of-factness in all matters of exchange. "Money," Simmel continued, "is only concerned with what is common to all, i.e., with the exchange value which reduced all quality and individuality to a purely quantitative level." Alluding to the deleterious effects of this system on human relations, Simmel cautioned: "All emotional relationships between persons rest on their individuality, whereas intellectual relationships deal with persons as with numbers, that is, as with elements which, in themselves, are indifferent, but which are of interest only insofar as they offer something objectively perceivable."[6] For those on board with Germany's capitalist future, or for those realists willing to accept it, a change in the definitions of art and artists was bound to occur.

Gropius's move exacerbated existing strife within the institution. The newly formed program of social constructivism effectively drove art production of a nonutilitarian slant underground. Ernö Kállai reported in 1930 that easel painting had become a somewhat clandestine activity: "Whoever glanced into the studios and rooms of the Bauhäusler at night was amazed by the many painters who were standing here and there at their easels, brushing away at their canvases—only in secret, like schoolboys...writing poetry, perhaps with a bad conscience, because they were not brooding over modern functional buildings, collapsible chairs or lamps."[7] And upon his resignation in 1930, Hannes Meyer sardonically noted: "As carpets on the floors lay the psychological complexes of young girls. Everywhere art strangled life."[8]

A great exception within this climate of rational application was the photographic output, and no one was more responsible for the experimental playfulness of Bauhaus photography than Moholy-Nagy. Moholy's entry into the Bauhaus is normally heralded as the victory of constructivism over mysticism. This, however, was not entirely the case. As at least one historian has noted, Moholy maintained only a "semblance of scientific method."[9] In his approach to the preliminary course, Moholy incorporated Itten's method of "learning by doing" as well as his exploration of the properties of materials. The only difference was that Moholy used glass and metals where Itten had used natural fibers. And while Moholy's official position was one of enthusiastic support for Gropius's union of art and industry, he demonstrated his support less through practical applications of artistic exploration than through artistic exploration itself. (One need only consider the practical applications of the *Light Space Modulator* to grasp this point.) Moreover, unlike his wife, Lucia Moholy, and later Walter Peterhans, Moholy did not participate in the documentation of Bauhaus workshop production for advertising or other purposes. Lucia Moholy's photographic records of Bauhaus production were the only applied photographs from the early part of the 1920s, when such ideas were first espoused, and it wasn't until 1929 that Peterhans began teaching the first official photography workshop. His method, founded on "logic, analytical thinking, and tabular principles," differed markedly from that of Moholy's in that photographs were made to serve as practical components in book design, advertising, and other forms of print media.[10] In the end, Moholy was a consummate "form master" and not a "workshop master," according to the institution's own pedagogical divisions.[11]

As noted, the creativity Moholy encouraged in the preliminary course was modeled on the play of children, for whom spontaneity and inventiveness were seen as biological necessities. In *The New Vision,* Moholy writes of the preliminary course's objectives: "to show the student the way to a universal outlook, to make [him] conscious of his creative power. The method is to keep in the work of the grown-up the sincerity of emotion, the truth of observation, the fantasy and the creativeness of the child."[12] The purposelessness of this activity Moholy understood as a necessary stage in the production of a new industrial society, whatever form that might take—for new forms had to be invented, a new world imagined, before it could be rationalized, systematized, and put into working order. This was the defense of art circa 1925. Others made the argument in headier terms.

Philosopher Ernst Bloch developed around this time a concept of art that he referred to as *Vorschein,* or anticipatory illumination. Part psychoanalytic theory, part utopian vision, and part Hegelian phenomenology, Bloch's concept valorized art and literature as expressions of hope in a capitalist void. Through art, Bloch argued, man unveils his hidden desires and thus envisions the redefinition of cultural values, aspirations, and ideologies. *Vorschein* is an immersion in an altered reality, or "wish-landscape," an experience of some other happiness not attainable in the present. Unlike romantic escapism, however, *Vorschein* serves a productive function by providing a previsualization of a better world to come. "Art leads and brings the world," Bloch wrote, "in its way."[13]

What Bloch is describing is essentially a phenomenological definition of play.[14] Michael Apter has described play as "a state of mind, a way of seeing and being, a special mental 'set' towards the world and one's actions in it."[15] Apter develops the concept further, opposing play to work and by defining play as a "protective frame" of one's choosing, a momentary escape from worldly obligations. Two terms help in differentiating these various states: the *telic,* from the Greek "telos," meaning goal or purpose; and the *paratelic,* introducing "para," meaning alongside. In the telic state, the ends determine the means; there is an awareness of the product or end result of one's actions. In the paratelic state, the action is primary; there is an absorption in process, leaving little concern for end result. Thus in the paratelic state (or play state), the common laws governing reality are temporarily suspended, allowing the creative manipulation of objects and situations to take place. Unbound from a sense of purpose, the imagination is unleashed and free to explore ideas in a nonsensical, irrational, and highly personal fashion.

Grounding such ideas in capitalist society, James Hans has argued that devalued, marginalized activities such as play—activities occurring outside the spheres of empirical science and economics—remain central to the health and evolution of modern societies. A hypothetical activity, imposing order upon experience that does not actually exist, play reconfigures objects and situations from the existing world for therapeutic and developmental purposes. "It is through play," Hans writes, "that man adapts to his changing world, that he constantly challenges and changes the rules and structures by which he lives."[16]

As is apparent from his writings, Moholy-Nagy was keenly aware of such dynamics. He also was quick to realize that the *Vorkurs* offered a rare temporal space in which he and students alike could indulge in pure formal experimentation, untroubled by the demands of the institution's goals or society's expectations. Thus, despite Moholy's political lip service to art's applied future, his own interests in art making remained fundamentally romantic and primal. Kállai recognized this duplicity in Moholy's actions early on, observing that "Moholy the constructivist is fascinated by the energies, the rhythms and technical power of new life," and in the same breath noted Moholy's "naïve admiration of the eternal-primitive child-barbarian."[17]

Moholy's working methods followed a two-part program. First was the stage of absorption in medium, a period of exploration and discovery. Next came the stage of assessment, where discoveries from the first stage were rediscovered, rearranged, and resolved through various techniques, such as montage, cropping, and, as often as not, rephotographing. Beaumont Newhall described Moholy's methods in 1946 this way: "He was not interested in capturing on film and paper an already discovered vision. On the contrary, he discovered beauty *after* the photograph had been completed." Newhall named Moholy's photographs "after-products of vision."[18]

Moholy's concept of the New Vision, of course, was founded on the objective principle that the camera lens sees more than the human eye and thus could be exploited as a means of seeing more or seeing differently. Such discoveries were often based on "so-called 'faulty' photographs: the view from above, from below, the oblique view," as he described them in *Painting, Photography, Film,* in 1925.[19] He thus encouraged actively breaking conventions of photography, from camera use to printing and beyond. This entailed not only disregarding photography's documentary function but, in some instances, dispensing with the camera altogether.[20] Afterward, he systematized his findings in prose, where these visual products of free association served as illustrations to his ideas; they became stabilized in a rhetoric of technology, finding application only—in truth—as illustrations in his books.[21] This practice had the effect of not only asserting Moholy's allegiance to the rational principles espoused by Bauhaus doctrine; it also provided his students with a kind of subversive manifesto, encouraging them to break with current photographic thinking and to invent for invention's sake.

Moholy was a prolific creator of new forms and this achievement was as much an assertion of subjectivity, an act of personal expression, as a proposal for a modern visual language. Moholy's photograms, which he began producing in 1922, had a machine-aesthetic and cadence, on the surface so dissimilar from the photograms created by Man Ray that same year. Whereas Man Ray's compositions often contained identifiable personal objects suggesting psychosexual relations, Moholy's comprised such inanimate forms as coils and gears. Yet on another level, these abstract compositions represented pure creativity as the end result of a process of free association. With their beautiful light effects and shadowy veiled forms, they conjured a mysterious, subjective vision of an emerging modern world. Their content could also be blatantly personal, as in a double self-portrait of Moholy and his wife, Lucia, or in any number of photograms featuring hands, a recurring motif in Bauhaus photography. While numerous other New Vision photographers adopted the eye as the movement's icon, Moholy tellingly emphasized the hand as the point of contact

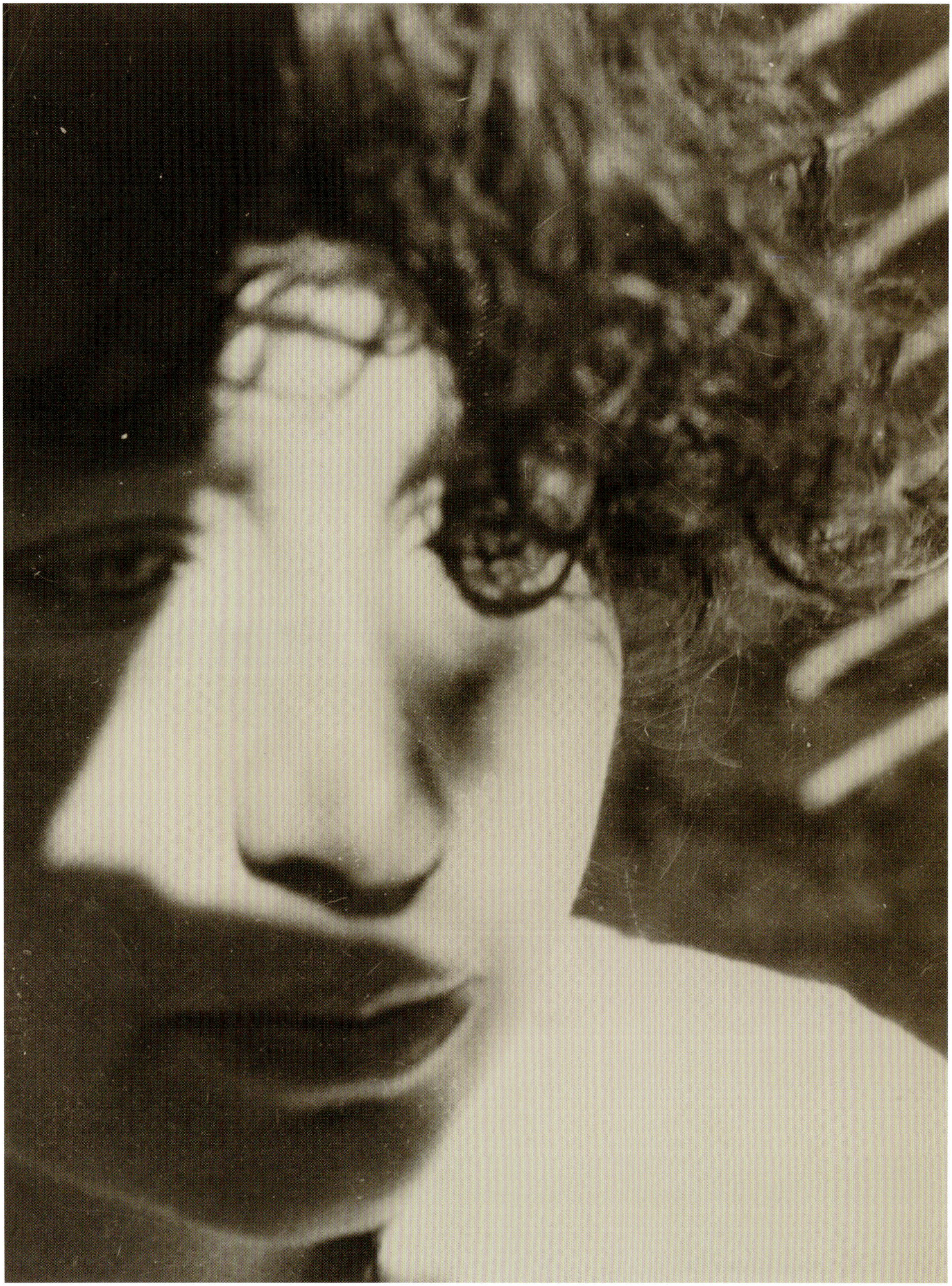

between the sentient individual and the mechanical environment in which he or she lived.[22]

Moholy's camera photographs embody a similar tension, their formal innovation being both aesthetically modern and radically subjective. His portraits and beach pictures in particular, produced during periods of leisure, carve constructivist compositions out of faces and ordinary bourgeois scenes. For example, a portrait of Lucia taken around 1925 (fig. 8) may be read on two levels: on a surface level of interlocking forms and on a psychosensual level, with the bleached skin and tousled hair of the subject emerging from a matrix of mechanistic forms—Constructivist aesthetics meet Surrealist content. In another beach picture, likely a portrait of Russian filmmaker Esfir Schub, with whom Moholy is thought to have had a brief affair in 1929, a geometric composition is created out of the foreshortened frame of the woman and the shadow of the boardwalk, atop which appears the photographer's own shadow.

Beyond such syntheses of perception, through which viewpoint and subject matter were conjoined in unexpected ways, narrative could be inserted into the composition, violating the surface of the photograph with elements cut apart and collaged. In these works, Moholy created the same tenuous mechanical-looking forms, yet they also contain some of the most obvious social and personal commentary. In *Jealousy* (1924–27), to cite one example, Moholy repeated his own silhouette, cribbed from the famous portrait of the artist as engineer. Variances in scale and tonality suggest altered identities and moods, each fixated on a common object of desire.

FIG. 8
László Moholy-Nagy,
Portrait, c. 1925.
Private collection, California.

Apart from proposing a new visual idiom based on the concept of objectivity, New Vision photography emphasized, paradoxically, subjective human perception. In this sense, one might see the movement as an extension of an arts tradition based in subjectivity—German Expressionism, most recently—here pushed right through the center of photography, modernity's most promising medium. Expressed is an ambivalent desire to at once embrace the technological future and a concomitant fear of losing sight of the individual. This accounts, to a large degree, for all the extreme angles, truncations, fragmentations, distortions, overlaps, collaging, montaging, and solarizations—each technique contributing in different ways to the notion of an idiosyncratic human vision. Yet besides vision—the particular way in which the exterior world is perceived—there was also man's physical relation to that world, and this became the subject of many Bauhaus photographs.

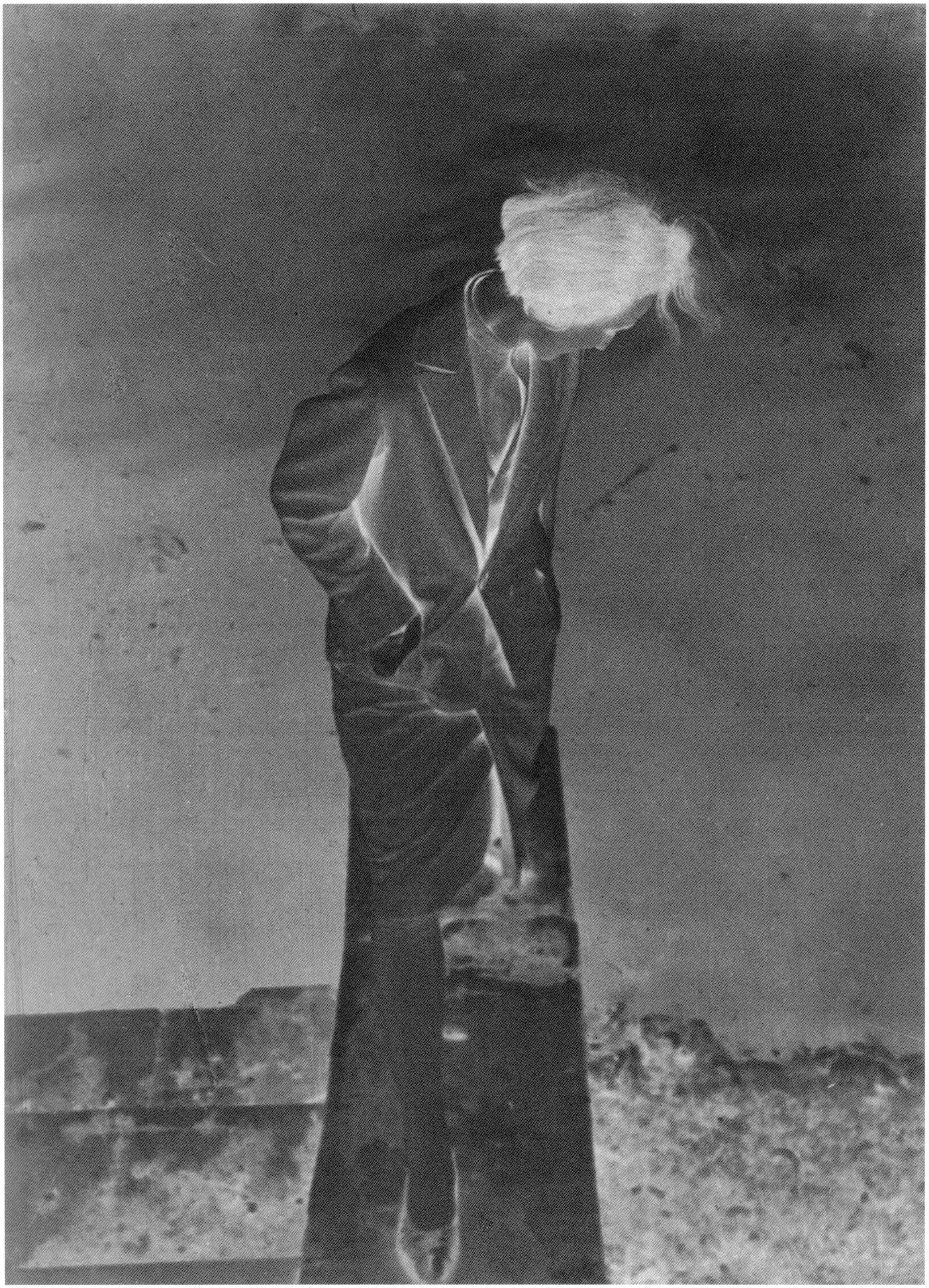

FIG. 9
László Moholy-Nagy,
Negative, c. 1927.
Private collection, Pace/MacGill,
New York.

Man's relation to the machine world was a hotly discussed topic at the time, framed most often within a dialectic between the organic and the inorganic, the human and the mechanistic. Moholy's rhetoric, for example, is rife with biological metaphors and frequent vilification of what he calls "technical civilization."[23] Indeed, witnessed across the broad spectrum of Weimar culture—from nudist cults, to a fear-obsession with robots and the automaton, to Siegfried Kracauer's concept of the "mass ornament"—is a preoccupation with the body and the limitations imposed by the modern environment.

Moholy's approach to teaching centered so specifically on the relation of the body to architecture that the *Vorkurs* might be seen as a laboratory for investigating this relationship. ("Photography," Moholy noted, "is doubtless a bridge.")[24] The use of photography to explore this problematic was obvious, for the camera could function as a kind of mechanical, optical prosthesis. Students approached the analysis of space in two ways: through a rational investigation into the structural properties of materials and through what Moholy described as the "direct experience of space itself."[25] In this combination of the physical and the sensory, one can see Moholy almost testing Gropius's conceptual model for modern architecture. Clear, functional architecture did not constrict individual vitality, Gropius contended, but inspired man to clarify and channel the disconnected impulses of his physical and mental being. Indeed, rational architecture itself was the organic product of man's "visions and brainstorms," he wrote. "All laws of the real, of the mental, as well as of the spiritual world find their simultaneous solution in artistic space."[26]

Reverberating in Gropius's remarks is a long tradition in German thought attempting to define man's exact relationship to the exterior world. Germane here is Friedrich von Schiller's "play impulse," a state in which both the sensual and the rational impulses are held in balance, allowing man to both sense and think simultaneously. For Schiller, the mediating object capable of inducing the desired state of suspension was the work of art. In the presence of art, "the object which afforded him this vision," man could both sense himself as matter and know himself as spirit, thus reconciling differing philosophical modes for comprehending one's existence.[27] Bauhaus rhetoric is full of such dialectics, most interesting perhaps as an expression of the vulgarization of German philosophy by the 1920s and the earnest attempts to apply such thinking to the crisis of modernity. Photography—"a bridge"—provided both the aesthetic and fluidity to attempt such a union.

Two compelling examples by Moholy: In an image titled *Negative* (c. 1927, fig. 9), Moholy fuses human form with architecture by reversing the tonal values and by shooting from an oblique angle. Within the dialectical framework of the light/dark reversal and in the ambiguous spatial play, the eye oscillates between two optical paradigms. In one, the woman appears as a figure standing on a wall extending over a body of water; in the other, she is a modern Daphne, a monumental form growing out of a solid, geometric pedestal, silhouetted against the sky.

In *Dessau* (c. 1926–28, fig. 10), human figures function as animated elements in a severe architectural environment. The reclining figure conforms to the balustrade on which she lies while functioning as a kind of organic ornament atop the plain architectural support. The other figure, radically foreshortened, violates the dominant plunging diagonal of the balcony rail. The conversing figures—one horizontal, the other vertical—communicate across distinct spatial zones, both mimicking and disrupting the patterns of the architecture. Their bodies compliment and complete the architecture, animating it through movement as well as form, thus achieving one of Moholy's express goals: "a balance between human existence and the technical world."[28] In truth, it was a balance achieved only within the frame of the photograph, a temporary, imaginary balance between sensual and rational modes. This may well be the most perfect vision of the biotechnical the Bauhaus produced.

STUDENT LIBERTIES

But what of the less perfect visions? What of the less well articulated photographs, particularly by Moholy's *Vorkurs* students, which seem to project an altogether different spirit of play, a spirit that sometimes seems to prefigure the synthesizing formal experiments of Moholy? As Andreas Haus has observed, Moholy's ideas were but paraphrased by his students "in liberated amateur fashion."[29] If the *Vorkurs* master's photographs demonstrated a search for a new biotechnological language of modernity, all the while reasserting the time-honored model of the artist as a divinely inspired creative being—an Expressionist in engineer's clothing—his students' work might be seen to embody some of the same while also suggesting a more refracted and irreverent constellation of activities associated with play.

While Moholy's subversion stayed well within the bounds of institutional diplomacy, that of his students careened easily out of bounds. If we compare two photographs of balconies, one

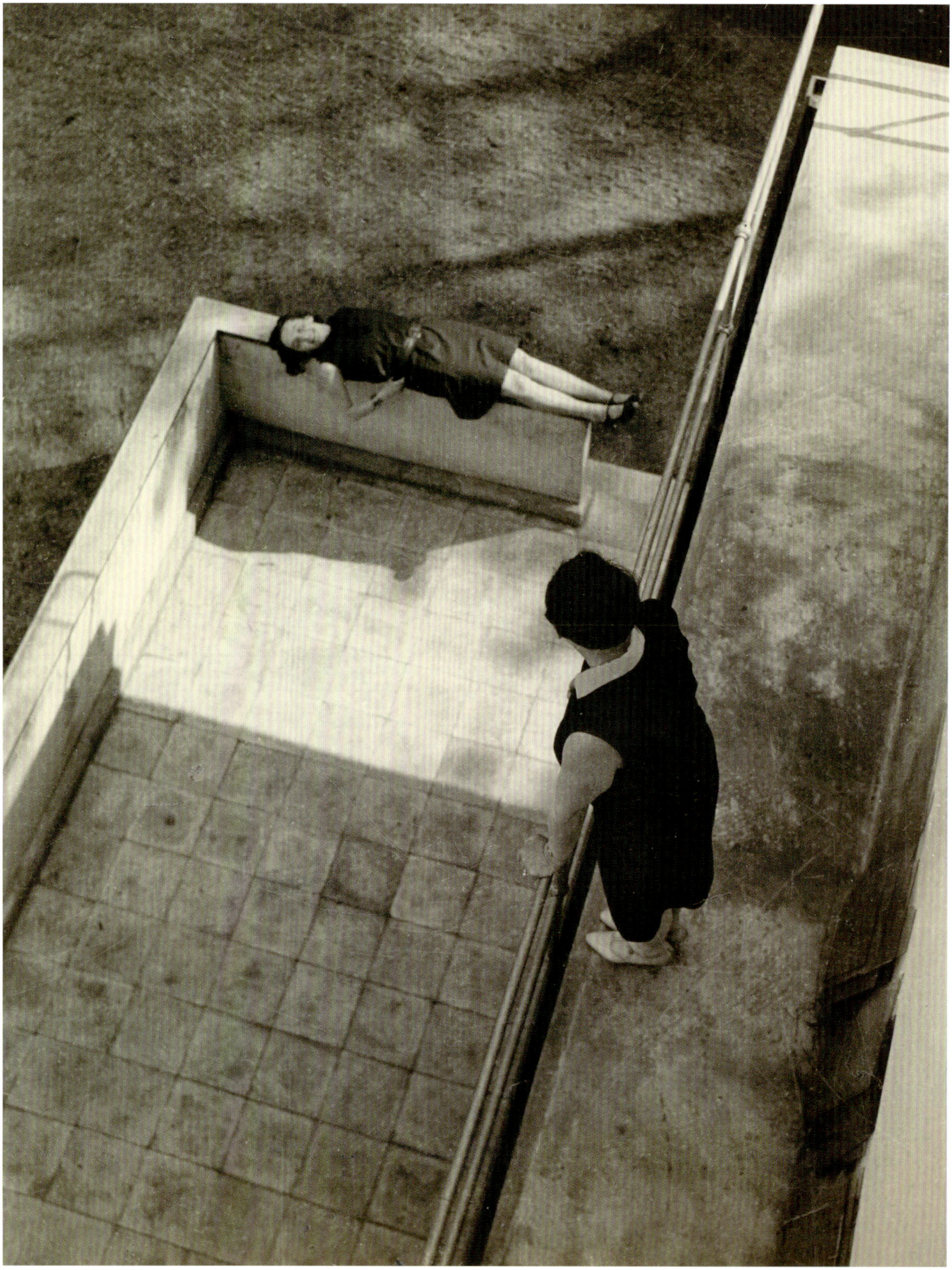

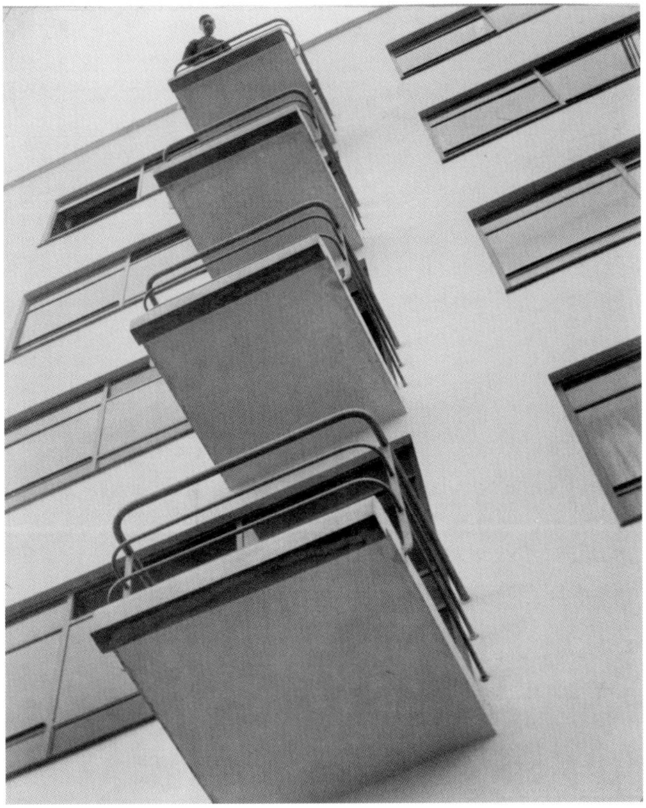

by Moholy-Nagy published in *Painting, Photography, Film* in 1926 (fig. 11), the other by student T. Lux Feininger from around 1928 (fig. 12), the differences are striking. Moholy's picture, captioned "The optical truth of the perspectival construction," shows the various properties one expects from the "form master"—for example, the unexpected viewpoint, restructured environment, and carefully placed human element. Here Moholy has achieved a textbook synthesis of both "the direct experience of space itself" and New Vision aesthetics. Feininger's photograph, by contrast, is a sloppy, spontaneous variant of the same idea, with awkwardly positioned appendages and a headless backside running interference with the rigid geometries of the architecture. The apparent naïveté and irreverence of this work suggests more than anything else posturing youth. In this case, the act of photographing for the students might be seen to approximate more closely conventional notions of play as an activity associated with children, for whom play exercises a central role in cognitive and physical development.

As Feininger's photograph suggests, *Vorkurs* students were engaged on a most fundamental level in a concentrated effort to assimilate the forms and ideas of their brilliantly original professor. To paraphrase the concepts of developmental psychologist Jean Piaget, assimilation occurs through repetition; it is through repetition that an accomplishment is consolidated within an individual's existing know-how and adapted to suit the specific needs of the individual.[30] (Drawing from Piaget's ideas and adding a pinch of Freud, Walter Benjamin wrote that to play was not "to act as if" but "to act again and again," in order to transform upsetting experiences into habit; habit, he stressed, is "the essence of all play.")[31] Unsurprisingly, many

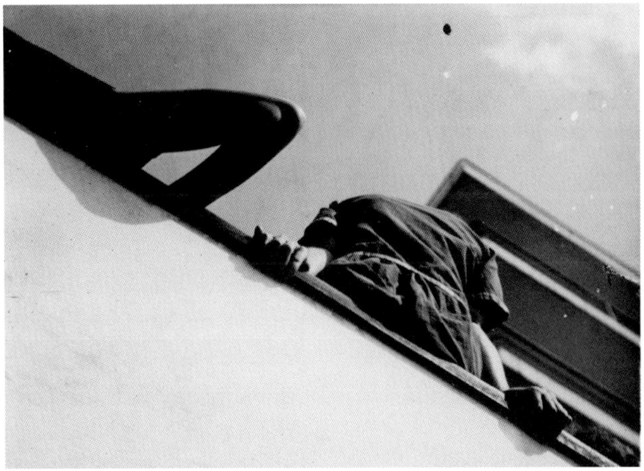

FIG. 10
László Moholy-Nagy,
Dessau, 1926–28.
Museum of Fine Arts, Houston,
Gift of the Prospero Foundation.

FIG. 11
László Moholy-Nagy,
Bauhaus Balconies, 1926.
George Eastman House, Rochester.

FIG. 12
T. Lux Feininger,
Human Elements in Architecture, c. 1928.
The Metropolitan Museum of Art,
Ford Motor Company Collection,
Gift of the Ford Motor Company and
John C. Waddell, 1987
(1987.1100.413).

of the same motifs Moholy repeatedly engaged appear in images by his students, but, as in the Feininger photograph just mentioned, results varied. Whether such images were intended as mischievous riffs on the master's prototypes or, conversely, failed attempts is impossible to say.[32] What is important is the role such images played in both students' indoctrination into Bauhaus principles and in their ability to flout such principles first encountered within the freewheeling context of the *Vorkurs* under Moholy's supervision.

A common use for the camera among Bauhaus members at every level was portraiture, which held special significance as a form of identity construction for the evolving institution. Students certainly worked in emulation of Moholy and others, who created images of themselves and colleagues as engineers, athletes, designers, dreamers, smokers, or, as in a series of portraits by Josef Albers, dynamic individuals emoting over sequences of frames. For Bauhaus students, the practice was somehow more fluid and experimental, due perhaps to an unusually heightened awareness of their participation in a self-conscious artistic revolution. Many portraits show a literal grafting of institutional identity onto personal image, as in Kurt Kranz's *Portrait and Bauhaus* (1930) and Lotte Beese's *Portrait of Otti Berger and Studio House* (c. 1930), both glamorous images that envision the artist as a kind of heroic, architecture-obsessed Hollywood pinup. Numerous self-portraits by Bauhaus women show subjects in unconventional poses and shot from unusual angles, engaging in a kind of spatial play favored by Moholy. This common motif of the compartmentalized figure transgressing his or her environmental surrounds appears most revealingly in a collage by Edmund Collein of the Gropius Atelier (fig. 13), which may be read as an assertion of both individual identity and *identification with* the institution, where the module and the multiple serve as common coin. Here, the search for individuality within conformity reflects the widespread anxieties of the period articulated by Simmel, Moholy, and others.

Clearly, an important aspect of play at the Bauhaus was purely social in function. Social theories of play recognize the importance of play as a mode of socialization in which competition and collaboration function as effective incentives for both order and individual achievement. In Johan Huizinga's famous study, the author describes play as hostility checked by friendship, out of which develops social virtues, such as chivalry, loyalty, and healthy competitiveness.[33] The creative applications of this sentiment squared nicely with contemporary understanding of capitalist incentives for productivity. Particularly within a highly regularized environment such as the Bauhaus, where the principles of mass production held sway, allowing for the emergence of variety within order was of fundamental importance.

Gropius first proclaimed the Utopian social goals of the Bauhaus in 1919, when he illustrated in bullet-point form the importance of group leisure activities at the Bauhaus. "Encouragement of friendly relations between the masters and students outside of work; therefore plays, lectures, poetry, music, fancy-dress parties. Establishment of a cheerful ceremonial at these gatherings."[34] Such activities are well documented within the Bauhaus photographic archive, where cross-dressing parties, band concerts, and amateur theatricals reveal a collegial spirit not all that different from undergraduate steam-letting at more conventional institutions. A more formalized interrogation of Bauhaus pedagogy may be observed in Oskar Schlemmer's theater workshop. In photographs of Bauhaus performances, one sees a sustained exploration of the relationship between human figures and modern architecture running parallel to activities undertaken with photography in the *Vorkurs*. Within these severely rationalized architectural environments, students were encouraged to experiment with costume and gesture in relation to space in much the same way Moholy's students explored such relationships through the camera's viewfinder.[35] However, in the theater workshop, such practices had a more direct, purposeful goal: the production of a staged event. Moreover, the radical perspectives and distortions produced through the photographic process were not available to viewers; audiences watched performances from a proscribed perspective, assimilating space in an optically conventional way. Significantly, photographs documenting Schlemmer's workshop performances have none of the experimental qualities one sees in the school's unsupervised photographic output. Feininger, one of the Bauhaus's most radically experimental photographers, relates that Schlemmer carefully directed him on how to document those performances, instructing him to avoid any hint of original perspective.[36]

Huizinga's ideas find a canny resonance in sport, a popular Bauhaus social activity that became a staple of experimental student photography. In Feininger's *Jump over the Bauhaus* (c. 1927; fig. 14), the relationship of the individual to the larger social body is expressed as well as the relationship of man to architecture. The dynamic colliding figures, frozen mid-air in the

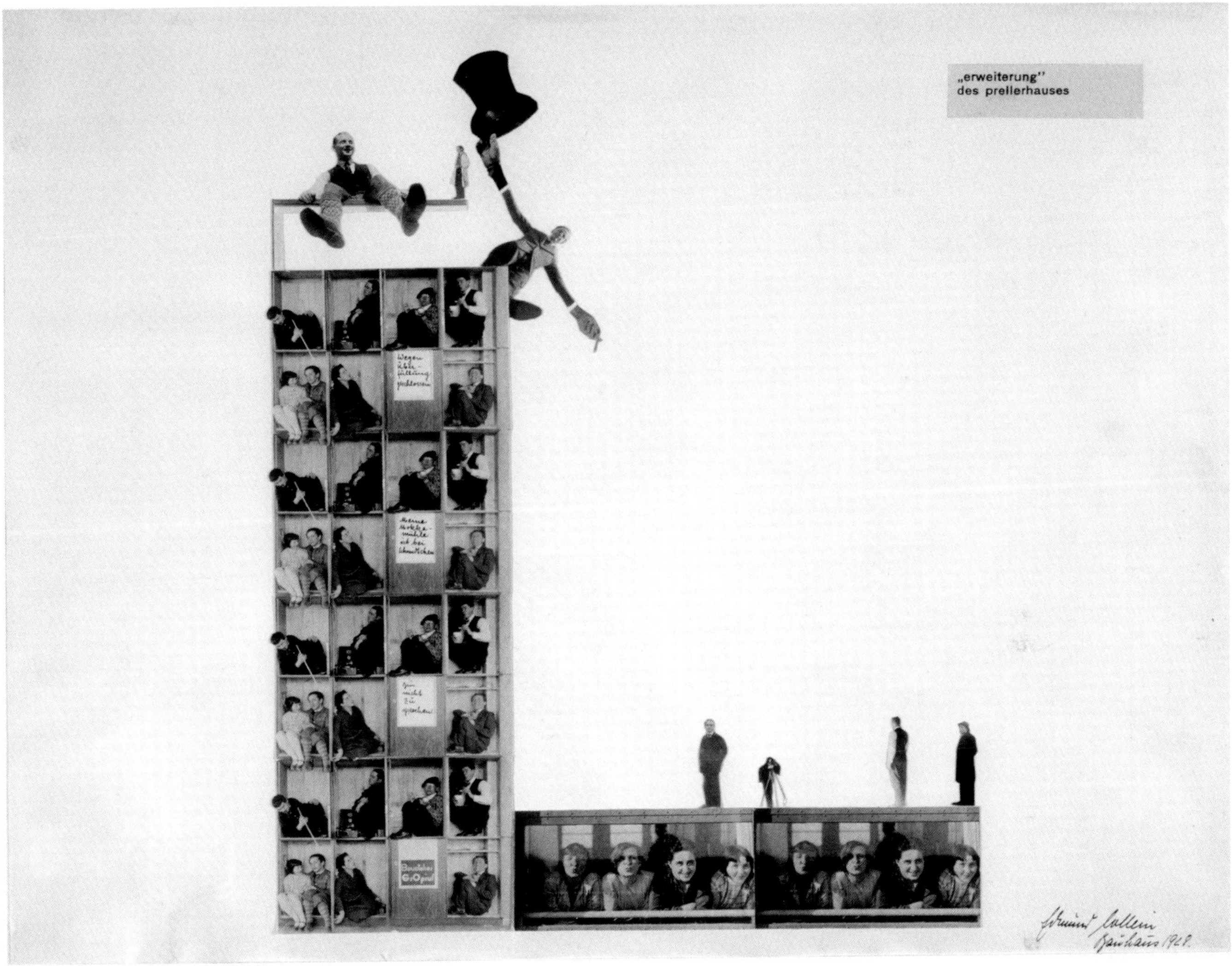

FIG. 13

Edmund Collein,
Extension to the Prellerhaus, 1928.
Bauhaus Archive, Berlin.

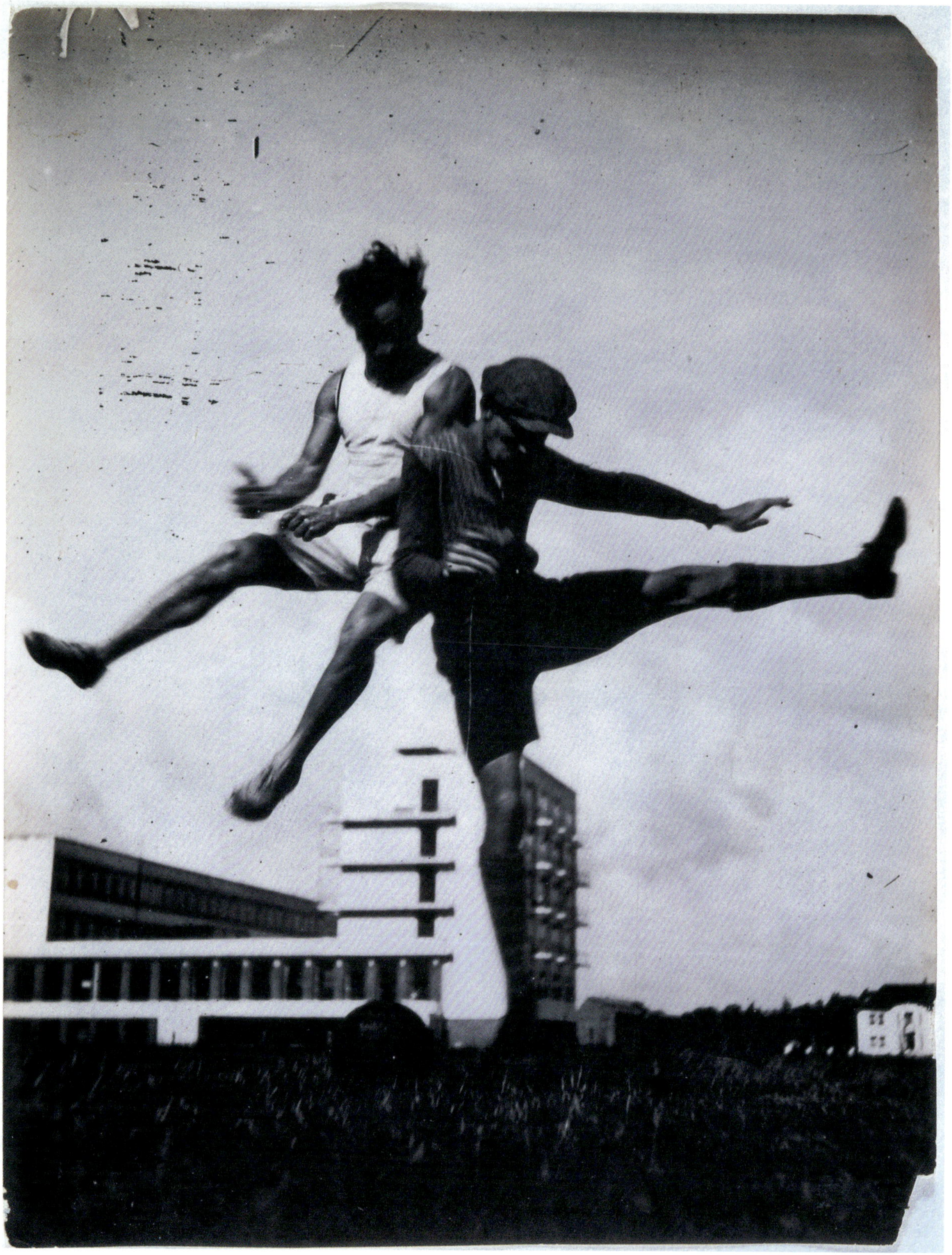

picture's foreground, capture the postures of athletes absorbed in competitive rivalry yet checked by the rules governing their activity—the players avoid using their hands. As they scrap for the ball, which lies stationary below, the figures are suspended momentarily in a perfect state of equilibrium between exuberant individual freedom and the rules governing their activity. Meanwhile, the players' relationship to Gropius's building in the background invites another meditation on the human form and modern architecture. Like Moholy's *Dessau, Jump over the Bauhaus* is an idealized image of Blochian *Vorschein,* a vision of a future in which man and modern geometric forms appear as perfect complements, with arms and legs both mimicking the cantilevers of the architecture and bursting with uncontrolled energy, an apt counterpoint to the building's grounded stasis. Emerging here in a single photograph, where movement is represented in stasis, scale is inverted, and subjective human vision dominates the cool eye of the camera, play finds purpose. In photographs such as this, the modern Utopia found its most perfect, if ephemeral, materialization.

FIG. 14
T. Lux Feininger,
Jump over the Bauhaus, c. 1927.
Bauhaus Archive, Berlin.

An idiosyncratic branch of the New Vision, Bauhaus photography embodies more than a youthful rebellion against documentary purity. Photographs by both Moholy-Nagy and students represent an exception within the Bauhaus's manifest purpose to tame art, to herd its past expressive impulses into the production of functional design. Made within the protective frame of the *Vorkurs,* which offered both students and professor exempt status from the school's applied-art mandate, Bauhaus photographs show a striking degree of irreverence and personal expression. In their unsystematic deconstruction of Bauhaus pedagogy, often taking the form of visual assault on Gropius's Dessau building itself, the Bauhaus photographers reasserted the primacy of the individual artist and the centrality of personal creative expression within the broader philosophy of technology-based capitalism. These pictures represent more than an irreverent protest against Ford-style productivity; they also make a case, if unwittingly, for such "unproductive" values as purposelessness, aimlessness, recklessness. The results boldly countered the artist-as-engineer philosophy promulgated by the Bauhaus, especially within the archetypal persona of Moholy-Nagy, declaring instead a determination to preserve a place for individual creative expression within an increasingly rationalized industrial society.

4

SERIOUS PLAY: GAMES AND EARLY TWENTIETH-CENTURY MODERNISM

CLAUDIA MESCH

Twentieth-century artists and cultural theorists have energetically pursued the analysis and exploration of the realms of "play" and games, aspects of culture that had been marginalized during the Enlightenment and ignored or denigrated by high-modernist critics. For example, in 1938, partly in response to the contemporary political situation, the Dutch philosopher Johan Huizinga recognized in his cultural theory of games fascism's barbarous and "puerile" censorship of play and games. At the same moment in the late 1930s, the cultural theorist Roger Caillois broke off his affiliation with the surrealist circles of both André Breton and Georges Bataille. Twenty years later he responded to aspects of Huizinga's analysis as well as to the Surrealists in *Man, Play, and Games* (1958), where he attacked the conceptual foundation of the postwar surrealist games Breton began publishing in 1953. Viewing games by the French Surrealists and by Marcel Duchamp through the lens of Callois's surrealist-inspired game theory, this chapter considers how games by these artists challenge modernist art production. More particularly, where the Surrealists used games to resist the restrictive political and intellectual conditions brought about with the rise of fascism, Duchamp eschewed such direct engagement. In his last years, Duchamp redefined his own art-chess as a primarily visual event. He thereby secured a place for himself within the modernist canon but also confined art-games to the autonomous realm of high art.

Art historians have recently pointed to the importance of play and games in the eighteenth century and to the period-style of the Rococo. It has been argued that the Rococo's "frivolous" artistic exploration of play and games is soundly rejected in the Enlightenment in favor of the "serious" delineation of aesthetics by philosophers such as Diderot, Kant, and Schiller. Jennifer Milam has, however, claimed that the "ludic impulse," as creative process and as "active engagement with the image," was central to Enlightenment thought and to the formulation of modern visual experience.[1] Within the history of twentieth-century modernism, little critical attention has been paid to the game as a structure common to the historical avant-garde. We might trace this continued repression of the game within critical discourse to the influential canon-constructing views of midcentury critics such

This chapter was first published under the same title in the journal *The Space Between: Literature and Culture, 1914–1945* 1, no. 1 (2005): 9–30.

as Clement Greenberg or Frankfurt School philosophers Max Horkheimer and Theodor Adorno. These thinkers rigorously distinguished the realm of visual modernism from the dross of mass culture as mere entertainment, a state destructive of authentic art. Greenberg's postwar art criticism had strictly segregated play, amusement, and entertainment from classical modern art. In order to champion the Kantian aesthetic tradition, Greenberg categorized the play of amusement as part of the corrupting effect of mass culture or kitsch, which must be contested and negated within the serious realm of art.[2] This absolute demarcation of the realms of high and low art willfully ignored Dada and surrealist experimentation with the game.

In contrast to the high-modernist critics who were their contemporaries, cultural theorists recognized games as a marker of civilization and acknowledged their place within epistemology. The cultural theorists' views on games perhaps indicate their debt to the disciplinary concerns of anthropology and sociology, on the one hand, and their reaction to the increasing power of fascist demagoguery, on the other. The burst of cultural theory centered on games in the twentieth century can be said to begin with Johan Huizinga, and with his first lecture on the play element in culture in an address in 1933; his *Homo Ludens: A Study of the Play-Element in Culture* was published in Leiden in 1938. Huizinga's resounding condemnation of the cultural and intellectual perversions of Nazism is also a modern-day tale of cultural decline that recalls the pessimistic pronouncements of Oswald Spengler's *The Decline of the West* (1920–22) and precedes those of the Frankfurt School. Huizinga mourned the dissipation of play in the twentieth century, and with it a code of ethics and a corresponding quality of human decency. He identified the "play impulse" as an inherent characteristic of human society and as an underlying structure of culture, not only in the creative act of poetry and art, but also in the waging of war in accordance with a "code of honor" and "the law of nations." Beginning with Plato's identification of human play activity as a kind of holiness, Huizinga sees play as central to ritual and inseparable from it; he discusses the use of masks in archaic cultures in marking the realm of "sacred play," a quality he claims has never wholly disappeared from social life and can still be manifested as "sheer play."[3] He goes on to chart the epistemological function of play within world history.

Huizinga then identifies five core qualities of human play throughout world history: (1) it is voluntary in nature; (2) it is separate from "real life"; (3) it has a beginning and end and must be repeatable; (4) it creates order in shifting between the states of tension and resolution of conflict; (5) all human play has *rules.* Huizinga traces the end of play activity in the sphere of the visual arts, where he dismisses contemporary art as overly esoteric and too concerned with the proliferation of "isms"—the "game" of a specialized critical discourse around modern art as it hurls itself toward the evermore "new." In a passage that recalls the contemporaneous analyses of Walter Benjamin, but lacks his radicalism and familiarity with the avant-garde, Huizinga notes how changes brought about in art by photographic reproduction work against the development of a "play-element" in art. In his view, art becomes at once too self-conscious and too connected to the market to retain its "eternal child-like innocence."[4]

Huizinga concludes with a powerful critique of the "friend/foe principle" outlined in the political philosophy of Carl Schmitt, which, Huizinga argues, destroys the ethical workings or "fair play" aspect of international law.[5] Huizinga explains how Schmitt's theory recasts the relation between states:

The theory refuses to regard the enemy even as a rival or adversary. He is merely in your way and thus is to be made away with. If ever anything in history has corresponded to this gross over-simplification of the idea of enmity, which reduces it to an almost mechanical relationship, it is precisely that primitive antagonism between phratries, clans or tribes where…the play-element was hypertrophied and distorted. Civilization is supposed to have carried us beyond this stage. I know of no sadder or deeper fall from human reason than Schmitt's barbarous and pathetic delusion about the friend-foe principle. His inhuman cerebrations do not even hold water as a piece of formal logic. For it is not war that is serious, but peace…. Schmitt's brand of "seriousness" merely takes us back to the savage level.[6]

Thus, Huizinga writes, Schmitt provides the intellectual foundation for the adolescent "puerilism" of fascism and its culture in 1938, a perverse "boy scoutism" without playfulness but that thinks itself beyond competitiveness; a world of yelled greetings, the wearing of badges and "political haberdashery," of "collective voodoo," crude sensationalism, pleasure in mass meetings and parades—simply, the "bastardization of culture."[7] However, he finally trusts that moral consciousness (a "drop of pity") will return with the awareness that human action may be "licit as play": "But if we have to decide whether an action to which our will impels us is a serious duty or is licit as play, our moral conscience will at once provide the touchstone."[8] Huizinga trusts that the play-instinct will reject thinking such as Schmitt's and compel a reentry into the sphere of ethics and civilization.[9]

Perhaps due to his aversion to the economic totalizations of Marxism, Huizinga did not theorize the place of games within the capitalist economy. Caillois's *Man, Play, and Games* (1958) pointed critically to Huizinga's decontextualized and teleological narrative of play-as-drive that established it as an enduring human quality throughout all of world history. Well before Foucault, Caillois advanced a nuanced theory of power that is more optimistically based upon the rise of competition and its dialectic with *alea,* or the chance advantages of a privileged birth. Caillois raises the possibility that power in modernity flows not unidirectionally but circulates and is actively contested in democratic society.

To formulate a less abstracted study of play culture, Caillois developed a taxonomy of existing games, which he delineated on two axes: (1) *ludus,* games that are subordinated to the disciplining framework of rules, and (2) *paidia,* games that consist of spontaneous and even tumultuous activity. On the other axis, Caillois places the categories of: (1) *agôn,* games of competition; (2) *alea,* games of chance; and (3) mimicry, games of simulation, and play behavior—such as the playing of a role in theater, in children's games, or by means of the process of identification with another within the act of spectatorship, as in, for example, the cultlike worship of film stars or athletes; (4) *ilinx,* or games that pursue vertigo, disorder, and physical disorientation, as is offered by amusement park rides like the roller coaster.

Caillois's taxonomy claims a wider berth for games within human society, and in the animal kingdom, than Huizinga's. He does not ascribe rules or an ordering function to all games, as he understands that *paidia-* and *ilinx*-type games may not operate on rules or may even strive toward disorder. In fact, he concludes that games either have to do with rules or they have to do with "make-believe," with "acting as if." Caillois tracks the development of civilization, or democracy, in the shift from *paidia* to *ludus,* across numerous world cultures, and in the "struggle against the prestige associated with simulation and vertigo" in democratic societies.[10] He understands the use of masks in ancient society along these lines; he describes how the mask is used as a symbol of superiority, furthering the inequity of power by instilling terror in political inferiors in the "reign of mimicry and *ilinx.*"[11] When, for example, the Greeks began to understand the universe as ordered through the use of mathematics, *agôn* and *alea* also began to structure social life. Regulated competitions thus take on significance, relating to the founding of numerous games—Olympic, Pythian, the Aztec game of *pelota,* and Chinese archery contests. Further, competitive examinations come to determine a bureaucratic elite. According to Caillois, social power comes to be achieved rather than ascribed; it becomes dominated by the shift from inheritance to merit, or by competition and chance. Soon regulated competition becomes dominant, even between social classes. The game takes on the function of clearing a social field by establishing conditions of pure equality.

Huizinga seems to have been either unaware—or possibly dismissive—of the activities of the Dada and surrealist avant-gardes within the realm of visual art. In contrast, Caillois's expanded theory of games in modern society can also be attributed to his involvement with the Surrealists and to their rethinking of hardened polarities such as seriousness / nonseriousness or work / leisure. However Caillois finally broke with the Surrealists exactly because of the radicality of surrealist thought, particularly as Georges Bataille developed it. Earlier, Caillois participated in four "Recherches Expérimentales" in February and March of 1933, sessions that also included Salvador and Gala Dalí, Alberto Giacometti, André Breton, Paul and Nusch Éluard, Tristan Tzara, and Benjamin Péret.[12] Caillois's *Man, Play, and Games* is a pointed response to Huizinga and to Bataille in that it clearly distinguishes the ludic from the sacred realm, which Huizinga had not. In drawing this major distinction, Caillois initiates what has been identified as his secular postwar "new humanism," where the ludic realm figures centrally.[13]

Caillois was involved in a number of Bataille's "secret societies" or quasi-experimental alternatives to democracy, including the Contre-Attaque Group, the College of Sociology, but finally not Acéphale, where Caillois seems to have been aware of the rituals Bataille envisioned for the group and therefore finally refused to participate.[14] Infamously, human sacrifice was central to the collective and "masterless" bond that Acéphale was to achieve, according to Bataille. However, as no member would volunteer to act as executioner, the plan failed.[15] During their period of close intellectual contact, both Caillois (in *Man and the Sacred,* 1939) and Bataille shared a major concern with the realm of the sacred. Inspired by pagan or archaic ritual, the sacred was key to realizing Bataille's utopian collective bond of "la vraie vie" or authentic life. In contrast, Caillois regarded the realm of play and of playful transgression—and not sacred transgression—as the second realm central to civilization. It is the case that Caillois rejected Bataille's radical appropriation of certain ideological devices that the fascists used in order to fight fascism. He recognized Bataille's idealized, quasi-pagan ritual-as-murder-pact in the fascists' ideological exploitation of this same idea on the battlefield, in their mythification of quasi-sacred, collective military death. This was one contributing factor to his break with Bataille's Surrealism.

Many of his postwar writings, including *Man, Play, and Games,* widened this fundamental rift with Surrealism in turning critically to Breton's practice. In other essays, Caillois commented, sometimes negatively, on both Breton's and Duchamp's manipulation of the game within the realm of art.[16] In his later years, Caillois mounted a constant vigil against what he called "totalitarian" art and thought. By this he meant theory that tended to totalizing claims: Caillois attacked psychoanalysis, Lévi-Strauss's structuralism, and Breton's games under this conceptual umbrella. By the 1950s he therefore recognized the significance of Breton's reengagement with surrealist automatism but did not approve of it. Caillois rather insisted that postwar thought and culture follow his own presumably open and antitotalizing schema for a "diagonal science," itself firmly anchored in his own reworking of the surrealist legacy.[17] In strong contrast to high-modernist critics, Caillois thereby acknowledged the cultural significance, and even the dangers, of both the ludic impulse and of Breton's postwar reengagement with surrealist automatism.

By the 1950s, Breton had recognized that the Surrealists had, by means of the games they devised, reconfigured the process of art-making *in toto* and even the workings of knowledge and language. Huizinga apparently prompted Breton, in the interviews that make up his memoirs (*Entretiens,* 1952) and in a number of essays in *Médium* (beginning in 1953), to reclassify almost the entirety of surrealist practice as the playing of games. Breton claimed that while the group (that is, *he*) first understood games merely as a kind of social glue and collective entertainment, and in embarrassment concealed their games as "experimental" activities, he only later realized the epistemological "discoveries" it could generate. In his catalogued list of surrealist games, Breton did not separate the automatist games of *dessin* or of the visual arts, such as the collective "Exquisite Corpse" (*Cadavre exquis*), from those involving language: the exquisite corpse is described as "written or drawn"; the "recipes" of the visual

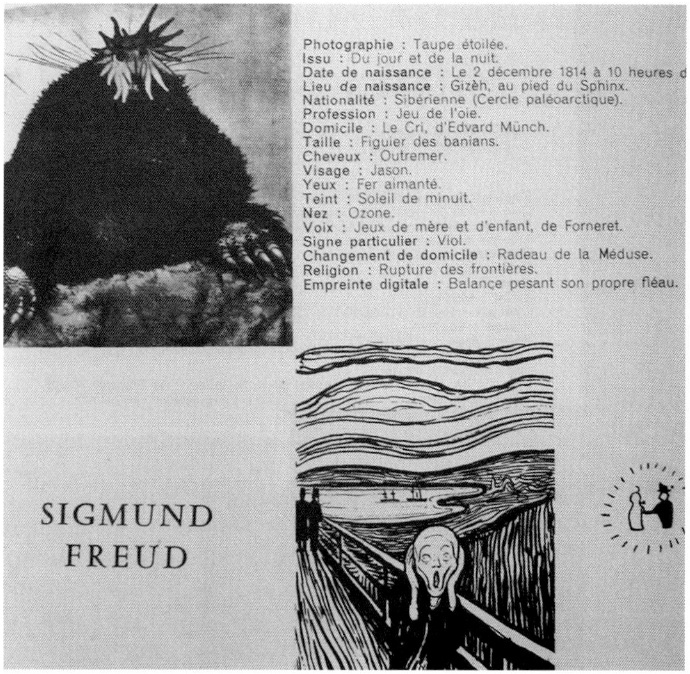

FIG. 15

"Cartes d'Analogie" [*Cartes d'Analogie*], 1959, from *Le Surréalisme même*, no. 5 (Spring 1959): 21.

FIG. 16

Joan Miró, Man Ray, Yves Tanguy, and Max Morise, "Exquisite Corpse" [*Cadavre exquis*], 1927. Private collection, Paris.

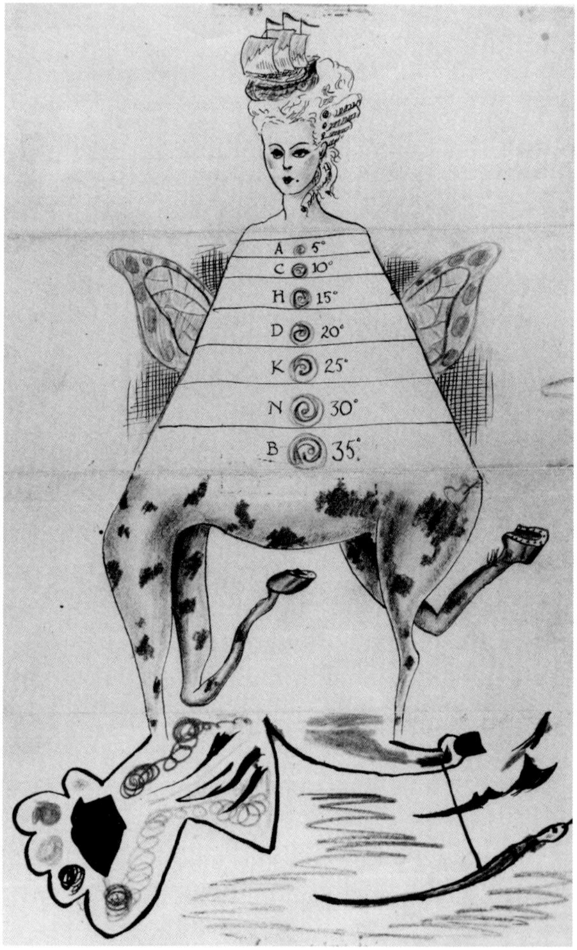

arts, listed as "collage, frottage, fumage, coulage, spontaneous decalcomania, candle-drawings, etc.," allowed, so Breton remarks, "greater satisfaction of the pleasure principle" in that such games could put the possibility of art-making in anyone's hands.[18]

In contrast, Philippe Audouin's analysis of surrealist games establishes another category, *games of objects,* under which he groups the "Experimental Research," the "Drawn Exquisite Corpse," the "Marseille Game," and the "Analogy Cards" games. Audouin would later distinguish as surrealist language games the game of "Definitions," the "Game of Conditionals—if...when...," and the "Exquisite Corpse," from what he called "games of options or opinions," such as "Scholarly notation" and "Would you open the door, or the Visitor."[19] Breton's 1954 comments on Huizinga and surrealist games appeared with his description of the "One into another" game he developed with Benjamin Péret,[20] and a year earlier Breton had published "Would you open the door?" (*Ouvrez-vous?*), a new collective game.[21]

The surrealist games that Audouin determined to be concerned with the visual often had to do with the construction or circulation of cards, either playing cards of the "Marseille Game" or the fictional and collectively fashioned "identification papers" of the "Game of Analogy Cards" (*Cartes d'Analogie,* fig. 15). One of these "portrays" Sigmund Freud according to customary categories of a passport of the 1940s: his photograph depicts a "star-nosed mole"; his domicile is "The Scream by Edvard Munch," his place of birth is "Giza, at the foot of the Sphinx." Both sets of cards engaged with the immediate wartime experience of the surrealist circle: the state of physical transience of travel, their forced relocation and exile to New York and other locations, and the continued demand to present identification papers while traveling in occupied France. Perhaps the cards also have to do with a sense of being pitched into the realm of pure *alea.*

The "Exquisite Corpse" (*Cadavre exquis,* fig. 16), a procedure devised so that a collective could by means of automatism assemble or "compose" a singular work and avoid the conscious control of any individual author, opened, as Breton saw it, a "strange possibility of thought, which is that of its pooling."[22] However, in including as its pool of players only practicing visual artists, the game (or Breton) did presuppose the seriousness of artistic training as its basis. Surrealist games can then be best understood as tools toward automatism, as strategies that attempt to pool a process of collective thought unmediated by the individual ego, or to short-circuit the conscious workings of the individual mind as it works its way through and applies the rules of the game to the actions at hand. Sometimes, as in Robert Desnos's plunges into hypnotic states, games of *ilinx* (physical and mental disorientation) are instead pursued. In Surrealism, the ends of *agôn,* that is, the regulated and antagonistic relation between powers and the drive to win, are repositioned such that the id, either individual or collective, might, with the proper surrealist discipline and perseverance, be summoned as a reluctant opponent and be forced to reveal itself in language and in image.

The "Marseille Game" (*Jeu de Marseille,* figs. 17a and b) is most interesting in that it is the collective project/game undertaken immediately before many of the contributing Surrealists—Breton, Victor Brauner, Oscar Dominguez, Max Ernst, Jacques Herold, Wifredo Lam, Jacqueline Lamba, and André Masson—began their exile from fascist-controlled France. Incorporating a woodcut by Alfred Jarry and drawings by these artists, this playing card deck included new court cards—genius (in lieu of king), siren (queen), and magus (jack)—and new suits: flame (love), star (dream), wheel (revolution), and lock (knowledge).[23] The "Marseille Game" featured personages including Baudelaire, Lautréamont, Sade, and Hegel as Genius; Lewis Carroll's Alice, and Hélène Smith (a nineteenth-century clairvoyant) as Siren; and Novalis, Freud, Pancho Villa, and Paracelsus as Magus. The source for these cards in the "magical arts" of alchemy and tarot is clear: the suits flame, star, wheel and lock, as well as the figures of genius, siren, and magus, point to the traditional tarot deck. It is not coincidental that the famed "Tarot de Marseille" of the late fifteenth century, regarded as the source for many later tarot decks, is the origin for this surrealist game.[24] As the tarot is usually used for fortune-telling purposes—it is said to have been brought to Western Europe by Roma—the Surrealists' turn to divination in a time of upheaval perhaps underscores their tenuous situation but also their continuing desire to navigate their future, so to speak, through the influence of other revolutionary minds. By contrast, this game recognizes card-playing as a means of passing the time, and as characteristic of waiting; the Marseille Game also wills that skill and ability can begin to structure an uncertain, even treacherous situation. Card-playing is a game that combines both *alea* and *agôn;* in certain card games, *agôn,* in terms of the experience and strategy of the card player, can determine the winning hand.[25] The surrealist card game, undertaken in transit and a time of great

FIGS. 17A AND 17B

"Marseille Game" [*Jeu de Marseille*], 1940–41, from *V.V.V.*, nos. 2–3 (March 1943). Court cards by Brauner, Breton, Dominguez, Ernst, Herold, Lam, Lamba, and Masson. Redrawn for publication by Robert Delanglade. Courtesy of Special Collections, Department of Archives and Manuscripts, University Libraries, Arizona State University, Tempe.

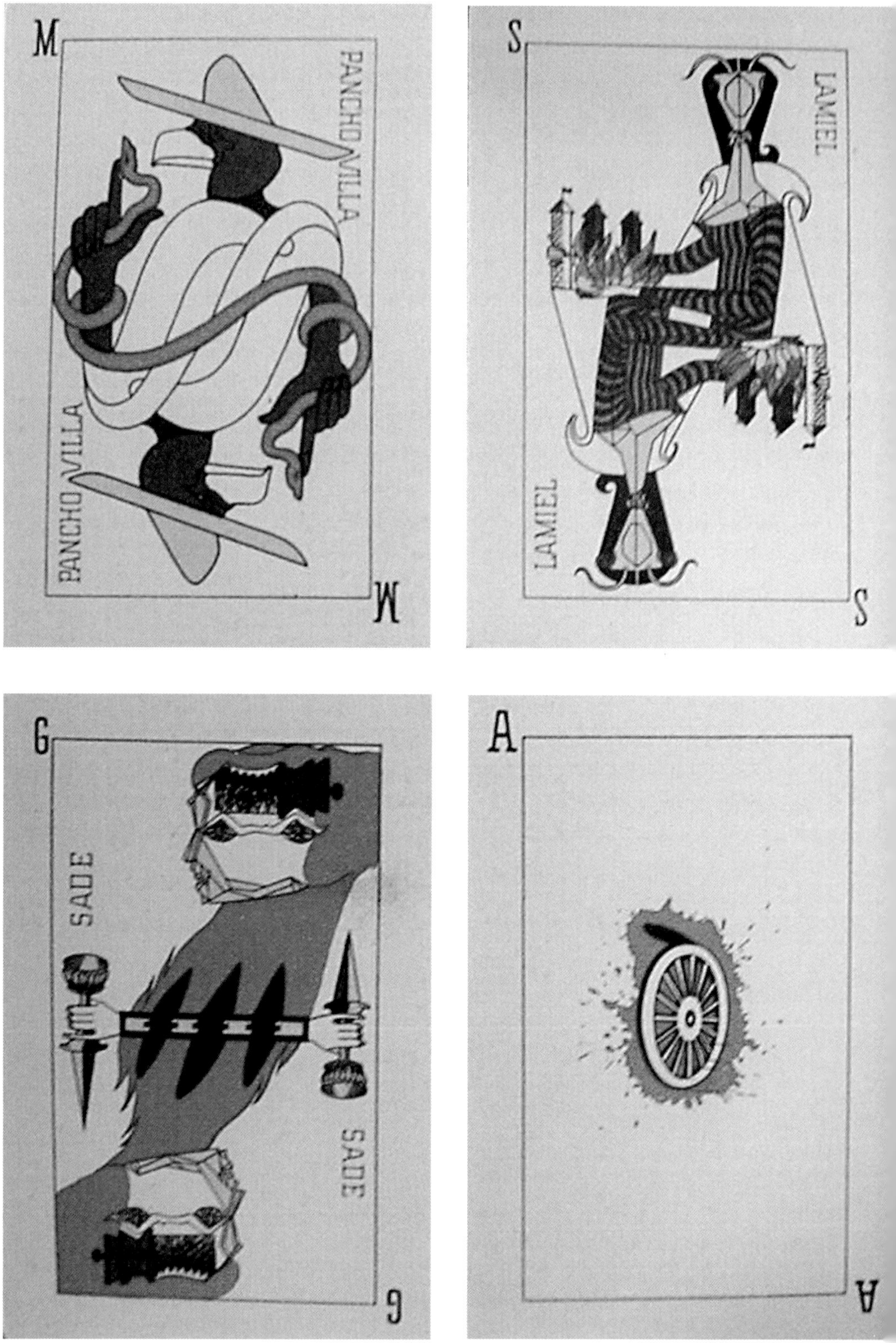

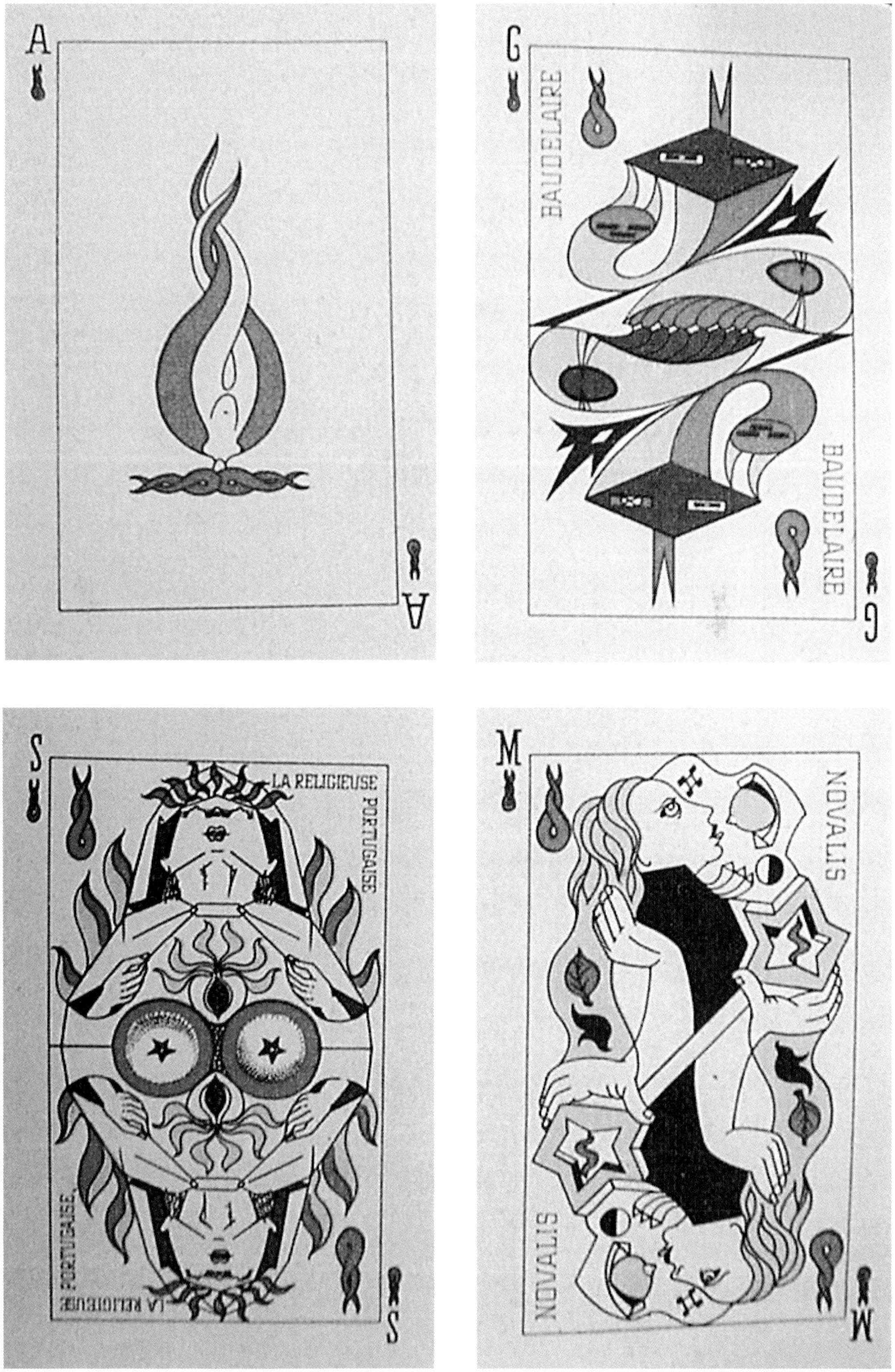
A
G
BAUDELAIRE
S
LA RELIGIEUSE PORTUGAISE
M
NOVALIS

uncertainty, works to foreground human agency in the situation where fate, chance, or the specter of totalitarianism seems to have overtaken it.

Certainly the slippery interchange between chance, on the one hand, and ability, on the other, was well known to Marcel Duchamp. Perhaps more so than any other artist of the twentieth century, Duchamp concerned himself with this divide and with the structure and process of *agôn,* as it delimits human action and as it is personified in the game of chess. He understood that the ludic impulse and the agonistic structure of the universe take place on the plane of eros, and within the tensions, resolutions, and displacements of sexual play. In his art Duchamp, systematically introduced the element of gender and tied the confrontations and negotiations of eros to the field of *agôn.* Beyond this Freudian confrontation with the game, Duchamp at first positioned chess-playing as a realm outside of art practice, but one that by reason of his activities within it became part of the sphere of avant-garde art: his familiarity with the chess community and the remaining chess scores that document his chess performances radically expanded the field of visual art. Surrealist artists Alberto Giacometti, Max Ernst, and Man Ray also made reference to chess in their art, but the game did not buttress the entirety of their artistic production the way it did Duchamp's. Duchamp's engagement with *agôn* by means of chess was continuous and spanned his involvement with the divergent artistic practices of Cubism and New York Dada.[26]

Late in life, Duchamp used chess as a stage for public art performances, part of his elaborate "comeback" to the American art scene in the 1960s. Faithfully documented in photographs, he played chess against a number of younger opponents on stage and in art museums. Most spectacularly, he played against a nude female opponent at the Pasadena Museum. He thereby explicitly reconnected his art to the high-art tradition of the female nude within Western painting. In a retreat from the collaborative and readymade aspect of chess that he had earlier emphasized, Duchamp's late art staged chess as a visual and aesthetic experience that could fit comfortably, as an autonomous practice, within the history of Western art.

Chess, one of the oldest and most rigidly competitive games of *agôn,* is, as Caillois understood it, an ultimate contest of *agôn,* in requiring players to compete as rigorously and intensely as they can with the goal of winning.[27] Winning is required of a player in order to achieve ranked status in chess, which Duchamp pursued aggressively in France during the 1920s. "Wouldn't you rather win?" Duchamp is said to have dryly asked Walter Hopps in 1963 as they deliberated around the roulette tables at the Golden Nugget Casino in Las Vegas. As chance would have it (at least according to Hopps), Duchamp's instructions at the tables resulted in a considerable win.[28] Can we then also understand Duchamp as one of the most competitive artists—that is, one who was most concerned with winning—in the twentieth century? This reading goes against a prevalent postmodernist understanding of Duchamp's involvement with the game, as the possibility of endless "beautiful" play without result or concern for an outcome.[29] In the 1950s, Duchamp himself insisted that he was more interested in investigating how the language of chess could visually realize the beautiful than in outplaying an opponent, yet this was surely not Duchamp's view as he played competitively in the 1920s.[30] One can make the claim that the recasting of all human interaction, including heterosexual sexuality, into the guise of *agôn,* and thereby creating situations that could be mastered and possibly won—a process of conversion that one can read across his entire oeuvre, even in his final epic work, the installation *Etant donnés*—seems to have interested Duchamp the most.

One might also consider the chess game as a parallel and analogue to Duchamp's series of readymades, which he is said to have begun producing in 1913. He first exhibited the readymades in New York in 1916 and the famed *Fountain* in 1917. Duchamp realized that he could take up the popular culture phenomenon of chess like a found object and use it as a subject and a structure for his art. Chess was perhaps Duchamp's most compelling assisted readymade, one he could reconfigure almost endlessly but always in accordance to its established boundaries and rules. The chess game might be considered Duchamp's master readymade, and one that unifies almost his entire oeuvre.

Duchamp's love of chess, the game most removed from the workings of chance, is apparent in his art. One can trace an origin of Duchamp's concern with chess and *agôn* in the iconography he developed early in his career while he worked within the medium of painting. His Cézanne-esque paintings of his brothers at the chessboard of 1910 and 1911, and the paintings of the following year that removed these figures and focused exclusively on the movement of the chess piece in play, *Le Roi et la Reine traversés par des nus vites* and *Le Roi et la Reine entourés de nus vites,* are all representations that focus on chess. Duchamp famously declared in 1923, a point that coincided with the "completion" of his earliest epic work, *The Large Glass,* that he had stopped being an artist and would in the future only concern himself with chess.[31]

Indeed, in the late teens and 1920s, he played competitively in Argentina and then as a ranked player in France, and produced chess pieces and other chess paraphernalia.[32] For a time thereafter, Duchamp worked directly on the problem of reconfiguring or transforming *alea* (roulette) into pure *agôn* (chess). While the intellectual challenge of the task attracted Duchamp to the project—it is quite impossible, which he later recognized—he was clearly also motivated to "break the bank," that is, to garner a huge profit by means of gambling. One might even conclude that had his model succeeded, he would have reconfigured the functioning of the capitalist economy.[33] He co-authored a treatise, "Opposition and Sister Squares are Reconciled," on an obscure chess end-game problem in 1932, and produced a "pocket chess" assemblage in 1944 for Julien Levy. Impressed by Duchamp's foray into chess theory, Caillois first commented on Duchamp's essay in 1937 and returned to it in 1970 in his aptly titled collection of essays, *Cases d'un échiquier* (The Squares of the Chessboard). Caillois was finally most intrigued by one implication that Duchamp raised—that a voluntary failure might bring victory or vice versa. Effectively Duchamp was working to destabilize the notion of zero-sum play, the agonistic cornerstone of chess, in this theoretical work.[34]

It was in and around his Pasadena retrospective exhibition of 1963 that Duchamp began to present himself as a chess player *within* the realm of art, a reversal of his earlier insistence that his activities in these two domains were wholly separate. One asks why Duchamp seized upon this radical reversal shortly before his death.[35] In addition to the reissue of many of his readymades and the assemblage as multiples, and the permission to produce duplicates or "replicas" of many major works for the 1963 exhibition,[36] Duchamp posed while playing chess during a number of highly publicized appearances both during and after the 1963 exhibition. Many of these appearances are captured in Julian Wasser's series of photographs of Duchamp, as well as in the film *Jeu d'échecs avec Marcel Duchamp* by Jean-Marie Drot, all of which were completed during and shortly after the Pasadena exhibition.

FIG. 18

Marcel Duchamp and Eve Babitz at the Pasadena Art Museum during Duchamp's retrospective exhibition. Photograph © 1963 Julian Wasser. All rights reserved.

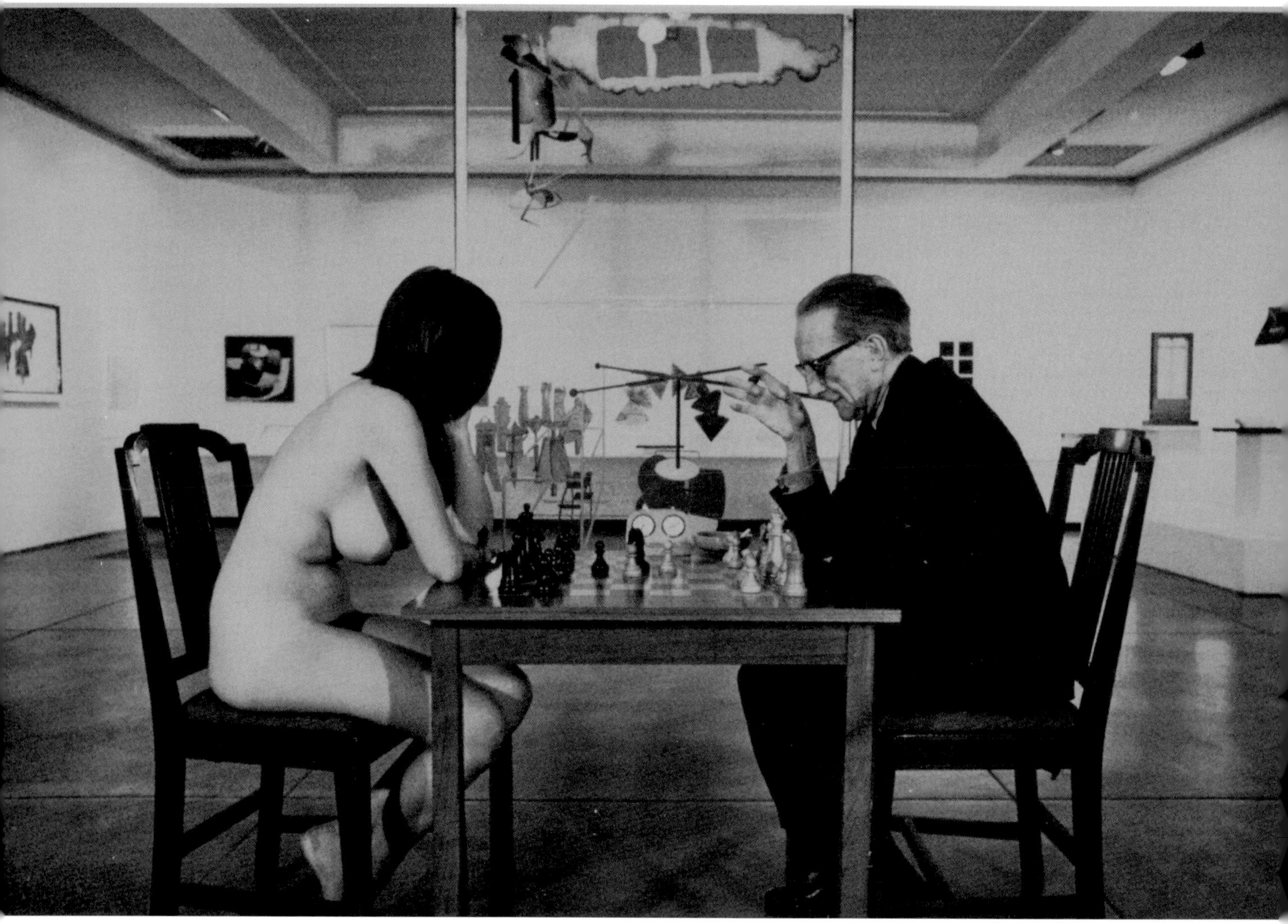

The most widely disseminated image by Julian Wasser of the chess match between Duchamp and the nude Eve Babitz, a female friend of Hopps's, was shot on October 18, 1963, in the Pasadena gallery that featured *The Large Glass* and related works in the Duchamp exhibition (fig. 18).[37] Wasser and Duchamp staged this game before *The Large Glass* in order to emphasize its composition or even in a sense to perform it. For the exhibition, Hopps had placed the early chess-related drawings and paintings in the second gallery. Dickran Tashjian claims that the Babitz/Duchamp match was a chance event whose genesis cannot be traced to any one person, but it was an idea that Duchamp agreed to.

It seems a highly deliberate decision to have staged for the camera and before *The Large Glass* a chess game between Duchamp and a female nude named "Eve," the biblical ur-bride. Tashjian suggests that several aspects of this event are purely "serendipitous." Duchamp had already related the biblical female nude to the movement of chess pieces across the board: with a nude "Eve" depicted within his earlier painting *Paradise* (1910–11), which featured a nude model posing as Eve, a painting that further became the verso of *King and Queen Surrounded by Swift Nudes*. The Wasser photograph also recalls Duchamp's theatrical appearance as the nude Adam to Brogna Perlmutter's Eve in Francis Picabia's "CinéSketch" of 1924, recorded in a famous photographic image; the Wasser photograph is also reminiscent of a 1936 photograph of Duchamp at the chessboard in front of *Nude Descending a Staircase;* and the image interacts with the complex iconography of *The Large Glass* itself, its segregation into female and male domains and its direct references to chess in, for example, the *Nine Malic Moulds* of the lower panel.[38] While Duchamp may not have arranged the event himself (as Babitz's account suggests), it is likely that given the resonances of the image there, he would have suggested that the game should be staged before *The Large Glass.*

However, Babitz's image and her own recollection of the event have effectively disappeared from art history. Her essay "Me and Marcel" remained unpublished. In Wasser's photograph, Babitz's hair has fallen over her face in her absorption in the game, erasing her as an individual adversary or player from the scene. In contrast, the camera captures Duchamp's absorbed gaze and his gesture, as though he is explaining or gesticulating a recent move. Wasser's arresting image of an urbane and elegant Duchamp engaged in chess with a voluptuous younger gaming partner reconnects to Duchamp's investigation of the eros of *agôn* (or the *agôn* of eros) in *The Large Glass* by displacing the onanism of the grinders of the *Glass* onto the movements of the pieces in the game between himself and Eve. However, in the process of rendering this game as a photographic image, she disappears as a subject and also as an opponent within the game of chess. The photograph transforms her into a representation of a female nude, a familiar image with a long history in Western painting. Babitz's image is therefore taken out of the realm of *agôn,* where adversaries confront each other under ideal conditions. She is instead put into the recognizable context of high art and its representations of the female body, which were traditionally offered as an object of the (male) viewer's gaze. Duchamp also used the photograph of his game with Babitz to relate himself and his art to recognizable genres of modern painting. This traditional subject matter may have enlightened more conservative museum administrators and trustees and also the American public as they deliberated his art, in grounding it in a traditional high-art genre.

Duchamp had indicated his new postwar conception of chess as a primarily visual event already in the 1950s. In his address to the New York State Chess Association in 1952, Duchamp outlined what he called the "three main aspects of chess": first, as *agôn* or as an intellectual competition; second, as a realm for the development of "scientific methods" for chess, a game "already too complex for the limitation of the human mind."[39] He declared that the third aspect, the "artistic side of chess," was most important to himself. Duchamp notes that chess pieces might be thought to produce an actual visual design within a game, although "with no visual aesthetic value." Yet he then suggests that chess offers two distinctly aesthetic pleasures. The pieces and their function elicit human thought as language might. As they are moved by the winner, the pattern that emerges "tell(s) an ideographic story through a series of moves and become(s) a real visual pleasure."[40] In this short address, Duchamp emphasized the *visual* patterns of the winning player's moves as they are registered across the horizontal playing surface. He described these winning moves as an aesthetic pleasure that is at least in part experienced visually. One might also question why the movements of an opponent who ultimately may not win the game do not enter into Duchamp's considerations or count as "sensuous pleasures" in their own right, independent of win or loss.

Keeping these comments in mind, we might return to the Babitz / Duchamp match and consider the complex horizontally based pattern the match produced as an essential visual element within the installation of primarily vertically oriented visual patterns, that is, Duchamp's chess-related drawings and paintings in the same gallery space. Schwarz recounts that Duchamp won the game against Babitz.[41] Given his association of the aesthetic qualities of chess with a winning player's moves, did Duchamp then guarantee that he would remain the singular author of all the images, objects, and events in the Pasadena gallery in 1963?

Wasser's photograph of the Babitz / Duchamp match visually conforms to a long lineage of female nudes retinally transformed into objects by male artists.[42] In chess, a condition of equality is assumed between players regardless of gender; equality must be taken as a point of departure in the game. The Wasser photograph negates this essential aspect of *agôn,* which had previously always concerned Duchamp. It simultaneously renders the scene recognizable as high art. Duchamp had of course previously used photography to explore cultural assumptions regarding the modern-artist persona, and to deploy his female alter ego, Rrose Sélavy.[43] Given his earlier subversive use of photography, the photograph of the Babitz / Duchamp match is all the more disturbing for its gender-conventionality and, if we can believe it, for Dickran Tashjian's claim that the Wasser photograph was Duchamp's favorite.[44] As a result of the Wasser photograph, the chess match is transformed into a retinal event of the type Duchamp had earlier disparaged. In it Duchamp relegates chess to the autonomous realm of art.

Duchamp was also photographed playing with Hopps in the museum's galleries with people crowded around them. Five years later, in an auditorium at Ryerson Polytechnic in Toronto with his fully clothed wife, Teeny, at his side, Duchamp and Teeny were photographed at play in a series of two chess games against John Cage (he lost one, but Teeny won the second). Cage titled the series "Reunion," a musical composition, and connected the chessboard to light and sound sensors that issued sounds corresponding to the moves of each player.[45] In returning to the foundation of his art in chess late in his career, Duchamp configured himself publicly as a challenger to, or even a collaborator with, avant-garde artists of the 1960s such as Cage. Duchamp's phrase "Tous les joueurs d'échecs sont des artistes" further reminds us of the realm of precision and beauty that *agôn* should and can occupy and of the importance of games as a sphere proper to *art,* where the agonistic impulse can be tapped as a creative force.[46]

While modernist art criticism did not recognize the cultural centrality of games during the rise of fascism in Western Europe, artists and game theorists did. Huizinga and Caillois elevated play and the game as markers of civilization; Duchamp and the Surrealists claimed the game as a structure for modern art. At least for a time, these artists deployed the game as a means to dramatically expand the realm proper to art. The game-as-art would also, in Breton's conception, lessen the control of a singular creating author/ego behind the artwork. At times, Duchamp, like the Surrealists, used the game to bend the conditions of fate, uncertainty, and even chance to human reason, and to will human agency into existence amid chaos or the unknown.[47] And while Bataille, Breton, and Caillois had differing views of how it should be pursued, the Surrealists explored the game within art, even as a kind of sacred ritual, in order to contest the absolutism of fascist ideology.

Duchamp at first explored chess as a readymade and attempted to apply its agonistic aspects not only to art but to the real, or to all human interaction, in order to create situations that might be mastered or "won" through sheer analytic ability. However, late in his life and production, Duchamp turned against the surrealist notion of collective authorship via the game in privileging the moves or visual patterns produced by the zero-sum victor in chess. He absorbed chess into the realm of art in his final years, but in doing so Duchamp notably kept his distance from another aspect of the "real," that is, from the realm of politics. Unlike the direct attacks launched against fascism by surrealist circles, Duchamp formulated his art (and what became his art-chess) as autonomous from other spheres of social life. Duchamp's notion of autonomous art also squared well with American art criticism's development of a similar idea of art's autonomy during the Cold War. His earlier interest in challenging the zero-sum situation (as he had explored it in his 1932 treatise) seems therefore to have evaporated as Duchamp struggled to assure his own legacy within the history of modern art. This challenge necessitated a return to the notion of a singular, producing author of art. Duchamp's late emphasis on the singular victor/author went hand-in-hand with his own strategic recasting of chess as a visual experience through which he could claim his rightful place, victorlike, within the canon of modern art. In the end, one can confidently say that though they theorized the game structure in dramatically different ways and for vastly different ends, the extended and consistent engagement of Huizinga, Caillois, Duchamp, and Breton with the game is an important if belittled chapter in the history of the twentieth-century avant-garde.

SURREALIST GAMING: RULES AND THE REST

MARY ANN CAWS

Gaming is about chance and rules together—perhaps in every view, but most certainly in the surrealist view. Let me take chance first: think of that so important method called "objective chance"—*le hasard objectif.* Now its rule is the necessary leaving of yourself open to possibility: "L'état d'attente" or "disponibilité." You come across in the outside world the answer to a question you didn't know you had. Ignorance is part of it: not knowing. And that of course is the point of André Breton's fulmination against the already seen and the already known. It is no good to know or even predict something—for that removes the point of open possibility and makes it into the very dull and almost closed probability.

Joseph Cornell is hands down the supreme craftsman of what could be thought of as a kind of surrealist game. Never mind that he considered surrealism to aim at black magic and that his art was aiming at white magic. Never mind: seen more or less *sub specie aeternitatis,* his entire way of being and doing and thinking was game, seriously considered—and considered under the stars, as Kirsten Hoving has recently discussed.[1] All those boxes with wires, globes, bubbles, rolling balls, grids, bottles, things all lined up, collected, arranged to move about.... Yet we might think that such a tight frame as in his famous boxes would militate against any openness—don't they fence in what they include? No, indeed they work against any settling down into clarity and done-ness. Their feeling of fragmentation—their reliance, say, upon the piece of fabric from a beloved ballerina's dress, all those snippets of nostalgia—leaves the suggestion open, and its wholeness (as opposed to the whole dress) intact. Such a very Mallarméan concept: the leaving intact and untouched of the garment by the partial indication of a bit of it. This is advanced semiotics in the dress code before Roland Barthes was even born. Each included thing serves as metonymy for more. No one was ever more Mallarméan than Cornell, for whom he was the primary icon. Or then see, in a box dedicated to the *Romantic Ballerina,* the way a few rhinestones and a brief text can sum up a whole legend of Taglioni's dancing for a highwayman at night. As Louis Marin thinking of Poussin would have it, this is a form of *delectatio,* of utter delight in allegory and in its working out and through.[2]

All those boxes working specifically as games! You put a ball in the top, and it rolls majestically down the zigzag slope, falls into a trough, and you start over. Or then you push a little metal ball along a wire, choosing the rhythm of its motion by a manipulation of the box from side to side. His invalid brother Robert may have loved to play with this just as with his trains and the other constructions Joseph made for him, but then so do we. Philosophical toys, he said. There is a peculiar joy to a Cornellian game, as to a Mallarméan conceit. Their plays on white and on the idea of nothing can be thought of as a double play. In these games, as in these notions, less or at least what we could see as minimal is generally a great deal more.

What do we ignore here, if part of the chance depends on what we ignore? Everything in the outside world beyond the box: everything we know of a particular diva's temperament, perhaps, or the workings of physics or of highwaymen, or of diamonds. To play by a Cornellian method, you have to accept what you are given, and let the box open up the possibilities of your mind.

But is that not true of the entire surrealist enterprise of gaming? The rule is there, and that is exactly what makes the freedom of chance open up into the freedom of your own imagination, along with that of the other imaginative players.

The game of all surrealist games is of course the collective and surprising *cadavre exquis,* played with such enthusiasm both in drawing and in words—so hovered over as a concept and so universally enjoyed in groups from the most elementary school exercise to the university seminar and beyond. When, several years ago, New York City's Drawing Center sponsored a publication on the topic (*The Return of the Cadavre Exquis*),[3] there were more than six hundred entries by artists eager to participate—and that was simply by word of mouth, the best surrealist word that ever was.

As automatic drawing and speaking took over the café games of the neo-surrealist groups, many of us were surprised and, actually, disappointed, by the way the rules predominated over the spontaneity. Unforgettable for me was an evening we were sitting, surrealist-style, some would-be latter-day surrealist types and moi, at La Coupole in Paris, and it was my turn to manifest my automatic thoughts. I was somewhat embarrassed by the project. I might have written at some length and in some places about such games, but didn't know I would ever be called upon to participate. I mumbled something or other—we were doing this orally, alas—only to hear my neighbor (an over-the-top qualified latter-day *surréalisant)* reprimand me with: "How dull that is." Now I had believed that you weren't supposed to think it out and just blurt out something that would be received unjudgmentally. I was clearly wrong. So much for individual spontaneity. Group spontaneity was of a different order, perhaps, but this was demonstration of the self for the others. Of course, when I started to pore over various surrealist documents of those first glory days, I saw with my own perhaps pre-surrealist eyes that re-touchings existed: oh, yes. My lips were sealed and remain so.

In any case, collectivity was the thing, and often anonymity. A medieval cathedral—as John Ruskin knew—had all the supreme strength of the collective craft and of the sacrifice of the individual name. Ruskin loved irregularity, from building textures down to sugar cubes. But alas for the ideal, the ex-surrealist poet René Char told me of constructing a poem of triple authorship, intended to be anonymous, by Paul Éluard, André Breton, and himself. The surprise, to him, and then to me (idolizing Breton as I did then) was that Breton was the one to rule against anonymity. So much for rules and freedom.

Moving beyond the Cornellian frame and the exquisite corpse to other ways of framing the surrealist game and ruling it, we might still think of how a set of built-in rules and constraints give extra play to one's mind by all the possibilities opening out from the tight certainties. This was and is the case with the celebrated work and play of OULIPO (the *Ouvroir de Littérature Potentielle*), and in its famous example, Georges Perec's novel *La Disparition,* written without the use of the letter "e"—by far the most frequent letter in the French language.[4] It turns out to be a veritable marvel. Its difficulty somehow facilitates its openness.

Some of us have spent ages, years, poring over the kinds of rules, limits, and constraints of surrealist gaming—even when we aren't trying to re-create any of it or them. They repay endless consideration, generally where we wouldn't expect it. For example, one could think of the ways that rules get followed by remembering the word plays of Robert Desnos, who borrowed Marcel Duchamp's alter ego, Rrose Sélavy, for his own. When Desnos asked Duchamp's permission to use his muse, Duchamp replied that he had no rights over her. Desnos's special skill in the early 1920s lay in the hypnotic sleeps: those trances in which, when queried, he answered so singularly. How does this play on the nerves of the spectator? It certainly played on Breton's nerves, provoking in him an intense jealousy. When we read the accounts of these sessions, the peculiar mysteriousness of Desnos's responses are provocative even for us: just listen…

SLEEPS

Breton: Desnos, it's Breton here. Tell us what you see for him.
A. The equator (draws circle and horizontal diameter).
Q. Is this a trip Breton will take?
A. Yes.
Q. Will it be a business trip?
A. (he shakes his head. Writes:) Nazimova
Q. Will his wife travel with him?
A. ????
Q. Will he go to find Nazimova?
A. No.
Q. Will he be with Nazimova?
A. ?
Q. What else do you know about Breton? Speak.
A. The boat and the snow—there is also the pretty telegraph tower—on the pretty tower there is a young…

Ernst's hand replaces that of Breton:

Q. This is Ernst's hand. Do you know him?
A. Who?
Q. Max Ernst.
A.
Q. Will he live long?
A. Fifty-one years.
Q. What will he do?
A. He'll play with madmen.
Q. Will these madmen make him happy?
A. Ask that blue woman.
Q. Who is that blue woman?
A. THE.
Q. The? What?
A. The tower.[5]

What isn't to love about that? The questions, the answers, the way we wish we were there—Desnos's drawings have the same charm about them, and the same mysterious reference. We see a tower, we see a line with an arrow indicating a voyage, we see a star, or a bottle of ink and a pen. Their self-referentiality is potent.

But about rules: Breton's own rules irritated the life out of many in New York during his period of exile. Sitting around the café table, the surrealists were required to raise their hands to ask to speak. ("X has the floor.") Good grief. What room did this leave for spontaneity, for speaking out, when you had to be ruled in each time? Where was the place of oddity? How to be singular when everything was about groupiness?

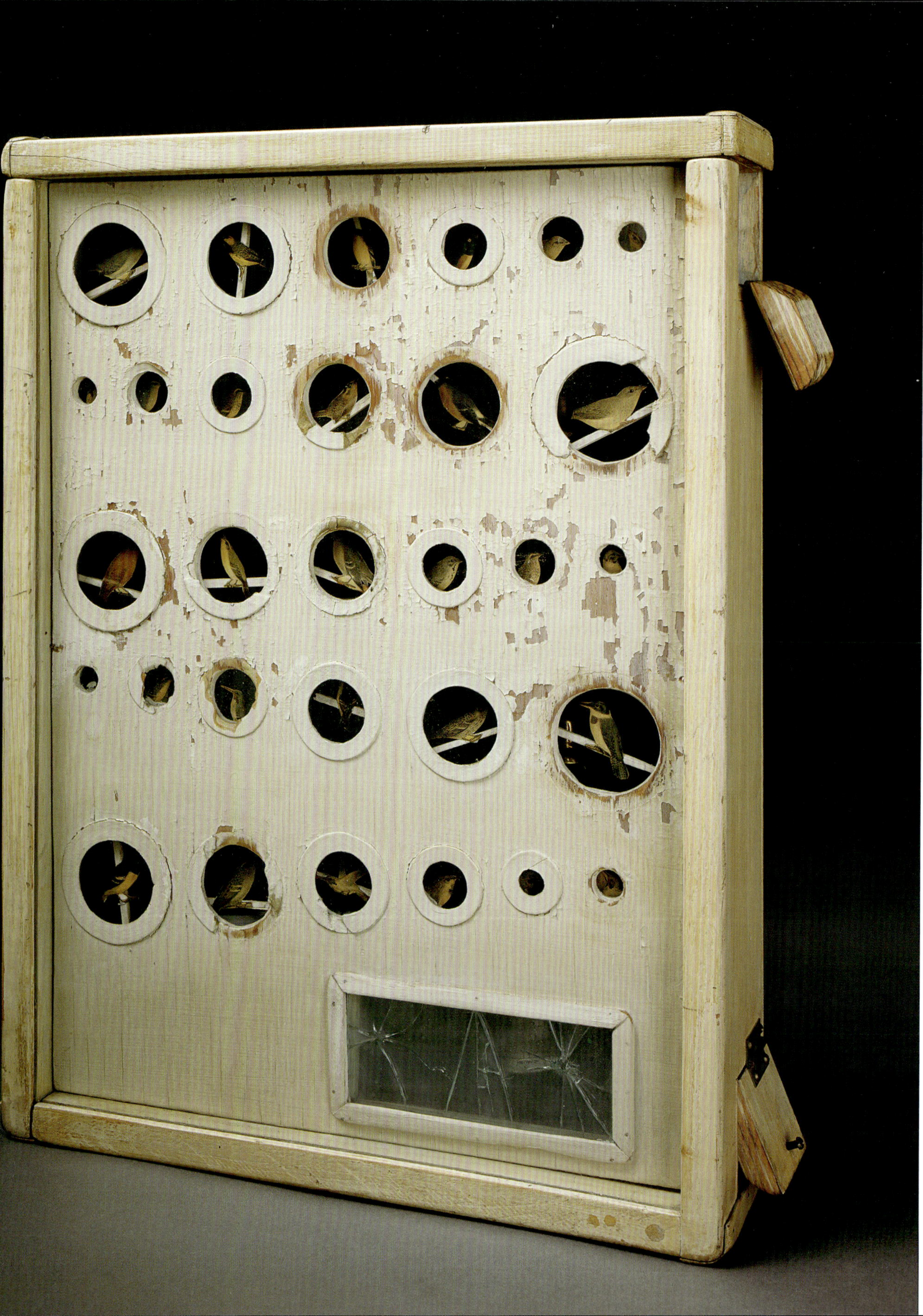

FIG. 19

Joseph Cornell, *Untitled (Forgotten Game),* c. 1949, box construction, $21\frac{1}{8} \times 15\frac{1}{2} \times 3\frac{7}{8}$ inches. Lindy and Edwin Bergman Joseph Cornell Collection, 1982.1852. Reproduction, Art Institute of Chicago. Art © The Joseph and Robert Cornell Memorial Foundation / Licensed by VAGA, New York.

FIG. 20

Joseph Cornell, *Untitled (Penny Arcade Portrait of Lauren Bacall),* 1945–46. Bergman Collection. Courtesy Bergman Collection. Art © The Joseph and Robert Cornell Memorial Foundation / Licensed by VAGA, New York.

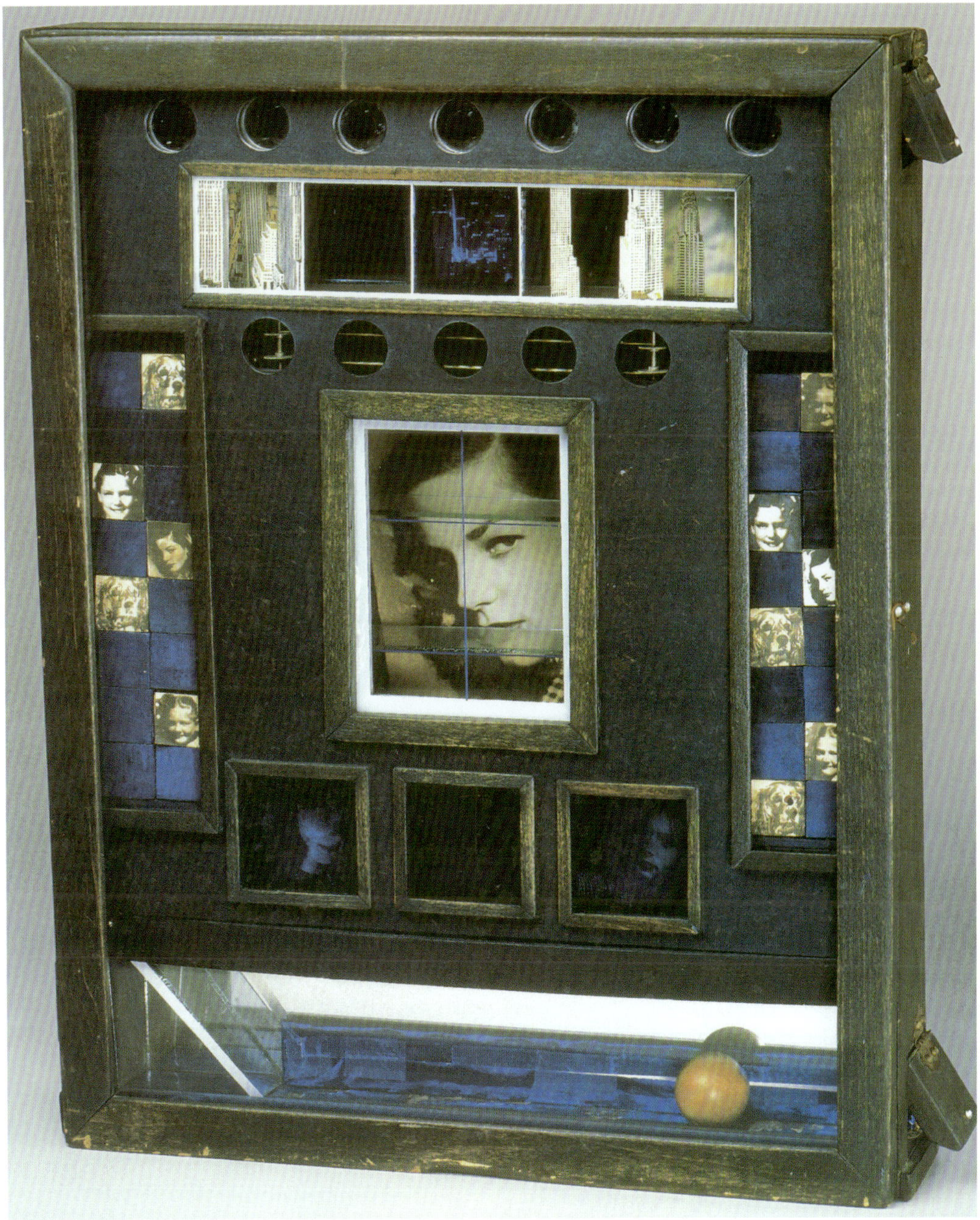

When we now read all those records of the oral games, such as *The Game of Truth* or *The Game of One in the Other,* or when we think, then and now too, of the recounting of surrealist dreams as a kind of game, we notice two things each time. That they are all, ideally, directed toward a play of the mind and spirit. This is the case with a game such as *"l'un dans l'autre,"* in which the players have to get from one element to another so radically removed from it—say, from a match flame to a lion (the answer is something like the lion's mane in its orange gleam). The constraint of the rules, in fact, extends your thinking apparatus, like a visual crossword puzzle. Drawing on life and personality, however, their most immediate potential may be, as in *The Game of Truth,* that of great embarrassment. I remember one that begins with Benjamin Péret asking Breton what the woman would prefer when making love, to which Breton responded: "Goodness, does that matter?" Well, rather a lot, I would think. And never mind what Breton thought.

What has grabbed me recently are some rereadings of the collective descriptions among the surrealists of individual paintings, because I find in them not just the automatic responses we would expect, but also something extraordinary about the way they many times give us a feeling of the personality of the person responding. Why was I surprised? And delighted, because in fact this works out as a kind of lyricism of the game. Listen to these descriptions of one of Giorgio de Chirico's paintings, *The Enigma of a Day* (1914), some of which are clearly structured to be simply oppositional, but in which others give us the full flavor of the poet speaking—that is, the rules of the game, despite the restrictions they place on the poets, nevertheless allow the individual personality to manifest itself (much like the way Perec's novel was required to be more adventurous in its avoidance of the letter *e*). I am saying "poets" here because in such experiments they all turn out to be poets. They SOUND like poets. That is, after all, the important thing.

Listen to Breton, René Char, Éluard, Alberto Giacometti, Maurice Henry, Benjamin Péret, and Tristan Tzara discuss De Chirico's painting:[6]

Where is the sea?

Breton:	Behind the statue.
Char:	Everywhere in the conversation of the two personages.
Éluard:	In the porticos.
Giacometti:	Very near, behind the first arcades.
Henry:	On the spectator's side.
Péret:	On our side, but we turn our backs to it.
Tzara:	Ten miles away behind the chimneys.

Where would one make love?

Breton:	Inside the plinth of the statue.
Éluard:	On the plinth of the statue.
Giacometti:	Under the porticos at right.
Péret:	Standing, in the middle of the square, regardless of the two personages, who are dead.
Tzara:	The painting behind being blind, love would be made in the sun.

Whom does the statue represent?

Breton:	Lincoln.
Éluard:	The father.
Giacometti:	A disciple of Cavour.
Henry:	A furniture mover, famous in the country.
Péret:	The inventor of decalcomania.
Tzara:	A celebrated inventor in matters of baking.

What time is it?

Eleven.
Noon.
Three am. The sun is false.
Noon.
Four-thirty pm/am.
Five pm in summer.
Between six and seven pm in June.
The midnight sun.

And finally, I like to think of the responses to *Enquiries* as superb examples of the so different personalities emerging from the game of response—the collective somehow brings out the individual character, as in the "Responses to the Enquiry on Love" from 1929:[7]

What do you expect of love? What about passing from the idea of love to the fact of love?

Luis Buñuel	If I love, all hope. If I don't love, none. For me, only the fact of being in love exists.
Paul Éluard	The hope of always being in love, whatever may happen to the being I love. The idea of love depends too much, for me, on the fact of being in love, for the passage of the one to the other to be envisaged.
Paul Nougé	Love—then I would answer that I expect nothing from it. Nothing that could be held, by any right whatever, as a consequence, a result of that love; nothing that could be named outside of it.... The lack of adherence of idea to fact has here an exemplary value.
Suzanne Muzard	The hope never to recognize (for myself) any raison d'être outside love. The transition from the idea of love to the fact of loving. It's about the discovery of an object, the only one I deem indispensable.

Clearly in this case as in others—in all surrealist games as in what I hope are our lives, those of us reading and rereading surrealist texts—poetry can be made by all.

6

PLAYING IN THE SAND WITH PICASSO: RELIEF SCULPTURE AS GAME IN THE SUMMER OF 1930

DAVID J. GETSY

André Breton once referred to Picasso as the creator of toys.[1] In many of the anecdotes supplied about him by his friends, family, and acquaintances, Picasso was lovingly depicted as a trickster, a joker, and a player. These characterizations are echoed in the scholarly literature on Picasso, where his heterodox artistic practice has at times been seen as mischievous, whimsical, or mercurial. Play and games, in other words, were recurringly associated with Picasso's practice and with his fashioned persona. The implications of this theme, however, have only rarely been considered seriously in his work.

In this chapter, I will examine one particular moment in Picasso's career—the creation of the so-called sand reliefs in the summer of 1930—by attending to the ways in which play operated in his practice and, more specifically, how a specific group of works can be considered as a game. The works in question make up a small set of objects that Picasso created when he was on vacation at the beach on the French Riviera. Each measuring only some eleven by fourteen inches, these assemblages were composed of canvas, cardboard, found objects, glue, paint, and sand. When viewed through the major methodological lenses that have been used to scrutinize Picasso's work, they have come to seem rather commonplace. That is, they have been seen to provide relatively little new information when analyzed in relation to larger contextual narratives of style, of biography, of the semiotics of visual communication, of the political debates of his era, of the deployment of gender norms, and of the other primary methodological perspectives from which Picasso's work has been studied. Consequently, these objects have a fairly minor place in the Picasso literature.[2] As vacation works, they are frequently downplayed in assessments of his career precisely because of their playfulness, casualness, and overall nonseriousness. They were, after all, done at the beach. Their playfulness, however, is precisely what I want to take seriously. These eight works derived from a ludic process and from, I would argue, playing a game. This game was local and particular to Picasso's work at the time as well as suggestive, more broadly, of the complexities of relief sculpture in modernism from which Picasso took his guiding rules. It was his play in both these registers that made these objects useful to him, for a time.

As I discuss in the introduction to this volume, games are characterized by a set of rules loosely or stringently defined, which individuals negotiate in order to enter into this alternate zone or "temporary world" of game-play.[3] To put it simply, a game is based upon a set of limiting structures by which players agree to abide. The enjoyment of the game and the pleasure of its identificatory possibilities occur through the creative navigation of these rules and the agreement to be governed, for a time, by them. In short, the limitations imposed by this artificial system constrain the agents within in it while also providing the framework for their activity and creative solutions. Games can be either finite or infinite—that is, with a goal to be won or with the continuation of play as the aim. For either of these types, however, the end results must be to some degree open-ended and variable. Indeed, games are most successful when they have the capacity to be repeated. Players continue to play because of the variability, cumulative skill, and pleasure that the game, despite its rules and limitations, continues to engender.

The sand reliefs occupy a limited and entirely unique place in Picasso's body of work. Their procedure was not replicated among the thousands of other works he created. They are the result of a particular and limited process, and I refer to them as a game because, like games, they each work with a shared set of imposed rules, a few of which I discuss below. As a group, they evidence the repeated negotiation of those rules. Rather than understand them as merely a series, they are divergent solutions to the obstacles Picasso set for himself in his game.

This approach affords a deeper understanding of Picasso's turning point in 1930 as one implicated in game-play as artistic method, yielding four interdependent conclusions: (1) that the sand reliefs were not merely casual but were also developed according to an adaptive logic that is best understood through the framework of rules and games; (2) that the process of game-play and the particular parameters he set for it relied upon and interrogated specifically the medium of relief sculpture; (3) that while these works were playful, their diversion nevertheless managed the specific content that was foremost in Picasso's mind during this summer (his affair with Marie-Thérèse Walter); and (4) that these investigations, in turn, facilitated his reengagement with traditional sculptural practices. In short, by using games as a method to interpret this moment, these informal little artworks are revealed as mediating larger issues crucial to Picasso's life and work in the early 1930s.

A central concern of mine in dealing with these works is to place them in the context of the medium of relief sculpture, for it was its limitations and possibilities that shaped the contours of Picasso's game-play and gave him his starting point. Even though these works are neither modeled nor carved, they nevertheless fall within the central defining traits of relief. It may be, in fact, simpler just to refer to these works as "objects," but this generic term does not highlight—as "relief sculpture" does—the complex set of representational issues that working in between two- and three-dimensional systems raises.

Relief sculpture has an uneasy place in modernist narratives. In the hierarchy of media that reached its most rigid codification in the nineteenth century, relief sculpture was often considered an ancillary subcategory of sculpture, much in the way that watercolors have been sometimes subordinated to painting. Beginning at the end of the nineteenth century, however, a rapid increase in the number and kinds of works that could be considered relief sculpture flourished concomitantly with the emergence of modern art in Europe. This historical phenomenon has gone relatively unremarked in histories of twentieth-century art, and the subsequent art-historical literature has rarely registered the ubiquity and variety of reliefs.[4] The term "relief sculpture" as I am using it includes a more expansive range of formats and materials than the traditional associations it has with carved stone or cast bronze. Following Picasso's lead, relief sculpture in its modernist mode was frequently independent of architectural decoration, intimate in scale, and incorporated techniques of assemblage and construction. The category of relief sculpture became vastly more elastic in this period, but it retained certain fundamental traits: a general flatness, shallowness of actual and of depicted depth, a vertical orientation in relation to the wall as support, and a compromise between pictorial depiction and sculptural physicality.

At base, a hybridity of two- and three-dimensional modes of representation gives relief sculpture its particular character and limitations—in other words, its rules. It is an intermedia partaking of both pictorial and sculptural strategies and tools. However, it can never achieve the degree of illusionism that either a painting can in two dimensions or a sculpture in three. There must be, by definition, passages of compromise in between these modes in a single relief work. That is the basic rule of relief sculpture. Because of this limitation, it is often left out in many narratives of modern art, seeming too subordinate, too marginal, too liminal, and ultimately not serious enough compared to the "proper" pursuits of painting and sculpture. Traditional modernist accounts that privileged discrete media drew teleological lines of development for painting, for sculpture, and so on. In such accounts, the intermedial format of relief sculpture fell in between the lines and consequently has often been consigned to the margins.

Relief sculpture had of course been a central part of Picasso's earlier practice. Related to his work in collage and assemblage, Picasso had early in the century created a number of constructed works that conform to many of the traits of relief sculpture. In particular, the constructed guitars and violins from 1912 and after have been considered one of Picasso's major breakthroughs. Relatively shallow in depth and hung on the wall, these objects have furthermore been cast as a major innovation in the history of sculpture and, more specifically, a fundamental step in the development of Cubism. In addition to the guitars, works such as *Still Life* (1914, Tate Gallery) operated in between pictorial flatness and sculptural solidity.

In making his sand reliefs, however, Picasso developed a novel procedure for himself. He began by taking small stretched blank canvases and turning them around. In the shallow box created by the stretcher frame on the verso, he combined various objects—sticks, seaweed, toys, his own cardboard creations, and, in one, a stuffed glove. To unify these agglomerations, Picasso then covered them with a layer of glue and sand, making a monochrome (and somewhat stony-appearing) surface. On some of these, he then painted the sand, from a faint triangle of light blue on one to a fuller polychromatic treatment on the last object. This multistaged process, shared across the series of works, evidences a self-conscious play between pictorial and sculptural modes: the moves from the inverted flat canvas to the addition of assemblage elements to the unification of the surface approximating stone relief, and to the painting of this surface all can be understood as a chain of inversions between surface flatness and three-dimensional projection from that surface.

These "deliberately lowly and yet uncanny works" (as Yve-Alain Bois called them) occupy a unique position in Picasso's career.[5] Picasso had earlier incorporated sand into his works, and assemblage remained a central sculptural practice for him throughout his career. He did not make works like these again, however.[6] They remained part of his own collection until his death, then becoming part of the Musée Picasso in Paris. Many of his most experimental objects he kept for himself, and he had a jealous attachment to certain things he had made. For many years, these reliefs were kept together as a group in a small room adjacent to the sculpture studio in his apartments at Rue des Grands-Augustins. This room contained, among other things, his "museum," in which he kept many of his playful sculptural experiments and casual constructions, as well as antiquities such as his much-prized Egyptian fragment. They remained there through World War II, and we have an account of them from Françoise Gilot, whom Picasso once tried to seduce with this little cabinet of curiosities. She recounted:

> **The most curious things, though, were a number of reliefs built up, surrealist-fashion, by groupings of heterogeneous objects—matches, a butterfly, a toy boat, leaves, twigs—and covered with sand. Each one was about ten by twelve inches. I asked him what they were. He shrugged. "Just what they look like," he said. "I had a spell of doing things like that about ten years ago, on the surface or the underside of small canvases. I assembled the compositions—some of those things are sewn on—covered them with glue and sanded them."[7]**

While not very illuminating, Picasso's quoted casual description of the works nevertheless does stress the importance of the flipped stretched canvas as the defining characteristic of these works.

In thematizing a relationship between the flatness of the canvas and the three-dimensionality of the object, these works exemplify the interlaced relationship between the pictorial and the sculptural in relief sculpture. Some of the core traits of relief sculpture, in other words, provided Picasso with the rules he subsequently took on as the opening parameters for his playful experimentations. The repeated format of these works resulted from the game Picasso played with himself within the framework of constructed relief sculpture: take a canvas, flip it, fill it with objects of one's choosing or making that must then be made monochrome through the layer of sand and glue. He played this game of artistic solitaire eight times, each with very different results and often building upon his previous solution. His process was open-ended and explorative, and it was in the playing of this game that Picasso came to terms with the limitations and possibilities of this format, as I discuss below. In what follows, I will examine one issue among many—the use of shadow—in order to track the nondirected exploratory play that Picasso allowed himself through these works.

Some brief descriptions of the reliefs will be helpful as a starting point to an analysis. The first work, from August 14, 1930, is one of the most complex in the series (fig. 21). In it, a round face stares out at the viewer as its hands grasp the frame in a gesture that seems to pull the figure outward. Behind the seemingly detached

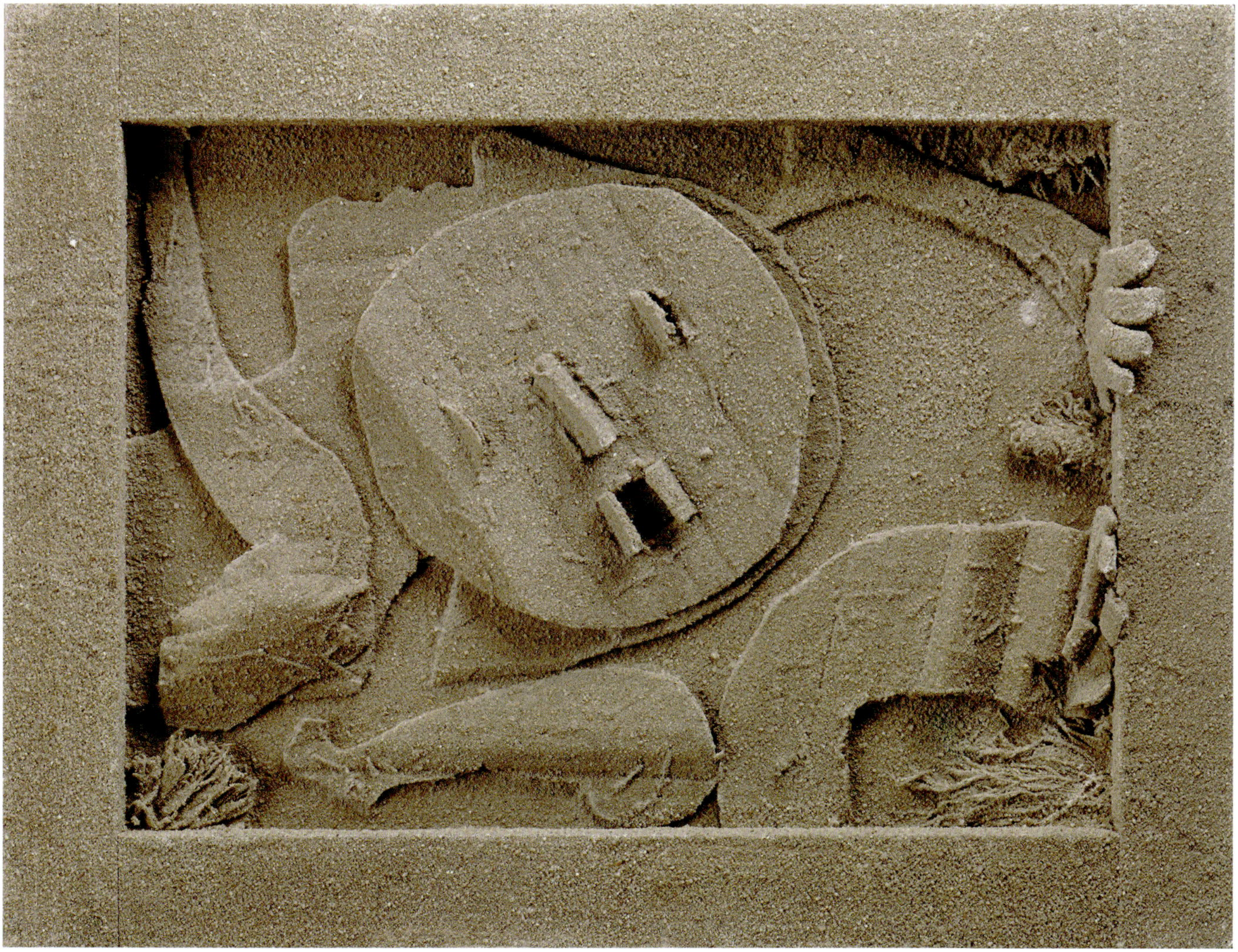

FIG. 21

Pablo Picasso, Relief 1: *Bather and Profile* [*Baigneuse et profil*], Juan-les-Pins, August 14, 1930, sand on back of a canvas and stretcher, cardboard and plants, 27 × 35 × 3 cm. Musée Picasso, Paris.

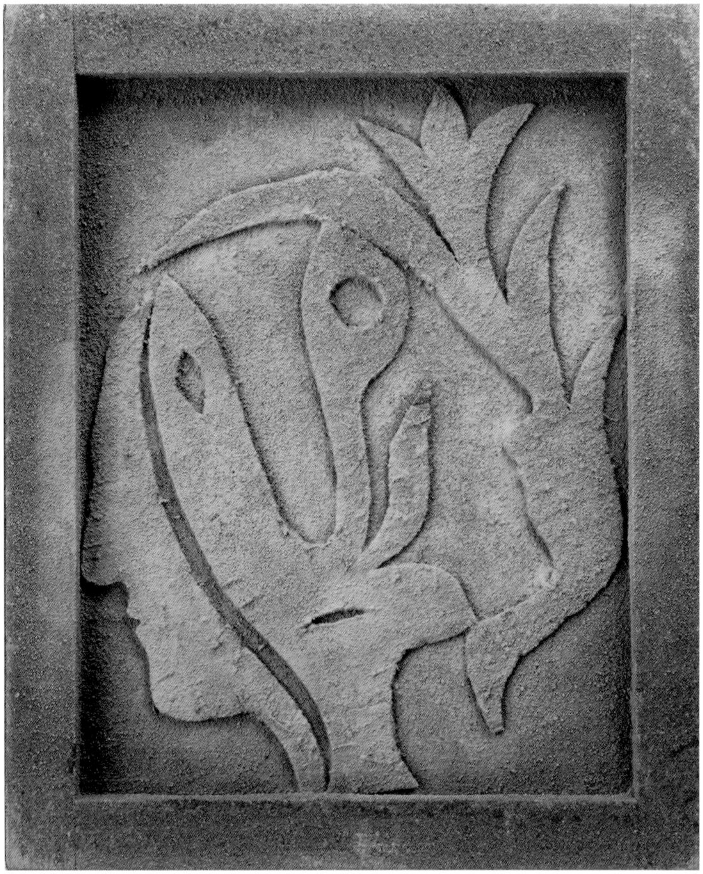

FIG. 22

Pablo Picasso, Relief 2: *Face with Two Profiles* [*Visage aux deux profiles*], Juan-les-Pins, August 14, 1930, sand on back of canvas and stretcher, cardboard pasted and sewn onto canvas; sand partially painted, 41 × 33 × 1.5 cm. Musée Picasso, Paris.

FIG. 23

Pablo Picasso, Relief 3: *Standing Bather* [*Baigneuse debout*], Juan-les-Pins, August 14, 1930, sand on back of canvas and stretcher, cardboard and plants sewn onto canvas, 33 × 24.5 × 2 cm. Musée Picasso, Paris.

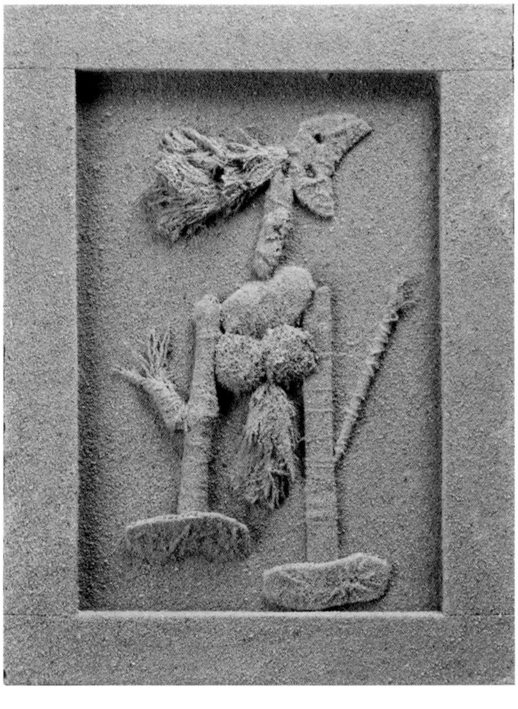

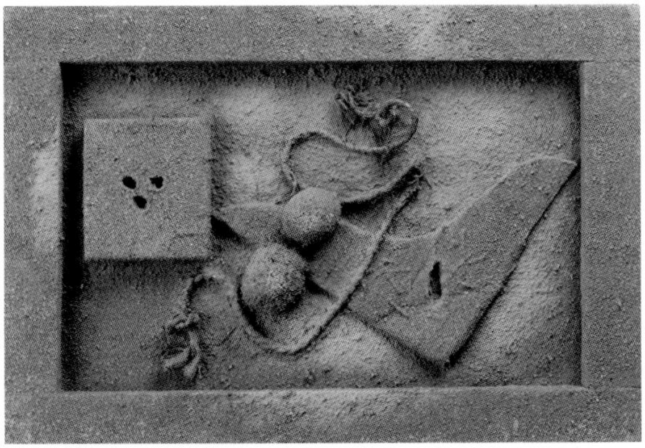

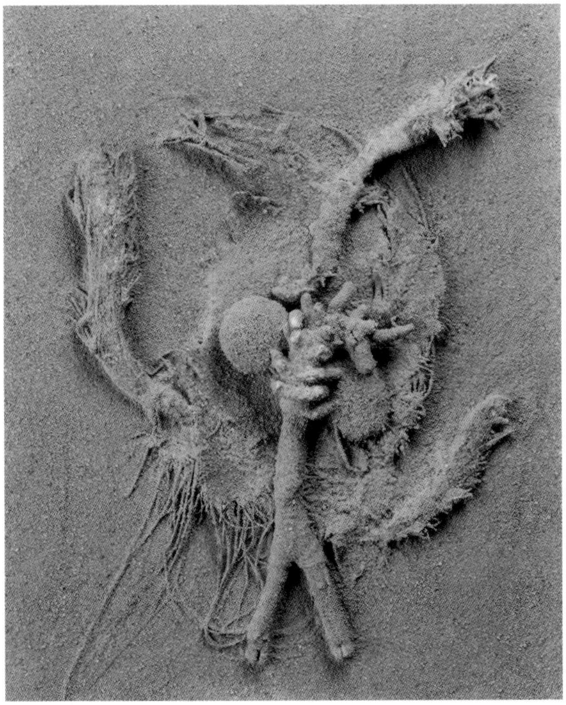

FIG. 24

Pablo Picasso, Relief 4: *Reclining Bather* [*Baigneuse couchée*], Juan-les-Pins, August 20, 1930, objects, string, and cardboard sewn and glued to back of canvas stretcher and coated with sand, sand partially painted, 24 × 35 × 2 cm. Musée Picasso, Paris.

FIG. 25

Pablo Picasso, Relief 5: *Composition* [*Composition*], Juan-les-Pins, August 21, 1930, sand on canvas, wood and plants sewn and glued to canvas, 35 × 27.5 × 3 cm. Musée Picasso, Paris.

limbs of this figure lies a profile silhouette, rotated ninety degrees. This silhouette is taken up in the second of the works, also from that same day (fig. 22). Here it is transformed into a comparably flat composition with a Janus-headed double profile that, in turn, holds the eyes, nose, and mouth of a more abstracted face. Like the previous relief, this rudimentary and flat face stares out at the viewer. The third relief, also from August 14, moves in a different direction (fig. 23). An assembled female figure with a gaping or screaming mouth has been constructed from sea detritus. This particular work has often been seen as analogous to Picasso's many images of women at the beach of this period. The fourth relief, done after a hiatus of six days, depicts a reclining bather whose body has been rudimentarily, and crudely, depicted (fig. 24). The next day, Picasso created another example, this being the only one of the eight attached to the front, rather than the back, of a stretched canvas (fig. 25). Though much more ambiguous, the implication is that this, too, is a female figure like the others in the series, placed this time against a backdrop created by the seaweed sewn onto the canvas. The sixth combines an actual glove, exhibiting a sculptural fullness, with a cutout cardboard form that is most frequently interpreted as a distorted woman's face with a toothy, open mouth (fig. 26). The last two reliefs, done on August 27 and 28, use smaller objects to give a greater sense of depicted, yet still claustrophobic, space. The unexpected combination of the woman sitting on the bench and the floating cabana, with the form that separates and threatens to overwhelm both, has been one of the objects that suggests a comparison to Surrealism (fig. 27). The last, brightly colored, relief combines toy boats to create a tightly packed image of the harbor (fig. 28).

In his catalogue raisonné of the sculpture, Werner Spies saw the innovations of the sand reliefs primarily in relation to representational space: "While Picasso's sculptures up to this point had been marked by a clear relationship to space or to the relief ground as well as by the sharp contouring of individual forms, in these works he established imperceptible transitions between background, low relief, and high relief."[8] That is, Spies saw Picasso's engagement with imaging as the central innovation of the sand reliefs. Indeed, the strategies of the sand reliefs return again and again to a basic question: How does one maneuver between the differences and possibilities for imaging offered by a two-dimensional medium, such as painting, or a three-dimensional medium, such as sculpture? Picasso addressed this question by taking on some of the key issues for the format: the

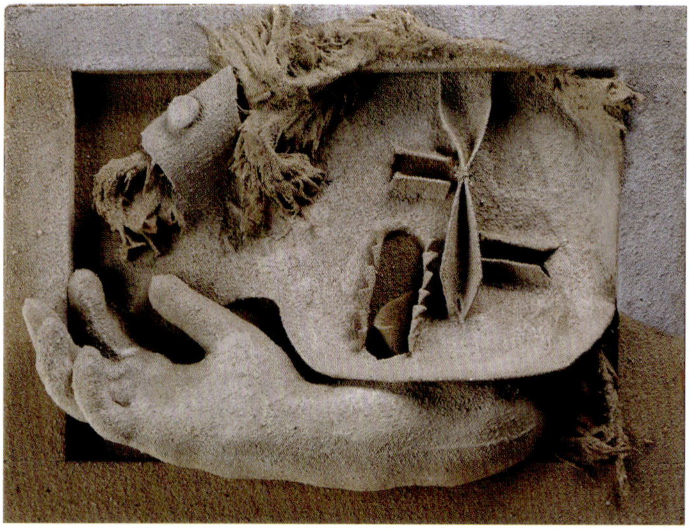

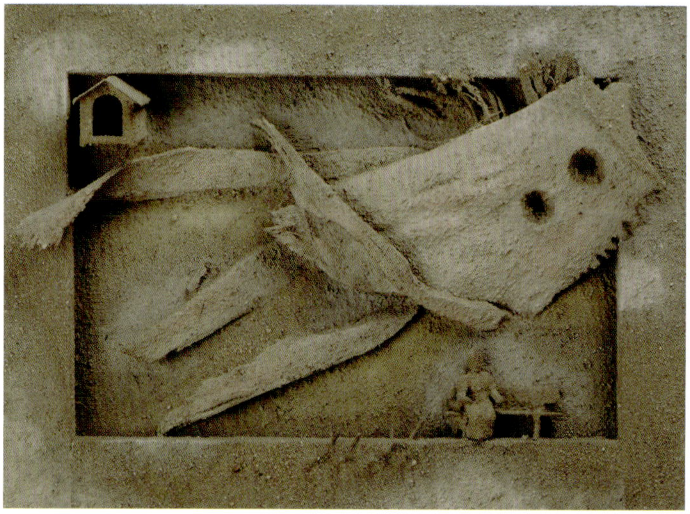

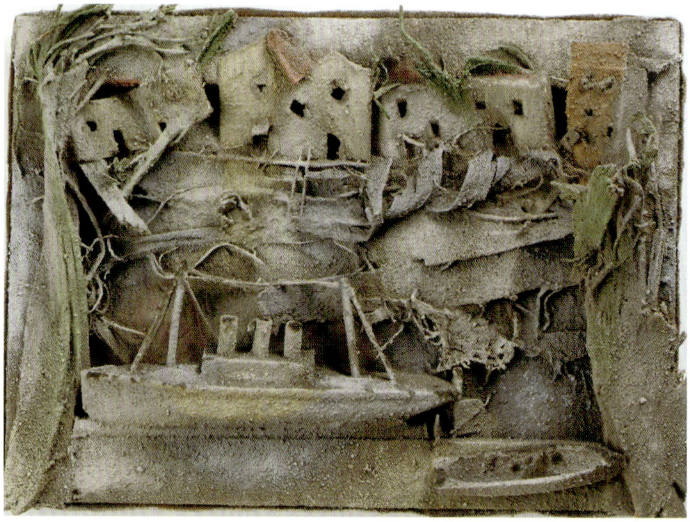

FIG. 26

Pablo Picasso, Relief 6: *Composition with Glove / Construction with Glove* [*Composition au gant*], Juan-les-Pins, August 22, 1930, glove, cardboard, and plants sewn and glued to back of canvas stretcher and coated with sand, sand partially painted, 27.5 × 35.5 × 8 cm. Musée Picasso, Paris.

FIG. 27

Pablo Picasso, Relief 7: *Object with Palm Leaf* [*Objet à la feuille de palmier*], Juan-les-Pins, August 27, 1930, cardboard, plants, nails, and objects sewn and glued to back of canvas stretcher and coated with sand, sand partially painted, 25 × 33 × 4.5 cm. Musée Picasso, Paris.

FIG. 28

Pablo Picasso, Relief 8: *Landscape with Boats* [*Paysage aux bateaux*], Juan-les-Pins, August 28, 1930, plants, cardboard, and two toy ships sewn and glued to back of canvas stretcher and coated with sand, sand partially painted, 26.5 × 36 × 7 cm. Musée Picasso, Paris.

flatness of the relief plane, the importance of projection from the back plane for relief sculpture, the issue of monochromy, and the importance of shadows to depiction in relief sculpture. It is not merely a formalist exercise to attend to these tactics, for it was the question of imaging in between two and three dimensions that generated and sustained Picasso's play in these works.

Each of the eight works could warrant an extended analysis of its representational strategies and its vacillation between pictorial and sculptural modes of imaging. Rather than exhaustively detail these particulars eight times, I will instead examine one issue from the list above—the role of shadows—in order to discuss how the art-theoretical questions that motivated Picasso's game-play were not solely contained within the development of forms but also intersected with other contexts and meanings for him. Attention to the play of shadows, in other words, helps to illuminate the back-and-forth play occurring across the series of sand reliefs, but it also points to their role within Picasso's career at the time.

At the most basic level, all of the sand reliefs rely on shadows created through the outward projection of elements from the flat vertical plane. That is, they are created through an accumulation of material objects on and through spatial *projection* from the material surface of the back of the canvas, which operates not as pictorial field but as physical support for the assemblage. Picasso's projective space and figures invert the spatial recession and pictorial illusionism that the picture plane normally facilitates, using it instead as a staging ground for varying degrees of projection into three dimensions.

Projection from the back plane is one of the basic tools of relief representation, and Picasso further emphasized its importance through his reliance on the monochrome material surface of the works. The neutral layer of sand and glue covers the surface of each of the reliefs, giving it a grainy texture. Even though that layer has been subsequently painted in some of the examples, any color or staining is clearly supplemental. It should be noted that in almost all of Picasso's earlier, extensive experiments with relief sculpture or analogous formats, he often used vivid polychromy in order to break apart any material homogeneity for the object.[9] By contrast, the assembled objects and constructed elements in the sand reliefs from 1930 are often difficult to identify as independent components, having been integrated with the sandy covering. Whereas Picasso often maintained the independence and component-status of each of the elements in his earlier relief constructions, the works from 1930 reversed this tactic. Heterogeneous objects have been made to look as if they were all sculpted from the same material.

The deployment of a base monochromy in the sand reliefs, combined with the emphasis on outward spatial projection, highlights relief sculpture's reliance on shadow. With its images created primarily from different degrees of projection from the flat ground, relief sculpture is an art of drawing with shadow.[10] Traditional relief sculpture presents a challenge to the artist because of the difficulty of using degrees of shadow to create subtle pictorial images or solid physical entities from elements as shallow as faint incised lines to outstretched figures in high relief. For a medium in which neither coloristic modeling nor three-dimensional plenitude was fully realizable, images both shallow and deep had to be created in relation to the real light sources in which a work was to be placed. Consequently, the artist is challenged to compensate for different viewing positions, different lighting sources, and moving viewers in creating a coherent image through relief. Picasso's deployment of monochromy in these works indicates his engagement with the parameters of relief sculpture. He restricted himself to abide by its basic rules, making all of these works approximate the look of a carved relief even though they had been made through his idiosyncratic process. Again, we can see across the eight examples of these works a consistency in certain founding rules Picasso set for himself to direct his playful experimentation within those constraints.

Shadow operates in the sand reliefs as more than merely a tool for articulating the projecting shapes and forms. Picasso allegorized the fundamental importance of shadow for relief sculpture from the very beginning in these works. As the base layer of the first relief of the series, he included a different type of image that shares with relief sculpture its reliance on drawing with shadow—the silhouette rotated ninety degrees.

A silhouette's profile is created by a shadow that falls onto a flat surface, condensing the three-dimensional complexity of an object such as a face into a bold, iconic contour. In this regard, it is an extreme example of the translation that occurs in the process of representing the three-dimensional world on a two-dimensional surface. By definition, the silhouette is the flattest of images, lacking modeling or even variations in hue or value. Despite the radical transformation of three-dimensionality into an utterly flat and unmodeled shape, the silhouette is nevertheless often still recognizable as that person. This is the reason the silhouette has been understood as a precedent for photography in its creation of a recognizable image of a person through light. While one can certainly draw a profile without the use of a shadow, it is nevertheless the implied presence of the individual in the form of her or his shadow that gives the silhouette its evocative power as an image of both that person and of their absence. In Greek mythology, the story of the Corinthian maid Dibutade, who traced the profile of her departing shepherd lover, is itself a myth about the origins of art.[11] She fixed the image on the wall as a way of holding the fleeting shadow. In this myth, the shadow's immaterial presence already contained within it the imminent absence of the beloved. The origin of art, following this story, involved the shadow's re-presentation of that which would soon be no longer present.

For Picasso, the silhouette served as such a metaphor for conjoined absence and presence, as I will discuss below. In the years leading up to 1930, he had been preoccupied with the silhouette. It came to be a vehicle for self-portraiture, for portraiture, and, more generally, for a rumination on art.[12] While it was a recurring feature of his painting in the late 1920s, its appearance in the sand reliefs was more than merely another manifestation of a motif. This image had to be translated into the restricted format that Picasso had set for himself: the shallow monochrome assembled relief. In a medium like relief sculpture that images through the use of shadows, Picasso transformed his use of the silhouette from his paintings into the contradictory presence of a sculpted shadow that would, itself, be made visible by the shadows it created in relation to the flat relief ground.[13] It was, in other words, no casual addition.

The second relief of the series takes up the silhouette from relief 1 as its central image. In this work, Picasso cut the silhouette from a single piece of cardboard, thereby making two mirrored contours, one positive (on the left) and a negative contour created from a piece of cardboard whose positive form resembles a plant. This act created two identical, yet physically different, silhouettes facing in different directions. Again, one could relate this to his earlier Cubist practice of using negative and positive cutout shapes in his *papier collées* as well as to his focus on the imagery of the doubled head in the late 1920s and early 1930s. In this work, however, the silhouettes operate as the flat, yet slightly raised, profiles as well as the outer boundaries

FIG. 29
Anonymous, Marie-Thérèse Walter at the age of nineteen on the beach in Dinard, 1928. Musée Picasso, Paris.

of a third face that, like the face peering out from relief 1, looks outward into the projecting space. Here is an example of Picasso's play. The silhouette and its negative cutout become transformed into a third face through Picasso's combination of them within the constraints provided by the shallow space of the flipped canvas as ground for these works. Again, one can see the guiding influence of the rules he set for himself in relation to the medium of relief sculpture, as the initial reliefs work with flat cardboard cutout shapes and their relationship to three-dimensional space.

Picasso put the silhouette as image aside in the subsequent reliefs, which become increasingly more sculptural and three-dimensional. In the back and forth of the first two reliefs, the silhouette stands as the initial, and exemplary, token in Picasso's play. Even though it disappears after the second relief, the flatness it emblematizes continues as a theme throughout. In the paradoxical play between the silhouette as immaterial image and physical ground in the reliefs, Picasso signaled the importance of this element. The silhouette, however, is not just a type of image that Picasso used in his reliefs. It represents a specific person who had a central role in Picasso's life at this moment—his lover Marie-Thérèse Walter (fig. 29). Walter's facial features and strong straight nose—what Françoise Gilot called her "arresting face with a Grecian profile"—are clear and closely related to the many other profiles of Walter that Picasso covertly incorporated into his work in these years, such as the 1927 *Guitar Hanging on a Wall* (Alsdorf Collection) with its conjunction of a similar silhouette of Walter with her and Picasso's initials.

Although still married to his wife Olga Kholkova, Picasso had been engaged in an affair with the much-younger Walter beginning in the late 1920s.[14] There was almost a thirty-year difference in their ages—in 1930, Picasso was forty-nine and Walter was twenty—and Picasso kept his relationship with her obscured and secretive long after they had parted. Public awareness of a very young mistress would have posed a major difficulty socially and financially, in addition to being grounds for an expensive divorce from Kholkova. Despite or because of this taboo, Picasso felt compelled to keep Walter near, even when on vacation.[15] It later became known that when he and Kholkova were vacationing at Dinard in Normandy in 1928, Picasso put Walter in a nearby pension for adolescents so that he could slip away and visit her surreptitiously. Similarly, she was kept nearby in the summer of 1930 at Juan-les-Pins.

Especially at the beach, Walter was both close and far, accessible and out of reach. Picasso had to limit himself to relatively brief episodes with her, making the issue of her proximity a source of frustration and desire. Over the past three years, he had become increasingly obsessed with Walter, and her image crept into many of his works.[16] He had depicted her silhouette many times before and after, from the beginning using it as a dual sign of her presence and absence. As with earlier works about her, Picasso found coded ways to allude to Walter through her silhouette and the often-repeated cryptograms of their initials.[17] In the summer of 1930, their relationship came to a head, and the situation changed drastically the following month. Soon thereafter, Picasso installed Walter in an apartment down the street from his marital residence at 23 rue La Boétie.[18] More significant, just two months before—in June of that year—Picasso had just purchased the chateau at Boisgeloup, which would soon become the primary place where Picasso and Walter could be together without fear of discovery. Accessible only by car, the chateau provided a refuge where Picasso could more freely be with Walter. The stables were converted into a

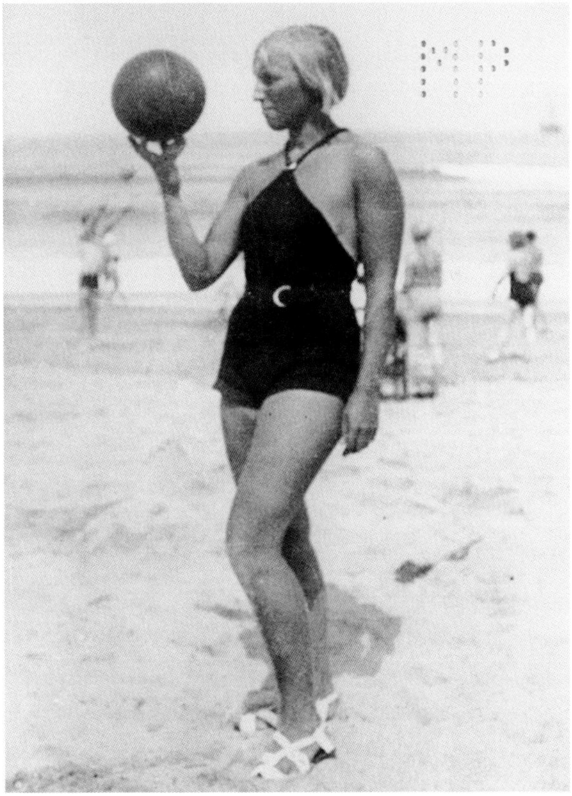

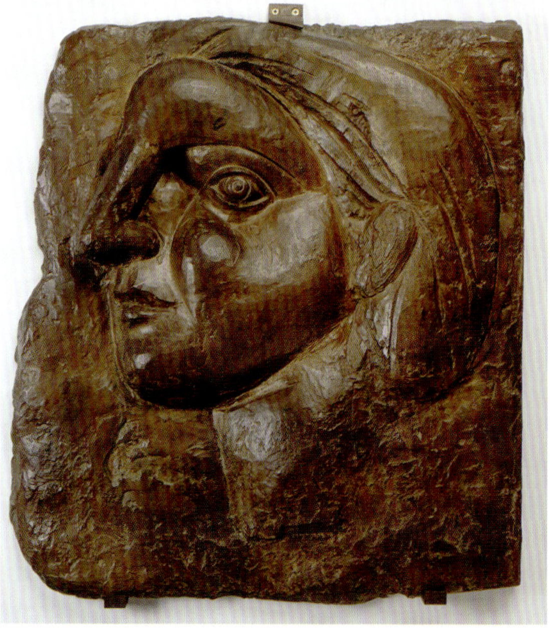

FIG. 30

Pablo Picasso, *Head of a Woman, Left Profile (Marie-Thérèse)*, 1931. Musée Picasso, Paris.

FIG. 31

Brassaï, *Bust of a Woman (Marie-Thérèse) and Female Head (plaster, 1931) in Picasso's Studio, Boisgeloup, 1932*, silver print, 23.6 × 17.3 cm. Musée Picasso, Paris.

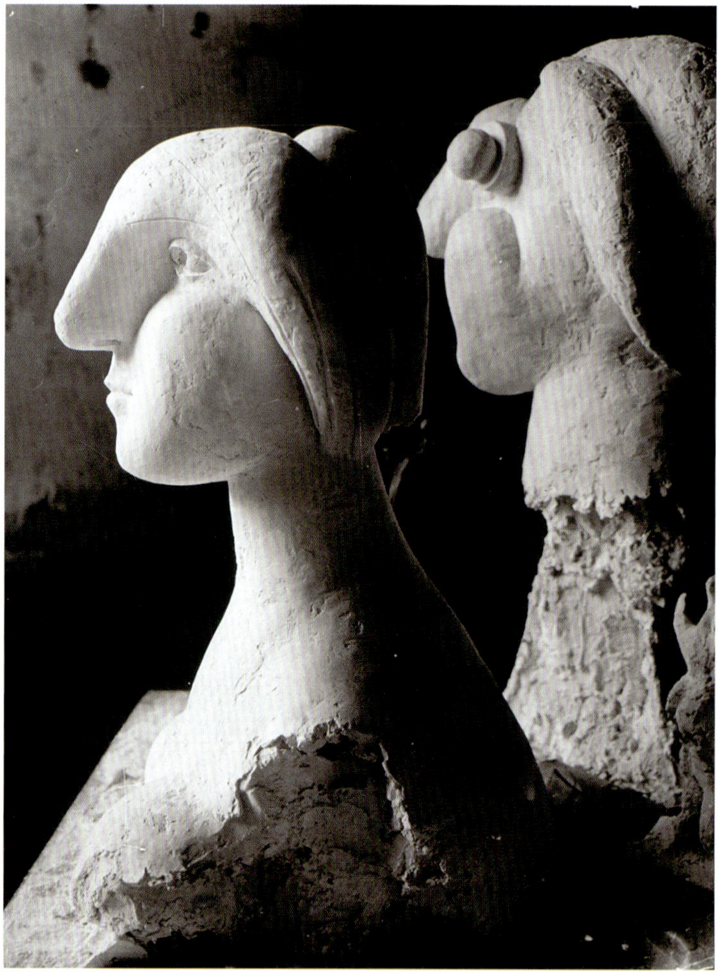

large sculpture studio in the autumn of 1930, and it was here that Picasso created the series of monumental heads of Walter. Whereas she had been a presence in his paintings in the years leading up to 1930s, beginning at Boisgeloup he monumentalized her in sculpture.

Picasso's play was, from the start, tied up with the issue of Walter, and we can understand the incorporation of her silhouette as the background to relief 1 in relation to these events and concerns. That is, while relief sculpture provided the rules and the terms of Picasso's work on the sand reliefs, Walter was, at least in part, its initial subject matter. The content of the sand reliefs has often been disregarded as merely playful, but when placed in the context of Picasso's biography at this time, they take on a different cast.[19] I do not mean to suggest that the entire series can be read, reductively, as merely a reflection of this biographical context. Quite the contrary, the works move in expansive and contradictory ways across the set, and there is ultimately no single theme that is consistent across them. Nevertheless, they share a family resemblance in following the rules of relief sculpture and the limitations Picasso set for himself in exploring it. The role of Walter's image in the initial reliefs signals that this play, however, was not meaningless but rather mediated and couched these questions that were foremost in Picasso's mind. Walter returns, as I discuss below, not in the sand reliefs themselves, but as part of the outcome of their play in Picasso's return to traditional sculptural solidity and techniques.

The terminology of game studies can prove helpful here. Play can be either telic or paratelic—that is, directed toward a goal or undirected.[20] Paratelic activity—nondirected, exploratory, and indulged in for the sake of playing—is what Picasso was engaged in when he made the sand reliefs. Paratelic activity is also a central means of distraction. That is, one escapes into a game that can continue, that can be repeated endlessly, that has infinite outcomes.

The summer of 1930 was not a productive summer for Picasso. While he did create many sketches for sculpture, he did not produce any significant paintings. The distractions of his secretive relationship with Walter would only be alleviated in the fall with the opening of the studio at Boisgeloup. The sand reliefs, in their casualness, offered a form of distraction, and Walter's spectral presence in the initial ones can be taken as an indication that these were a way of filling his time away from her. That is, it is possible to understand the repetitive strategy of the sand reliefs as just such a paratelic diversion.

The sand reliefs are not *about* Walter in any singular or direct way, and identifying her silhouette does not foreclose their meaning. The silhouette emerges as more than Walter; it becomes a figure of two-dimensionality that Picasso ultimately balanced later on with the sculptural fragment. Picasso may have invented this game to distract himself, but his paratelic explorations led him to self-reflexively test and toy with the medium in which he was working. Not all artistic activity is paratelic. One could argue that illusionistic work, by definition, has to have the predetermined image as a goal. Modernist imaging practices, however, can more easily accommodate the paratelic and the exploratory, as with Picasso's sand reliefs. Scholars have failed to come to a convincing iconographic reading of these works—or even to tie in all but the most superficial ways to the motifs of this period in Picasso's oeuvre—precisely because the goal was not the creation of an image but was the process of imaging itself.

The hybridity of two- and three-dimensional imaging practices that is particular to relief sculpture facilitated this paratelic play. Picasso arrived at new options, I contend, because of the possibilities created by play within the experimental zone of intermediality that relief sculpture afforded. The ultimate result of this was a reconfiguration of his attitude toward sculpture. When looked at as a group, one can see an ever-increasing role for three-dimensionality in the sand reliefs. Even though all the elements combine the flat and the solid, we can see, in general, a move toward the sculptural in Picasso's later works in the series.

If, in the early examples of this game, Picasso explored the ways in which flatness and shadow could be put to use in relief sculpture, by the end of the series he toyed with sculptural fullness and presence. This can be seen in the introduction of such elements as the toy boats and blocklike cabana in the last two reliefs, but is clearest in the presence of the life-size hand in relief 6. The physicality of this body fragment is strikingly literal in comparison to the rest of the elements in the series. It offers the fullest three-dimensionality as well as the greatest degree of verisimilitude of any passage in these works. Regardless of the scale of the relief overall or the objects within it, the glove is resolutely life-size and, thus, related to actual bodies in both its appearance and volume.

In their inclusion of sculptural solidity and fully three-dimensional components, the final reliefs in the series stand as the counterparts to the exploration of flatness in the early examples. These two moments represent the opposite ends of the spectrum within which Picasso moved, yet neither are entirely freed from the shallow projective space of relief. The hand in relief 6, turned in and caressing the stretcher frame—like the gripping hand of the first relief—calls attention to the framing element of the stretcher. Even within this relief, however, the sculptural presence of the hand has been balanced with a reminder of the pictorial limitations of relief. A triangle of light blue, painted just on the stretcher frame itself, on top of the sandy ground, gives a subtle, but nevertheless recognizable, horizon line over the projecting elements of the monochrome relief. Through the introduction of this painted element, the sculptural projection and actuality of the hand became reincorporated into the hybrid playground of relief sculpture. This work, in particular, illustrates the back-and-forth activity of Picasso's process. From flat canvas to projecting frame, to solid monochrome objects, to painted surface, there is a movement between two-dimensional and three-dimensional modes of imaging.

For instance, if we look at a work like relief 4, we can see how Picasso further capitalized on the in-betweenness of relief. The reclining bather is composed of clearly flat forms as well as objects that have a sculptural fullness. The head of the woman conflates these two possibilities, being a square box with an utterly flat facet into which holes have been drilled to indicate the face. This head is both projective and flat. The body itself has been reduced to an irregular shape, resembling a dress perhaps, into which a somewhat brutal slit has been cut to signify the genitalia. The flatness and depth of the lower part of the body is given its inverse in the treatment of the breasts, which balloon out cartoonishly. In sum, the whole body is composed of elements that move between utter flatness, real depth, and projection.

One could track this back-and-forth play across the whole series. By the end of the two weeks, and the completion of relief 8, it seems that Picasso had done all he could with this game. The final reliefs are crowded with sculptural fragments, real toys, and three-dimensional encrustations in a way the earlier ones are not. It is as if, by the end of the period of game-play, he had moved from flatness to object-making within the cramped frame of his flipped canvases.

Until this time, Walter had not appeared in Picasso's sculpture—only in his painting and drawing. Immediately after the summer of 1930, however, Picasso prepared the sculpture studio at Boisgeloup and began—in the first concerted push for almost two decades—modeling in the manner of a traditional sculptor. His earlier work had been assembled and constructed, and he deliberately subverted monolithic sculptural solidity. In the series of works of Walter done in 1931, however, Picasso demonstrated himself to be just such a monumental sculptor. Appropriately, his first proper sculpture of Walter was a modeled relief (fig. 30). Walter, in other words, was the driving image for Picasso's return to sculpture, and we can see an earlier prefiguration of this centrality in the play across the sand reliefs that start with Walter's image and end up with sculptural three-dimensionality (fig. 31). This can help explain a comment relayed by the artist's granddaughter, Diana Widmaier Picasso. Discussing the move to Boisgeloup after the summer of 1930, Widmaier Picasso noted:

> **The work sculpted by Picasso at Boisgeloup is inextricably linked with the figure of Marie-Thérèse, *whose shadow it was, he said, that had inspired him to take up sculpture in the first place.* If the anecdote does not sound very plausible—inspired as it is by myths about the origins of painting, applied here to sculpture—it nevertheless shows what Picasso meant to make of his sculpted work: the symbolic expression of the amorous fusion between Marie-Thérèse and himself, between the model and the sculptor.**[21]

Whereas Widmaier Picasso is skeptical of the importance of Walter's shadow, a close analysis of the sand reliefs provides support for Picasso's claim. It was Walter's silhouette, which Picasso incorporated into a number of works during the years before and after 1930, that became the initial token of Picasso's diversionary play in the sand reliefs. Toying with the silhouette and its flatness in the arena of relief sculpture and its projections facilitated Picasso's greater exploration of the potential of sculptural solidity and three-dimensional representation. I would not claim that the play during these two weeks in the summer of 1930 is the exclusive reason for Picasso's sudden addition of traditional sculptural modeling to his repertoire of assemblage and welding techniques. Nevertheless, a close attention to these works reveals that they staged such issues across the instances of his constrained game-play. There is no unlinear trajectory of progress from relief 1 to relief 8. Rather, the general rules were kept in place as the artist explored and abandoned certain avenues. The silhouette drops out after the relief 2, but the challenges it raised in transforming the utterly flat image into a sculptural relief set the terms for subsequent play. The later reliefs take up different questions, yielding different solutions. The nondirected play of these diversionary works, that is, was highly productive in proposing new questions to answer.

In other words, in their staging of the moves in between flat image and sculptural solid, the sand reliefs reflect, on a microcosmic level, the larger issue of Picasso's newfound interest in monolithic sculpture and traditional practices of carving and modeling. Just at the moment when his relationship with Walter would become more concrete and accessible, he placed her silhouette into the sculptural matrix afforded by relief sculpture and began to shift his representations of her from the pictorial to the sculptural. Relief sculpture and Picasso's paratelic play within it facilitated this move to sculpture. The relief format was the playground for a reconceptualization of his practice precisely because of its intermedial propping of the pictorial onto the sculptural and vice versa. His paratelic, open-ended, diversionary, and repetitive practice allowed him, at this moment, to explore intermediality not just for its formal and art-theoretical traits but also as a metaphor for his further investment in Walter. In his play, her image, like all the women Picasso turned into his muses, became another token in his game. The transformations in her image register the new options Picasso generated from his activity in between two- and three-dimensional imaging.

In conclusion, I should say that I have attempted myself to play between three different levels of analysis in this chapter. First, I have sought to unpack some (but not all) of the imaging strategies and organizing motifs of the sand reliefs as a means to demonstrate their complexity. Second, I contend that the sand reliefs, understood as a game, provide an emblematic case for an understanding of relief sculpture's appeal within modernism. Their specific parameters point to the rules and possibilities of this format more generally. And, third, I have argued that taking these works seriously as a game—via the methodology of games studies and play theory—demonstrates how intermedial exploration and media transgression facilitated a shift in Picasso's practice. From these perspectives, these humble, casual, playful works done at the beach in the summer of 1930 suddenly begin to demand serious attention.

7

JOSEPH CORNELL'S DANGEROUS GAMES

STEPHANIE L. TAYLOR

Everything in his world is a secret, and the games are still the game of love, the game of hide-and-seek, and the chilly game of solitude.

—CHARLES SIMIC, "SECRET TOY," *IN DIME-STORE ALCHEMY*

Much of the artistic production of the American artist Joseph Cornell (1903–1972) was linked to childhood and the games played by children. This essay problematizes the large number of sculptural assemblages, two-dimensional collages, and films that Cornell made that can be considered "gamelike." This beginning, which constitutes a close look at a handful of his works, suggests a wide range of possible meanings that are often ignored in Cornell scholarship in hopes that they will enhance our understanding of this enigmatic creator and help us connect him to the history of modern art, from which he is all too often estranged. I will address the darkness that often lies beneath the surface of even the most innocent of Cornell's game constructions. In this chapter, I will argue that the label of *"jouet Surrealiste,"* which was used to market Cornell's work in the 1930s, rather than being an insult, actually serves to categorize Cornell's art as complex in its connection to the strangeness of the surrealist sensibility he clearly shared. With this label in mind, it becomes possible to seek out the kink in Cornell's game boxes, to wrest them away from the idyllic land of sweet childhood innocence and untroubled dreams to which they are all too often relegated, and to point out the possibility of an adult sensibility that was surely driving the artist in the creation of such distinctive objects. I argue that it is important to remember that, while childhood memories and children's activities often inspired Cornell's art, his works were always filtered through a knowing, adult, and often surrealist sensibility.

CHILDREN'S GAMES

Object (Hotel Theatricals by the Grandson of Monsieur Phot Sunday Afternoons), a mixed-media construction Joseph Cornell made in 1940, is typical of his boxed assemblages in terms of format, materials, and function.[1] While other artists had and would use the box format, Cornell made it his signature form, and it is the

Parts of this chapter were presented in a lecture at the San Francisco Museum of Modern Art in January 2008. I appreciate Frank Smiegel, Associate Curator of Education, for inviting me to speak there.

type of work for which he was and remains best known, despite the large number of two-dimensional collages and experimental films he created during his lifetime. This particular box encloses a grid composition that features photographs of a young man striking a series of charade poses. Cornell emphasizes the sequential nature of the boy's actions both by including multiple photographs that show a dramatic narrative unfolding from left to right ("Jacob Wrestling the Angel," "The Visit of the Queen of Sheba to Solomon," "The Finding of Moses in the Bulrushes," "The Triumph of Galatea") and by including colorful marbles that have been left free to roll along the horizontal "shelves" of the glass-enclosed, three-dimensional and boxed composition. If allowed to handle the box, as Cornell intended, the viewer would have added action to the otherwise static sculpture by shaking or tipping it to make the marbles move. Adding the element of motion to this work is reminiscent of the early cinematic experiences that Cornell had as a child growing up in the first decades of the twentieth century. He would have seen the slow (by today's standards) clicking frames of the nickelodeon machines, and would have played with still photographic images by viewing stereoscopic cards and lantern slides as well. The grandson's clothing, a sober dark suit including a stiff vest and high collar, and his surroundings show that he is from the past. Even the game he is playing marks him as the inhabitant of a long-gone era, one in which grandsons played parlor games to amuse their elders and to while away long Sunday afternoons.

All of these elements of the box are apropos the topic of this chapter and this book: the child pictured is playing a game of charades, the marbles are favored toys that have been collected over the years by millions of children around the world, the viewer who is lucky enough to manipulate the box gets to activate it both physically and imaginatively. Selecting and holding a Cornell box is often redolent with the pleasure we experience when pulling a favorite game off of the shelf and beginning a round of play.

Many of Cornell's boxes *are* playful. They are "spectacular" in that they are sometimes colorful and make noise, and they often contain whimsical objects and inspire happiness. They invite not just a look but a touch and a shake, and sometimes a knowing shake of the head. But thinking of them as *just* toys, or as *just* children's games, belies their complexity as well as more infinitely complex notions of childhood and play. Any adults who imagined and enacted the active sex life of their Barbie dolls, or played out the murderous rampages of a marauding G.I. Joe, in their childhood know the complexity of which I speak. One does not need to rely on the imagined traumas of childhood posited by Sigmund Freud to understand the difficult nature of this stage of development. Even in an idyllic childhood, such as the one Cornell is purported to have had, it seems to be impossible to avoid the typical stresses of that age: we all remember feeling small, insignificant, powerless, perhaps forgotten, at some point in our early life. It comes with the territory of being a kid.

Toys and play are at the heart of many classic children's tales, but that does not make them purely happy or joyful either. Consider the toy house offered by Herr Drosselmeyer in *The Nutcracker.* It is an enchanting object, and Clara, to whom it is given, adores it and adores the godfather who gives it to her. Eventually, the toy leads to the object of Clara's desire, a real-life prince whom she loves. But danger is implicit in the toy; battles with horrifying creatures must be fought in Drosselmeyer's dream house, and while it is a beautiful object, it is simultaneously terrifying.[2] Psychoanalysis and psychology give us an inking of the fraught nature of childhood, and they point out that we have important needs fulfilled by such scary stories as told by the classic ballet and fairy tales. Even contemporary children's literature follows this trend, albeit often in an updated, suitably ironic, and postmodern style. Consider Lemony Snicket's *Series of Unfortunate Events,* a set of books in which the sadistic author repeatedly places the heroic Baudelaire children in a nightmarish world of danger and disaster, all the while claiming allegiance with them as their steps are dogged by misfortune.[3] Or J. K. Rowling's child wizard Harry Potter, chronicled in seven famous books that tell the story of his life from the age of nine to sixteen. Throughout the series, Harry loses to death many of the people he loves, and more than once he is called on to fight battles against terrible evil that eventually cost him his innocence as well.

Joseph Cornell's own childhood was in many ways quite awful—a fact his biographers all too often ignore. While he was born into a situation of wealth and relative privilege, the disease and death his immediate family suffered had a profound and disastrous impact on his formative years. He was the eldest of four children, and his earliest years were spent in a large house in Nyack, New York, a small town on the Hudson River, which had been the birthplace of his ancestors. Despite the privilege he experienced in his early childhood years, however, and the reported closeness of his family, there were profound problems and events that occurred at this time that changed the course of his life. For example, his younger brother, Robert, was born with cerebral palsy, an affliction that made it impossible for him to walk and difficult for him to express himself verbally. Robert was a blessing to Cornell, who found joy and inspiration in his brother's company throughout his life, but he was also a burden: Cornell was Robert's primary caregiver for most of their lives.[4]

Cornell's childhood was also marred by the death of his father, who succumbed to leukemia in 1917, when Joseph was just fourteen years old. This led to financial straits for Cornell's family, since Joseph Cornell Sr. had died in debt and intestate, and the money worries of the widow Cornell were compounded by a swindle perpetrated by a close friend of the family. Cornell's mother supported her small family in Nyack by baking cakes and making sweaters to be sold in Manhattan, and by playing the stock market.[5] She moved away from the comfortable upper-class hometown of Nyack with her children not long after her husband's death, resettling with her children in rented houses in Douglaston, Long Island, and then Bayside, Queens, finally purchasing a house in Flushing, Queens, in 1929.[6]

Cornell and his sisters did what they could to add to the family's monthly income. For example, while Cornell was sent away to board at Phillips Academy in Andover, Massachusetts, immediately after his father's death in 1917, he did so with the financial aid of his father's former employer, and he worked campus jobs in the dining hall and the library to help ease any financial burden on his mother. The years he spent in Andover were lonely and isolating, and Cornell often felt fearful and unhappy while he was away from his family. He did not excel academically, nor did he participate in any extracurricular clubs or teams. "Prone to nightmares and stomach problems, Cornell was perceived as a sensitive youngster who needed special attention," writes Lynda Hartigan.[7] Cornell skipped college in order to find full-time work in 1921: like his sisters, he shared his income with the family in order to support the home that his mother was making for them.

Knowing this, we might expect Cornell's art, especially the boxes that stem from childhood games, to be slightly sulfurous, though few scholars have picked up on this element. Pepe Karmel is one critic who did take note of Cornell's dark side when he wrote that Cornell's work was "seeming so sweet the bite goes unnoticed."[8] It is the bite that can be discerned in such works as *Untitled (Bébé Marie),* a box from the early 1940s in the collection of the Museum of Modern Art.[9] Like the *Object* showing the grandson of Monsieur Phot playing charades, this box can be seen as simply a doll enshrined for posterity, or perhaps more complexly as a visual rendition of the classic fairy tale of Sleeping Beauty, who was enshrouded in thick briars and left to sleep until awakened by her prince charming. (The vertical presentation of the box forces us to use our imagination in this regard, but Bébé Marie is in fact a classic dolly that "closes" its eyes when it is reclined.)

Charles Simic captured the darker overtones of this work in a poem he included in his 1992 collection of ruminations on Cornell's life and work, *Dime-Store Alchemy.* The poem, named after the box, describes a "chubby doll in a forest of twigs" who has been naughty. While her mother wasn't looking, the doll got into her makeup and smeared it all over her face. "Now," writes Simic, "she's to be punished." The end of the poem describes her fate, and its effect on the poet:

> **A spoiled little girl wearing a straw hat about to be burnt at the stake. One can already see the flames in her long hair entangled with the twigs. Her eyes are wide open so she can watch us watching her.**
>
> **All of this is vaguely erotic and sinister.**[10]

In a recent catalogue essay about Joseph Cornell and the art of play, Dickran Tashjian puts it succinctly: "Keep the savvy artist distinct from the child."[11] For all the nostalgia packed into his assemblages, and the strong connection made between the artist, his art, and his childhood, Joseph Cornell did not look back and remember all of his early life with great fondness. In fact, there are two important lacunae in his reminiscences—which we have in the form of his obsessively kept journals, his voluminous correspondence, and his recorded commentary—that reflect areas of memory that the artist rarely disturbed or discussed. For example, despite spending four years at Phillips Academy, he does not reminisce about that phase of his life, and rarely, if ever, mentions the people he knew there. As someone who cast his social net far and wide in his adult years, and kept up lively written and phone communications with a large number of various friends and acquaintances, it strikes me as telling that Cornell did not keep up with any friends or acquaintances that he made at boarding school. Another large hole in Cornell's self-reportage is an engagement, or lack thereof, with the memory of his father, who appears fleetingly but extremely rarely in his diaries. Cornell loved his father, and often recalled with great fondness the early childhood when his family was intact and living in Nyack, but he does not often write or muse about his dad, nor does he dream about him.[12] It is as if he had forgotten large parts of his childhood.

Of course, it is natural to forget, or misremember, the early phase of our lives. Dreams can be remembered as reality, and events that were upsetting or damaging may be relegated to memory as a dream or a nightmare in order to distance the psyche from the harms inflicted by the real world. But Cornell's work tells us that he never forgot the fragility of children or childish innocence.

And so, a work like *Untitled (The Crystal Cage: Portrait of Berenice),* a dossier that Cornell worked on from c. 1934 until 1967 that is full of descriptions of an enchanting and brave little girl who is a scientific explorer and astronomer, cannot be seen as a simple celebration of childhood. This is because it is predicated on the fact that Berenice's parents built her a glass pagoda in which to pursue her studies and experiments, and by doing so they isolated her from childhood friends and games and, worst of all, the family circle of affection. With this in mind, the *Portrait of Berenice* becomes a story about a brave but also terribly lonely little girl, trapped in a "crystal cage," who is not allowed or expected to act like a little girl at all.[13]

Cornell's understanding of the fraught nature of childhood appears again and again in his work, such as in his haunting 1957 film, *Nymphlight,* which was shot in and around Bryant Park in Manhattan with the help of Rudy Burckhardt. The narrative arc of the film follows two young girls. The older child can be read as a metaphorical or dream figure: she dances nimbly into the *mise-en-scène* and seemingly controls the movement of different characters through her active gaze. The gauzy dress she wears and the strange prop she carries (a broken umbrella) mark her as some sort of surreal allegorical figure. She watches a younger girl who walks haltingly along the paths of the park, fidgeting with the tie on her dress and acting as if she were oblivious to her surroundings. The older girl was the child of a friend of Cornell's: she was hired for the occasion and fully aware of the fact that she was being filmed. The younger girl simply happened upon the scene that day in Bryant Park, and Cornell incorporated her into his film, which became a story of the shift between innocent childhood and a more complex and aware adolescent understanding of self.

MYSTERIOUS GAMES

Cornell wrote a paper about Harry Houdini while he was a student at Phillips Academy, and told his family back home about it on two occasions: in one letter, he mentions that he was prepared to recite the paper he had written about the famous magician if called on in class to do so; in the second, he expresses his disappointment that he had not been called on to share his work with his classmates.[14] In the essay, Cornell describes his favorite Houdini act as the one in which he made an elephant disappear. He concluded that "there is hardly likely to be a person so clever and mystifying as Houdini for many centuries."[15]

Cornell's early attraction to magic and mystery did not die with the end of his childhood and adolescence, but remained a source of fascination and interest for him throughout the rest of his life. It is an interest that is evident in his work as well as his reading materials and his journals, where he often discussed both his memories and his current ideas about his thoughts and experiences. Once could even surmise that Cornell's eventual participation in the world of Surrealism was a part of realizing the possibilities that his early interest in such mysterious figures as the Great Houdini opened up for him at a young age.

Cornell maintained a close connection with the major artistic movements of his lifetime. This of course includes his participation in Surrealist exhibitions, such as the 1932 Julien Levy Gallery *Surrealisme* show, the purported impetus for the Wadsworth Atheneum's first exhibition of Surrealist art in America just months earlier. Cornell had works included in both exhibitions, and designed the exhibition catalogue cover for Levy's gallery. While Cornell would later deny a close connection to what he perceived the "black art" of European Surrealism, I think he was heavily influenced by it throughout his career. This includes his early objects (thaumotropes, pillboxes, word shakers, empty boxes or envelopes) christened *"jouets Surrealistes,"* or "Surrealist Toys," by Levy, as well as his early film experiments. For example, it is hard to imagine a film that fits the Surrealist ethos of chance encounters and sublime accidents as well as *Rose Hobart* (1936), a work that Cornell made from a B-movie that he had unearthed at a junk shop, cut up, spliced together, slowed down, and set to dreamy bossa nova music. In fact, Cornell's experiment was so successful that it enraged Salvador Dalí, who accused Cornell of stealing an idea that would have made him money. Later works continued to mine a Surrealist vein, including several iterations of the silly and strange *Pantry Ballet for Jacques Offenbach,* all of which feature plastic lobsters in tutus swaying among miniaturized cutlery.[16]

As adults, we go back to our childhood haunts and childhood belongings and we wonder at their size and their function. We ask ourselves: Could I ever have been small enough to sit comfortably in that chair? What was it about that stuffed animal, or that particular book, that made it a favorite? What was the object of the game played hour upon hour with friends or siblings or alone? *Untitled (Forgotten Game),* c. 1949 (see fig. 19), causes us to ask all of these questions and more. Its worn facade and broken elements speak to a period of hard play and long use, but its title also reminds us that this game has been abandoned, forgotten, one that remains unknown and unknowable even in its rediscovery.[17] How do we play this game, the rules of which were misplaced or thrown out years ago? Perhaps this forgotten game is a memory machine, but its broken-down air only serves to remind the viewer that memory is fragile, incomplete, unreliable. It reminds us of childhood but remains a mystery to our disconnected adult mind.

DANGEROUS GAMES

Childhood is a fragile time for girls and boys, and Cornell's work often shields them from the potential harm of real-life experience. But these dangers could not be ignored, and the Joseph Cornell Study Center archives are full of newspaper clippings that attest to the horrors perpetrated upon the young that Cornell read about in his daily newspapers and took note of in his journal entries.

There are dozens of examples of Cornell's attention to the dangers of childhood, but a particularly compelling one appears on the reverse surface of one of his late collages titled *Missing Girl* (1962, figs. 32a and b). The front of the work suggests beauty and enlightenment, featuring as it does a chandelier hanging above a rain-slick and colorful surface, and an angel clipped from a reproduction of a Renaissance painting. On the verso of the collage, Cornell has included a typed journal entry that alludes to the coziness of "Dutch interior" paintings and the children often pictured in them blowing soap bubbles. He also mentions the "wonderland" that the deserted, rainy streets of Manhattan could be for the missing girl, whom he calls here "a wandering, wondering tot." The terrible fate of the young girl is spelled out in a newspaper reproduction of the City of New York Police Department report that is also pasted onto the back of this collage. It appalls the reader with details of four-and-a-half-year-old Edith Kiecorius's life. The report includes a picture that features her dimpled smile, but the police description of her tells us that Edith can also be recognized by a cigarette burn on her right cheek. This awful detail reminds us of what Cornell knew: life was not, and is not, easy for children. It certainly was not for Cornell, and he remained empathetic and aware of the dangers that children faced. This awareness appears repeatedly in his so-called childish art, a label that I argue must be enlarged to include *all* of the experiences of childhood, not just the pleasant and innocent aspects. For every well-loved child, there could be one that was scarred by the absence of love, the death of a father, or the burning end of a cigarette.

Beyond the perilous nature of childhood itself, there are many Cornell works—boxes, collages, and films—that are charged with an adult sexuality that cannot be explained if the artist's construction as "innocent" remains intact. Cornell's art and journal entries and papers often illustrate his knowledge and conviction that the world of children was full of dangers that could compromise their innocence if they became lost in the mirrored world of the arcade or the beautiful fantasy of the darkened movie theater. It is as if Cornell sensed that the young children and teenagers he watched were prey to many dangers, not just the worry he had that they would lose an innocence that he found to be an inspiration.

In the *Medici Slot Machine (Object)* (1942, fig. 33), the cubes included in the composition look like dice and can be connected to the illicit activity of gambling, while the jacks featured at the bottom of the composition are unstable. The "Medici Prince" centered in the box is actually caught in a set of crosshairs that Cornell has carefully inscribed onto the glass: he is either watched by a telephoto lens or he is being sighted down the barrel of a gun. "Trained on the images of children," writes Lynda Hartigan, "the sight lines that are painted on panes of glass in these boxes evoke the moving targets featured in arcade shooting galleries."[18]

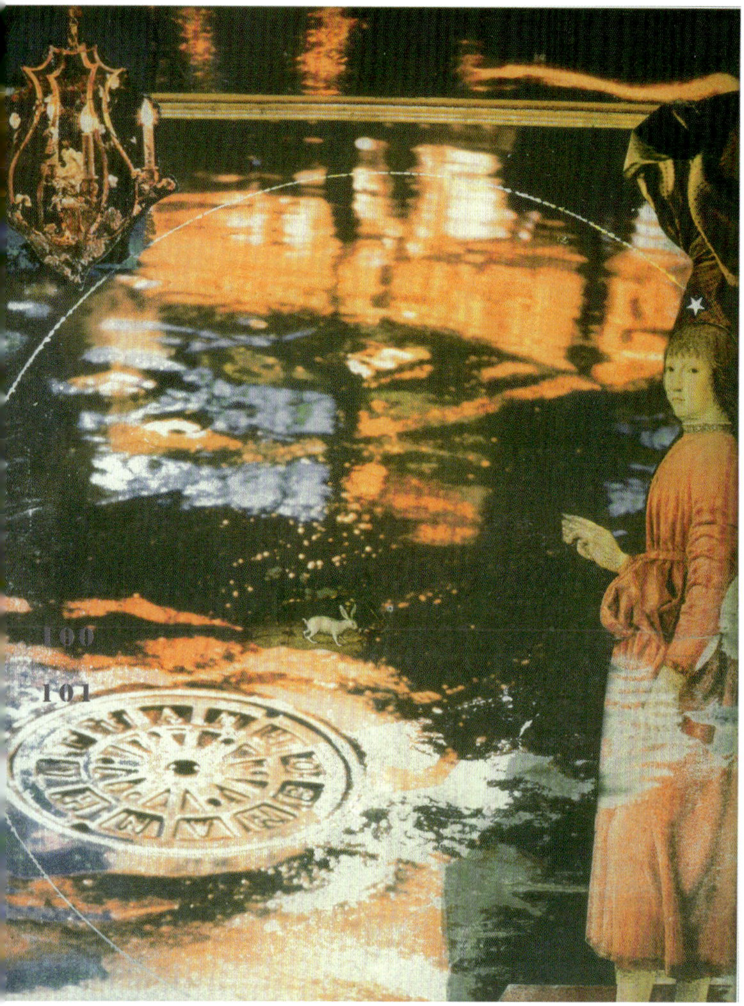

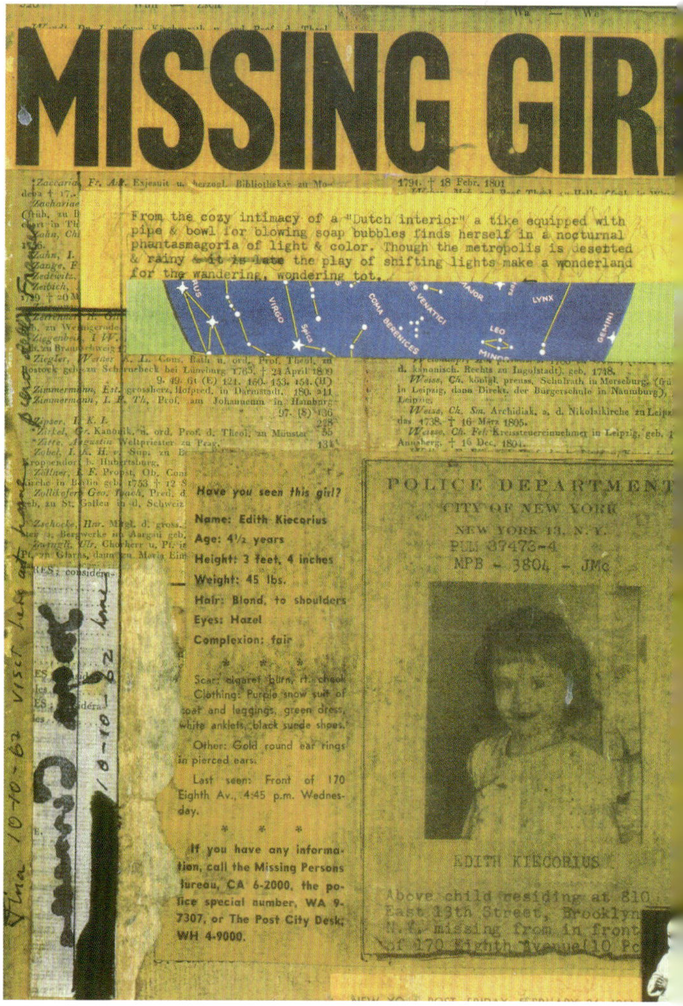

MISSING GIR
1791. † 18 Febr. 1801
From the cozy intimacy of a "Dutch interior" a tike equipped with pipe & bowl for blowing soap bubbles finds herself in a nocturnal phantasmagoria of light & color. Though the metropolis is deserted & rainy & it is late the play of shifting lights make a wonderland for the wandering, wondering tot.
VIRGO
Spica
COMA BERENICES
VENATICI
LYNX
LEO
GEMINI
Have you seen this girl?
Name: Edith Kiecorius
Age: 4½ years
Height: 3 feet, 4 inches
Weight: 45 lbs.
Hair: Blond, to shoulders
Eyes: Hazel
Complexion: fair
Scar: cigaret burn, rt. cheek
Clothing: Purple snow suit of coat and leggings, green dress, white anklets, black suede shoes.
Other: Gold round ear rings in pierced ears.
Last seen: Front of 170 Eighth Av., 4:45 p.m. Wednesday.
If you have any information, call the Missing Persons Bureau, CA 6-2000, the police special number, WA 9-7307, or The Post City Desk; WH 4-9000.
POLICE DEPARTMENT
CITY OF NEW YORK
NEW YORK 13, N.Y.
MPB - 3804 - JMc
EDITH KIECORIUS
Above child residing at 810 East 13th Street, Brooklyn

FIG. 32A

Joseph Cornell, *Missing Girl,* 1962 (recto), collage, 12 × 9 inches. Collection of Robert Lehrman, Washington, D.C. Art © The Joseph and Robert Cornell Memorial Foundation / Licensed by VAGA, New York.

FIG. 32B

Joseph Cornell, *Missing Girl,* 1962 (verso), collage, 12 × 9 inches. Collection of Robert Lehrman, Washington, D.C. Art © The Joseph and Robert Cornell Memorial Foundation / Licensed by VAGA, New York.

FIG. 33

Joseph Cornell, *Medici Slot Machine (Object),* 1942, box construction, $15\frac{1}{2} \times 12\frac{1}{4} \times 4\frac{3}{8}$ inches. The Menil Foundation, Houston. Art © The Joseph and Robert Cornell Memorial Foundation / Licensed by VAGA, New York.

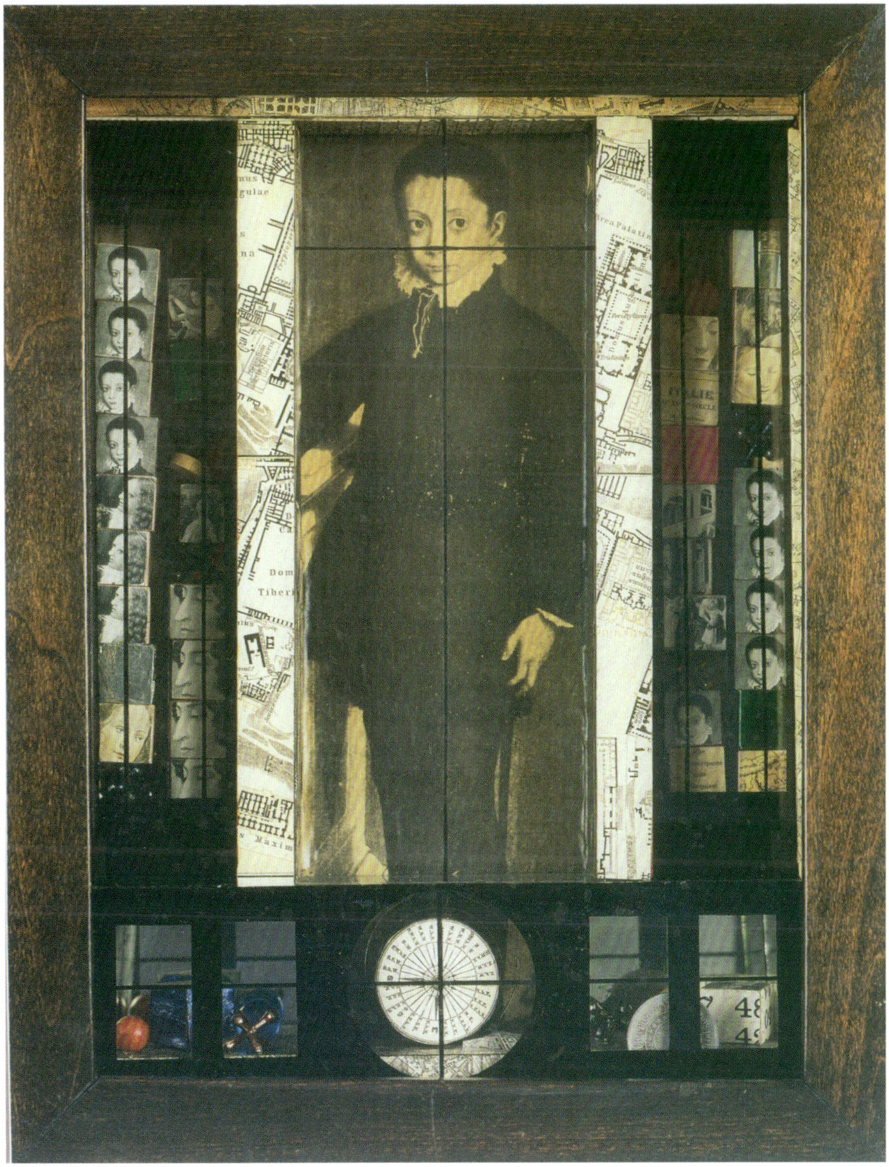

A slightly less horrifying read of this object could be related to the world of movie theaters and Hollywood films, both of which Cornell was enthralled with throughout his life, as children often are as well. The stacked wooden cubes or dice rising along the right- and left-hand compartments in this case might equally be read as film strips (other iterations of this series include numbers, reminiscent of those used to count down to the beginning of films in prevideo days), and the crosshairs as focusing elements for a movie camera trained on the young boy, the "star" of the box. But movie theaters, and the movie business, can be rough for young children, as current celebrity headlines seem to attest on a daily basis.

A slightly more elegiac paean to the dangers (and delights) of the movies than our current obsession with former child actress Lindsay Lohan can be found in Frank O'Hara's poem "Ave Maria," which was first published in his 1964 collection *Lunch Poems*. Simultaneously funny and chilling, O'Hara's poem encourages mothers to send their children to the movie theaters, despite the dangers that lurk there in the form of strangers with candy.

Mothers of America
let your kids go to the movies!
. . . .
they will know where candy bars come from
and gratuitous bags of popcorn
as gratuitous as leaving the movie before it's over
with a pleasant stranger whose apartment is in the
Heaven on Earth Bldg
near the Williamsburg Bridge[19]

In a similar vein, Charles Simic describes the not-so-innocent possibilities in store for this young prince in his 1992 poem about this work, which he reminds us is part of a game, a slot machine, that is meant to be manhandled, manipulated, played. "The name enchants, and so does the idea—the juxtaposition of the Renaissance boy, the penny arcade, and the Photomat in the subway," writes Simic. He describes the boy as friendless and "lost in revelry"; he is surrounded by "panhandlers, small-time hustlers, drunks, sailors on leave, teenage whores loitering about" in a Times Square subway station, where, Simic writes, "His picture is repeated in passport size on the machine." The poem continues: "Outside the penny arcade blacks shine shoes, a blind man sells newspapers, young boys in tight jeans hold hands. Everywhere there are vending machines and they all have mirrors." This hostile environment might not matter to Simic, who also envisions the young prince as "stubborn and cruel," already in possession of "secret vices," but it does threaten the idyllic innocence that many interpreters of Cornell's work cling to in such works. If nothing else, the extreme political danger that was at the heart of the lived experience of such historical children as the Medicis, whom Cornell often featured in such boxes (not to mention the incidences of death for mothers in childbirth and increased instances of childhood mortality in the premodern medical age) should open our eyes to the darker odds that may roll up in such artistic slot machines.[20]

Such alternative readings, one hopes, will open viewers to the possibilities of understanding and appreciating the complexity of Cornell's art, and will remind us to think twice about such simple labels as "childish" or "innocent" when dealing with an artist with a curious nature and a long history of intellectual and emotional pursuits. The mirror world into which Alice fell taught her hard lessons: we all know that children experience these hard lessons even in our advanced, capitalistic society.

The notion of toying with Cornell's "games" can also pack a more overt sexual punch, as evidenced by his *Untitled (Penny Arcade Portrait of Lauren Bacall)*, 1945–46 (see fig. 20). To play this game, one inserts the wooden ball into the hole at the upper-right corner of the glass-covered box. Gravity sends it plunging and clattering down hidden interior ramps, behind reproductions of Hollywood publicity photographs and amateur snapshots of the young starlet, finally depositing it into a receptacle at the bottom of the sculpture. Often posited as one of Cornell's "toys for adults," and a work intimately tied to such traditional turn-of-the-century playtime pursuits as penny-arcade games and nickelodeon movies, Joseph Cornell's *Penny Arcade* complicates the accepted notion that the artist was innocent and childlike.

The box, a modern-day *retablo* of sorts,[21] houses multiple photographs of Bacall, many of which are attached to the surface of stacked wooden blocks, like those found in the *Medici Slot Machine*. These images establish her background, including pictures of her puppy and dioramic representations of the Manhattan skyline, which signal her beginnings in that metropolitan area. Made in the same year that Bacall debuted in the Warner Brothers release *To Have and Have Not*, Cornell's assemblage reads like a shrine to the fresh, young actress whose movie-poster image had caught his eye one rainy afternoon outside a cinema. In a journal entry dated April 1945, Cornell wrote about Bacall and his ideas for the boxed homage he was creating for her, writing, "The original inspiration for this box portrait was the surprise of the ORIGINAL quality of this actress after the smoke screen of the usual cheap Hollywood publicity." Cornell continued: "As far as the fans are concerned [Bacall is] a new, slinky, sultry, sexy siren of the silver screen, but underneath all of this cheesecake [is] a girl of Botticellian tenderness. [. . .] And so a box, a game, a portrait or a machine that belongs in a penny-arcade—as genuinely [. . .] American as herself,—but one with a shiny clean look, fumigated of Hollywood booze, cigarette smoke and slow-motion mugging."[22]

What is most astonishing about this description is that Cornell's presentation in both the box and diary refuse to face facts. In both of these sources, Cornell completely overlooks the reality of Bacall's life, as well as the behavior of the character she portrayed in the movie that inspired his art. After all, this was a very young woman at the time, one who had garnered the provocative nickname "The Look" from her sexually charged stare well before her twentieth birthday. Ignoring the memory of this *noire* heroine uttering a classic come-on line ("You know how to whistle, don't you? Just put your lips together and blow"), Cornell presents Bacall as innocent, not a "sexy siren of the silver screen" but a "girl of Botticellian tenderness."

The actress herself, writing in a 1978 autobiography, was clear about the type of woman she played in her first movie role, describing her as everything from a "know-it-all, experienced sexpot" to a "wanton, life-bitten woman of the world."[23] Bacall's real life at the time was also scrubbed "shiny clean" by Cornell, negating any hint of the scandal that then surrounded her. Thus, the affair that she was conducting with Humphrey Bogart, her married and much older co-star in the movie and a man who reportedly liked to call her "Baby," is predictably fumigated from Cornell's assemblage, along with the booze, smoke, and "slow-motion mugging."

But is this representation of Bacall as pure, hermetically sealed, and "under strict control" as Cornell scholar Jodi Hauptman reads it in her 1999 study of this work?[24] Was the maker innocent in his transformation of the woman, Bacall, into a machine to be manipulated, a game to be played? Are we never allowed to remember Bacall's svelte figure as it moved across the screen, her sexy stare or her husky voice, as we peer into and manipulate this box? Could Cornell's assemblage ever make us forget her smoldering sensuality?

And what about the mechanism of this game? Play involves inserting a ball into an opening at the top of the box—a mouth—and retrieving it from an opening at the bottom of the box—a lower bodily orifice perhaps? Continuing play means repeating that action, again and again. This continuous "balling" of a woman whose private life was splashed across the tabloids because of her precocious sex appeal, and whose onscreen characters certainly knew how to "have a ball," forces the viewer/player into an invasive and controlling relationship with the subject and object at the center of this activity. As the player, you literally hold Bacall's life—her glamorous image, her city, her childhood, her puppy—in your hands. This goes beyond the "philosophical gaming" that Richard Vine has mentioned in reference to this box,[25] and suggests the importance of an investigation into the not-so-innocent nature of many of Cornell's game boxes.

Cornell extended his play into areas of his life beyond his art process, including the seemingly endless and imaginative revisions of reality that can be seen in his journal keeping and letter writing. These documents—correspondence with poet Marianne Moore, painter Pavel Tchelitchew, and many others—contain layers of narrative that often feature many different versions of reality mixed with fantasy. As a Cornell scholar, I can attest to the fact that I too have been forced to play with the archival materials that Cornell has left behind, to seek the hidden, to detect the bluff and proceed blindfolded, to connect the dots as I attempt to understand this artist and his art.

Joseph Cornell has also been pictured—and often posed himself—as a player, an adult who was interested in games. In photographs taken by Hans Namuth, Duane Michals, Terry Schutte, and many others, we see this side of Cornell's personality emerge, in images of mirror play, imaginative play, and playful posing. Entire contact sheets of the artist mugging for the camera can be found in the Namuth files at the Center for Creative Photography in Tucson, making public Cornell's private mirror play. He stands and acts a part; he grins and mugs; he "reads" a book in a completely imaginative and original way, holding it (upside down) to his cocked ear. In a self-posed photograph taken by Ernst Beadle in 1948, he pretends to hold back a giant boulder that is threatening to crush a small doll he has placed nearby, and in another, by Duane Michals, he plays with kitschy backyard animal sculptures in his tiny backyard.[26] Cornell poses as, and remains for many, the naïf—an artistic innocent who created "*jouets Surrealistes*" and communed most readily with figures of fantasy and enchantment, such as the ballerinas and actresses he included in his art and the neighborhood kids he befriended over many years in Flushing, Queens.

I believe that Joseph Cornell played the game himself, presenting the most palatable artistic image he could in order to downplay or distract the viewer from some of the more disturbing qualities of his work. Like a skilled prestidigitator, like Houdini, he knew that success lay in diverting the attention of his audience. He presented a palatable front, sweet and innocent, while all the time the shiny coin was neatly concealed in the palm of his fast-moving hand as he reached to pluck it from behind our unsuspecting ear.

8

PLAYING WITH DADA: HANNAH WILKE'S IRREVERENT ARTISTIC DISCOURSE WITH DUCHAMP

DEBRA WACKS

Satire is a lesson, parody is a game.

—VLADIMIR NABOKOV, *STRONG OPINIONS*

I really don't look like I'm serious, but I'm very serious... humour is much more difficult to attain than humourlessness... it's hard to make a joke...jokes are like the most serious things in the world.

—HANNAH WILKE

Hannah Wilke (b. 1940) produced sculpture, paintings, performances, videos, and photographs until her untimely death in 1993. Although she often declared the importance of feminism to her life, Wilke did not belong to any women's group in particular. Instead, both her feminism and her art were cultivated on her own terms, which almost always included humor. This humor operated in constellation with play, puns, parody, and the carnivalesque as a means to convey her serious sociopolitical observations. Humor provided an irreverent tool with which Wilke could chip away at established ideas and hierarchies. As part of this subversive process, Wilke challenged all sorts of authority, including that of a most venerated "father" of both twentieth-century avant-garde art and of the pun—Marcel Duchamp. For he was the one to compete with in order to play the postmodernist game.[1] In this chapter, I will examine Wilke's periodic unrequited art dialogue with Duchamp, one that lasted for years.

Wilke is perhaps best known for her public and private performances of *S.O.S.—Starification Object Series* (1974–79). The private performances—what Wilke called "performalist self-portraits"—are documented through a series of photographs depicting Wilke as she parodies clichéd representations of femininity.[2] In most of the images, Wilke appears partially nude, yet she is always covered with small vaginally shaped chewing-gum sculptures that work to interrupt the scopophilic gaze as well as point to the parodic nature of her gestures.[3] Parody is understood here in terms of Linda Hutcheon's definition, as "repetition with critical distance, which marks difference rather than similarity."[4] It follows that one must acknowledge the *difference* Wilke produces through her parodies in *S.O.S.* as well as her other works in order to recognize their critical elements—that is, their ability to question and to deconstruct problematic stereotypes.

For their thoughtful comments regarding this chapter, I would like to thank Kathleen Wentrack and Debra Kalmanowitz, with additional gratitude extended to Stuart Spencer and Donald Goddard.

At about the same time that Wilke began working on *S.O.S.* in the mid-1970s, French feminist Luce Irigaray was extolling the subversive power of parody in her 1975 essay "Pouvoir du discours/subordination du féminin."[5] Here she urged women to "play with mimesis," for she explains that to "assume the feminine role deliberately...means already to convert a form of subordination into an affirmation, and thus to begin to thwart it."[6] By playing with mimesis (or parody), one can invert the power structure defining the feminine.[7] Rather than the passive wearing of femininity, Irigaray calls for an active use of feminine mimicry as a conscious citation and parody of male discourse. Although Irigaray writes in regards to language, an intentional parodic play with visual culture proves to be a likewise formidable strategic method.

Similarly interested in the rebellious potential of play, Susan Rubin Suleiman observes in her book *Subversive Intent* that whereas men regularly use play in their avant-garde work conservatively to reenact patriarchal scenarios, women who play through their art depart from the status quo to produce something innovative. Suleiman praises the liberating effects of laughter, parody, and play in the art and writing of progressive women. For "it is in playing that the 'I' can experience itself in its most fluid and boundaryless state."[8] "I believe," continues Suleiman, "that women—women artists in particular—must be strong enough to allow themselves this kind of play."[9] Later in the text, Suleiman envisions a time when women and future generations of women play together to rewrite traditional psychological and social patterns.[10] This notion of play—as potentially subversive, even transformative—underlies my reading of play in Wilke's art.

Originally, Wilke created her *S.O.S.* images literally to be played with in her work / game entitled *Mastication Box* (1974–75, fig. 34). Taking a cue from Duchamp's *Boîte-en-valise* (1941), the piece consists of a black box that contains a variety of chewing gum flavors, game instructions, playing cards, and the thirty-five *S.O.S.* photographs of Wilke.[11] As a game, *Mastication Box* requires the players to chew the provided gum and then, following Wilke's photographic examples, produce their own witty parodies. In terms of wordplay, "Mastication" clearly puns on the act of chewing gum, while "box" evokes the slang term for vagina. The most obvious pun, however, "masturbation box," parallels contemporary 70s feminist calls for self-pleasure (like those of author Betty Dodson).[12]

Pleasure, language, and the body meld together in most of Wilke's work, particularly through the multiple meanings afforded by the pun. For example, the title of *S.O.S.—Starification Object*

Series conveys Wilke's multivoiced sentiments: referring not only to different types of scarification but also to the objectification of famous figures (stars), as well as a dire call for assistance (SOS). Wilke's vaginal-scarification also may be viewed as a response to Duchamp's earlier version of self-starification, when in 1921 he had shaved a star shape onto the back of his head and sacrilegiously called it *Tonsure.*

Such ironic wordplay appears in the work of both artists throughout their careers. With puns, words are placed within a context that suggests layered readings based on similarities of look, sound, or meaning. Strict language systems cannot accommodate the various meanings fostered by puns, which "totally undermine the explicit."[13] Puns fundamentally exploit the ambiguities of language and contradict the concept of singular, unquestionable meaning.[14] From a semiotic perspective, a pun has great potential for causing disorder and confusion because it inherently suggests the disruption of language. Indeed because language is a critical ingredient in the foundation of society and the formation of individuals, then the manipulation and breakdown of words and their meaning should be seen as a socially radical gesture.

Yet Joanna Frueh notes that while the puns in Wilke's work incorporate the sociopolitical and the personal, Duchamp's wordplay is, by contrast, "that of indifference."[15] There is a kind of "cool" detachment in the way Duchamp uses language, whereas Wilke's puns—and her use of humor and play in general—are intrinsically linked to the "hot" context provided by the women's movement in the United States.[16] This was a time when 1970s feminists employed humor strategically. For instance, the November 1973 cover of *Ms.* magazine confronts presumptions concerning feminists' humorlessness with a comic-strip-style cartoon. A bubble over the man's head reads: "Do you know the women's movement has no sense of humor?" To which the woman answers: "No.... But hum a few bars and I'll fake it!" Marie Severin's mocking image succeeded because it used playful humor as the means by which the woman articulated a defense against the criticism implicit in the initial question.

Strategic or "serious" play was also central to more public actions involving the women's movement. In August 1970, fifty thousand women marched down Fifth Avenue in New York City to celebrate the anniversary of women's suffrage. Simultaneously, thousands of people participated in rallies across the country. Photographs of the marches show women laughing and chanting as they take over public streets—all in the name of changing society. By acting en masse against the status quo, these women created contemporary parallels with Mikhail Bakhtin's theories concerning carnival.[17] He believed that carnival activity provides a site for social and linguistic transgressions in which the populace employs humor to rebel against and alter established sociocultural norms and authorities. "Anything goes" during carnival because it is a time of upheaval, blurred boundaries, laughter, and irreverent play. Moreover, once a carnivalesque act occurs, according to Bakhtin, its radicality has the potential to forever alter society as well as the constantly renewing cycle of life and death.

Carnival supplies both a method and a space for change. I am suggesting that, during the 1970s, the women's movement fostered a carnivalesque context that stimulated sociopolitical transformations.[18] In turn, this carnivalesque spirit was embraced and cultivated by feminist artists, particularly by women performance artists. There are many examples of this carnivalesque play; for instance, Linda Montano's *Chicken Dance* performed on the crowded streets of San Francisco in 1972.[19] Dancing around dressed like a chicken, Montano created a playful, yet disruptive, communal spectacle.[20]

Similarly, Wilke deployed play while embodying the carnivalesque spirit in her performances, as in *Through the Large Glass* (1976). In this case, parody acts as Wilke's challenge to Duchamp's monumental sculpture, *The Bride Stripped Bare by Her Bachelors, Even* (also known as *The Large Glass,* 1915–23) (see fig. 7). According to Duchamp's notes, his sculpture depicts an abstracted narrative about sex, or the lack thereof.[21] The work is explained as a "machine" divided into two parts: the upper register for "the bride," the lower for her "bachelors." The bride, however, forever remains a virgin in Duchamp's onanistic plot. She is caught in the endless cycle of stripping, which is mechanically produced by the frustrated bachelors.

In contrast to Duchamp's representation of masturbation as doomed sexual failure, Wilke had earlier linked it to pleasure and games in her *Mastication Box.* In *Through the Large Glass,* she went further when she erotically played with Duchamp's words and literally stripped *through* the glass sculpture in a performance at the Philadelphia Museum of Art.[22]

Wilke's performance has been captured in a three-part, color art film, *Through the Large Glass.* The first two segments track Wilke as she enters and examines *The Large Glass* while wearing

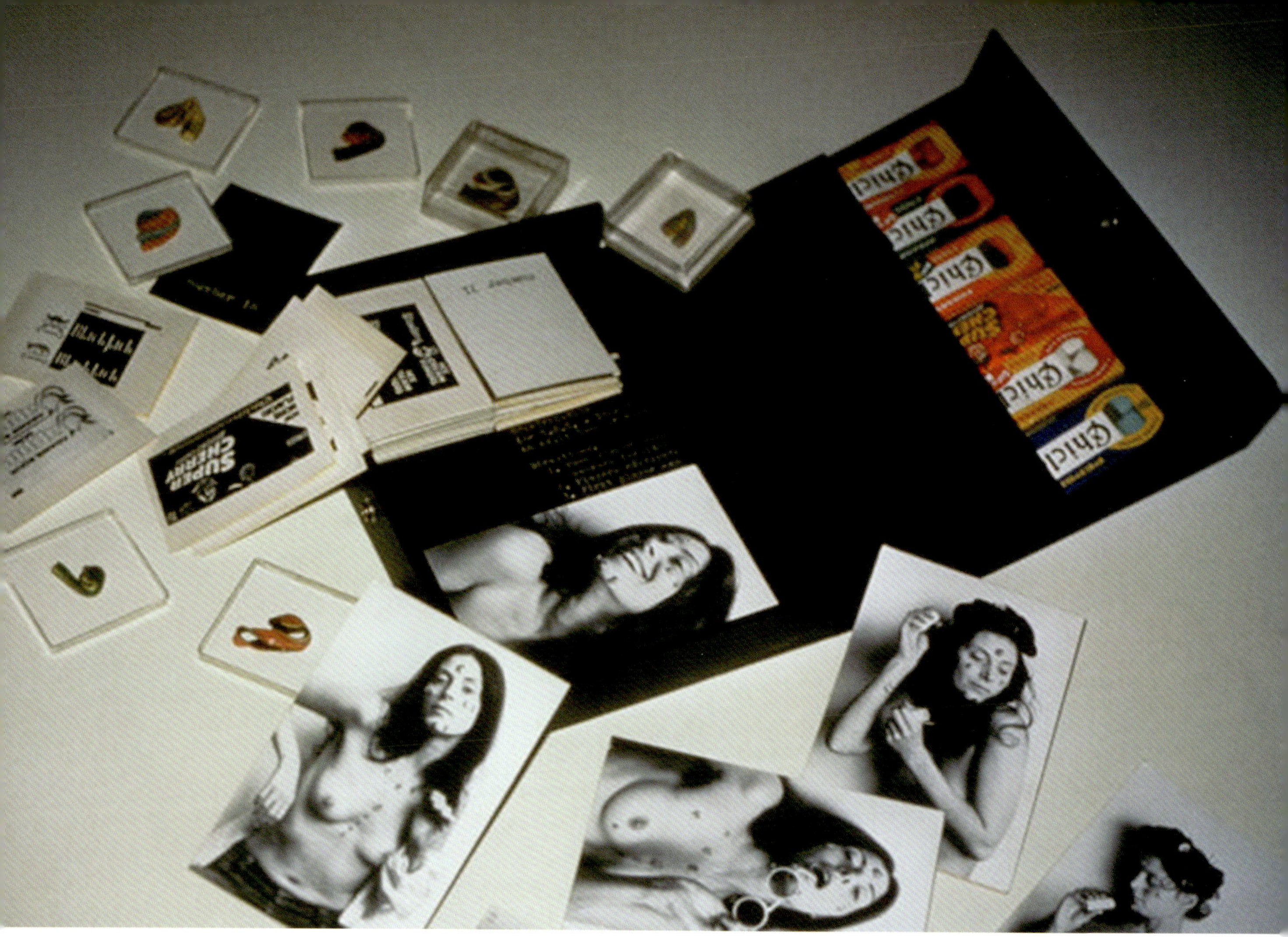

FIG. 34

Hannah Wilke, *S.O.S.—Starification Object Series, Mastication Box,* 1974–75, chewing gum, black-and-white photographs, playing instructions, and playing cards, 12 × 8 1/2 × 2 inches.

FIG. 35

Hannah Wilke, *Through the Large Glass,* 1976, still from the film *C'est la Vie Rrose.*

a white three-piece suit, scarf, heels, and fedora hat— an outfit that she associated with her masculine persona (fig. 35).[23] In response to the glass sculpture, Wilke strikes a series of both sexy and silly poses that intertextually recall gestures from her past works, as well as the curved hands from Duchamp's famous self-portrait as Rrose Sélavy (1920–21). Wilke then rhythmically removes every piece of clothing, except for the hat—a marker of her play with gender and a symbolic link to criticality—which always remains on her head. The strip is effortless and graceful, made simpler by the lack of any undergarments. But before she discards her scarf, the camera consciously zooms in on the initialed letter "H," which brands it like a signature on a work of art. Wilke's authorship is made clear.

The third and final segment of the *Through the Large Glass* represents Wilke's performance as a series of snapshots, the movement between poses now removed. This steady and abrupt slide show theoretically parallels the spirit of mechanization fundamental to Duchamp's narrative of *The Large Glass.* Yet Wilke's sexuality remains undeniable, ultimately serving only to contradict the asexuality of Duchamp's "bride."

Throughout Wilke's performance, the camera/viewer stays in front of *The Large Glass* with Wilke remaining behind it. Like the chewing gum in *S.O.S.,* elements of the sculpture (a cone, a sieve) always interrupt any direct viewing of Wilke. Her body is constantly negotiated through Duchamp's work, ensuring that it becomes part of his work and vice versa. Wilke's seduction, however, visually asserts itself and the sculpture eventually slips into the foreground, like a metaphorical scrim. And although Wilke's contemplative gaze stays fixed on Duchamp's sculpture (for the strip is first and foremost in heated dialogue with the work of art), *she* becomes the spectacle—the one to watch.

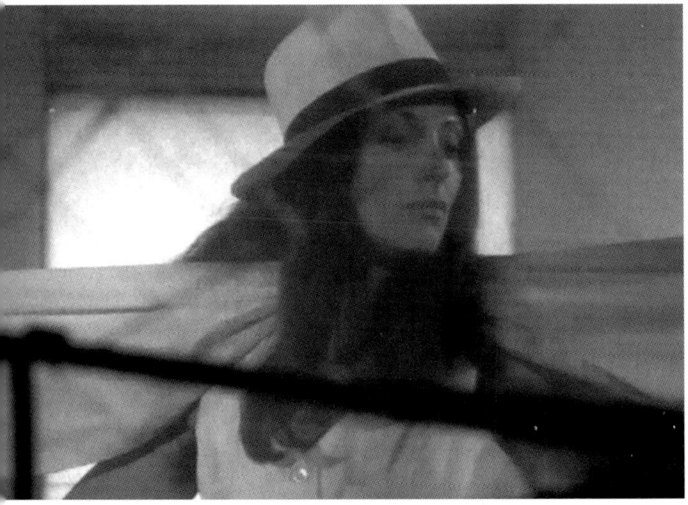

Whereas essayist Octavio Paz partially described the bride's striptease in Duchamp's *Large Glass* as "a spectacle," Wilke's performance clearly out-spectacles both the bride and her bachelors.[24] Duchamp's sculpture cannot help but appear inert in its role as prop, while Wilke intentionally turns her self / body into a spectacle. In a chapter entitled "Female Grotesques: Carnival and Theory," Mary Russo speaks of "making a spectacle out of oneself," and writes that feminist parody is most disruptive when women employ mimesis to aggressively repeat the feminine.[25] This aggression not only redefines the feminine as a visible force but also produces excessive, subversive *difference.*

Building upon Russo's ideas and writing about hyperbolic, visible femininity, Kathleen Rowe observes that although women have traditionally been objectified and rendered powerless via the spectator's gaze, "in a postmodern culture of the image and the simulacra, power also lies in possession and control *of* the visible."[26] This affords them the power of aggressive visibility in contrast to passive objectivity. In her dual function as artist and model, Wilke deliberately demonstrates her power to (re-)create parodies of femininity in order to skew them (differentiate them). Rowe further explains that women (like Wilke) who purposefully become spectacles engage the carnivalesque and may be labeled "unruly"—one who disturbs social and gender norms, behaves disorderly, and acts out of turn.[27]

Wilke's unruly parody of *The Large Glass* was initially produced for and edited into the German film *C'est la Vie Rrose,* in which Wilke plays herself (1977).[28] The idea that someone else might have more control over the representation of one of her works, however, bothered Wilke enough to simultaneously make her own videotape, a black-and-white "auto-documentary" of *Through the Large Glass* entitled *Philly* (1976). The latter video records Wilke's actions leading up to and during the actual performance and includes some closing scenes as well. As can be expected from Wilke, wordplay contributes to the meaning of the video. The title, *Philly,* not only puns on the site of the performance but also on "filly," a slang term for a vivacious young woman. It plays with the suffix "phile," which connotes "one who loves" when added to another word. And it alludes to the specific Latin word for "love," as in Philadelphia, the city of "brotherly love."

Meant to be viewed together, the film and the auto-documentary not only contrast in appearance (color versus black-and-white, stylized versus documentary) but also in sound.

Through the Large Glass is silent, while *Philly* showcases Wilke's voice. She is heard analyzing art with the museum's curator (Anne d'Harnoncourt), choreographing shots with the film's director (Hans-Christof Stenzel), and chitchatting with the video's cameraman (Andy Mann), all in her noticeably cheerful New York accent. Her instructions are constantly self-interrupted by jokes, double entendres, and carefree laughter, regularly punctuated by her steady champing of chewing gum.

The gentle clash between Wilke's rebellious spirit and the traditions represented by the imposing beaux-arts architecture of the Philadelphia Museum is underscored by a scene from the video that begins with a spotlighted nude bust of a woman. From out of the darkness Wilke's arm can be seen placing her fedora hat onto the sculpture's head. The juxtaposition of the stylish, contemporary man's accessory on the idealized, nude body of the "lady" is not only visually ironic, but also calls attention to constructions of gender—still a novel concept in the 1970s. The hat, however, transforms the timeless beauty from passive object and activates her—emulating the way Wilke complicates her own classically beautiful image. This defiant moment, however, is soon interrupted by an annoyed, off-camera male voice, who asks Wilke to "please remove the hat."

Acute confrontations continue throughout *Philly,* as does Wilke's preoccupation with Duchamp's work. For instance, Wilke is seen walking through the Duchamp exhibit at the museum. She enthusiastically discusses the French titles of the works, all the time holding a vaginal gum sculpture that she playfully threatens to stick to one of Duchamp's pieces. A voice of authority is heard again, this time instructing Wilke "not to touch anything"—unequivocally contrasting with Duchamp's wall sculpture *Prière de toucher* (*Please Touch,* 1947).

But once Wilke enters the private space of the women's restroom—to change into her "male character"—she is free to ignore standard rules of public decorum. She casually discusses Duchamp's work with the unseen cameraman, who pans around the bathroom and excitedly notes similarities between the restricted space he has entered and a typical bathroom for men. When Wilke points to the lack of urinals, the camera purposefully turns to focus on a water fountain, creating a visual pun with Duchamp's notorious porcelain sculpture, *Fountain* (1917). After Wilke mischievously urinates for the camera, she gradually removes her jeans and blouse and dons her white suit. It is not without irony that Wilke undresses and dresses for the camera while describing the voyeuristic elements of *Etant donnés.* As a finale, Wilke aggressively spits out her gum onto the bathroom floor. She laughs hardily before retrieving the debris and folding it into a familiar vaginal form. With obvious pride, she then sticks the tiny sculpture onto the bathroom wall—surreptitiously ensuring that the Philadelphia Museum of Art displays at least one of her works.[29]

Along similar unruly lines, another scene from the *Philly* video catches Wilke as she plants several steamy kisses onto *The Large Glass* itself, leaving traces of breathy lip marks across the impotent mechanical figures.[30] Wilke's passionate yet sympathetic kisses appear to ameliorate the sculpture of its sexual woes. Bride and bachelors alike are temporarily, simultaneously eroticized by Wilke, whose sensual body transgresses the *Glass'* isolated gendered registers. In this manner, Wilke one-ups Duchamp at his own game—echoing his risqué and antiauthoritarian alteration of Leonardo's painting with *L.H.O.O.Q.* (1919). Just as Duchamp had scandalously sexualized *Mona Lisa* with a moustache, Wilke co-opts and transforms Duchamp's masterpiece for her own irreverent sexual scenario.

The Large Glass moves from foreground to background in the final scene of *Philly,* in which Wilke sits at a table playing chess with another woman (I Sa Lo) (fig. 36). Wilke is nude, except for her white hat and high-heeled shoes. She embodies the collapse of traditional mind/body dichotomies and represents a type of thinking nude. Her female companion is dressed androgynously in black. Together they represent a gamut of gender possibilities. Occasionally whispering to each other, they concentrate intensely on the game before them. Reminiscent of Suleiman's feminist vision, they are women playing together and they are rewriting traditional social patterns. Wilke moves a piece and smiles as she says "checkmate." The video cuts to black and ends.

The sense of competition and play in Wilke's chess scene, however, references something beyond the video skit. This performance parodies a famous 1963 photograph of Duchamp playing chess in front of *The Large Glass* at the Pasadena Art Museum (fig. 37).[31] In the photo, he sits at a table with a visually anonymous woman, who is not only completely nude (no hat or shoes), but her face is obscured by her hair, making her identity appear inconsequential.[32] Comparing a film still of Wilke's chess-playing scene (that was used as a promotional image) to the Duchamp photo, one sees that the curved body of the Pasadena nude looks inactive next to Wilke's upright and physically engaged position. Wilke's raised arm is poised to move, which actually mimics Duchamp's ready pose. Compositionally, the images mirror each other, but the firmly maintained gender codes in Duchamp's photograph are ultimately parodied, conflated, and rejected by Wilke's representation.

The relationship between Wilke's work and that of Duchamp sometimes appears to be a game of tug-of-war. As Suleiman suggests: "A double allegiance characterizes much of the best contemporary work by women: on the one hand, an allegiance to the formal experiments and some of the cultural aspirations of the historical male avant-gardes; on the other hand, an allegiance to the feminist critique of dominant sexual ideologies, including the sexual ideology of those same avant-gardes."[33] Through her art, Wilke obviously pays homage to Duchamp as a "father" of both pre-postmodernism and the artistic pun, acknowledging his importance to her work specifically and to art history in general. At the same time, of course, she also misbehaves as a disruptive "daughter."[34] She reiterates, manipulates, and radically alters Duchamp's work, all the time suggesting a kind of heretical play; refusing to follow any law of the father (especially sexual), blurring boundaries, and exaggerating feminine stereotypes. She is an artist jockeying/joking with the / her father's body of work, subsequently providing a feminist / artistic slant to Roland Barthes' bold claim that a "writer is someone who plays with his mother's body."[35]

And so it goes. Wilke continues her parodic/critical challenge to Duchamp's work when she next takes on his final grand piece, *Etant donnés: 1 La Chute d'eau, 2 Le Gaz d'éclairage* (1946–66) with her *I Object: Memoirs of a Sugar Giver* (1977–78, fig. 38). As mentioned earlier, voyeurism is key to *Etant donnés.* Its three-dimensional tableau—which depicts a hidden-faced, disfigured, nude woman sprawled out on a bed of twigs, holding a lighted lamp—can only be seen through two peepholes set in a forbidding wooden door permanently installed at the Philadelphia Museum of Art (fig. 39).[36] Wilke responds to the eerie female body with two poster-sized, color performalist-self portraits that together act as a pseudo book jacket belonging to her (not yet formulated) autobiographical text, "I Object: Memoirs of a Sugar Giver."[37]

On what is understood to be the "back cover" of the imagined book, Wilke's foreshortened feet are in the foreground; her eyes are hidden and her nostrils exposed. The central focus of the photograph is occupied by the relaxed open thighs of Wilke's appealing nude body—boldly reaffirming Wilke's

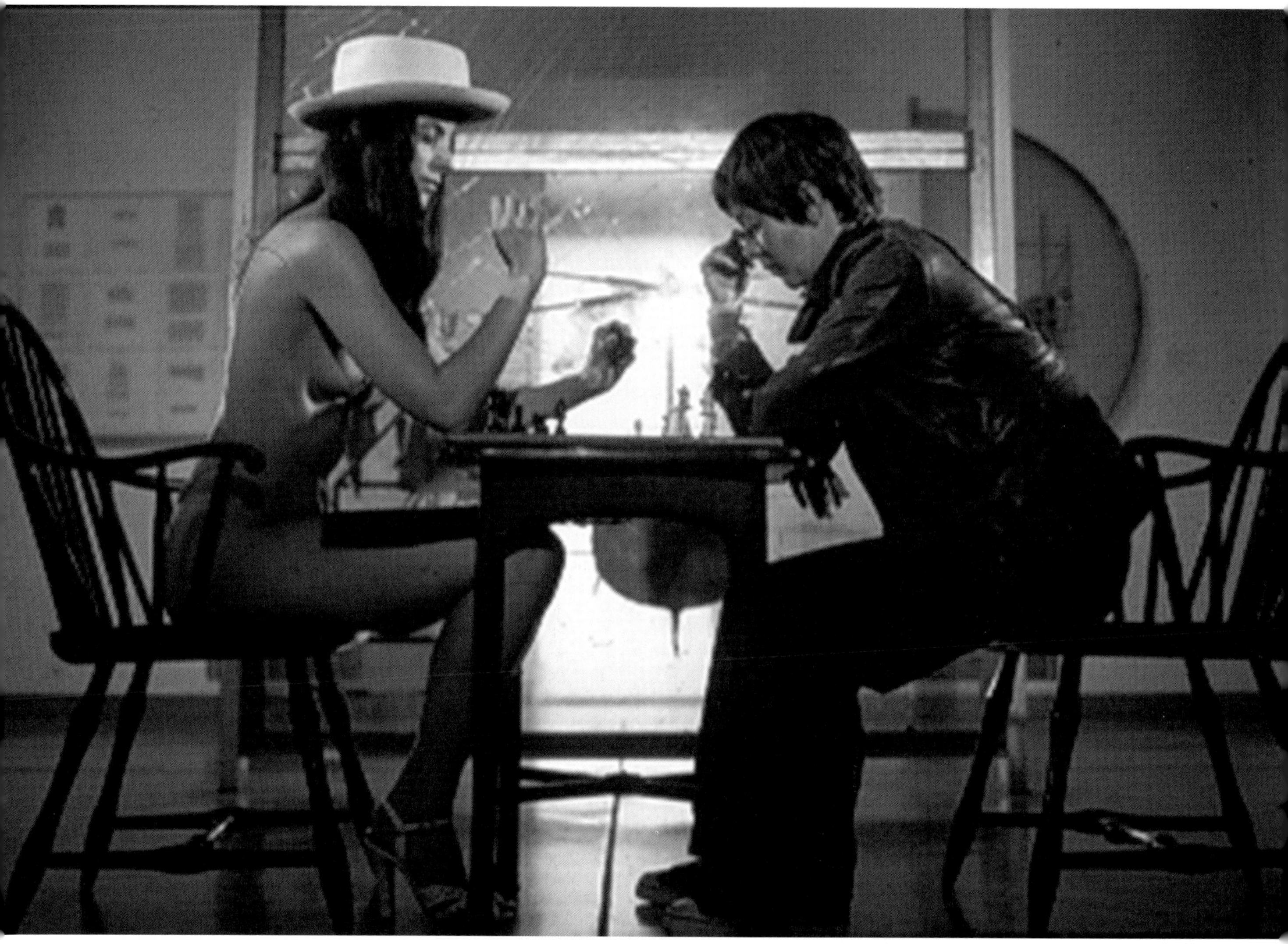

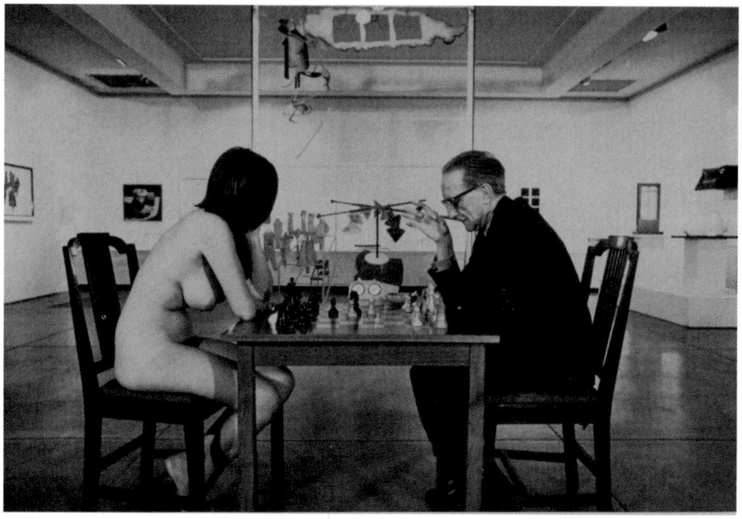

belief that "the pride, power, and pleasure of one's own sexual being threaten cultural achievement."[38] While she mimics the crotch-shot perspective of *Etant donnés,* here the sense of menace is avoided, the female body is healthy and whole, and the representation is integral to the subject's autobiography (reaffirming Wilke's individual subjecthood).[39] Tellingly, Wilke produced these photographs during a trip to Europe, physically trespassing on Duchamp's territory to pose on rocks that were once part of his home in Cadaques, Spain.[40]

Wilke makes apparent that her nakedness on the rocks results from yet another stripping, as evidenced by the strewn wardrobe surrounding her in a way that recalls model Victorine Meurent's crumpled dress in Édouard Manet's 1863 painting *Luncheon on the Grass.* Posing as herself and without shame, Meurent's confidence exudes from her gaze. Wilke echoes that striking gaze on the "front cover" of her "memoir," where a bird's-eye-view captures Wilke flat on her back as she peers past a rock to stare at the viewer. This time her head appears at the bottom of the image with her feet at the top—literally turning Duchamp's tableau figure on its head. Inverted, Wilke lies among her staged still life as both object and producer of objects, as sexually desirable and self-possessed.

The title and author of the "book" are printed in bright white letters on this "cover" photograph. By using the name "Sugar Giver," Wilke reemphasizes her self-perception as a giver of pleasure, as "one who loves," and places herself in direct opposition to Duchamp, who used the pseudonym "Marchand du Sel" (an anagrammatic play on his name that translates into "salt seller") for his collection of writings.[41] Again, the work's punning title offers paradoxical and layered meanings: "I Object." The title may be read as just another fact: "I (am an) object," or as an acknowledgment of the visual pleasure Wilke offers: "eye object." Here, however, objectification is not a passive behavior. Another reading of the title requires a contortion in intonation and thinking: "I object!" As in a courtroom, Wilke raises an objection to Duchamp's *Etant donnés…,* its content and its unparalleled canonical status.

FIG. 36
Hannah Wilke, *C'est la Vie Rrose,* 1976–77, still from the film. © Marsie, Emanuelle, Damon, and Andrew Scharlatt / Licensed by VAGA, New York.

FIG. 37
Marcel Duchamp and Eve Babitz at the Pasadena Art Museum during Duchamp's retrospective exhibition. Photograph © 1963 Julian Wasser. All rights reserved.

By combining the rebelliousness of spectacle and unruly transgression with 1970s feminist politics and humor, Wilke, like her fellow women performance artists, tapped into the explosiveness of carnival. During the 1980s, however, as the carnivalesque spirit dissipated in the United States and feminism endured a powerful backlash, Wilke produced art that seems to have little to

FIG. 38

Hannah Wilke, *I Object: Memoirs of a Sugar Giver,* 1977–78, two Cibachromes, each 24 × 16 inches. Performalist Self-Portraits with Richard Hamilton. © Marsie, Emanuelle, Damon, and Andrew Scharlatt / Licensed by VAGA, New York.

FIG. 39

Marcel Duchamp, *Etant donnés: 1 La Chute d'eau, 2 Le Gaz d'éclairage,* 1946–66, mixed-media assemblage, 95 1/2 × 70 inches. Philadelphia Museum of Art, Gift of the Cassandra Foundation, 1969.

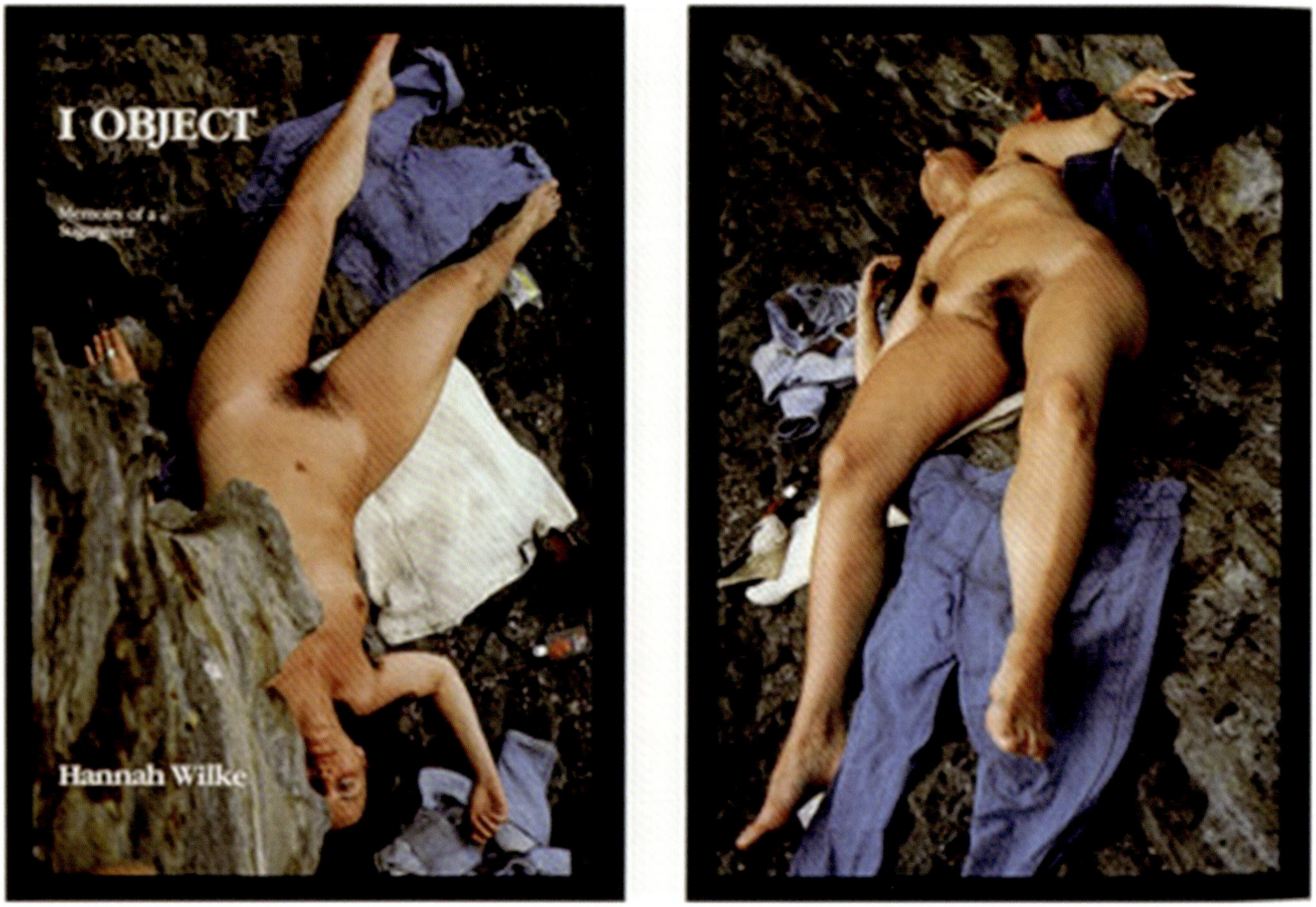

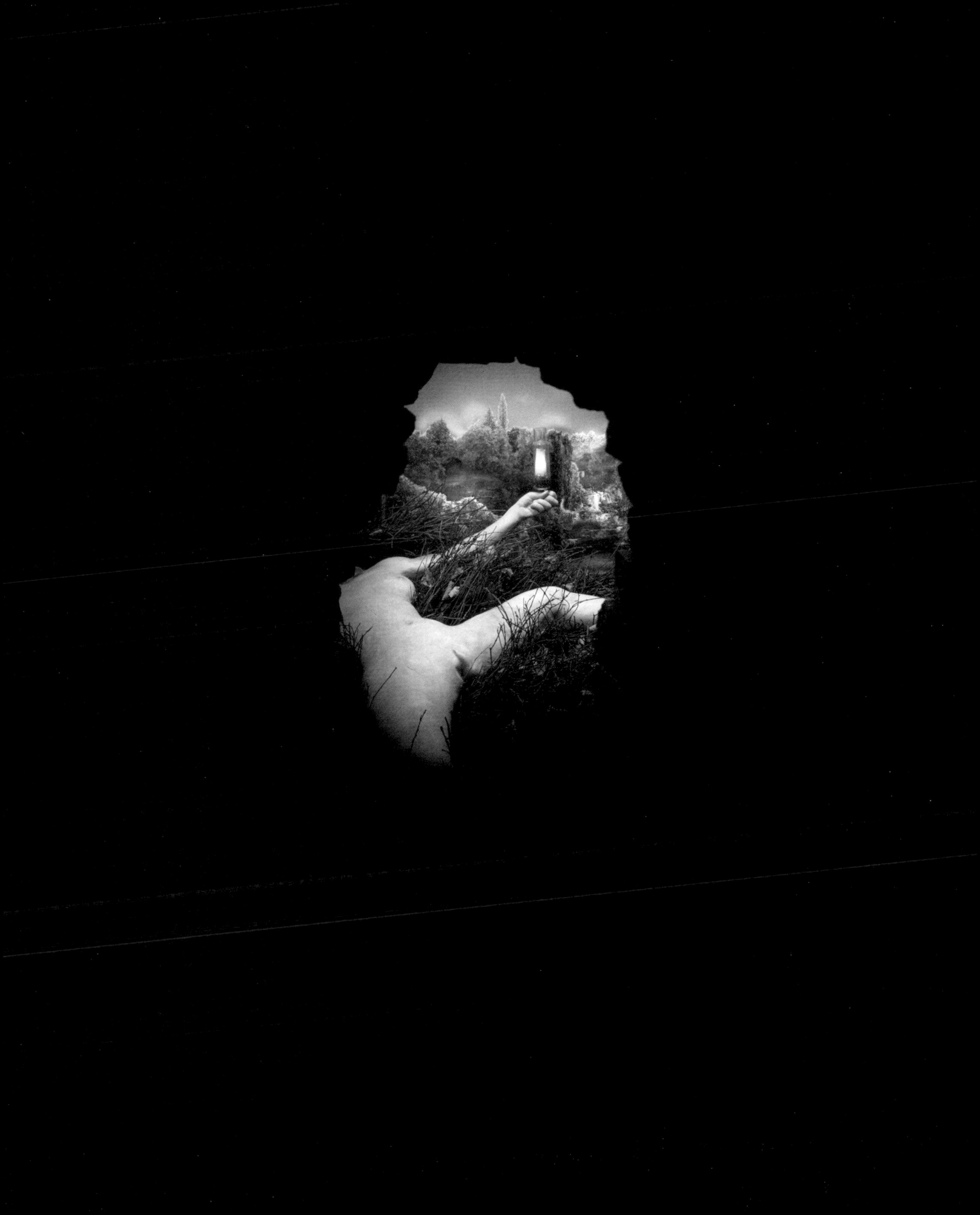

FIG. 40

Hannah Wilke, *Wedges of...*, 1992, two lead alloy radiation blocks, 3 × 6 1/2 × 6 inches. Courtesy Donald and Helen Goddard and Ronald Feldman Fine Arts, New York.

FIG. 41

Hannah Wilke, *Why Not Sneeze?* 1992, wire birdcage, medicine bottles, and syringes, 7 × 9 × 6 7/8 inches. Courtesy Donald and Helen Goddard and Ronald Feldman Fine Arts, New York.

FIG. 42

Intra-Venus Series No. 1 June 15, 1992 / January 30, 1992, 1992, one of two panels, 71 1/2 × 47 1/2 inches, Chromagenic supergloss. Performalist Self-Portrait with Donald Goddard. Courtesy Donald and Helen Goddard and Ronald Feldman Fine Arts, New York.

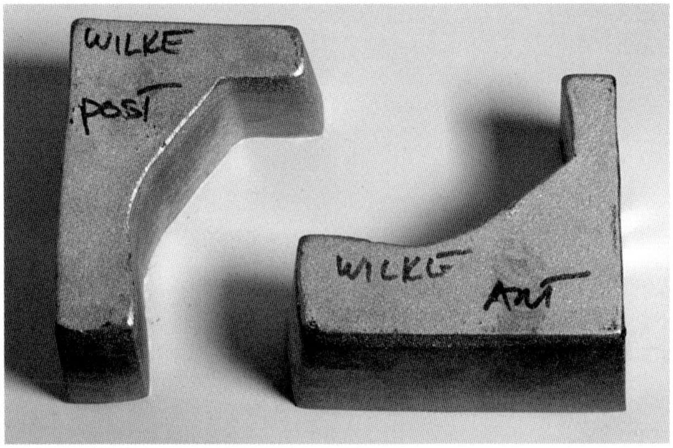

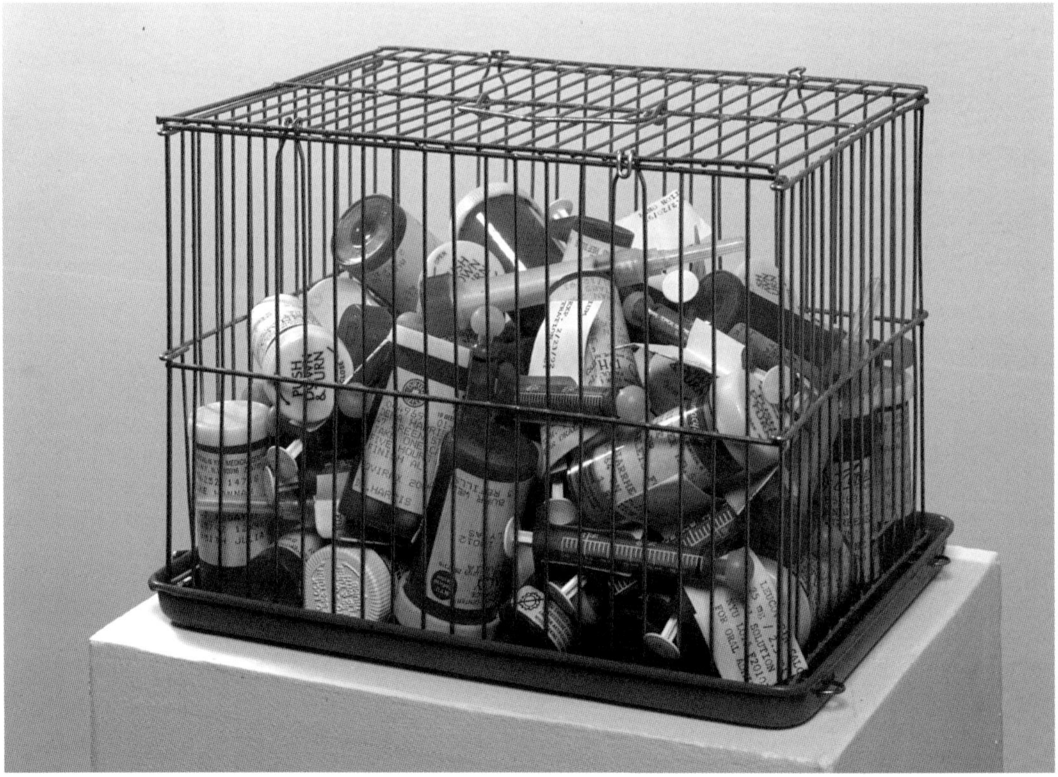

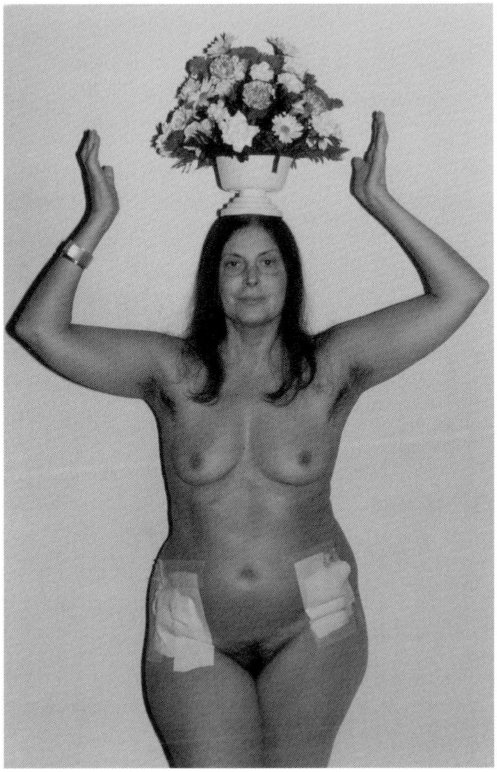

do with Duchamp. If anything, the carnivalesque became adopted instead by the queer movement. Yet Wilke continued to address her body via humor, even in the early 1990s, as she documented her failing battle with lymphoma.

It is under these dire circumstances that Wilke produced two found-object sculptures that finally conclude her games with Duchamp. The first, *Wedges of…*(1992), counters Duchamp's *Wedge of Chastity* (1954), a small sculpture consisting of a rectangular brick of galvanized plaster erotically lodged into a slab of pink dental plastic (fig. 40).[42] In an interesting turn of techniques, the latter sculpture was fabricated by Duchamp, but Wilke's work—two C-shaped, lead pieces—are readymades. They are neck radiation blocks used in Wilke's cancer treatment. And unlike the overt, generalized eroticism of Duchamp's work, Wilke does not attempt to suggest a palpable sexuality. Instead she directly references the growing loss, even the absence of her own, specific (and measured) body. Similarly, Wilke's *Why Not Sneeze?* (1992) (fig. 41) responds to Duchamp's *Why Not Sneeze Rose Sélavy?* (1921; see fig. 6). Here Duchamp's nonchalant nod to sickness assumes a serious reference. Rather than a generic thermometer and heavy marble cubes, Wilke fills her birdcage with her many empty medicine bottles and used syringes. The fantastic, fictitious persona of Rrose Sélavy is now symbolically replaced by Wilke's very ill, very real body.

The later work that Wilke produced continued to move away thematically from Duchamp's art. In her performalist photographic diptych *Intra-Venus Series No. 1 June 15, 1992/January 30, 1992* (1992), pain blurs with pleasure, beauty with the abject. Intrusive tubes and medical paraphernalia abound as cancer ravages the once-familiar body of Wilke in both images. One of the photographs displays Wilke at her most intense, clearly wrought with pain. The other image shows a nude Wilke with tacky hospital flowers on her head and oozing bandages on her bloated anticlassical form. Despite this, she raises her arms to parody a Greek caryatid figure (fig. 42).[43] The carnivalesque now simmers in a private and more grotesque manner. The latter was always considered by Bakhtin as crucial to cultural subversion—for he believed that the grotesque, especially when suggesting death, regenerates the cycle of life. Once and for all, Wilke blatantly rejects Duchamp's cool irony. And yet, Wilke still played with words. In a manner that is characteristically both personal and passionate, Wilke jarringly brings together invasive hospital procedures (intravenous) with her ongoing identification with Venus, the goddess of love.

9

DICK HIGGINS, FLUXUS, AND INFINITE PLAY: AN "AMODERNIST" WORLDVIEW

OWEN F. SMITH

Throughout the history of modernism, there are a number of "alternative traditions" to the mainstream notions of its practice. One of the most significant of these is that demarked by the trajectory from Dada to Fluxus. Their creative processes conjoined disparate elements from conventional meanings and actions in order to create new and unexpected possibilities. Dada and Fluxus attempted to establish multiple possibilities rather than to set new transcendent orders or associations. These artists and groups sought to open up potential out of a desire to participate in the world without fixed goals or definitive characteristics—that is, to reform, to associate, to create without a traditionally required predetermined end and, most important, to play.

At the risk of seeming to create yet another category of modernism (which is not my intent), I propose another tradition that has been a part of the modern-to-postmodern trajectory yet is conceptually and historically distinct from both. This is what I am labeling "amodernism." My point is not to argue for a taxonomy in and of itself, but rather to offer it as a means of interrogating both processes of production and paradigms of conceptual interaction in art over the last one hundred years. The amodernist project—what I am calling the artists and directions associated with this particular worldview—can be connected to four challenges to symbolic systems: (1) the dismantling of distinctions between subjective and objective definitions in discourse and throughout culture; (2) a focus on the structure of communication as opposed to enacting its operative function; (3) an engagement with a multiplicity of systems or forms of meaning and the apparent devaluation of specific meaning; and (4) the denial of historicity in social and linguistic change. These challenges are evident in most ideas, expressions, and work associated with amodernism. For this chapter, however, I will focus on one particular aspect: how these concerns are both evident in and enacted through a specific nexus, that of "play." After discussing some of the themes within amodernist play, I will focus on the fundamental importance of the writings of Dick Higgins and his conceptualization of Fluxus.

The general focus of much of amodernism is on the continuous destabilization of established meanings and the projection of new possibilities. Such a strategy seeks to affirm play in all its possibilities, references, and contexts. It should not be seen as a kind of romantic effort to replace one whole with another, more inclusive whole. As I will argue, the potential for the endless play of associations and difference in amodernist works is thus not a referencing of some higher or transcendent category, but instead attempts to deflect us back to a starting point—to the world itself with all of its vagueness, dislocations, and potentialities. Accordingly, the interest in physical materials, particular events, and even social and political occurrences by Fluxus and other amodernist artists is a dismissal of two dominant modernist principles: first, the romanticist vision of creativity as both nonmaterial and transcendent and, second, an engagement with art that seeks to escape into a world of its own creation as an expression of what Nietzsche described as a "dissatisfaction with reality."[1] The amodernist investigation of the concrete is not, however, a neo-Nietzschean exploration of the tragic, but rather a simple insistence on experience as an interaction between the subject (viewer) and the object (the performance, or work) that seeks to minimize any potential closure of play.

INTERACTIVITY, CHANCE, AND INDETERMINACY: FLUXUS AND JOHN CAGE

From Dada through Happenings and Fluxus, play has provided a formative principle and philosophical ground for a new tradition of art making. Play manifested itself as a creative exploration of humor, puns, gags, and games and was subsequently used as a mechanism of artistic praxis. I will discuss this play through reference to Fluxus and John Cage and through their key forerunners, notably Marcel Duchamp and Dada. Their play is more often evident as an attitude than as a reference to a recognizable format (such as playing a game). As I will go on to argue, it could be more aptly described as "infinite play."

Many of Duchamp's works in particular are founded on a conceptual reading of play—some directly, some not. For example, in *3 Standard Stoppages,* he dropped three pieces of string, each a meter long, and fixed the unique line each made by chance when it hit the ground. In this, he subverted the expectations about the conventional standards (here the standard meter) and playfully mimics the methods of an experimentalist approach.

The mechanism of production, although most often referenced to chance operations, is also based in play. Duchamp plays with our expectations about standards (the meter), he playfully mimics the methods of an experimentalist approach, and even the fall of the string and its subsequent shift from a straight line to a curved one. His work and working process additionally reference aspects of play used in describing tolerances and relations of mechanical parts, specifically variations within limits or parameters. Although probably not intended by Duchamp, the idea that this work is a reconsideration of the meter, and seeks to "play" with the concept of measure, suggesting not an exact length but instead a shifting parameter, is intriguing in the way that "para"+"meter" can be playfully seen as meaning not only "besides" and "resembling" but also "beyond" and even "incorrect," given the multiple meanings of "para."

Both Duchamp's work and play in general, however, are most significant in broad terms as a kind of model for engagement and as a way of thinking about the world that does not rely on essentialist paradigms or predetermined outcomes. In this way play is most important as an idea, approach, and means for creative thinking and acting. It is by its nature participatory. It offers a new way of interchange and interaction between the traditional "players" in a game of oppositions—the idea and the object, the spectator and the artist, the process and the product. Furthermore, play offers a way of collapsing barriers to meaningful interactivity.

Consequently, a certain openness can be seen in practice of artists from Duchamp to Fluxus that seeks to incite participation. In particular, many of the event scores of artists associated with Fluxus clearly demonstrate this shift in intent and aims to openness and play:

Albert M. Fine, *Ice Cream Piece,* 1966
Performer buys an ice cream cone and then (a) eats it, or (b) gives it to a stranger, or (c) waits until it melts completely, then eats the cone, or (d), on finishing the piece, buys another ice cream cone.

Ken Friedman, *Fruit Sonata,* 1963
Play baseball with a fruit.

Dick Higgins, *Danger Music Number Twenty-Nine,* March 1963
Get a job for its own sake.

Alison Knowles, *Proposition,* 1962
Make a salad.

Yoko Ono, *Lighting Piece,* 1955
Light a match and watch it till it goes out.

Mieko Shiomi, *Shadow Piece,* 1963
Make shadows—still or moving—of your body or something on the road, wall, floor, or anything else.
Catch the shadows by some means.

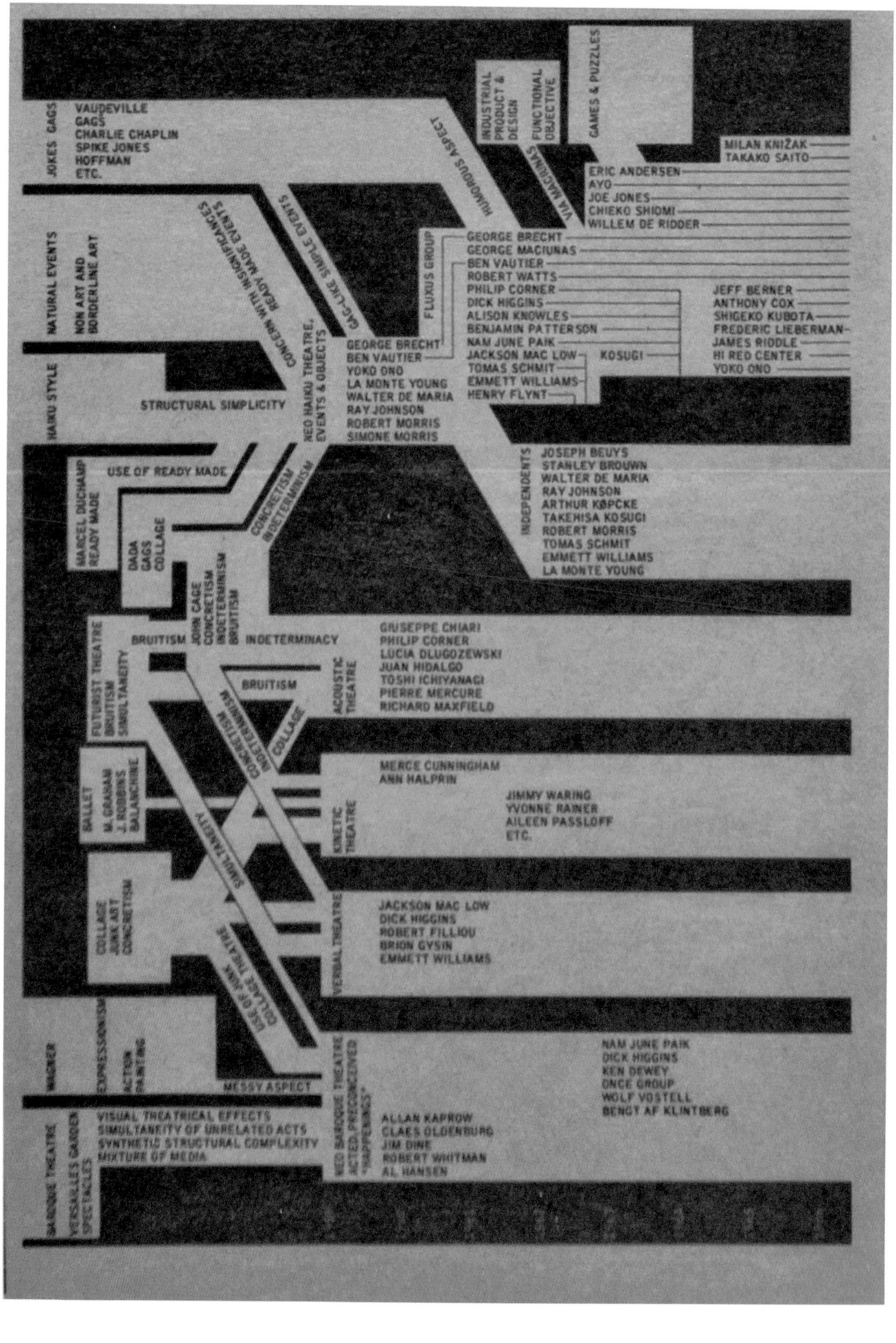

JOKES GAGS
VAUDEVILLE
GAGS
CHARLIE CHAPLIN
SPIKE JONES
HOFFMAN
ETC.
INDUSTRIAL PRODUCT & DESIGN
FUNCTIONAL OBJECTIVE
GAMES & PUZZLES
HUMOROUS ASPECT
VIA MACIUNAS
MILAN KNIŽAK
TAKAKO SAITO
ERIC ANDERSEN
AYO
JOE JONES
CHIEKO SHIOMI
WILLEM DE RIDDER
NATURAL EVENTS
NON ART AND BORDERLINE ART
CONCERN WITH INSIGNIFICANCES READY MADE EVENTS
GAG-LIKE SIMPLE EVENTS
FLUXUS GROUP
GEORGE BRECHT
GEORGE MACIUNAS
BEN VAUTIER
ROBERT WATTS
PHILIP CORNER
DICK HIGGINS
ALISON KNOWLES
BENJAMIN PATTERSON
NAM JUNE PAIK
JACKSON MAC LOW
KOSUGI
TOMAS SCHMIT
EMMETT WILLIAMS
HENRY FLYNT
JEFF BERNER
ANTHONY COX
SHIGEKO KUBOTA
FREDERIC LIEBERMAN
JAMES RIDDLE
HI RED CENTER
YOKO ONO
HAIKU STYLE
STRUCTURAL SIMPLICITY
NEO HAIKU THEATRE, EVENTS & OBJECTS
GEORGE BRECHT
BEN VAUTIER
YOKO ONO
LA MONTE YOUNG
WALTER DE MARIA
RAY JOHNSON
ROBERT MORRIS
SIMONE MORRIS
MARCEL DUCHAMP READY MADE
USE OF READY MADE
CONCRETISM INDETERMINISM
DADA GAGS COLLAGE
INDEPENDENTS
JOSEPH BEUYS
STANLEY BROUWN
WALTER DE MARIA
RAY JOHNSON
ARTHUR KØPCKE
TAKEHISA KOSUGI
ROBERT MORRIS
TOMAS SCHMIT
EMMETT WILLIAMS
LA MONTE YOUNG
FUTURIST THEATRE BRUITISM SIMULTANEITY
BRUITISM
JOHN CAGE CONCRETISM INDETERMINISM BRUITISM
INDETERMINACY
ACOUSTIC THEATRE
BRUITISM
GIUSEPPE CHIARI
PHILIP CORNER
LUCIA DLUGOZEWSKI
JUAN HIDALGO
TOSHI ICHIYANAGI
PIERRE MERCURE
RICHARD MAXFIELD
CONCRETISM INDETERMINISM
COLLAGE
BALLET
M. GRAHAM J. ROBBINS BALANCHINE
KINETIC THEATRE
MERCE CUNNINGHAM
ANN HALPRIN
JIMMY WARING
YVONNE RAINER
AILEEN PASSLOFF
ETC.
SIMULTANEITY
COLLAGE JUNK ART CONCRETISM
VERBAL THEATRE
JACKSON MAC LOW
DICK HIGGINS
ROBERT FILLIOU
BRION GYSIN
EMMETT WILLIAMS
USE OF JUNK COLLAGE THEATRE
WAGNER
EXPRESSIONISM
ACTION PAINTING
MESSY ASPECT
NEO BAROQUE THEATRE ACTED, PRECONCEIVED "HAPPENINGS"
NAM JUNE PAIK
DICK HIGGINS
KEN DEWEY
ONCE GROUP
WOLF VOSTELL
BENGT AF KLINTBERG
BAROQUE THEATRE
VERSAILLES GARDEN SPECTACLES
VISUAL THEATRICAL EFFECTS
SIMULTANEITY OF UNRELATED ACTS
SYNTHETIC STRUCTURAL COMPLEXITY
MIXTURE OF MEDIA
ALLAN KAPROW
CLAES OLDENBURG
JIM DINE
ROBERT WHITMAN
AL HANSEN

The contextual nature of these works (and of amodernist works in general) reflects a recognition that meaning results as a construct of the particular framework or situation in which it occurs. Fluxus works can never claim to be completely original or distinct entities. Given their situational nature, their meaning and relevance change in relation to the context in which they occur or are experienced.

Fine's *Ice Cream Piece* not only references daily life and commerce but also charges these references through the particular context of the ice cream cone and all its related associations with childhood and summer. Dick Higgins's *Danger Music Number Twenty-Nine* suggests not only a reconsideration of the necessity of work but also a reevaluation of the way in which we determine its value. Shiomi's *Shadow Piece* manifests the way in which experience, knowledge, and even existence are, like the shadow itself, "real" and at the same time only an immaterial projection, always held as a reference between other elements, things, or places. Such contextual relationships rely on a kind of plagiarism of a prior discourse—that is, of life itself. Thus, the work receives its own life and meaning from what it defines itself against (its difference), whether that be other objects (including works of art) or experiences and the expectations that prior experiences generate.

A primary concern for these artists was indeterminacy and its use in chance operations. Futurism, Dada, and Surrealism all took chance as both a reflection of an aesthetic point of view and as a particular mode of working. George Brecht, in his pamphlet *Chance Imagery,* described some of the uses of chance by Dada artists:

Duchamp's theories on the use of chance seem highly developed, but not exhaustive. Other Dadaists, especially Arp, Ernst and Tzara, later developed other important applications of chance:

Arp composed collages by picking up chance scraps of paper, shuffling them, and gluing them down just as they fell (example: the "Squares arranged according to the laws of chance," a collage of 1916).

Ernst developed the "decalcomania of chance," wherein, for example, ink was spread between two sheets of paper, which were then pulled apart.

Tzara composed poems by drawing words from a hat. ("To make a Dadaist poem / Take a newspaper. / Take a pair of scissors. / Choose an article as long as you are planning to make your poem. / Cut out the article. / Then cut out each of the words that make up this

FIG. 43

George Maciunas, *Fluxus (Its Historical Development and Relationship to Avant-Garde Movements),* Fluxus Editions, c. 1965.
Image courtesy of the Intermedia Collection, University of Maine.

> article and put them in a bag. / Shake it gently. / Then take out the scraps one after the other in the order in which they left the bag. / Copy conscientiously. / The poem will be like you. / And here you are a writer, infinitely original and endowed with a sensibility that is charming though beyond the understanding of the vulgar.[2]

As Brecht emphasized, for the Dadaists chance was both a process of artistic production and a means of escape, particularly from the limits underlying philosophical constructs of rational thought so dominant in Western culture. Like the Futurists, the Dadaists realized that the power of art existed in its potential for altering the practices of life. Life, however, was not defined as the life of rationalized cause-and-effect relationships but rather as ordinary daily-life experiences that included irrationality, chance, and inherent contradictions.

Many of these same views concerning the limits of rationality and the value of daily life were echoed in the work and ideas of musician and theorist John Cage. The unifying force of process and change in Cage's view integrates all life activities within the concept of nature. Thus, Cage came to believe that art should harmonize with nature and its processes. Art should utilize the operations of the natural world; accordingly, chance and change should be a part of the artistic process. The use of chance for Cage, and for many other artists, was a way to liberate the artist from taste, habit, and ego. This was echoed by George Brecht when he wrote that chance "in the arts provides a means for escaping the biases engraved in our personality by our culture and personal past history, that is, it is a means of attaining greater generality. The result is a method of approach with wide application."[3]

Cage was influenced by Zen metaphysics, in which there are no natural hierarchies. He concluded that art should mirror an equivalency of values instead of suggesting that "artistic" experiences are more elevated than "ordinary" experiences. In this way, art becomes important as a means to make one aware of one's actual environment. Jackson Mac Low, a poet associated with the Fluxus Group and a student of John Cage, reiterated the importance of chance operations. The intent of his own work, he stated, was to create situations that would allow meanings to arise spontaneously by letting the materials of the work speak for themselves. But he also remarked that such work is never fully egoless or meaningless:

> At first one thinks one can avoid the ego, make works that are egoless, by chance. This illusion passes after you work this way for a while. You realize that making a chance system is as egoic, in some ways, or even as emotional, as writing a poem spontaneously. But at the same time you realize that there is something more than just yourself doing it. & by interacting in that way with chance or the world or the environment or other people, one sees and produces possibilities that one's habitual associations [. . .] would have precluded.[4]

Chance, especially in the form of indeterminacy, establishes a significant basis for the amodernist critique of the cultural status quo and its overemphasis on rationalism and egoism. Almost all the artists who can be associated with amodernism indicate in their work a recognition of chance as an underlying factor for exploration. It is this interest in randomness and chance that is also one of the most direct links throughout this tradition. Additionally, such an interest in chance as both a mechanism of production and a means beyond social and cultural paradigms links this tradition to the ideas of Duchamp and Cage, who were two of its strongest advocates.

These ideas about the importance of indeterminacy, especially those forms drawn from Cage, established the significance of chance as a creative mechanism and as a philosophical concern for many amodernist artists in the 1950s and 1960s. The recognition of indeterminacy as a prevailing principle of nature, as well as a central aspect of the creative process, reinforced the attitude that the world is based on ambiguities, ruptures, and incongruities. Following from this, many amodernist artists realized that deterministic processes—and key among these is written language—were not a reflection

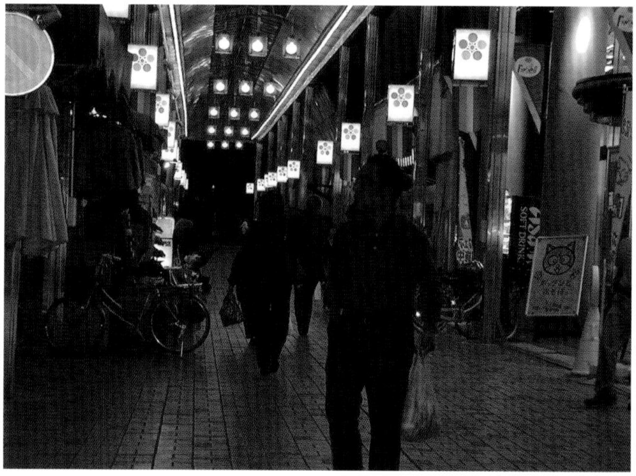

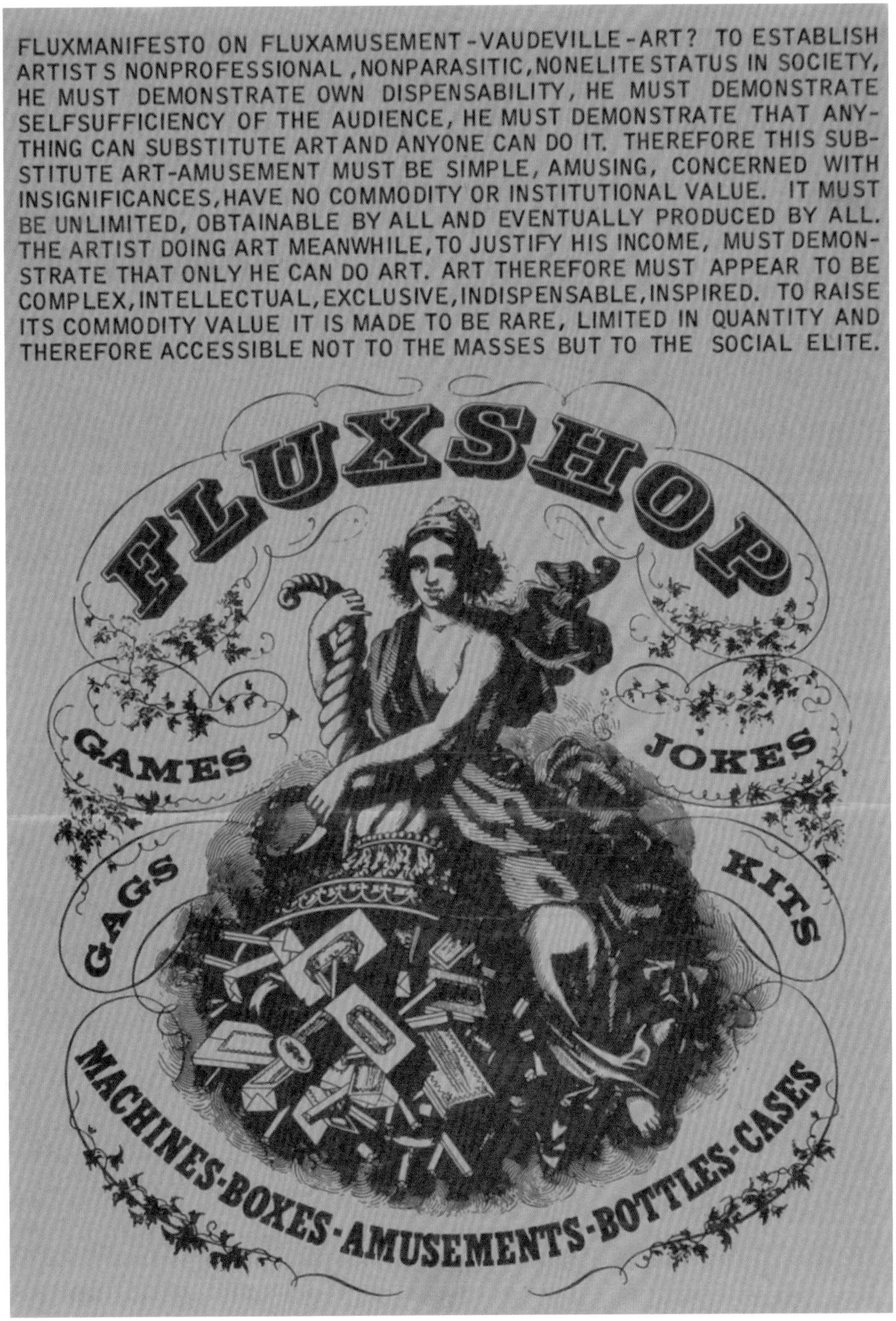

FIG. 44

Mieko Shiomi, *Shadow Piece,* 1963, night street performance, Nagoya, Japan, May 2002.

FIG. 45

Fluxus, *Fluxshop / Fluxorchestra Flyer* with *Fluxmanifesto* (detail), designed by George Maciunas, 1965. Image courtesy of the Intermedia Collection, University of Maine.

of reality but constructs reflective only of the "Western mind's" predilection toward structure and reason. The use of chance, which many if not most amodernist artists stressed, is important beyond its use as an artistic technique (chance as a means to produce some end). Rather, it reflected a recognition of the fluid and shifting nature of the world or, in the specific case of the group Fluxus (a central player in the amodernist tradition), the "flux" in "Fluxus."

This awareness is particularly important as it relates to the concept of "play" in a variety of forms. Although play is evident in many amodernist works in their use of specific quotidian forms of humor or games, it is most influential as a philosophical approach and an antiauthoritarian model for process, production, and even evaluation. It prioritized shifting relations, open-ended investigations, and modes of production and communication that emphasized the process over the result. In this process-oriented engagement, the traditional separations—such as those between the artist and the viewer, the process and the result, and even the concept and its realization—lose their validity. We are instead presented with a set of possibilities, not actualities, for which we seem to have little or no way of determining set notions of completeness, success, or efficacy. The contextual relationships of most amodernist work necessitate a denial of art as a special, separate activity. These works exist through an indexing of life in which the work receives its own fullness of meaning by its references and associations, not in spite of them.

The significance of infinite play, as contained in the amodernist worldview, is that the process of unending substitutions is an act of life, and the joy of such a recognition is that traditional systematics are no longer valid. One's field of awareness is of the potential for infinite possibilities of alternative, differing, and even contradictory meanings. In other words, the most direct connection between the use of indeterminacy and the other conceptual aspects of amodernism is the emphasis on life over art. Across the historical trajectory of amodernism, this particular aspect evolves in an interesting manner—from the use of life to question art to the acceptance of everyday life itself as being worthy of attention. In the early twentieth century, Dadaists such as Raoul Hausmann, Tristan Tzara, and Duchamp rejected the hierarchal elevation of art (and all culture by extension) over life and questioned the value structures that hold such beliefs in place. By the mid-twentieth century, Cage went further to argue that life gains value in and of itself. As he has advised: "Living takes place each instant and that instant is always changing. The wisest thing to do is to open one's ears immediately and hear a sound before one's thinking has a chance to turn it into something logical, abstract or symbolical."[5] In describing his working process as "purposeless play," Cage gave a specific connection between the significance of life and the creative process:

And what is the purpose of writing music? One is, of course, not dealing with purposes but dealing with sounds. Or the answer must take the form of paradox: a purposeful purposelessness or a purposeless play. This play, however, is an affirmation of life—not an attempt to bring order out of chaos...but simply a way of waking up to the life we're living, which is so excellent once one gets one's mind and one's desires out of its way and lets it act of its own accord.[6]

Like Cage, many artists in the amodernist tradition came to believe that art should equal daily life and daily life should equal art because it is within life that the things of greatest interest and fascination are to be found. Art continued to have relevance not as an end in itself or as something of intrinsic value but as a means of being attentive to what those elements of life might be. George Maciunas, the primary organizer of most Fluxus works and events, stated that "Fluxus people must obtain their 'art' experiences from everyday experiences, eating, working, etc.—not concerts etc."[7] Thus many works by artists associated with amodernism are concerned with simple, almost mundane occurrences; the fall of a piece of string (Duchamp's *3 Standard Stoppages*), a drip of water (Brecht's *Drip Music*), or the sound of falling snow (Higgins's *Winter Music*).

DICK HIGGINS, EXEMPLATIVISM, AND INFINITE PLAY

Dick Higgins was one of the artist/theorists who spent a great deal of concerted energy thinking and writing about the processes associated with the amodernist worldview and, in particular, Fluxus. He played many important roles in the art world of the 1950s, 60s, and 70s. He was a founding member of Fluxus, a leading practitioner of Happenings and Events, and the founder and guiding force behind Something Else Press. In addition, he coined the term "intermedia" and was the leading theorist of the concept.[8]

Higgins believed that experience holds the key. This is of course nothing new. The conceptualization of art as part of, or connected to, perceptual experience is well established, but what was different in Higgins's approach was the way that he situated this notion into a broader participatory frame. He wrote, "Our work is always at the center of an emanation of experience...we offer implicativeness [*sic*] as a goal—the work has not only its own integrity but suggests a whole vast range of further possibilities."[9] He argued that art should not be seen as some abstraction distanced from life or as a foil for personal exploration seeking to elucidate the place of the "I" in the world. Rather, art existed for Higgins in the realm of phenomena and through the mechanisms of human communication. What Higgins was working toward in his art works, writings, and other activities was an approach that was philosophical as well as applicable. This approach aimed to produce art that manifested a genuine engagement with the world as it is experienced. Such an engagement in art is at the core of his term "post-cognitive" (a term that Higgins uses in the same way I am using amodernism).[10] Although Higgins's terminology differs from the one I am using here, both describe similar ideas and processes.

From 1965 through 1968, Higgins worked out a set of interconnected ideas in essays such as "Games of Art" (1966), "Intending" (1966), "Boredom and Danger" (1966), and "Structural Researches" (1967).[11] These texts explored and elaborated on the creative and working processes central to many of the amodernist artists from Dada and Duchamp, through John Cage and Happenings, up to his own work in Fluxus and beyond. Later in his 1976 essay, "Exemplative Works of Art," he finally brings all these ideas together and labels this approach "exemplativism."[12] Key in these considerations, as well as throughout amodernism, is a shift from author to process and from a fixed product to a situational manifestation. Part of such a reconceptualization of artistic praxis was accepting certain risks, allowing for the determining or even, as Higgins put it, "fascistic control of the author" to slip away and be replaced by systems that set possibilities, then allow a shifting set of relationships to determine the details of the materials or the particulars of the work.[13]

Like Higgins's concept of intermedia, exemplativism is both a rejection of avant-gardist nihilism and a recognition of the formative significance of the space between concepts, categories, and things. Whereas intermedia signals the potentiality of thinking and acting in the spaces between traditional media, exemplativism

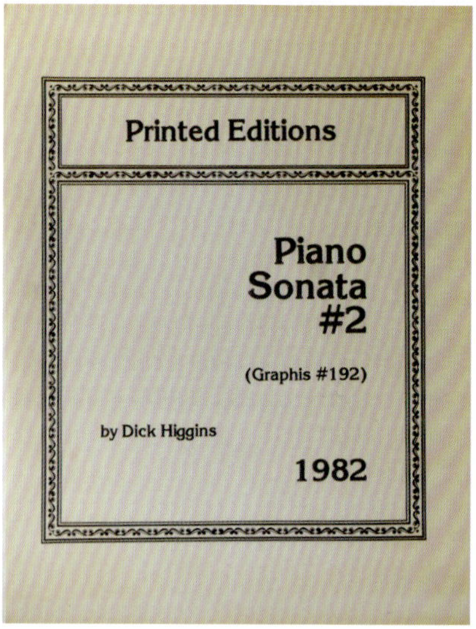

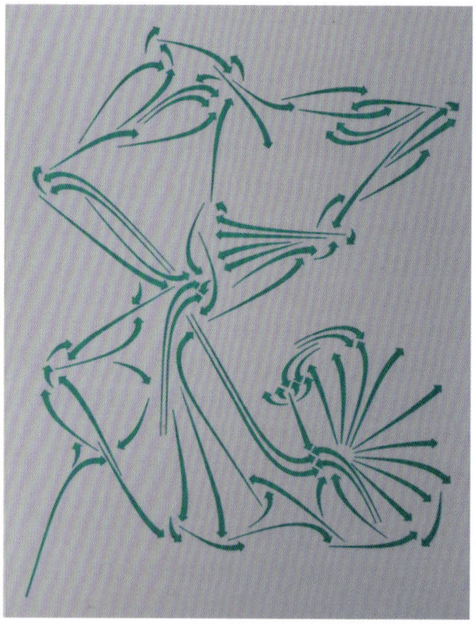

FIG. 46

Dick Higgins, *Piano Sonata #2 (Graphis #192),* 1982. Printed Editions, Barrytown, New York. Courtesy the Estate of Dick Higgins.

FIG. 47

Dick Higgins, *Five Traditions of Art History,* 1976. Courtesy the Estate of Dick Higgins.

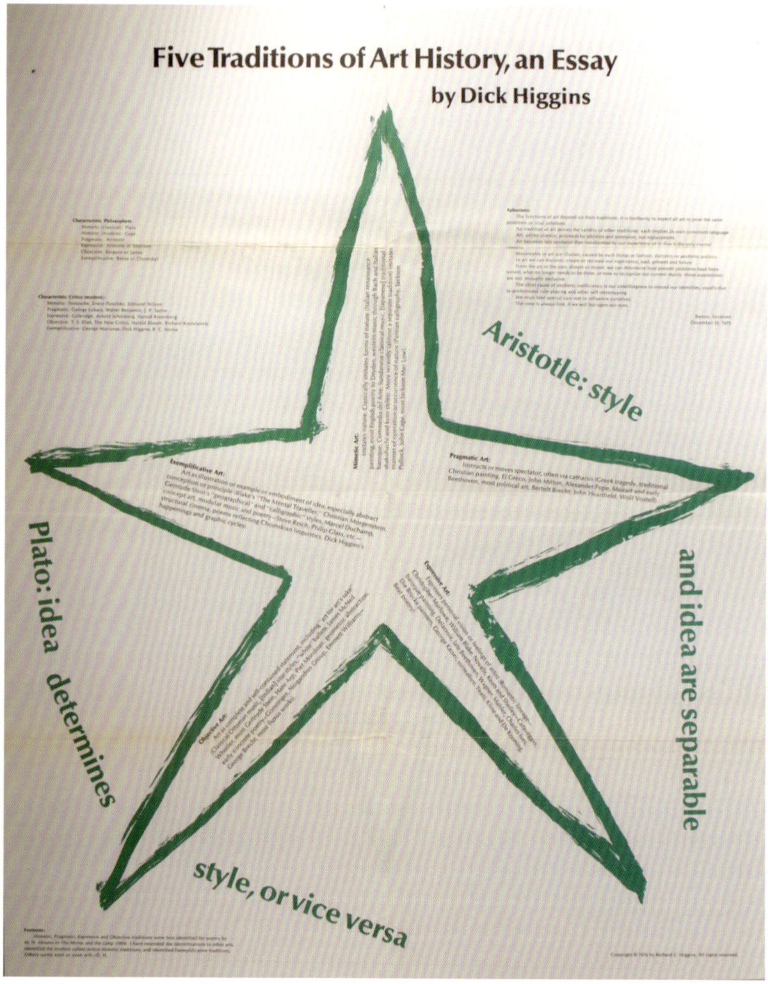

stresses the space of exchange —the intermedium between the artist and the viewer. Higgins states about the shift from traditional work to a new form that the "fixed-finished work began to be supplemented by the idea of a work as a process, constantly becoming something else, tentative, allowing more than one interpretation."[14]

Although one might connect Higgins's formation of the role of the artist to the postmodernist "death of the author," this is only partially correct. What Higgins envisioned was not the death but rather a shift in the author's role, or a de-centering from the traditional core authorial position. For in Higgins's view the author must relinquish some control, particularly over the specifics of a work, while retaining a direct and specific place for their intentions. "The specificity of the artist's intentions has to be passed along if the work is to suggest anything to think about, which is a normal requisite for comprehensibility and impact."[15] Thus the author does not vanish, but takes up residence in the intentions as manifested in the broad outlines of the piece and particularly in the procedures and processes of the work, all the while allowing the piece to remain open to shifting realizations. As Higgins himself writes about his work, "My poems tend to be exemplative—you could make a substitution of each and every word or image, but the poem qua poem is a poem of ideas…and it would remain the same as long as the relationship among its components was not interfered with."[16]

As with Higgins's *Five Traditions of Art History,* an exemplativist work is simply a work in which the form epitomizes at least a part of what it describes. Additionally, the aim of exemplativist art was, for Higgins, like much of the use of play throughout the twentieth century: to suggest and explore possibilities without overly delimiting potential experiences or reducing them to pre- and post-experiential evaluative measures. The form of presentation and the specifics used by the artist are functional rather than demonstrable. The nature of exemplativist work, as well as much work in the amodernist tradition, is neither to defend nor describe in detail but to suggest and infer. Fluxus event scores are key examples of this kind of positioning. Take, for example, Mieko Shiomi's *Boundary Music* from 1963: "Make the faintest possible sound to a boundary condition whether the sound is given birth to as a sound or not. At the performance, instruments, human bodies, electronic apparatus or anything else may be used."

This work is to be read as a score or as instructions to facilitate a performance, but it contains very little of the standard description of limited actions intended for a performer to enact. Instead, the words contextualize the area/aspect to focus on ("Boundary Music"), suggest a variety of performance means ("At the performance, instruments, human bodies, electronic apparatus or anything else may be used"), and infer the function of the act to be performed ("Make the faintest possible sound to a boundary condition whether the sound is given birth to as a sound or not"). The position of such works is a transitory one, dependent on the relation between the spectator and the artist. Duchamp referenced an aspect of this interconnectedness in "Creative Act," a talk he gave in 1957, as part of what he called the "art coefficient":

> **the personal "art coefficient" is like an arithmetical relation between the unexpressed but intended and the unintentionally expressed.**
>
> **To avoid a misunderstanding, we must remember that this "art coefficient" is a personal expression of art à *l'état brut*, that is, still in a raw state, which must be "refined" as pure sugar from molasses by the spectator…. The creative act takes another aspect when the spectator experiences the phenomenon of transmutation: through the change from inert matter into a work of art, an actual transubstantiation has taken place, and the role of the spectator is to determine the weight of the work on the esthetic scale.**
>
> **All in all, the creative act is not performed by the artist alone; the spectator brings the work in contact with the external world by deciphering and interpreting its inner qualification and thus adds his contribution to the creative act.**[17]

A similar act of transference is key to Higgins's idea of exemplativist art. He describes the work and processes in the following way: "[The] focus is the process of transferring his model to the reader or spectator. The detail is the example, not the defense of it. If the work is an essay, the process of the transfer is what is given…. An exemplative work is merely one which gets its crucial aesthetic impact from its transference of a model from the artist's mind to the spectator's."[18]

Exemplativism, and indeed all amodernist art, is based on a simple recognition of art as potentiality rather than as a fixed point in culture. Another statement by Higgins on exemplativism is useful: "So many of the artists became unhappy about this eternal, unyielding quality in their art, that they began to wish their work were more like shoes, more temporary, more human, more able to admit of the possibility of change."[19]

Throughout the twentieth century, artists, poets, musicians, and others began to shift away from traditional modes of thinking about and producing art. Play, however, remained a common context for their new ways of making art. Beyond the use of games and humor in many amodernist works, the more general importance of play was as a model for open-ended discourse that stressed relations over linear production or the mere communication of discrete pieces of information. In this way, play emphasized participation and had the ability to break down normal physical and conceptual barriers between the spectator and the work. To borrow a term from the philosopher Peter Carse, this was an aspiration toward "infinite play."[20]

The aim of an infinite game is its own continuation, without a fixed goal or definitive end point. Structured and goal-driven games can themselves be played within or as part of larger infinite play. In these cases, however, the fixed games are not played with the same earnestness. For instance, in works that make use of game structures such as *Fluxchess* by Mieko Shiomi, *Penny Arcade* by Allan Kaprow, or Tristan Tzara's "To Make a Dadaist Poem," the structured games (chess, for example) are central to the work, but the aim is not to win the literal game but rather to undertake the larger infinite play with the boundaries between art and life.

In all forms of infinite play, what is significant is an opening up of possibilities. Rather than having no focus at all, everything that happens is of potential consequence, and thus to be considered. For this reason, play's significance is transformative rather than formative. It is this aspect of the amodernist worldview that seeks (but does not always arrive at) a nonhierarchical density of experience. Because infinite play is expansive, the only motivation that exists is in the perpetuation of the process of play and to ensure that the players are kept in the act of play. What would be seen as the end in a traditional finite game structure (as either a goal or a specific desired end) is rejected in amodernist play in lieu of a preference for immediacy and for the intensity of experience found in the flow of the constantly changing present moments.

The overall concern was to enrich the experiential world of the spectator by "enlarging the repertoire of their over-all experience."[21] He argued that to do so requires not only a new mentality but also a new means of making art—art that remains intentionally open for the spectator or viewer to extend the process as a means of creating the greatest range of usefulness. The forms of presentation of a work and its particular details or materials are thus functional rather than demonstrable. "Ours is a mass society," he wrote, "and, while we do attempt to do what we do with maximum quality, quality has for us become one among other indications of integrity. Today we do not equate quality alone with the value of a work."[22]

Part of the significance of this statement for the artists was the establishment of new mechanisms in art that were participatory, open-ended, and educational. He argued that one could utilize these structures and tactics—"blank structures," as he called them—to call into question the traditional separations between artist / audience, active / passive, form / content, and process / object.[23] More often than not, he claimed, these separations are not only questioned but are broken or invalidated. This is a shift from more traditional conceptualizations of art as a statement-making process in which the artist by force of will or act of genius creates a singular, static object. Instead, art is seen as a shifting statement of possibilities—or even simply as a question that offers a sampling of possible realizations that the viewer is invited to complete. With regard to such processes, Higgins adds:

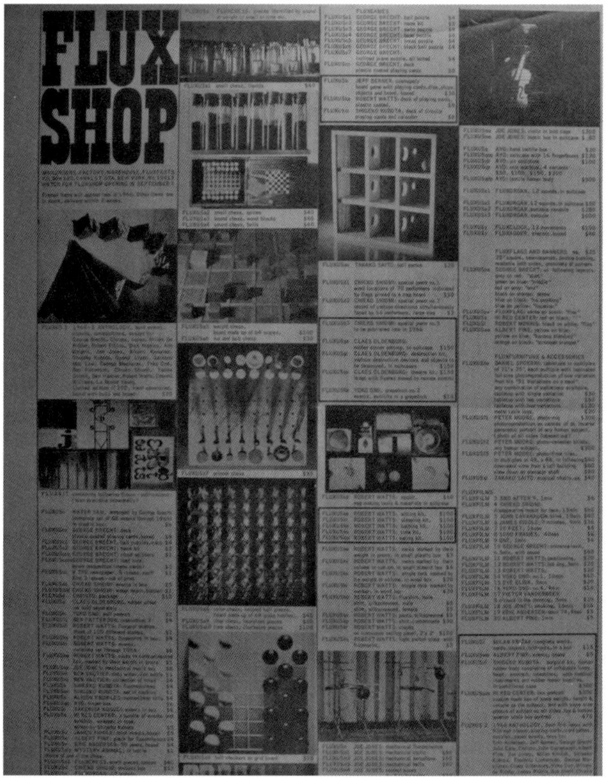

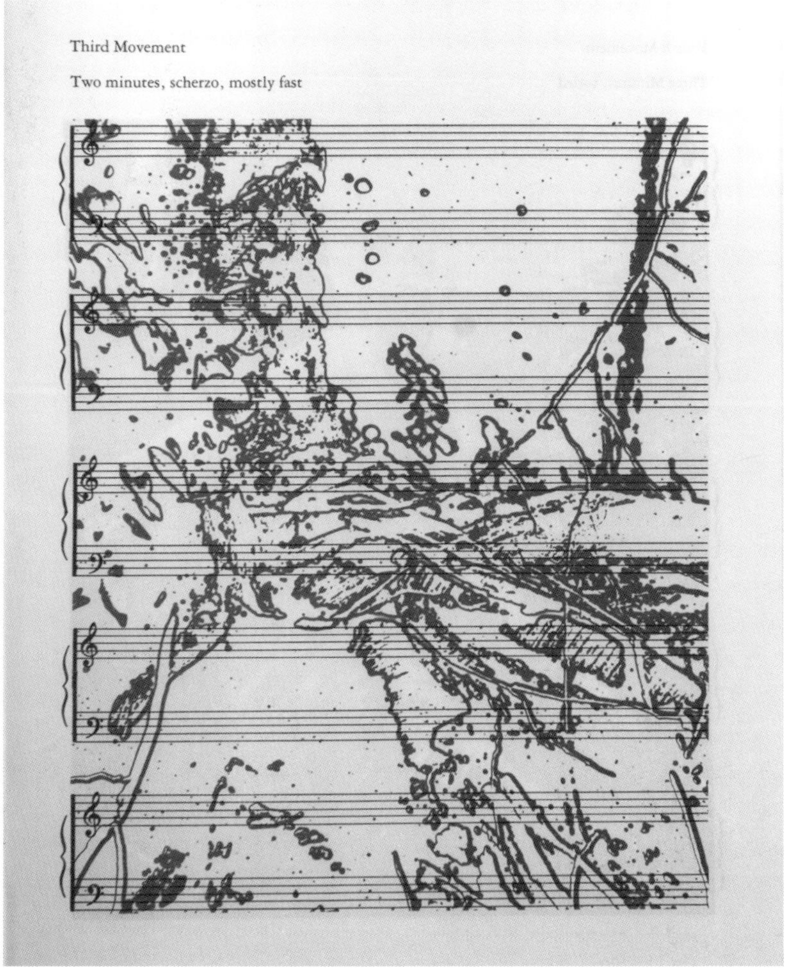

FIG. 48

Vaseline sTREet, Fluxnewspaper No. 8, May 1966, edited and designed by George Maciunas, 1965. Image courtesy of the Intermedia Collection, University of Maine.

FIG. 49

Dick Higgins, *Sonata for Prepared Piano,* third movement, 1982. Printed Editions, Barrytown, New York. Courtesy the Estate of Dick Higgins.

FIG. 50

Dick Higgins, *Homage à François Villon* (1988), Edition Conz, 1990. Image courtesy of the Intermedia Collection, University of Maine.

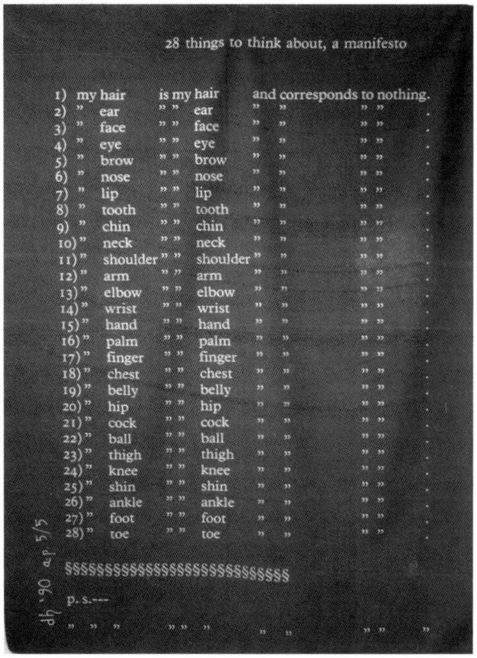

28 things to think about, a manifesto

1) my hair is my hair and corresponds to nothing.
2) " ear " " ear " " " " .
3) " face " " face " " " " .
4) " eye " " eye " " " " .
5) " brow " " brow " " " " .
6) " nose " " nose " " " " .
7) " lip " " lip " " " " .
8) " tooth " " tooth " " " " .
9) " chin " " chin " " " " .
10) " neck " " neck " " " " .
11) " shoulder " " shoulder " " " " .
12) " arm " " arm " " " " .
13) " elbow " " elbow " " " " .
14) " wrist " " wrist " " " " .
15) " hand " " hand " " " " .
16) " palm " " palm " " " " .
17) " finger " " finger " " " " .
18) " chest " " chest " " " " .
19) " belly " " belly " " " " .
20) " hip " " hip " " " " .
21) " cock " " cock " " " " .
22) " ball " " ball " " " " .
23) " thigh " " thigh " " " " .
24) " knee " " knee " " " " .
25) " shin " " shin " " " " .
26) " ankle " " ankle " " " " .
27) " foot " " foot " " " " .
28) " toe " " toe " " " " .

§§§§§§§§§§§§§§§§§§§§§§§§§§§§

p. s.---

" " " " " " " " " " "

dh '90 a.p 5/5

Nor need such work necessarily be only of the cooler, relatively cerebral kind, there can also be what I have called an "allusive referential" at work, a displacement between what one expects to see and what one does, in fact, see (or hear, or read). This displacement factor can generate the entire emotional panoply of which art is capable without any particular reference to the artist's or viewer's personal expression. We expect to see or hear A, instead of which we see or hear B, and this points us toward a new entity, C.[24]

In part, such a process leads to a potential fusion of the artist's and the viewer's horizons. Higgins argued that this created the greatest potential for "liberated processes of thought and feeling, as opposed to directed ones."[25] The most direct benefit of Higgins's "blank structures" or "blank forms" was that the mutability of the work's particulars allowed the work to retain a maximum relevancy to the time of presentation rather than the time of creation. Higgins writes of this immediacy and contingency that "by giving blank forms, the most relevant materials for a given time and mentality can be filled in, thus avoiding the appalling irrelevance of perishable materials that are no longer current."[26] In addition, this view aimed to reconsider the whole creative and evaluative superstructure by interrogating core assumptions (such as the separation of artist and audience) rather than peripheral manifestations. "Relativism [is] axiomatic," he wrote.

PLAY, ENGAGEMENT, AND CHANGE

Another model of play is important within the amodernist worldview: that is, play as a model for change and activism. As amodernism rejected some of the core notions associated with modernism, particularly its concern for autonomy, play and its associated strategies for transformation became models for engagement that sought to supplant modernism's model of estrangement. Higgins, and amodernists more generally, contended that the artist must seek to access the arena of social, political, and cultural debate. To this end, play offered a means to realign and reshape cultural practices on the level of engagement rather than alienation. Higgins called upon us as participant observers (as either "artists" or "viewers") to consider how we create or relate to art as well as what comprises our expectations of it. The relation of amodernist works and ideas to society is one of potential vagueness. The seeming indifference of this worldview indicates a shift from a concern for measurable utility (which has traditionally been the basis of recognized activism) to one that celebrates life and the potential engagement in infinite play (the free play of difference).

In this worldview, conceptual or physical boundaries cannot exist other than those that are internally defined in relation to the recognition of associations and difference. This is not to suggest that there are no boundaries in the amodernist worldview, but that they are less important and ultimately inconsequential in the processes of change and creation of possibilities. It is this aspect of amodernism that puts thought into play in such a way that it does not become fixed or predetermined—in the sense that it is developed for some specific utilitarian end, such as solving a problem. Additionally, although rules do exist in infinite play, they are initiating factors rather than delimiting agents. The rules of infinite play are situationally determined and must change through enactment to ensure an expansion of the processes of discourse. The rules of infinite play respond to traditional fixed or predetermined limitations (and social contracts), but only to the degree that they can be countered and the act of play allowed to continue. In children's games, this is clearly seen when the players change the rules in the act of play in order to respond to an event or even possible event that could potentially terminate the play. For this reason, it is impossible to determine how long infinite games can be played (as with amodernism itself), when or if they will end, and even when they started. The freedom inherent in this worldview can be identified with infinity insofar as it affirms a play that can be neither guaranteed nor controlled. Thus many of the works associated with Dada and Fluxus can be said to operate within a set of changing rules, but these rules exist only insofar as they will allow the participants or viewers potentially to continue the play/work infinitely.

A comment that Dick Higgins made in discussing his view of the value of Fluxus is relevant to our broader understanding of the significance that these changes of approach and attitude had for many artists:

I do not believe in amateurishness: that isn't what it is all about. But in amateurism, is simplicity. An art (by which I also mean non-art, if you prefer, so long as it is aesthetic in some way) on which one cannot hang a cycle of professional crafts and dependence. An art which by its very nature denies its perpetrators their daily bread, which must therefore come from somewhere else. Such an art must be given, in the sense that experience is shared: it cannot be placed in the market place and in this way it differs profoundly from the Fluxus-derived "movements" of earth-works or media-hype forms of concept art. Much of that work I enjoy—I even love… I must reject, not because it isn't officially Fluxus, but because it isn't free. It's just so many hat racks for careers to be hung onto. When the name of the artist determines the market value of a work and not its meaning in our lives—beware![27]

By rejecting the modernist notions of art as a professional and an exclusionary praxis as well as the romanticized frames of art as visionary and transcendent, Higgins himself (and amodernism in general) seeks to return to a more direct constitutive engagement. Art becomes not a way to become famous, a career, or even a way to make a living, but something more important—as a social act in its participatory or exemplativist nature. It becomes transformative as well because of this very same inclusivity. Although the open and often seemingly uncritical or playful aspects of Fluxus, mail art, and other amodernist work are sometimes dismissed as insignificant or lacking a serious motivation, this playfulness is, instead, of fundamental import. Through it, art becomes a part of our processes of cognition and gains a new existence as part of a particular time and place—that is, *as* part of our lives rather than as a comment on them. Art is no longer seen as timeless or as a diversion, but rather as a return to the real world. As participant observers in the amodernist experience, we are offered a place to act / play, a set of approaches with which to engage/play, and a value structure that makes sense of the constantly changing world through associations, relations, and participation. The lesson, then, of amodernism is that play is serious business if you understand its cognitive effects and creative potential.

10

SUBVERSIVE TOYS: THE ART OF LILIANA PORTER

FLORENCIA BAZZANO-NELSON

One can be a headless mariachi and still sing like Maria Callas. Many unusual things are possible through playacting in the miniaturized wonderland that Liliana Porter has created in *The Fox in the Mirror, Concert / El zorro en el espejo, concierto,* her most recent short film of 2007 (fig. 51). For example, the tiny wooden mariachi in a blue-painted folkloric costume projected on the shimmering screen holds a microphone up to his missing head, but neither his acephalous condition nor his apparent male gender pose insurmountable obstacles to the beautiful, flowing voice of Maria Callas. How should we read the image of this little singer, at once puzzling and disturbing, vulnerable and enduring? While we consider the matter, the camera lingers on the toy standing still in the midst of the white seamless background that characterizes so many of Porter's works in all media. The musical concert that follows this preliminary vignette unfolds through a series of shots of toys and figurines representing musicians, singers, and dancers. But not all of Porter's actors have been assigned neutral or celebratory roles. As the headless mariachi seems to indicate, signs of trauma and violence are also present in the musical performance, which raises pointed questions about what recent—and perhaps not so recent—historical contexts may be relevant to the many possible readings of this work.

In this chapter, I will examine how Porter uses the playful manipulation of toylike objects in her art as an effective creative strategy that invites viewers to resignify the items she displays in her pieces—especially in *The Fox in the Mirror, Concert*—and thus become actively engaged in the production of polysemic readings that serve to open the structure of the work. I will begin by discussing the integration into Porter's art of the toy as found object, a tactic that began in her silkscreened still lifes of the 1980s and continued in her later photographs and more recent short films. Next, I will address the ludic tactics Porter employs in her pieces and the implications of this methodology when viewed not only from an art-historical but also from a psychological perspective.

TOYS: FROM OBJECT TO ACTOR

When Liliana Porter moved to New York in 1964, the use of toys and play as creative strategies had not yet become significant aspects of her work. She was then a young artist from Argentina,

I would like to acknowledge Liliana Porter's assistance in obtaining the images here included and for generously answering my questions. This essay has also benefitted from the support of the Art History Program of the Newcomb Art Department of Tulane University, for which I am grateful. In addition, I would like to thank Daniel E. Nelson for insightfully editing this essay, and David R. Norris for his helpful suggestions.

where she had been born in 1941. After studying art in Buenos Aires and Mexico City, she finally settled in New York at a time when the art scene seemed to be bubbling with creative effervescence. Porter had already spent a few years refining her already considerable expertise in the technical aspects of printmaking, but the experimental environment she found in Manhattan inspired her to replace her earlier emphasis on technique with a progressively reductive, minimalist aesthetic.[1] By the late 1960s, her approach to printmaking became more conceptualized as she adopted photography-based processes, including silkscreening and photoengraving, and began to experiment with assemblages and installations.[2] Her subjects also changed from the expressionist depictions of anonymous urban dwellers of her earlier New York prints to a concern with humble, ordinary objects whose paradoxical coexistence as two-dimensional images and as readymades challenges our perceptions of everyday reality. At first, these works concentrated on a limited number of items, such as nails, strings, or wrinkled paper. But then, by the end of the 1970s, Porter began collecting small objects, including toys, in flea markets and featuring them in compositions organized as still lifes as she continued to break down barriers between assemblage art and printmaking, reality and fiction.[3]

Porter's earliest still lifes, such as *The Dangerous Game,* a silkscreen on canvas and assemblage of 1978, already depicted toys along with various items associated with studio practice, including crayons, small drawings, and geometric solids, all of which were usually presented in the midst of a seamless, mostly white background. *Alice in Wonderland,* of related interest for its connection with childhood whimsy, became a recurrent feature in the early 1980s, beginning with works such as *The End of the Journey* of 1980, a silkscreen, etching, and chine collé (fig. 52). In this piece, as in others inspired by this particular motif, Porter reproduced Lewis Carroll's book—open to a page in which a drawing of Alice by John Tenniel can be clearly seen—and arranged around it a few toys and other small items. The objects thus displayed functioned as suggestive yet rather static receptors of the imaginative gaze of the viewers.

However, an important change took place in Porter's art toward the mid-1990s, when her still lifes seemed to wake up and come to life. This subtle shift begins to appear in *The Simulacrum II,* an acrylic, silkscreen, and collage on paper from 1992 (fig. 53). In this piece, Porter surrounded three books lying on a white surface with a female dancer in a red dress, a commemorative plate reproducing Cuban photographer Alberto Korda's well-known image of Che Guevara, a small figure of Mickey Mouse, and a green Donald Duck toy. While the books present a static mystery to viewers, who may wonder what these volumes are (a book of poems by Jorge Luis Borges, Michel Foucault's *This Is Not a Pipe,* and Jean Baudrillard's *Simulacra and Simulation*), the arrangement of the three figures attracts the eye in a more dynamic way. They appear to move around the space as if they had a life of their own, especially the Disney characters, who seem to interact with their immediate context: thus we see Donald happily following a path marked for him on the ground and Mickey looking back toward Che with a friendly smile. The way Porter has displayed these found objects lends them a sense of inner energy, a metaphoric construction that can be modified by the knowledge of these characters as active personalities that viewers bring into their reading of the work.

Once Porter embraced the metaphoric nature of these toylike objects, she quickly simplified her creative process. Her complex manipulations of printmaking techniques were meant to call attention to the ambiguous nature of reality by contrasting originals with copies through the use of various media while at the same time making this self-referential process evident to the eye. But as she came to accept that all reality can be a form of representation—a simulacrum, on occasion—she began to work directly with photography and film.[4] Simultaneously, she adopted a new cast of anthropomorphized toys that no longer behaved like the passive objects of her earlier still lifes. Through her playful manipulations, these new characters were able to project a sense of inner life and engage the viewers in psychologically complex ways.[5] In part, this ability to connect with the public came from the sense of history and cultural specificity that these objects display. For while Porter collected them over the years in flea markets in New York, Latin America, and Europe, many of them look as if they were produced when she was a child, which probably explains why she was subconsciously attracted to their visual style. The illusion of an interior psychological presence is also generated when Porter presents the specificity of these figurines in the manner of "true studio portraits," in the words of art critic Gerardo Mosquera.[6]

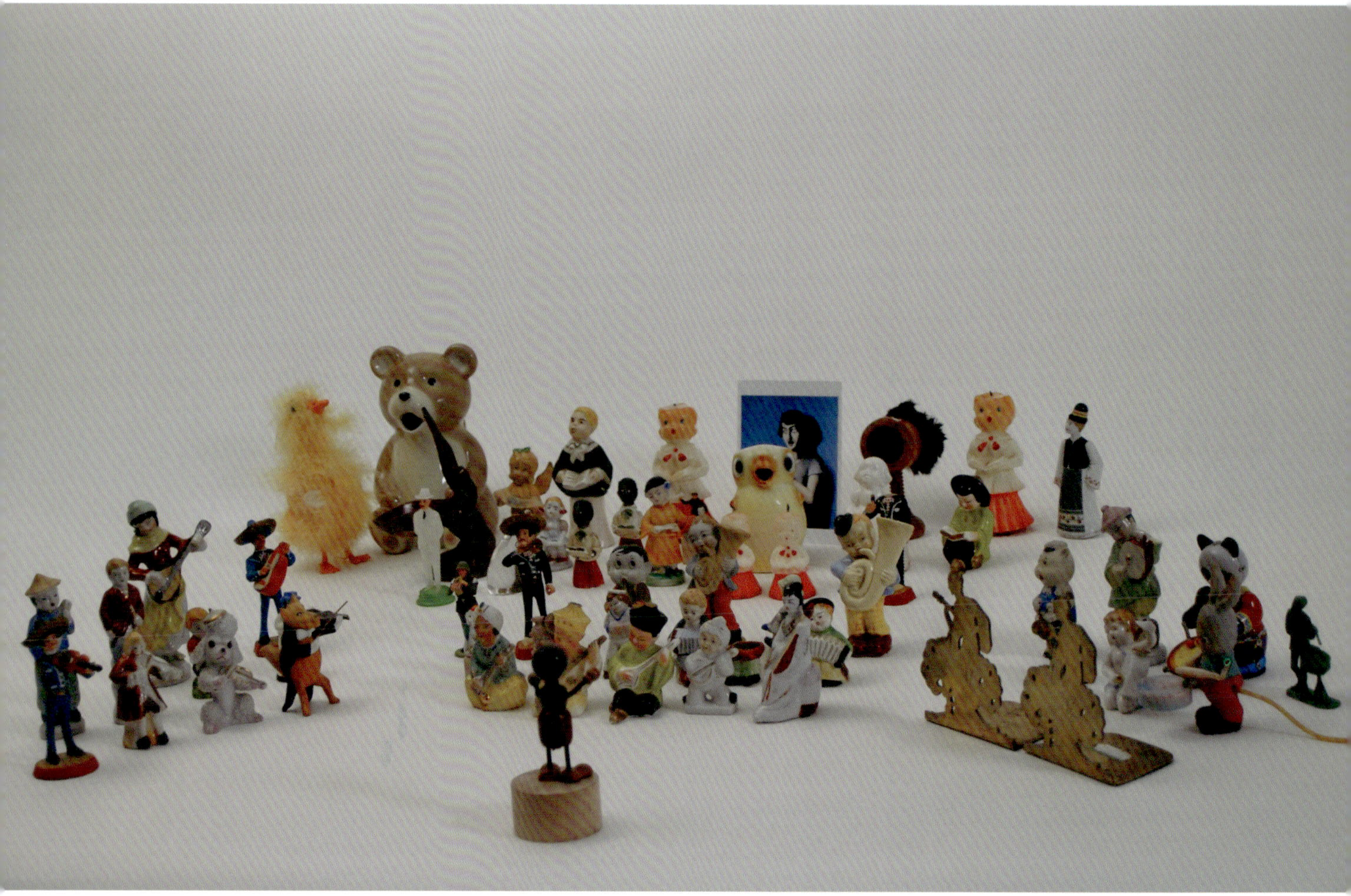

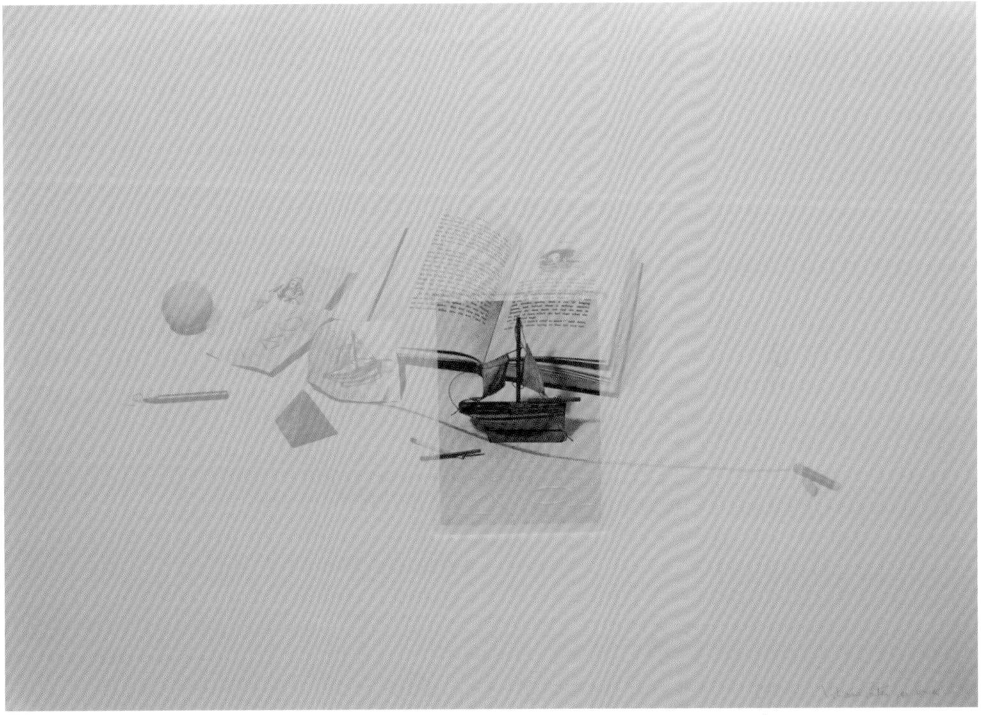

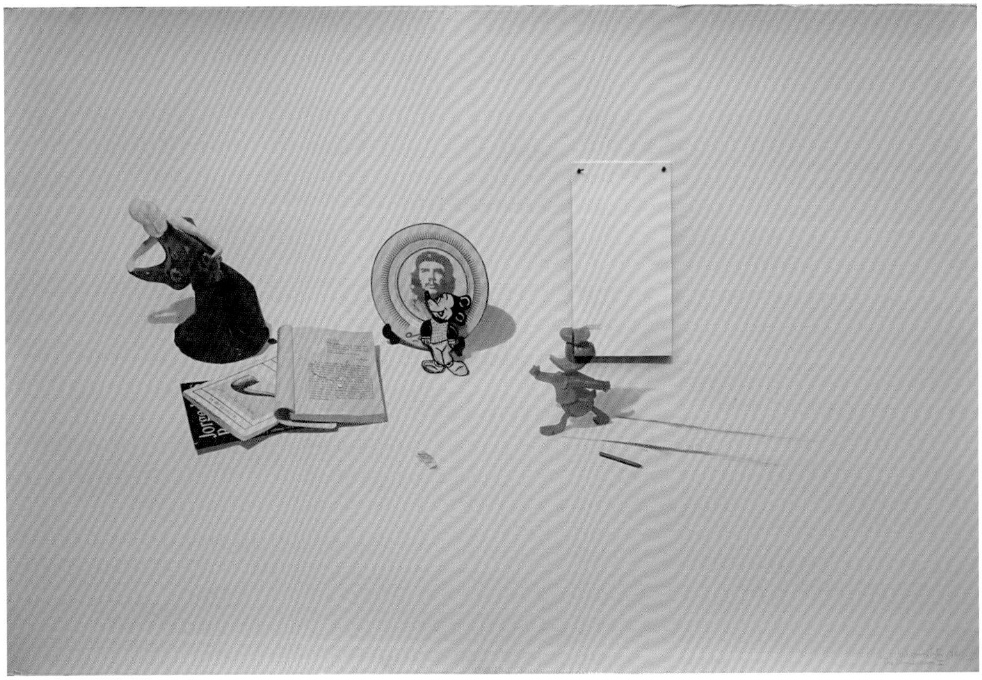

FIG. 51

Liliana Porter, still from *The Fox in the Mirror, Concert / El zorro en el espejo, concierto,* 2007, video, twenty minutes.

FIG. 52

Liliana Porter, *The End of the Journey,* 1980, silkscreen, etching, and chine collé, 25.5 × 38 inches.

FIG. 53

Liliana Porter, *The Simulacrum II,* 1992, acrylic, silkscreen, and collage on paper. Collection Yolanda Santos Garza, New York.

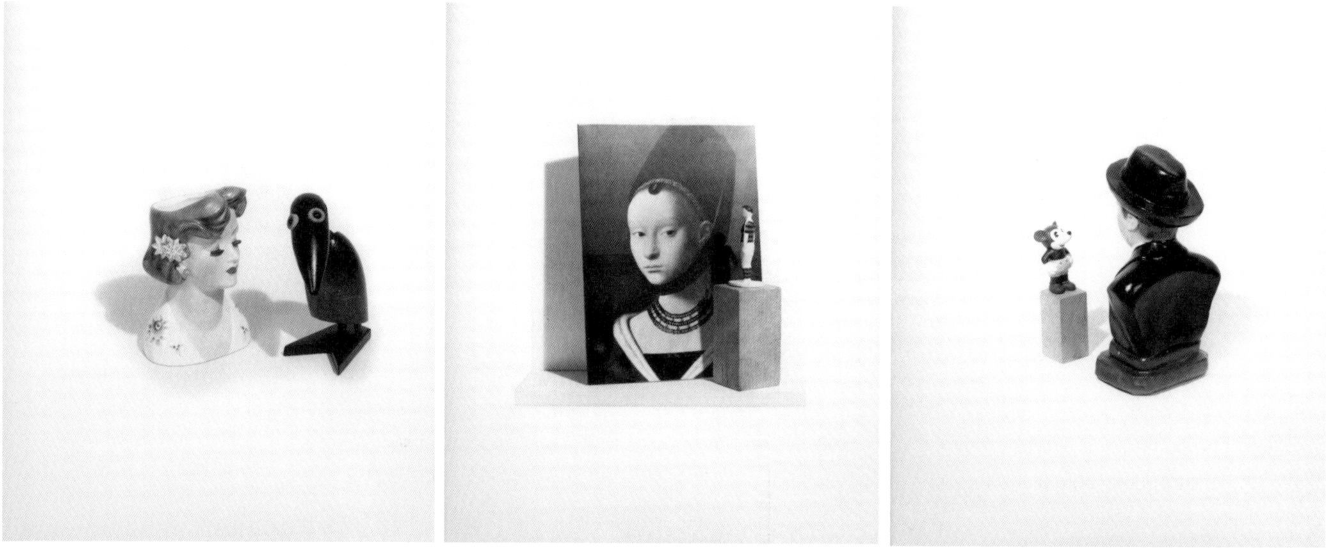

FIG. 54

Liliana Porter, *Dialogues (with Petrus Christus Postcard),* 1995, silver gelatin prints, 11 × 14 inches each, triptych.

FIG. 55

Liliana Porter, *Death Threat,* 1995, Cibachrome print, 16-inch diameter.

In the set of black-and-white silver-gelatin prints entitled *Dialogues (with Petrus Christus Postcard)* of 1995, the definition of each object as a character with a certain cultural specificity is an important aspect of the piece's complexity since the dialogical structure of the work must, in fact, bridge the divides of time periods, cultures, and even species represented (fig. 54). Through such playful manipulations, Porter brings together, for instance, a 1940s lady-head vase and a blackbird cardholder, a small Brazilian soccer player and a postcard with a fifteenth-century young woman painted by Petrus Christus, as well as a tiny, plastic Mickey Mouse and a polychromed plaster bust of the well-known Venezuelan popular saint Dr. José Gregorio Hernández. What might such dissimilar characters say to one another? What secrets might be exchanged in these dialogues? The viewer can only wonder. But judging from the type of wide-eyed looks, uneasy stares, and concentrated expressions on the faces of these figurines, Porter's chosen playthings rarely enjoy a truly happy or purely innocent existence, a fact that opens the door to even more unsettling questions.

This kind of complexity in the use of toys is far from unique in contemporary art. Toys have appeared with such surprising frequency in the art of the last fifteen years that cultural historian Eva Forgacs has affirmed that "an ocean of toy-based art works" has surged through contemporary art in the United States and

Europe.[7] Among those artists who have used toy-based imagery, one could mention Gottfried Helnwein, Mike Kelley, Takashi Murakami, Laurie Simmons, and Heidi Zumbrun. But their art is almost never exclusively about children or about childhood. In fact, as in Porter's case, it engages viewers at multiple levels and asks challenging questions about life experiences, creativity, cultural diversity, and even the status of toys as commodities in contemporary society. Thus, the reasons these artists have for working with toys are remarkably different, as are their ways of integrating them into their work.[8]

When examining Porter's oeuvre from the late 1970s to the mid-1990s, we see that the shift from including a few selected toys in her prints and assemblages to offering a more central role to the anthropomorphic playthings she portrays in her photographs and short films resulted in the development of what can be best described as the use of play as a creative strategy.[9] This creative play involved manipulating these toylike objects and turning them into active "characters" in the deceptively simple imaginary scenes captured in photographs such as *Dialogues (with Petrus Christus Postcard)* or *Death Threat* of 1995 (fig. 55). In the latter, a Cibachrome print featuring a yellow ceramic piggy bank and a small-armed man, Porter has set up a scene in which the rotund, smiling, unsuspecting pig is being threatened by the toy rifleman. Only in our imagination can we consider the various possible outcomes of this scene, but Porter herself gave it one possible resolution in her second film, *Drum Solo / Solo de tambor* from 2000 (16 mm, nineteen minutes). Like her first short film, *For you / Para usted* of 1999 (16 mm, sixteen minutes),[10] *Drum Solo* was also structured as a series of short vignettes, one of which was appropriately subtitled *Death Threat*. In it, we again encounter the friendly piggy bank accosted by a white rifleman. Suddenly a shot rings out as a small pile of yellow dust appears where the pig once stood. The unpredictable outcome—not without a touch of black humor—is quite representative of the subversive tone of these short movies in which the unexpected and humorous balance out the sentimental and dramatic.[11]

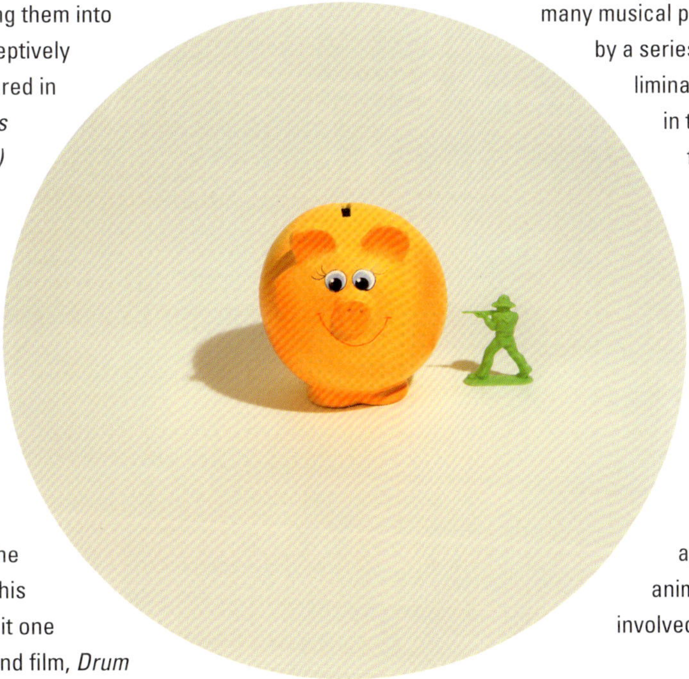

Only a small step separates the anthropomorphic tableaux of her photographs from the "playacted" vignettes in her films *For you* and *Drum Solo,* which involved minimal animation, creative editing, and special effects. Both movies were divided into brief segments—twenty-two and twenty-eight, respectively —with certain repeating themes that gave them a sense of unity. In contrast, *Fox in the Mirror, Concert / El zorro en el espejo, concierto* from 2007 (digital video, twenty minutes), is a more ambitious project because it is structured in a holistic way around the theme of a musical concert (figs. 51 and 56a and b). However, the type of creative play the artist used to work with her readymade actors in this film is the same as in previous works.

Porter directed and produced *Fox in the Mirror* with the assistance of a professional staff.[12] It follows the structure of many musical performances in that it is introduced by a series of brief vignettes labeled as preliminary and rehearsal scenes (nineteen in total). The second part of the movie, the concert itself, is divided into two halves separated by a short intermission. In the various scenes, the artist featured toys, kitsch figurines, functional knickknacks, and other readymades that have in common a musical theme. Thus most of the characters, with a few notable exceptions, are singers, dancers, or musicians who are presented—again, with minimal recourse to animation or special effects—as actors involved in a miniature musical concert.

PLAYGROUNDS AND TRANSITIONAL SPACES

The musical structure of the concert lends the film its narrative logic, but in reality Porter's manipulation of her toylike readymades is closer to the spontaneous quality of children's play than to the rule-oriented environment of organized games.

FIGS. 56A AND 56B

Liliana Porter, still from *The Fox in the Mirror, Concert/ El zorro en el espejo, concierto,* 2007, video, twenty minutes.

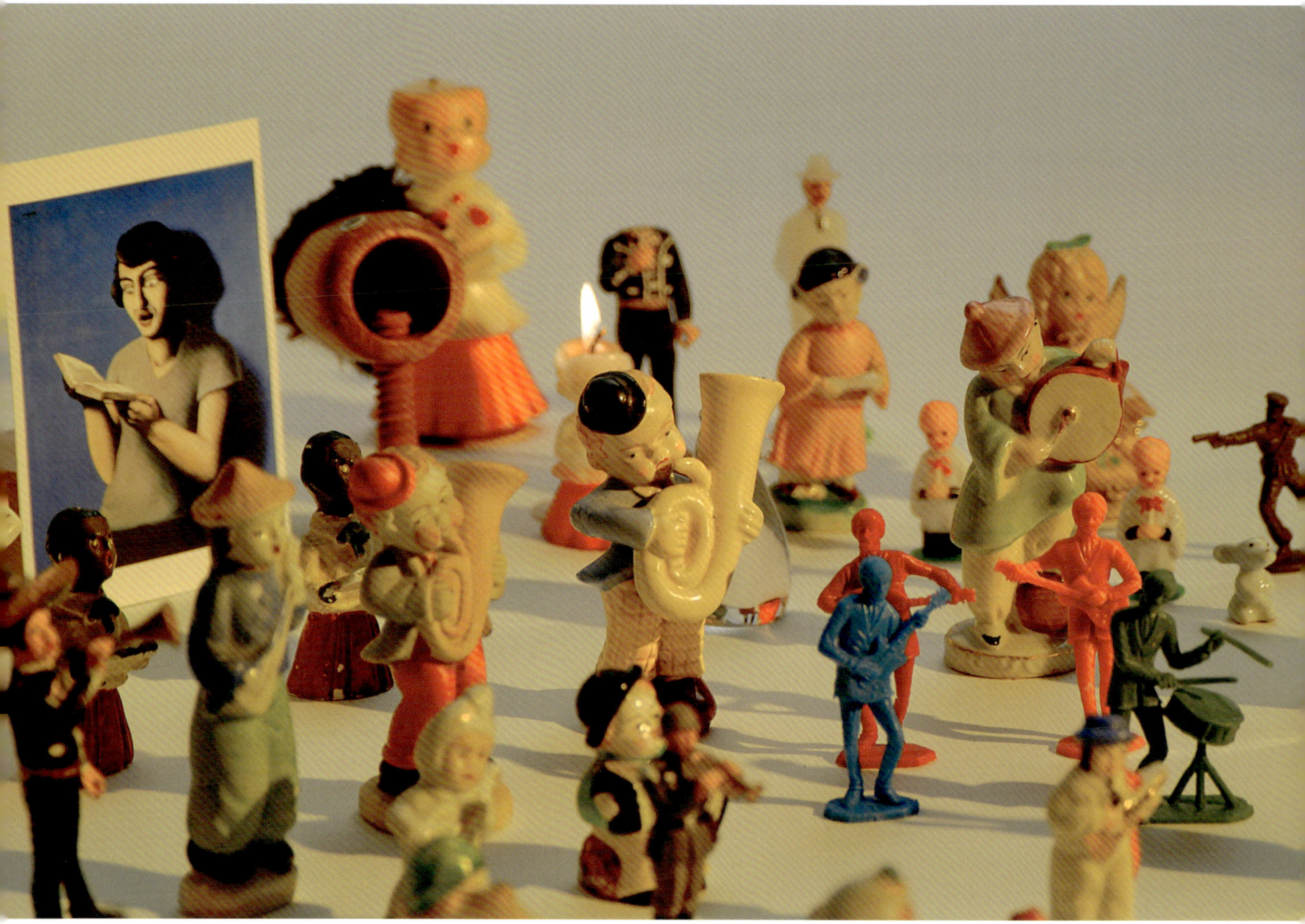

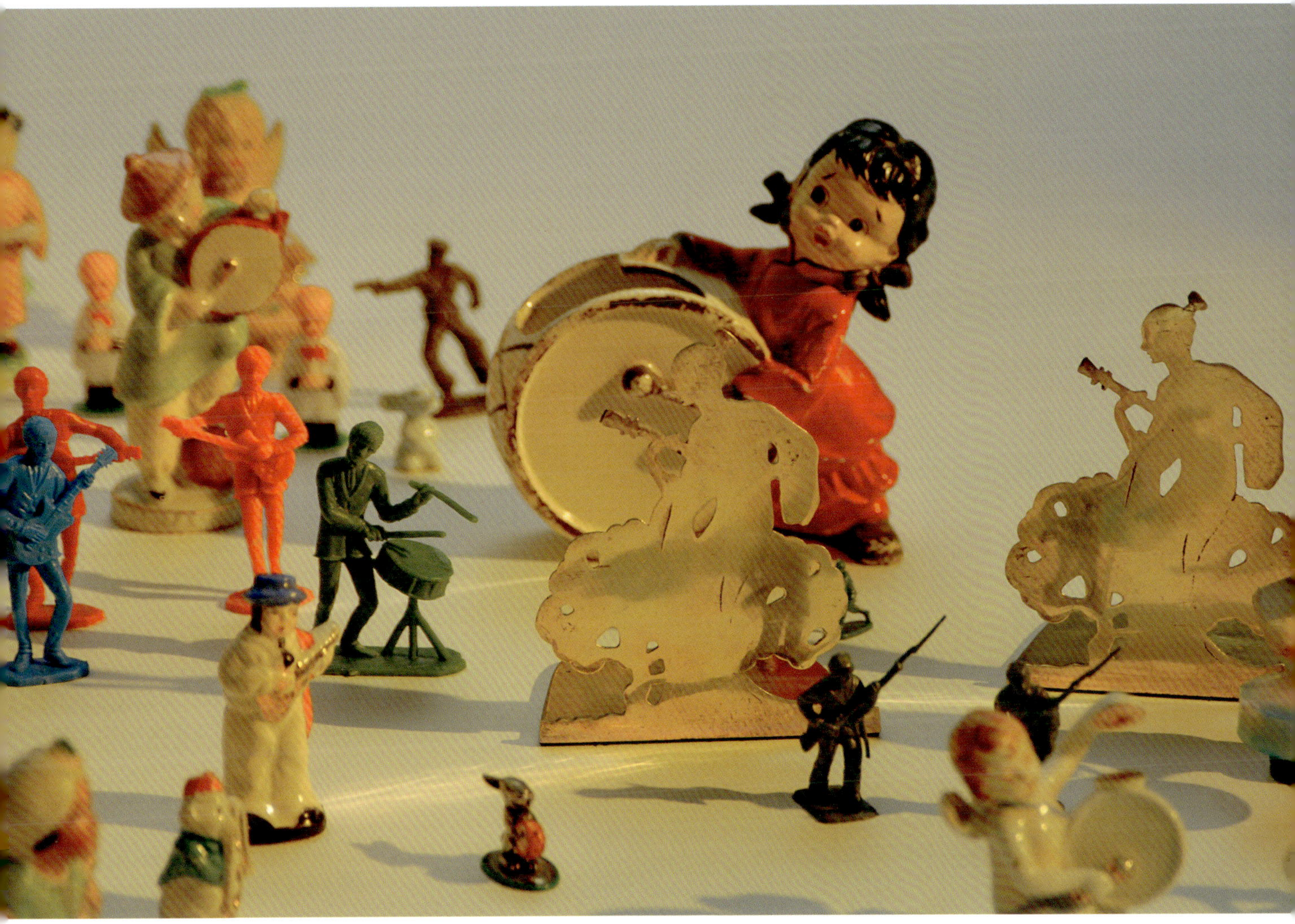

Charles Baudelaire, who has written quite perceptibly about children and toys, recognized early on that "all children talk to their toys; the toys become actors in the great drama of life, reduced in size by the *camera obscura* of their little brains."[13] Similarly, Walter Benjamin noted that "when children think up stories[,] they are like theatre-producers who refuse to be bound by 'sense.'"[14] In *The Fox in the Mirror,* the artist—either through the eye of the camera or through a pair of anonymous hands—plays with various figurines. She arranges them so they seem to be interacting with one another in the white, stagelike space that gives them room to move and at the same time isolates them as if they were actors performing in a play or musicians playing a concert. The overlap in meaning, at least in English, in reference to the word *play,* which can be used to signify participating in organized games, handling or using toys, acting in a theater, or performing music, is rather telling. In fact, *art* and *play* are interrelated activities comparable in their variety and vastness; therefore, defining them is a task that clearly exceeds the limits of this chapter.[15]

My own reading of *play*—following various scholars who have studied the subject from a psychological and cultural perspective[16]—is to consider it as a spontaneous and voluntary activity normally defined not by the content of the activity itself but rather by the experience of the player.[17] Only when we are in the midst of such an activity can we determine if it feels more constrained or alienating, and thus closer to capitalist labor, or more free and energizing, and thus more like play. When we play, we conceptually accept and follow a different set of rules from the ones we normally apply in everyday life.[18] Thus, play is an autonomous activity performed in a simulative mode that creates a degree of contrast between the simulation and the behavior from which it derives. However, according to Baudrillard, one could argue that clear-cut distinctions between simulative and nonsimulative realities are no longer possible.[19]

In terms of ordinary experience, in fact, there is no clear separation between play and reality, only relative perspectives. Depending on the context, play and games can function like serious business, as, for instance, in professional sports. On the other hand, any type of work can also become a pleasurable, playlike experience, as, for instance, in the arts. This is especially true if the activity is performed in contrast to other, more serious or compulsory duties by a player who, by following the rules of the game or by greatly enjoying the work, attains a temporary suspension of ordinary life comparable to a flow state or to the kind of suspension of disbelief that operates when we watch a movie or read a novel.[20]

Players willingly obey the illusion (from the Latin *illusio, illudere* or *inludere,* which means "in play") operating within a game in order to create "temporary worlds within the ordinary world, dedicated to the performance of an act apart."[21] According to the often-quoted Dutch cultural historian Johan Huizinga, who was among the first scholars to explore the historical relationships of play to law, war, poetry, philosophy, and the arts, this paradoxical relationship between reality and play has existed for centuries in Western contexts such as the Olympic games, other religious festivals, and carnival celebrations, in which the arts, including music and dancing, often played an important role in the process of establishing a temporary and separate space.[22] British psychiatrist Donald W. Winnicott argued that this space comes ultimately from the natural process of separation of the child from the mother. For as babies adopt specific items as transitional objects—security blankets or teddy bears, to name some common examples—they generate through their creative play an intermediary space between themselves and their environment. Progressively, this transitional space becomes the potential site for creative and cultural experiences.[23]

Play, by most accounts, is an activity that takes place in the world but at the same time is separate from prosaic existence. In my discussion of *The Fox in the Mirror, Concert,* I will show that while Porter generates in her movie a similarly paradoxical space—in which reality is banished on a temporary basis—she does so with a self-aware, often ironic intent, almost as if, in her own words, we were "watching a movie with the lights on."[24] Such an approach contributes to the humorous, dramatic tension of her pieces. Her toys, often mass-produced kitsch, subvert with their cultural or historical specificities the sense of separation that the space of play creates. Even more important, Porter's use of play as a creative strategy functions as an invitation to the viewers to enter, at least in their imagination, into the white playgrounds of the film and contribute to the meaning of the images by resignifying what they see with their own poetic or narrative readings.

In a general way, the vicarious manner in which Porter, through her playful action, makes viewers relate to her miniaturized world is reminiscent of Margaret Lowenfeld's "World Technique," also known as sandtray or sandplay therapy.[25] As first designed, this method of psychotherapy involved a large tray with dry sand, some water, and a cabinet containing little drawers filled with miniature versions of things one could find in the real world organized by type. According to Lowenfeld's somewhat Borgesian categories,[26] the classification began with people, divided into ordinary (regular people in various positions), military (including equipment), and special (ranging from gnomes to people from other cultures), and continued with houses, trees, fences, animals (wild and domesticated), transport (roads, rails, and boats), street signs, and miscellaneous.

All these items should be placed in a cabinet with drawers so the patients could access them without feeling overwhelmed by their variety and number.[27] As patients played with these items, they symbolically created a world of their own on the blank slate of the sandtray, thereby engaging in an activity that became part of the therapeutic process of analysis. Over the years, many other therapists have adopted different versions of this technique because of the usefulness of these toylike objects in mediating the healing process. In terms of Porter's movie, her miniature worlds seem to function in a comparable way by opening a door to the imagination so that viewers can create their own stories about the worlds they observe, even with regard to the most impossible things they encounter, like headless mariachis with beautiful voices.

WET DUCKS, CHINESE PROLETARIANS, AND DANCING COUPLES

The Fox in the Mirror, Concert opens with an introductory text by Emanuel Swedenborg from his book *Arquitectura del cielo* [*Architecture of Heaven*], which appears translated into both English and Spanish. Its English version reads the following way: "Even though things keep happening in sequence and progressing in heaven the way they do in the world, still angels have no notion or concept of time and space. The lack is so complete that they simply do not know what time and space are."[28] Porter had various reasons for choosing this text, including the fact that Swedenborg was often cited by Jorge Luis Borges, one of her favorite authors, but the reference to a group of beings who escape the basic constraints of ordinary life—time and space—seems particularly relevant to this toy wonderland that exists in the white, boundless space that frames most shots in the film.

The first part of this miniature concert consists of a series of vignettes organized into two groups entitled "Preliminaries / Preliminares" and "Rehearsal / Ensayo."[29] "Preliminaries" has ten vignettes titled by cardinal numbers, while "Rehearsal" has nine segments, some untitled and some titled simply by a punctuation mark. Beginning with the headless mariachi, they vary in their use of music (or lack thereof), the type of object featured, and even the range of motion the toys display. For instance, segment "IV" features a postcard with an image by the Belgian painter René Magritte, *The Subjugated Reader* from 1928. The camera slowly brings into focus the powerful image of a woman reading an open book that she holds in her hands, her face distorted in a grimace of horror or surprise. Nonetheless, she could be singing if the character is seen in the proper context. The stillness of this object contrasts with the following vignette, which features a roly-poly doll of the type that always rolls back and then rights itself when punched. Its back-and-forth motion adds a kind of hypnotic dynamism to the scene.

Like Porter's earlier movies, "Preliminaries" and "Rehearsal" feature a series of recurrent motifs that give a sense of thematic unity to the whole. These motifs can be divided into three categories: the figure of the chicken, images of couples, and labor-related images. In "Preliminaries," the duck—which seems a somewhat realistic version of a half-grown bird—appears as part of the "V–VIII" segments. It stands alone with its long yellow feathers blowing in a wind that is strong enough to topple it and blow it away out of the frame. The figure returns in segment "IX" along with the sound of distant sirens and a version of the song "Nobody's Baby" sung by Sylvia Meyer, the music producer for the film. Soon, water begins to fall from above, drenching the duck, until it stands in a pool of water looking rather pathetic. Viewers may read this segment in many ways, but coming from New Orleans, I can see how it would be easy to project many meanings regarding Hurricane Katrina and subsequent flooding onto the image of the soaked bird. "Rehearsal" begins with another duck vignette. In this case, the bird receives a kind of haircut: a hand with a small pair of scissors methodically cuts the duck's long yellow feathers, which fall, rather sadly, at its feet as we wonder what to make of these actions.

The second thematic group involves pairings, usually of couples dancing together, although they are shown in other forms as well. In "Preliminaries," two dancing couples appear in "V–VIII," but in spite of sharing the same choirlike music, they move at a different speeds, as if following dissimilar internal rhythms. The male figure in the larger couple, which turns slowly on its base, is a lighted candle with drops of wax rolling slowly down its face. The smaller couple is a windup toy. It goes round and round in the white space, moving much faster than the previous couple, coming in and out of the frame in a rather frantic way. The two couples return again in "Rehearsal," the male in the candle-couple still burning away, and the smaller couple moving even faster at the pace set by the animated music. Other pairings include two metal bookends in the shape of Asian musicians playing wind instruments, and a set of salt-and-pepper shakers, but one of the two figures is obviously missing. This lack is echoed in the music, based in part on popular nineteenth-century lyrics from Argentina (but that were actually brought from Spain) and presented in the form of a tango rather than in the expected folkloric musical style.[30] The female voice sings "I have curtains with black velvet to put my bed in mourning if you forget me."[31] The theme of the loss of a loved one will return again during the concert, which I will discuss below in "The Last Dance."

The third thematic group, loosely described as labor-related images, includes two kitsch objects from communist China that extol Mao's proletarian revolution. The first of these items, a watch bought in China and given to Porter as a gift by a friend, is featured at the end of the "Preliminaries" section. It shows Mao saluting while a female voice sings "So long, farewell," the song from the *Sound of Music,* a Rodgers and Hammerstein musical that was made into a movie in 1965, the year before Mao's "Great Proletarian Cultural Revolution" began in the People's Republic. The kitsch aesthetic of the watch and the obvious failure of Mao's ideals are humorously reflected in the leave-taking implied by the lyrics.[32]

The second item, featured at the very end of the "Rehearsal," is a rather complex polychrome ceramic object representing a group of five young revolutionaries, which Porter purchased in Chinatown in Toronto.[33] Whether they are students or members of the proletariat is impossible to tell without reading the Chinese ideographs they hold aloft along with Mao's *Little Red Book.* The idealism represented in this shiny knickknack contrasts greatly with Meyer's choice of music, a soulful African American gospel song entitled "Soon I Will Be Done with the Troubles of This World." The communist propaganda and sense of earth-bound hope of the revolutionaries seem to stand in opposition to the Christian gospel song and the implied pessimism of those preparing to leave this life in search of a more spiritual, heavenly home where there will be no more tears. Although both show different kinds of faith, according to Porter there is a great deal of sadness in this scene because of its sense of transience: ideals pass, optimism vanishes, life ends.[34]

The ironic critique implied in the perception of utopian revolutionary dogma as outmoded indicates that the young people represented in the sculpture—just as the people who made the sculpture—may no longer be interested in the same politics that failed them in the past and continues to fail them in the present. In fact, one needs only to recall the rampant spread of laissez-faire capitalism in many areas of China that has left the environment, workers, and consumers vulnerable to grave dangers in China and abroad. Porter did not personally connect these representations of a communist proletarian revolution with the theme of labor, which has emerged as an important motif in her recent art. But then, how do we read Porter's subversively paradoxical use of these objects made in communist China, which, according to Marxist theory, are the product of nonalienated labor and thus related to the notion of play? Given that the working conditions for most proletarian laborers in China are so far removed on many levels from what I would call play, I read these images of mass-produced propagandistic kitsch as carrying highly critical and ironic connotations that bring out the ideological dimensions of the relationship between play and labor.

For Porter, the issue behind the representation of workers is not one fixed by ideology alone, although such artworks easily lend themselves to more political or social interpretations, especially considering the configuration of Porter's pieces about labor. In recent years, she has developed a series of installations based on the notion of "forced labor," using figures involved in tasks such as shoveling a pile of dirt or moving a mountain of hay that is disproportionately much larger than the worker. However, for her, such constructed situations go beyond their immediacy as literal social critiques in order to function as metaphors for how the vastness of the universe overwhelms our attempts to make sense of it, thereby generating a cognitive and metaphysical process endlessly delayed.[35] Regardless of how the artist, critics, or viewers choose to read these works, in *The Fox in the Mirror* the situation becomes even more complex, since no simple contrast between labor and play is possible when musicians—or artists—are involved. In such cases, labor and play happen simultaneously, providing an interesting example of nonalienated labor in which a pleasurable flow-state is often attained among practitioners and performers, except when it is disrupted by traumatic or violent events.

THE LAST DANCE

Returning to the fictional world portrayed in the movie, after the nine vignettes of the rehearsal, the first part of the concert proper starts, its action advancing for several minutes without any pauses for titles—for time seems to move much faster now, as does the generally upbeat music. The beginning, accompanied by wind instruments, involves a quick succession of images showing a series of figurines, including the Asian bookends, a mariachi trumpet player, and the small couple rapidly spinning. Then, as the choir begins to sing, the toy fox, the orchestra's violin soloist, is introduced. He appears reflected under the spotlight in a round mirror, his face emphasized by dramatic camera angles. The conductor turns out to be a wooden Mickey Mouse lacking ears or perhaps any hearing all together. This is a metaphorically troubling situation for a leader who may not hear his people, but, as we know, it is not an insurmountable problem, for, in play, anything is possible.[36] He briefly looks at us before turning, through the magic of editing, to face his miniature orchestra, which stands around him in position supposedly playing the music we hear. As the camera gives us a general view of the group, we recognize many of the figures already introduced in the early sections of the film standing still with their instruments and some new musicians, who are members of the choir, such as a couple of burning candles in the shape of singing altar boys and a mariachi with a missing arm.

The first part of the concert seems to have two purposes: to introduce the musicians to the viewers, which happens in more detail as the concert progresses, and to get viewers used to playing the game of connecting the inanimate objects appearing on the screen with the sound of the music playing, thus developing their own mental narratives to explain the images they see in front of them. As the tempo of the music increases and the enhanced percussion makes it more rhythmic, the camera closes in on the different musicians and begins to play with the details of their faces and instruments.[37] Next, we see the dancers again. By now, the male in the candle-couple has burned down to his shoulders and is beginning to create a hollow with a rosy light, both lovely and increasingly sinister, shining within. The small couple spins quickly among the other dancers, which include two new pairs dressed in wedding clothes, one static, and the other, a music box, rotating on its axis. The tempo, emphasized throughout, becomes more accelerated, with most couples appearing to move at a faster pace, until a small porcelain girl joins in the dance, thanks to a basic animation technique, and the first part of the concert comes to an end.

The puzzling atmosphere created by the introduction of these characters presents an even more direct challenge to the viewer in the "Intermission / Intervalo." It begins with the figure of a small ceramic mouse in the middle of a white field accompanied by the same music as in the first part, which, paradoxically, has not stopped. Then, suddenly, a large metal hammer hits the mouse and pushes it through a hole in the surface of the white support. A hand with a pair of pliers tries to grab the figurine, barely visible inside the hole, but cannot as the camera closes in on the action and the animated music ends abruptly. This unforeseen event—a sort of kitsch version of "Bambi meets Godzilla"—and the black humor it implies by it jolts viewers into reconsidering the kind of sentiments they may be projecting onto these found objects.[38] Is it all an illusion, or should we read indications of trauma in the maimed bodies of the performers? Should we see a link between the different types of couples dancing and their emotional life? Are these representations related to notions of love and violence or labor and revolution? The blow of the hammer shatters our suspension of disbelief, forcing us to become more aware of the multiplicity of questions raised by Porter's images. This quick dissolution of the space of play is not only an expedient way to create a conceptual intermission but also helps set a more disconcerting mood at the opening of the concert's second movement.[39]

In terms of the music, the second part of the concert repeats the same short, upbeat composition Meyer created in the first half but emphasizes more voices and sounds meant to highlight various players as the camera focuses on them.[40] Very slowly, the viewer begins to notice standing among the musicians the figures of toy soldiers made of either dark plastic or metal and holding guns or rifles. They are especially noticeable around a group of four rock musicians that look like inexpensive plastic replicas of the Beatles. As soldiers surround the young rockers, the opera singer returns and the camera focuses on the head of a soldier. Then, the sound of cymbals establishes a subtle change of direction in the movie as it turns toward close-ups of the orchestra members, including images of physical injury, such as a candle singer melting away or a one-armed mariachi violin player. A general view of the orchestra does not seem to dispel the feeling of tension that begins to build up from the juxtaposition of such images; to the contrary, the sound of an emergency siren soon overwhelms the music for a few seconds, confirming the uneasy mood. In fact, in the next scene the figurines begin to accumulate rather chaotically around the fox playing in their midst, as if he had taken over the role of director while the couples continue to dance on the darkened stage. The small pair moves quickly about the space, but the concert ends with the image of the candle-couple, whose male partner has been almost completely consumed by the flame. The woman now dances holding a large hollow cavity in front of her. A weak reddish light glows within, illuminating the surrounding darkness until the music ends and the candle is extinguished.

I could weave many alternative narratives from what is essentially a work with the open structure that Porter has favored for many years. Her art has seldom been involved with politics in a direct or overt fashion, preferring rather to question our more fundamental assumptions regarding the way we perceive reality in the first place. However, in this film, suggestions of war and violence, disaster and trauma, death and loss, seem to become intrinsic parts of the narrative in a dramatically enhanced way that is new to Porter's oeuvre. We see here a significant iconographic shift, which is hardly surprising considering that the artist was involved in protesting in New York the spread of military regimes in Latin America during the 1970s and early 1980s. Just after that period of political activism, Porter moved her home and studio to Tribeca in Lower Manhattan, so the events of 9/11 were particularly stressful for her and her family. Perhaps many viewers will see in the siren blowing and in the disappearing candle figures references to those loved ones who were lost in these acts of violence.

Nor can one escape the constant news about the wars in Afghanistan and Iraq. Even Porter has recognized that this particular video involves "more evident themes, such as death, war, violence, inexorable time, the sensation that something goes on and on and there is no way to stop it. It is the influence of the context: one turns the television on and that appears all the time."[41] This interpretation opens a narrative that accommodates not only the more dramatic intrusions of the real—the sudden invasion of the soldiers, who seem to take over the concert—but also the more indirect signs of the war: the maimed bodies, the ravaged couples, and the loss of social harmony. However, since part of the process of suspending disbelief is to enter into the movie in our imaginations and play with the toys Porter projects onto the screen, alternative readings will no doubt emerge from the subjective experiences viewers bring with them to the work.

CONCLUSION: THE SUBVERSIVE LIFE OF TOYS

This process of resignification that Porter opens for her toys and figurines is rather subversive for various reasons. First, the artist often places objects that are clearly of popular or kitsch origin next to others that are part of what has traditionally been called "high culture," in the process completely obliterating their differences as well as the taxonomies that support such differentiations. Thus, all of her playthings become part of the same game and contribute in comparable ways to subjective interpretations that allow viewers to open the structure of the work. Second, by placing these mass-produced found objects into the separate realm of play, where they can become anything the imagination chooses them to be, Porter actively removes them from the commercial realm.[42] Finally, this subversive inversion of the mercantile order that created and discarded these items is complemented by the fact that the artist also engages play—the opposite of labor—as an activity that counters alienation, promotes therapeutic healing, supports critical thinking, and succeeds in enticing the inner child of the viewer into joining her in playing games and breaking rules.

CONTEMPORARY ARTISTS' VIEWS ON PLAY AND GAMES IN NEW MEDIA AND PUBLIC PRACTICES

Part II

1

DISSOLVING THE MAGIC CIRCLE OF PLAY: LESSONS FROM SITUATIONIST GAMING

ANNE-MARIE SCHLEINER

Due to its marginal existence in relation to the oppressive reality of work, play is often regarded as fictitious. But the work of the situationists is precisely the preparation of ludic possibilities to come.

—GUY DEBORD

In recent years, commentators on game culture and ludology have undertaken the task of analyzing and structuring play. Such work has been strongly influenced by the Dutch researcher Johan Huizinga's 1938 study of play, *Homo Ludens,* and Roger Callois's later structuralist elaborations of Huizinga's research.[1] In this chapter, I will draw on a different stream of thought from the mid-twentieth century (though one also informed by Huizinga, but not exclusively)—that of the Paris Situationist artists and architects, including Guy Debord and Gilles Ivain (also known as Ivan Chtcheglov). A number of important engagements with play and games by the Situationists are newly relevant today. Rather than offer a historical assessment of Situationism's theories, I will take cues from their writings to reconsider the potential of games in art. I find useful their critique of play within but nevertheless resistant to capitalism (and, by extension, imperialism and militarism), their architectural proposals for "player" navigation and transformation of urban "psychogeographic" zones (what we might call "ludic architecture"), their analysis of leisure and nonleisure activities, and their repurposing of Dadaist negativity. These proposals all have direct relevance to what McKenzie Wark calls our contemporary condition of "Gamespace."[2]

LESSON 1: FREEING PLAY

A promising tactic for the early Situationists was the unpredictable yet forceful potential of play—what anthropologist Victor Turner termed the "liminoid," or the freeing and transformational, moments of play when the normal roles and rules of a community or society are relaxed.[3] After these temporary situations, "players" settle once more into fixed roles. The Situationists proposed to adopt this liminoid "subjunctive mood" (when anything can happen) into a more general approach, a way of doing and being in the everyday, in order to transform material life with ludic actions. As Debord remarked, "We must develop a systematic intervention based on the complex factors of two components in perpetual interaction: the material environment of life and the behaviors which it gives rise to and which radically transform it .... Our action on behavior, linked with other desirable aspects of a revolution in mores, can be briefly defined as the invention of games of an essentially new type."[4] Situationist games do not respect the boundary between play and work, leisure and nonleisure, between "real life" and Huizinga's "magic circle," the separation from "normal space" that facilitates immersion in games and play. Situationist games are not sports and are not relegated to sports stadiums, arcades, or Playstation home entertainment setups. Situationist games bleed into the city, the workplace, the buyplace, the personal computer, the mobile phone, public and private transportation and communication, and into and inside escapist rule-based game environments themselves. In transgressing the "magic circle," a Situationist gaming tactic attempts to give transformative potential not just to play but to "normal" life.

LESSON 2: WRETCHED WINNINGS, OR CHALLENGING COMPETITION

The feeling of the importance of winning in the game, that it is about concrete satisfactions—or, more often than not, illusions—is the wretched product of a wretched society.

—GUY DEBORD

As Debord's quote above indicates, the Situationists were critical of the competitive aspects of play, what Caillois called "agon." For them, competition was complicit with capitalism, with the British working-class fans' mindless absorption in football, with the struggle to obtain material goods, with doing whatever it takes to be the last Survivor on the island, and playing to get the biggest family home in the Sims neighborhood. The Situationists, like avid gamers, rejected the modern division between production and consumption, active work versus passive leisure. Nevertheless, they did acknowledge that an element of competition might be necessary in their games: "The only success that can be conceived in play is the immediate success of its ambiance, and the constant augmentation of its powers...play cannot be completely emancipated from a competitive aspect."[5] In our adaptation of Situationist games, perhaps we allow for a degree of competition, among other motivating playful components. Moreover, for the Situationists, ludic actions were also "moral choices," and therefore the competitive drive should be questioned.

LESSON 3: VIRTUAL GAME WORLDS: TOWARD A LUDIC ARCHITECTURE

The architecture of tomorrow will be a means of modifying present conceptions of time and space. It will be a means of knowledge and a means of action.

—GILLES IVAIN

Situationist Russian architect Gilles Ivain imagined a "playful-constructive" movement through a city's "psychogeographic" zones—urban zones defined not only by streets, buildings, and businesses but also by how people inhabit the city and the collective psychic ambiances they project. Or as Guy Debord later wrote, while describing the now-famous Situationist notion of dérive, or drifting through a city, "from a dérive point of view cities have psychogeographical contours, with constant currents, fixed points and vortexes that strongly discourage entry into or exit from certain zones."[6] High-speed surveillance cameras tracking shopping patterns in stores like the Gap map these hidden currents, effectively becoming a time-based techno-capitalist development of the study of psychogeographic zoning that the Situationists did not forecast for their fledgling "science." "With the aid of old maps, aerial photographs and experimental dérives, one can draw up hitherto lacking maps of influences, maps whose inevitable imprecision at this early stage is no worse than that of the first navigational charts. The only difference is that it is no longer a matter of precisely delineating stable continents, but of changing architecture and urbanism."[7]

Beyond the remapping of existing cities as psychogeographic zones, new city forms were imagined. In "Formulary for a New Urbanism," Ivain described a futuristic Situationist city's quarters. It contained public and private architecture that would be in continuous flux and modifiable according to the whims of the inhabitants, including zones such as a Bizarre Quarter, a Happy Quarter (specially reserved for habitation), a Noble and Tragic Quarter (for good children), and a Sinister Zone. It is this last example for which have provided countless imaginings, and Ivain described the Sinister Quarter in a way that predicts the contours of many video-game worlds: "The Sinister Quarter, for example, would be a good replacement for those hellholes, those ill-reputed neighborhoods full of sordid dives and unsavory characters, that many peoples once possessed in their capitals: they symbolized all the evil forces of life. The Sinister Quarter would have no need to harbor real dangers, such as traps, dungeons or mines."[8] In contrast to a current rule-based "algorithmic" emphasis in academic ludology publications, some game researchers such as Chaim Gingold and Henry Jenkins have made convincing arguments for the importance of spatial poetics in structuring game-play.[9] This latter approach can be informed by the psychogeographic characterization of the city provided by the Situationists. Rather than seeing games as solely algorithmic rule machines, there is a significant attraction in players' exploration of virtual game spaces provided by games like *Grand Theft Auto, Tomb Raider,* and the classic exploratory *Myst.* Activities within these games incorporate spatial puzzles and goals tied to specific psychogeographic locations within the virtual game environment or city. For level design of more action-based shooter games like *Halo* and *Quake,* ludic architectural design of multiplayer fighting terrains (for hiding, for sniping, for jumping, for flying), and the placement of enemies and obstacles are a significant portion of game level design. The avid gamer's extensive time involvement in level modification, as was once common with PC games like *Doom, Quake,* and *Unreal,* is motivated by a desire to focus on and transform not the telic aims of the game but the paratelic space of the game world itself, invoking the Situationists' call for modifiable, changeable architecture: "Architectural complexes will be modifiable. Their aspect will change totally or partially in accordance with the will of their inhabitants."[10]

LESSON 4: SITUATIONIST GAMES BEYOND THE VIRTUAL: INTERVENING IN REAL CITIES

Situationist games are not necessarily confined to virtual digital game space. Guy Debord described the original Situationists' playful exploits into Parisian city space:

Our loose lifestyle and even certain amusements considered dubious that have always been enjoyed among our entourage—slipping by night into houses undergoing demolition, hitchhiking nonstop and without destination through Paris during a transportation strike in the name of adding to the confusion, wandering in subterranean catacombs forbidden to the public, etc.—are expressions of a more general sensibility which is no different from that of the dérive. Written descriptions can be no more than passwords to this great game.[11]

FIG. 57

Blast Theory, *Can You See Me Now?* Collaboration with Mixed Reality Lab, University of Nottingham, first manifestation 2001, Sheffield (detail of play).

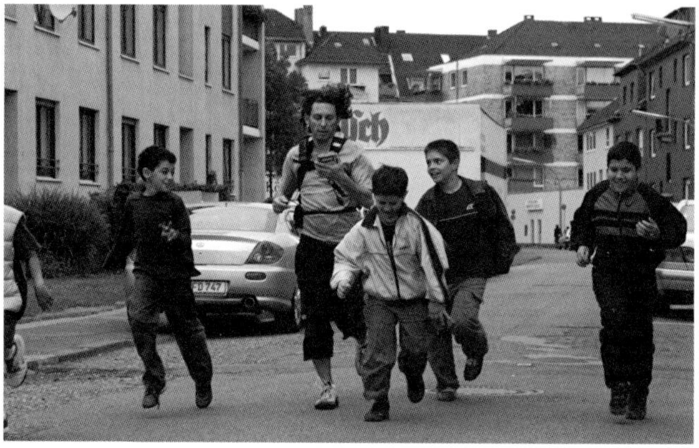

This description, like much of the Situationists' practice, anticipates the emergence of new forms of play as art practice today, most clearly in the example of the London-based artist collective Blast Theory. Blast Theory projects *Can You See Me Now?* (first manifestation, 2001) and *Uncle Roy All Around You* (first manifestation, 2003) reinscribe urban space with the rules and scenarios of their games. *Can You See Me Now?* players carry GPS-modified devices that contain a simple graphical *Pacman*-style game interface displaying the location of other players in the city. Running panicked through the city streets of Rotterdam in the first performance of *Can You See Me Now?*, players tried to escape these noncorporeal pursuers, who were less restricted by the actual geographic and urban obstacles such as traffic and traffic lights, pedestrians and hills. Similarly, *Uncle Roy All Around You* repurposed existing city infrastructure like pay phones and car rides to play a mysterious detective-style game on the streets of London. Clues and game-play advance through text instructions to players' mobile computers and planted "actors" (who seem like artificial intelligence players in a computer game played by humans). As Blast Theory explained, "The city is an arena where the unfamiliar flourishes, where the disjointed and the disrupted are constantly threatening to overwhelm us. It is also a zone of possibility; new encounters."[12]

The convergence of ludic activities and "real" city space are not the exclusive domain of Situationist-inspired artists. The Situationists did not foresee that megaplayers within the "superstructures" would also engage in playing their games. For instance, during the annual E3 game industry conference in 2003 in Los Angeles, the U.S. army staged a "playful" publicity stunt for its free recruitment shooter game, *America's Army*. They catapulted soldiers from a helicopter into downtown Hollywood. Passersby on the street were confused and frightened, as civilian city space was militarized through an intervention blurring the distinction between a soldier's job and playing soldier in a game. The use of game tactics and play to equivocate and familiarize urban warfare has become increasingly common in the wake of 9/11. *KumaWar* is a hyperreal, life-is-stranger-than-fiction attempt to maximize the blurriness between soldiering and play. This episodic game enterprise released shooter-game missions based on current American military events in Iraq. The designers of *KumaWar* regularly solicit advice from a retired U.S. general, and the player always is an American soldier battling "insurgents" in Iraqi cities. Distinguishing civilians from insurgents becomes an important skill for success in the "game." Again, city space (civilian space), military space, and game space are conflated.

A Situationist-style game more covertly complicit with the militarization of civilian space through ludological means was the innovative *I Love Bees,* designed by Jane McGonigal. Microsoft hired McGonigal, then a doctoral candidate in ludology at the University of California at Berkeley, to design a viral marketing campaign and Alternate Reality Game (ARG) for its upcoming Xbox release of *Halo 2.* In public places like pay phones, players of *I Love Bees* retrieved information and advances in the game story (a sci-fi "War of the Worlds"–like scenario leading into the story line of *Halo 2*). When they received game information, players would make an ironic military salute (echoing the gestures of futuristic American-style soldiers in *Halo*) and were thus able to identify other *I Love Bees* players in public places such as concerts and streets. *ILB* players posted numerous photos of this military salute on the Internet. Overall, the civic space of the city became militarized—even if for a fictional conflict.

LESSON 5: A DASH OF DADAIST NEGATIVITY: ILLEGALITY AS PLAY

Debord, after describing the role of Dadaism in combating "stale bourgeois culture" and fascism in post–World War I Europe, postulated that a dadaist-type negative aspect would be a necessary component of Situationism as long as undesired social structures were still in existence. "The dadaist spirit has nevertheless influenced all the movements that have come after it; and any future constructive position must include a dadaist-type negative aspect, as long as the social conditions that impose the repetition of rotten superstructures… have not been wiped out by force."[13] These "rotten" conglomerates continue today in the form of rapid globalization, imperialism and militarization, border closures, and increasingly hedged-in civil liberties in the post-9/11 War on Terror. In contrast to the complicit works described above, Situationist tactics have also been adopted as tools in activism.

One artist group that has been playing some urban interventionist, Situationist-like games with a dose of Dadaist negativity is Yo Mango, an Italian/Spanish art collective based in Barcelona. Yo Mango, slang in Spain for "I steal," regularly stages playful actions such as potlucks, where every dish must contain an element of stolen food, tango dancing in a chain supermarket while stealing, and distributing stylish "Yo Mango" patches to cover the holes left in stolen clothes by cutting out the plastic security clip. (The group recommends stealing only top designer, brand-name fashions.) Some members of Yo Mango are also loosely connected with the European Squatter Movement, an organized youth movement in opposition to private property that also participates in other activist activities, such as protesting against gentrification.

Mexican artist Rene Hayashi also creates ludic interventions in public space. In Indonesia and Argentina, he has realized playful architectural structures for street children. In 2006, in collaboration with Mexico City–based artist Eder Castillo, Hayashi created Guatemex, an imaginatively constructed island with computers with Internet access for illegal immigrants, floating on the river dividing Mexico from Guatemala. (His own laptop keyboard was water-damaged during this project.) Like the anticorporate antics and publicity stunts of the Yes Men and RTmark, the older public interventions of Critical Art Ensemble, and many of the political art actions that took place during the 2004 Republican National Convention in New York, Yo Mango's and Rene Hayashi's artwork can be described as ludic activism in which societal rules (laws) are willfully broken. Within activist culture itself, perhaps since the anti-WTO demonstrations in Seattle in 1999, Dadaist humor and ludic activities have become more prevalent.[14]

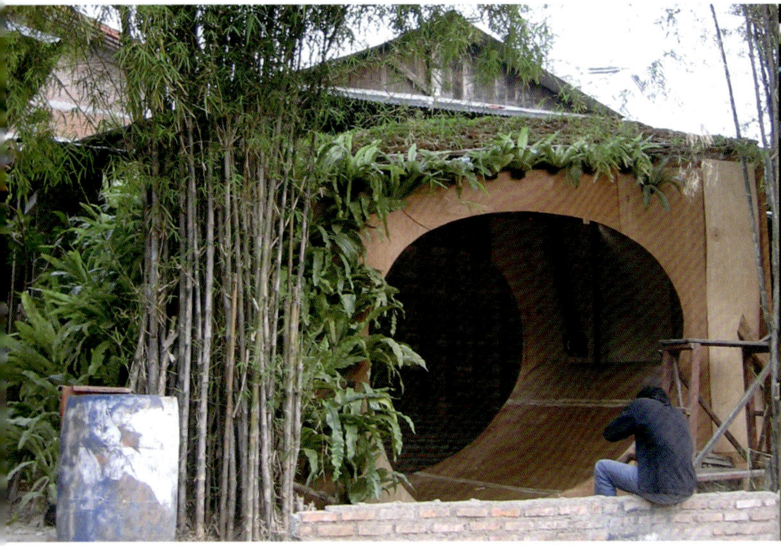
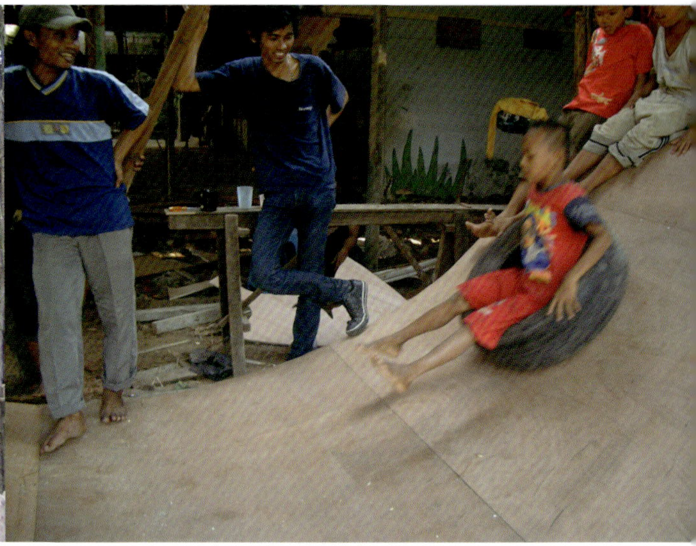

LESSON 6: GAMES WITHIN GAMES: INTERVENTIONIST TACTICS IN VIRTUAL SPACES

In their handbook for game designers, Katie Salen and Eric Zimmerman repeatedly emphasize the importance of the "magic circle" and the investment of the player in a separate, pretend space of play (whether abstract or photorealistic, virtual or non-digital).[15] They stress the pleasure in following the rules of games within the clear-cut boundaries of this magic circle. Situationist gamers, however, are more akin to the creative cheater, the game "griefer," or the hacker. They blur the peripheries of the magic circle, taking pleasure in changing the rules of the existing game space, which they see as problematic in a fixed state. Situationist mods and hacks intervening inside preexisting games can be more entertaining than the original game. For instance, the popular Massively Multiplayer Online Role Playing Game (MMORPG) *Second Life* has been playfully manipulated by the avatar Gazira Babeli, one of the members of the Second Front collective of Second Life artistic hackers. Her *Grey Goo* hack was an infestation of Second Life space with out-of-control repetitive, self-replicating objects, inspired by nanotechnological disaster scenarios. *Grey Goo* took various forms, from endless Mario-character replications to rampant Velvet Underground bananas. One day it effectively slowed down Linden Lab's game servers, interfering with game-play systemwide. Babeli's *COME.*

FIG. 58

Rene Hayashi, images from projects in Indonesia.

FIG. 59

Gazira Babeli, *Grey Goo,* 2006, still from hack of *Second Life.*

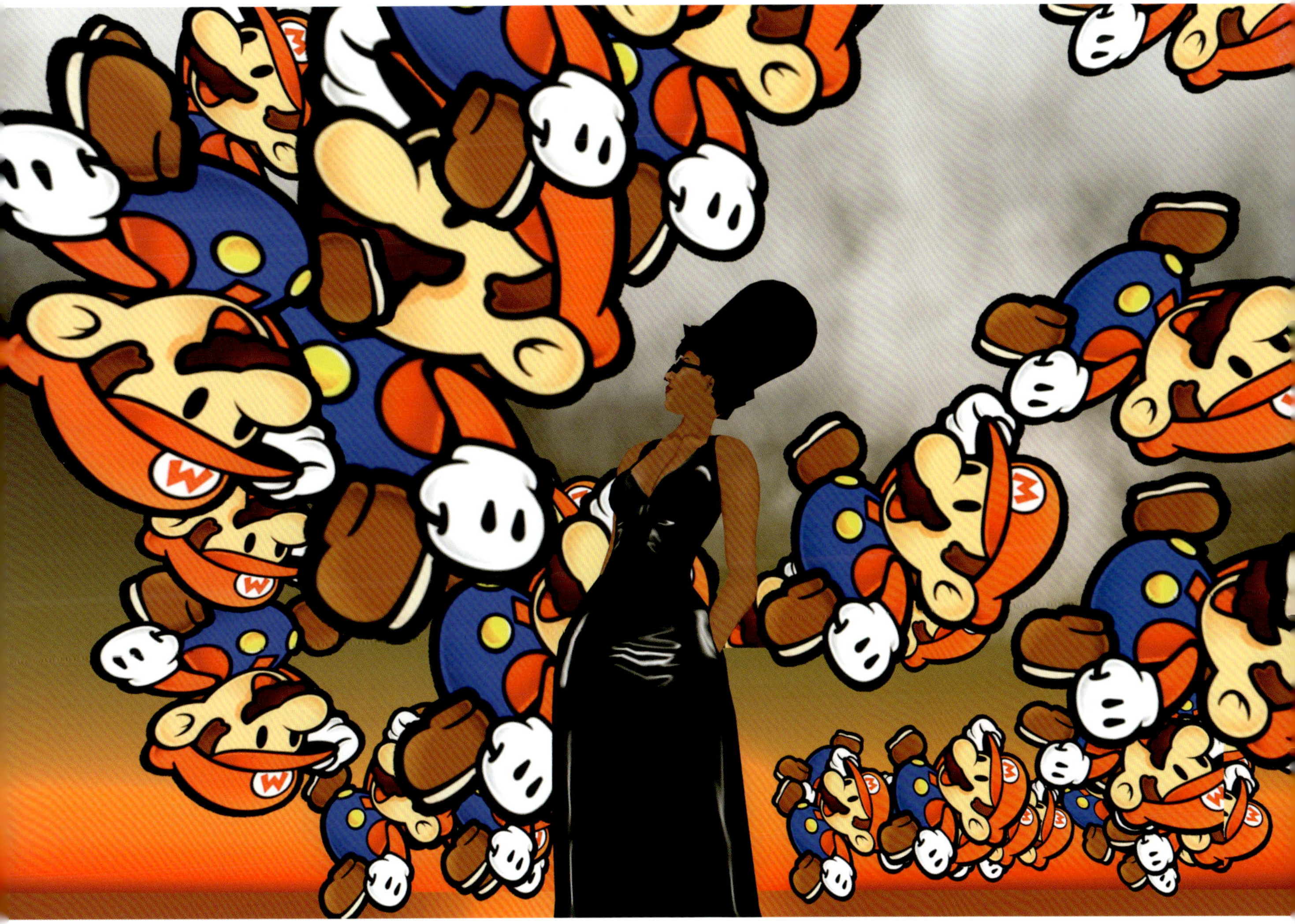

TO.HEAVEN similarly exploited a loophole in *Second Life,* allowing players to create gigantic avatars in proportion to the Second Life world, resulting in unexpected, interesting glitches. While the identity (or identities) behind the Babeli avatar is kept secret, the code for her Second Life interventions is always made public by being posted online so that others can learn from the code and reuse it.

A similar, Situationist-themed interventionist game strategy has been developed by Pierre Rahola, a French gamer and DJ. During the early phase of the Iraq War, Rahola and his collaborators would spray antiwar graffiti inside online shooter games. When I interviewed him in Paris in 2005, he admitted that "intervening in games is more fun than playing the game." About the same time Pierre and his friends were playing online shooter games with an activist edge, I began a body of work I would describe as Situationist gaming. In collaboration with the artists Brody Condon and Joan Leandre, we initiated *Velvet-Strike,* tagging the then-popular online soldier shooter game *Counter-Strike* with antiwar graffiti. *Velvet-Strike* was not only visual modification but also included "recipes" for disruptive actions designed to interfere with regular *Counter-Strike* game-play, such as one for making friends with your enemy.

RECIPE FOR FRIENDSHIP

1. **Find a *Counter-Strike* server with 0 or 1 other player on line. (If you go to an empty one, most likely someone will show up to see who you are.)**
2. **Shoot a few times at your enemy.**
3. **Tell them you are a newbie and ask them to show you how to plant the bomb.**
4. **Ask them which country they are from.**
5. **Ask them all about themselves.**
6. **Arrange to meet another time.**

Operation Urban Terrain (OUT) was another project I initiated to alter the dimensions of an existing game space—the free U.S. army propaganda game, *America's Army.* With OUT, I wanted to counter the convergence of military and civilian space with a kind of activism that merged virtual urban game space wirelessly with city space. I invited gamers, activists, and artists whom I had met online through *Velvet-Strike* to participate, including Chris Birke, one of the original *Counter-Strike* game texture artists, Mexico City architect Luis Hernández, and Pierre Rahola. We projected our live performances onto the walls and surfaces of Manhattan and Brooklyn, connected wirelessly to five players around the world during the Republican National Convention in 2004. I matched virtual locations within the *America's Army* game servers with physical New York City sites, projecting a live performance of a virtual sit-in inside a tunnel with yellow taxis onto a building in midtown Manhattan, where there were many yellow taxis, and pairing a red-brick warehouse in the game with a brick building in Harlem. For the last location, I merged a live soldier dancing performance in the popular *America's Army* map "Bridge" with projection onto the Manhattan Bridge in Brooklyn.

Riot Gear for Rollartista, another game within a game, was a series of machinima performances calling attention to European and British police abuse of Islamic and African immigrants, with players wearing padded "riot gear" costumes designed in collaboration with artist Talice Lee. In the first performance of the project, two player/performers roller-skated around the small Spanish city of Castellón projecting the Playstation2 games *Narc* and *Mechwarrior* from an ultralight projector attached to one of the player's helmets (technology had developed since the heavy battery and projector of OUT). At each projection location in the city, one player "roller-danced" and handed out flyers with stories of immigrant abuse to interested passersby, while the second player performed with a portable Playstation, controlling a dancing policeman character who violently beats up civilian city dwellers.

CONCLUSION: LEARNING THE LESSONS

The Situationists predicted an age of expanded ludic possibilities for artists and for anyone. Paraphrasing and remixing both gamer Rebecca Cannon and Situationist architect Gilles Ivain, we are bored with shooter games. We are bored with the suburbs, the stale imperialist sexist engineering-biased corporate game industry, and with new academic ludology that reifies existing conditions. We are ready to play reality TV off camera. We are frustrated with the imperialist military terrain of game cities. We don't want to play by rules we never agreed upon in the first place. Anyway, even if we enjoyed playing those games to begin with, it is now more entertaining to dismantle them, or to invent new unsanctioned games inside game space. If big players are intervening in game space, then it is time for Situationist gaming.

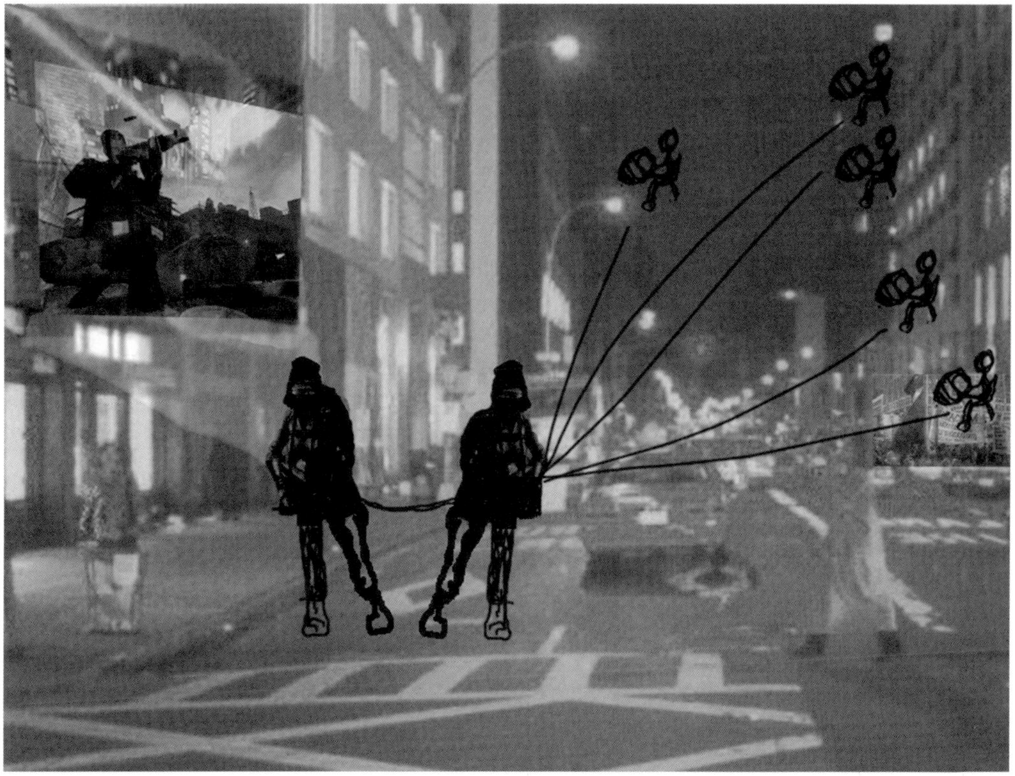

FIG. 60

Anne-Marie Schleiner, *OUT,* New York, still.

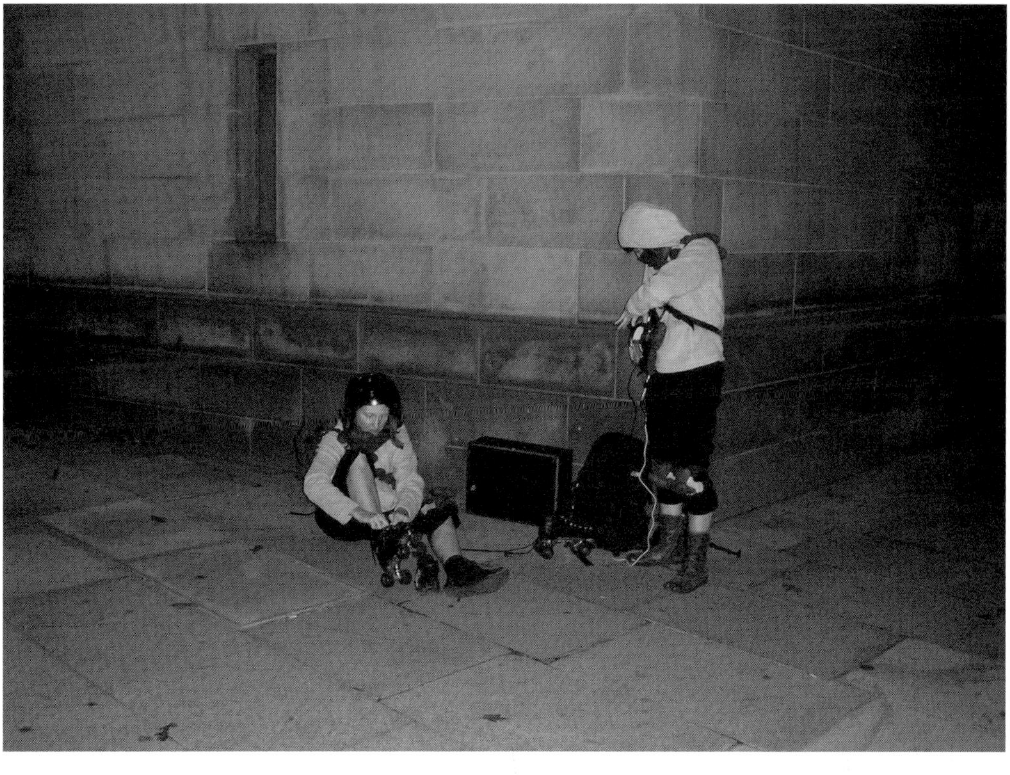

FIG. 61

Anne-Marie Schleiner and Talice Lee, *Riot Gear for Rollartista,* Manchester, 2007.

12

RUNNING AND GUNNING IN THE GALLERY: ART MODS, ART INSTITUTIONS, AND THE ARTISTS WHO DESTROY THEM

JON CATES

In the 1990s, many factors combined to enable artists to develop and manipulate video and computer-based games as a new mode of artistic practice. This activity exists at the intersection of new media art and computer games, particularly in a genre of computer games known as "first-person shooters." This specific intersection itself became known as a genre of artistic theory-practice called "art mods," a subcategory within the more general area of art games.[1] Art mods are modifications of existing commercial games. These games, first-person shooters, are modified to create artworks that are themselves playable as art games and were made possible by the technological and cultural changes that took place during the 1990s.

In the 1990s, a moment of genre formation occurred and new media and digital art cultures began to recognize the emergence of the genre of art games and art mods. As Christiane Paul stated, "Games are an important part of digital art's history in that early on they explored many of the paradigms that are now common in interactive art."[2] Gaming was a significant factor and force among media art histories and traditional art histories during the twentieth century. New media and digital art in particular feature this strong influence since the basic tool sets (of software, programming, rendering) and development environments (of computer hardware, video processors, operating systems) are the same in commercial gaming. In the 1990s, video and computer-based art games became exciting forms for those involved in these media art theory-practices. For generations of media artists who had reached adulthood by passing through the rise of arcades, video games, and computer games, the form, content, context, and implications of game culture became a natural home, holding promising possibilities for contemporary art making.

In this chapter, I will focus on the art mod as a subset of art games rather than attempt a general overview of digital or code-based art games. Further, I will concentrate mainly on a specific discourse within art mods. Already, within the slightly more than ten-year history of these new media art forms, a discourse has developed that places various projects in conversation. Through their modification of commercial games, these projects undertake to model or simulate a gallery, museum, or art space that physically houses the project. In these art mods, players can then play game levels inside the real galleries, museums, or art spaces that are being rendered or simulated. Such works began in the mid-1990s, when the commercial first-person shooter games became popular as a genre. These games take place in 3D-simulated digital spaces that are constructed as more or less complex mazes filled with monsters of one kind or another. Technical developments in these commercial games pushed their engines (their underlying code bases) to render increasingly "realistic" depictions of these mazes and monsters—the 3D environments and characters that provide the contexts, challenges, and obstacles in these games. Depictions of increasingly "realistic" violence in these games have been and remain a politicized issue of the first-person shooter. Artists who engage in this ongoing conversation have played with, altered, and critically commented on these structural conventions and cultural implications through the art mods they produce.

One important and influential art mod, *Museum Meltdown,* a project made in three versions by Tobias Bernstrup and Palle Torsson from 1996 to 1999, continued and extended a specific conversation that remains deeply influential and inspiring to artists in the field. Projects such as *Arsdoom* by Orhan Kipcak, Curd Duca, Rainer Urban, XRay, and collaborators (which preceded *Museum Meltdown* by a year) and the series *Everything I Do is Art, But Nothing I Do Makes Any Difference,* initiated by Chris Reilly in 2005, are two points of articulation in this conversation that connect the emerging technical possibilities of first-person shooters with critical artistic considerations. I will locate and discuss the emerging technical possibilities in these first-person shooter games in an important but not technologically deterministic role regarding the formation of the genre of art games and the subgenre of art mods.

Technological changes that occurred in the 1990s shifted computing, gaming, and online networking into peoples' homes and artists' hands. Consumer computing and video and computer games became familiar household activities rather than specialized activities taking place in designated social spaces outside the home (such as video arcades or university campuses). As these digital systems and games became domesticated, the Internet and World Wide Web became popular commercialized social spaces. The subsequent explosion in activity on the World Wide Web created social situations where digital files (such as art mods) were more easily exchanged through online communities dedicated to specific aspects of computer cultures (such as gaming). The core technologies of these digital products, the hardware (such as video processing cards and increased power for graphics) and software (the games themselves), developed rapidly, encouraging artists in these computer cultures to consider the systems as both players and creators or modifiers.

In 1992, id Software introduced *Wolfenstein 3D,* a game in which the player travels through the mazelike architecture of Castle Wolfenstein, as seen through the first-person perspective of an American soldier fighting Nazi soldiers, attack dogs, zombies, cyborg mutants, and a cybernated Adolf Hitler. Through the form and structure of the game and game-play, *Wolfenstein 3D* established the first-person shooter as a popular genre of 3D computer games. The first-person perspective of this and all subsequent games in this genre positions the view of the player inside the main character's perspective such that players see the main character's hands (holding weapons such as knives, machine guns, and crowbars) in front of them. The character's outstretched hands and weapons frame the experience of moving through the architectural mazes and enable the viewer to contend with whatever monsters he or she may encounter. This subjective point of view and embodied virtual camera position with its presence and directness of action contributed to the cultural interpretation or perception of the "realism" of *Wolfenstein 3D* in particular and the first-person shooter genre in general. This aspect of the first-person shooter also contributed to the cultural critiques and the potential effects of the violence of these games.

The game *Doom* by id Software followed *Wolfenstein 3D* in 1993 and further codified the genre of the first-person shooter. With *Doom,* id Software advanced the core technologies of the game (including the aspects of game-play, physics, and rendering). Through these technological advances, id Software further delineated the distinct genre of first-person shooters. To a greater degree, *Doom* allowed players to extend and customize the game. Extensibility became important to id Software as well as to the first-person shooter genre and contributed deeply to its popularity. Technologically, extensibility created the platform on which players could become a community of developers, building, editing, and sharing their extensions (their modifications or mods) with one another and playing each other's game levels (the mazelike maps that constitute the architectural spaces inhabited and traversed in these games). In later editions of *Doom,* id Software improved authoring tools, and the developer maintains a supportive attitude toward hacks, modifications, and creative recontextualizations of its games. As Tilman Baumgaertel wrote in 2004, the recent history of id Software's openness to these principles, combined with the hard work of a dedicated community of players and the Net / Web, has facilitated rapid developments in providing improved tools for making mods and led toward the realization of art mods as an area of artistic activity.[3]

Modifications, and thereby the principle of reprogrammability, became software features in these and subsequent games. The gaming culture valued these features as primary principles of the first-person shooter genre. Increasingly, editing levels to create these mods did not require comprehensive or advanced computer programming skills—just simple familiarity with the conventions of computer and game cultures. Being familiar with operating the GUI (Graphic User Interface), navigating online networks, installing and configuring software, selecting and applying properties from menus, and other such actions that most often are acquired through playing computer-based games and exploring computer operating systems are the skill sets required to make mods. Time and patience are also important, especially when the community-developed tools are less than stable or require idiosyncratic or poorly documented measures to be taken in producing mods. Even so, in cases such as those, support for the scripting (written in specific computer programming languages or following particular conventions) that is needed for modding is often available online. The community of modding enthusiasts, developers, and artists often offer their knowledge for free to those who are interested in tutorials and cultural resources online. As Baumgaertel wrote, the approaches and possibilities that "computer games offered their creators did not remain hidden for long, especially from artists who worked with new media or the Internet."[4]

Doom's relevance to media art histories was particularly highlighted when the ZKM Center for Art and Media in Karlsruhe, Germany, included *Doom* in its *Media-Art-History* exhibition in 1997. The ZKM, an important international site of media art research, exhibition, and publishing, included the *Doom* software as a commercial application rather than any specific art mods built using *Doom*. As such, the *Media-Art-History* exhibition ascribed cultural meaning and significance to the game and game engine itself. As stated in the exhibition catalogue, *Doom* "gained cult status because it links up with primeval human experiences (of being hunters and collectors) and thus produces a feeling of being alive (due to the fight for survival in a hostile world), with which every player is familiar. Contrary to reality, however, the possibilities of adapting the game to one's own abilities in *'Doom'* are almost un-limited."[5] In this quote, the combination of modification as well as the basic aspects of the first-person shooter that *Doom* codified generate cultural importance for this commercial game to be included among media art works in an early and influential tracing of current media art histories. The *Media-Art-History* catalogue identifies the way in which *Doom* changed the culture of gaming and media through id Software's development of the network functionality for multiplayer online play of *Doom,* as well as through the modding of *Doom* that was undertaken by the community of "enthusiastic *'Doom'* players." By the time the catalogue was published in 1997, artists had already joined this enthusiastic community as *Doom* players themselves and developers of art mods.

In 1995, *Arsdoom,* an art mod that runs on the *Doom* engine, was exhibited at Ars Electronica in Linz, Austria. The *Arsdoom* project, by Orhan Kipcak, Curd Duca, Rainer Urban, XRay, and their collaborators, appears to be the first large-scale art mod exhibited in an art space that it models. Baumgaertel goes further, stating that *Arsdoom* appears to be the "first attempt by an artist to use a computer game as an artistic medium."[6] While this larger claim is contentious and impossible to substantiate, *Arsdoom* undoubtedly did open a dialogue between digital and new media art and gaming cultures through level editing or modding. Julian Oliver (one of the founders of *selectparks,* a critical Web-based resource for art games) has called *Arsdoom* activities "practically a tradition of work of this kind."[7] In this chapter, I want to position this "tradition" as an ongoing conversation that can be charted as beginning with *Arsdoom* and continuing through the 1990s to the present. This conversation exists through the social networks of the Net/Web and runs on the game engines that were developed in the early 1990s. Further, art modding (as an ongoing conversation) continues to feed back into the technocultural influences that gave artists these possibilities. The conversation continued through the late 1990s with *Museum Meltdown* by Tobias Bernstrup and Palle Torsson, the next most visible art-mod project, which connected to projects such as *bio tek kitchen* by Josephine Starrs and Leon Cmielewski and *Q3* by Feng Mengbo (both from 1999), then crossed the threshold of the millennium with projects such as *Everything I Do is Art, But Nothing I Do Makes Any Difference* by Chris Reilly in 2005 and 2006. Narrating this media art history helps to locate points of articulation in this conversation, which began in the twentieth century and continues into the twenty-first.

Arsdoom, the work that initiated the conversation among art mods, involves the basic art-mod principles: the re-creation/simulation/modeling of the exhibition space using a game engine; the technically unaltered rules of game-play inherited from the game engine itself (whose meaning is culturally shifted by being relocated and recontextualized inside the simulated exhibition space); an engagement with questions of "realism" and violence raised by the first-person shooter as a genre; and the mobilization of institutional critiques. *Arsdoom* accomplished these aspects of the art mod by modeling the Brucknerhaus in Linz, a concert hall and important venue for exhibitions and events related to the Ars Electronica Festival. Inside this 3D-rendered model/simulated exhibition space, players could choose between characters/artistic identities such as Joseph Beuys, Arnulf Rainer, Georg Baselitz, or Jeff Koons and wield weapons such as a "color gun and water hose."[8] As the online archive for the Ars Electronica Festival details, this project was intended to create the conditions for "the desperate efforts of a misguided will to create—trapped in a loop of desperate creativity, tapping the aesthetic arsenal—and at the same time, destruction."[9] *Arsdoom* played during the festival and was available online from the Ars Electronica servers as a downloadable level for *Doom.* As Axel Stockburger wrote in 2006, this project inverted the relation of the digital object and its exhibition. Stockburger writes: "Rather than bringing an object from outside the art context into the white cube, the gallery or museum space itself was presented as a model that could be opened up."[10] In this opening-up, the potential exists for mobilizing an institutional critique of the festival itself, which is found in the game within a game. *Arsdoom* plays at breaking the rules, order, and values of the festival. As documented by various writers, players particularly enjoyed destroying an image of the exhibition director Peter Weibel. Weibel's role as the most desirable target for destruction is a simple illustration of the carnivalesque inversion of the social order or hierarchical power structures of the festival.

Museum Meltdown by Tobias Bernstrup and Palle Torsson was produced in three different versions from 1996 to 1999. It extends the conversation that began with *Arsdoom.* By relying on the basic principles of art mods, *Museum Meltdown* itself modifies the art-mod genre in these early moments of the development of computer-based art games. Its extension and modification lie in the simplicity of the act of reproducing a multilayered 3D-rendered reproduction of the physical exhibition space while maintaining the rules of play inherited from the commercial games that are being modified. Installations of *Museum Meltdown* are playable in the game space that reproduces the conditions of its exhibitions. Like *Arsdoom,* it appropriates the games and the exhibition spaces in which it runs. Players of *Museum Meltdown* stand at this intersection between game worlds, which are controlled by the rules of play for first-person shooters and the art worlds created by the museums that exhibit the projects. Bernstrup and Torsson extended and modified *Museum Meltdown* in three different versions, using updated digital technologies. These versions involved a transition through various game engines and authoring environments to model the museums in higher degrees of "realism" and with greater destructive abilities for players to violently express their desire to destroy the exhibition spaces and their collections while battling the inbuilt monsters of the games.

As Lev Manovich writes with regard to the subject of variability, "A new media object is not something fixed once and for all but can exist in different, potentially infinite, versions."[11] Manovich goes on to describe new media as "characterized by variability," stating that different versions typically replace identical copies in new media art.[12] *Museum Meltdown* is certainly variable in this sense, having existed in multiple instances or instantiations of the larger project. Still, the artists intended each installation/exhibition of *Museum Meltdown* to be understood as an individual work of art as well as part of the larger project. As Bernstrup stated in an interview with the author in 2007, "Each museum/game was a new different piece."[13] Each individual piece was created for the institution that exhibited the work, virtually modeling that institution inside the art mod, and as such they were, according to Bernstrup, "site specific" and engaged with every particular museum's "long or short history." Playing with these museums, the versions of the *Museum Meltdown* project created a new media art form based on recoding the relationship between the art institution and the artist. Rather than exhibiting the artists, the museums are exhibited by the artists who have been invited to model them. The models are then virtually defaced and destroyed by the forms of play that the art-mod project requires or encourages.

As each version of *Museum Meltdown* was built with a more advanced system, the game-play in subsequent versions was enhanced. The first *Museum Meltdown* modeled and was exhibited at the Arken Museum of Modern Art in Copenhagen as a part of the *Borealis 8: The Scream* exhibition in 1996. In this version, only details of the architectural interiors of the museums could be destroyed during play, which was inherited from *Duke Nukem 3D,* the game engine on which this art mod ran. As Bernstrup writes, they included architectural details such as "glass, and a mezzanine floor that would explode" and toilets that could be "smashed to cause a little fountain" to erupt. This version was partially a technological limitation of the times as well as an artistic decision. The physical architecture of the Arken Museum inspired Bernstrup and Torsson to take this approach. As Bernstrup explains, they were "struck by similarities between the museum and a 3D shooter game. The museum interior had a lot of gamelike texture details, such as fake metal panels and big sliding metal doors." Or as Torsson recounts, they "paired together the concrete setting of the postmodern architecture" through its resemblance to the first-person shooter games they were playing. Torsson states that they "felt like the fake metal panel and distorted perspective for the museum could be mapped to the in-world textures of games" because to them the museum was already a simulated space of game-play, the game in this case being the socially constructed worlds of institutionalized art making, sales, and exhibition.

The second version of *Museum Meltdown* introduced the capacity to destroy the museum's collection of artworks—in addition to its architectural elements. This version re-created the Contemporary Art Centre in Vilnius, Lithuania, in 1997. The context of the museum becomes a prerequisite for the possibility of playing at destroying art inside the art institution. Gunning down, exploding, or otherwise destroying recognizable artworks in the museum space can been understood as an attempt to mobilize an institutional critique. The digital objects that functionally render/represent the artworks were given properties by the artists so that the game engine would interpret them as destructible. The destruction becomes the game within the game, as with the destruction of the representation of Peter Weibel in *Arsdoom.* This game of institutional critique within the game of the art mod can occur within the existing rules of play that game engines offer (as an existing and available structure), relying on and replying to the context of the museum. In this way, *Museum Meltdown* addresses both the game presented by the game engine and

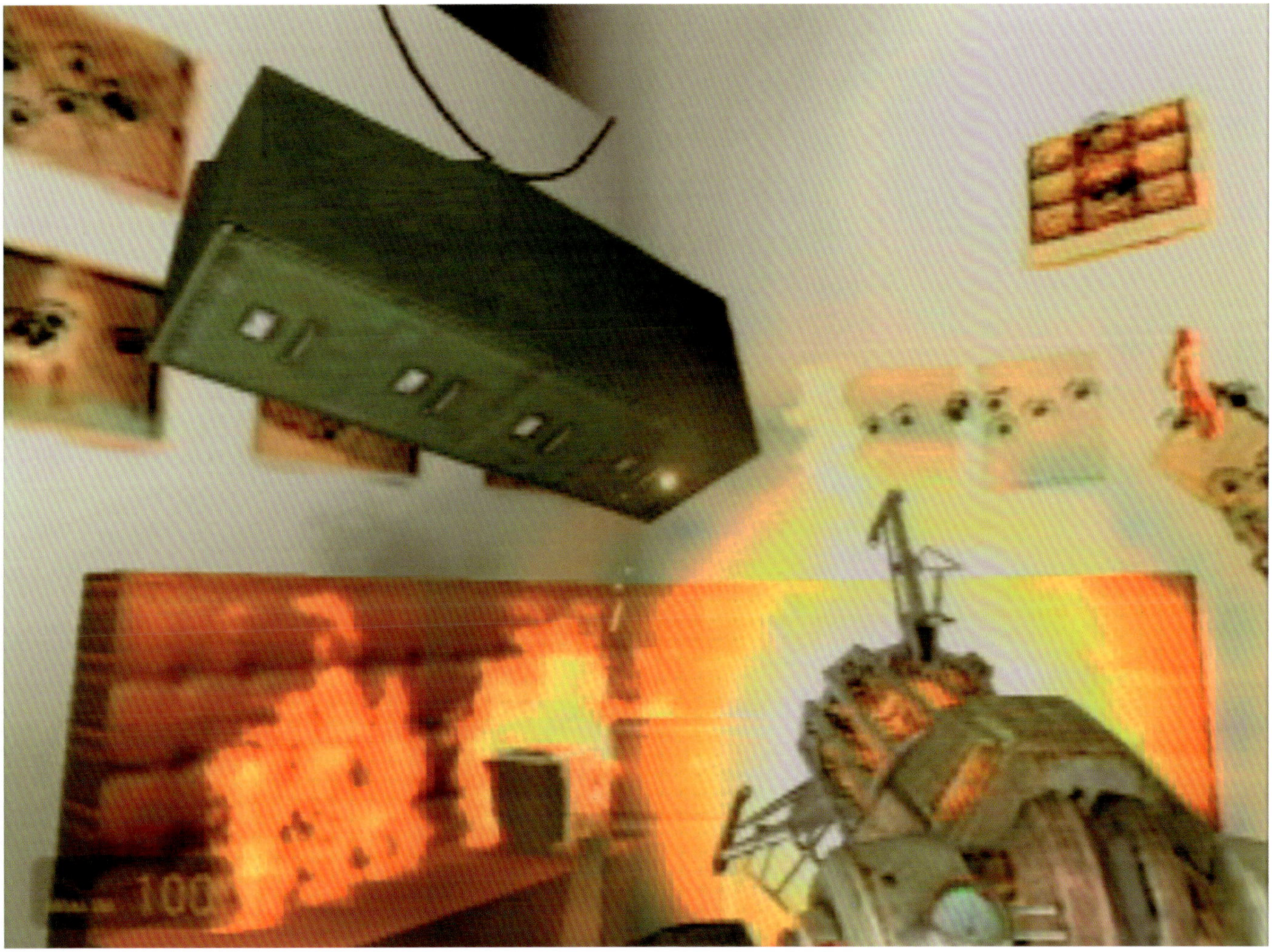

FIG. 62

Chris Reilly, screen shot from *Everything I Do is Art, But Nothing I Do Makes Any Difference,* 2005–6.

the game of the institutional art world operating in the specific art institutions where *Museum Meltdown* was installed. Torsson explains that they took this approach because it allowed them (as artists) and participants (as players) "to crack the codes and use them as you would in any social sphere." Torsson identifies these codes as the "hierarchical self-manufacturing artworld where power upwards works as an isolating layer to the access of production of meaning." Confronting this game world of the institutional art world, *Museum Meltdown* gave players a chance to exercise or experience an institutional critique by "blowing up masterpieces."

The symbolic violence of *Museum Meltdown* connects this project to parallel institutional critiques and anti-art gestures from various art histories. Positioned as more or less threatening in their depictions or realizations of violence, these parallel histories provide points of connection and distinction. Art movements such as Dada, Fluxus, and the Situationist International are all punctuated by (real / symbolic) threats against art-world institutions. Specific works of art from the twentieth century, such as Jean Tinguely's self-destructing *Study for an End of the World,* Richard Serra's *Prisoner's Dilemma* performance / video, or Chris Burden's *Samson* installation, present related moments created from mechanized or virtualized games of self-destruction and an interest in potentially nihilistic critiques of specific art-world institutions and contexts. An important distinction with art mods lies in their dual functionality as art and as mod, placing them solidly in the fields of both media art histories and game culture. Both of these fields relate to "realism" through representation and the rendering of simulations. The violence of art mods becomes more "realistic" as computing power increases.

The third and final installation of *Museum Meltdown* in 1999 rendered the Moderna Museet in Stockholm. Here Bernstrup and Torsson upgraded to *Half-Life,* a game that is famously known for its engine's ability to render increasingly "realistic" representations of space, characters, and violence. According to Bernstrup, they rendered "about 75% of the original works hung according to the collection. The debris was more realistic, for example when breaking Duchamp's *Large Glass* with a crowbar you would see both scattered glass and wood!" Torsson discusses how the simulations, "realism," and violent implications and suggestions crossed over from the virtual / digital to the real / analog worlds at the exhibitions of *Museum Meltdown.* Torsson relates a range of such experiences, from witnessing a child "pointing his finger formed as a gun at one of the real guards of the museum," to playing at shooting them as if in a first-person shooter, to how the head of security at one of the museums expressed anxiety that the project could be "used as a way to learn to master a robbery of the museum."

Players move at the intersections of these models (the material of the art mods) and the installation of these projects in the museums that exhibit them. Players literally stand and move through the simulated game space and the physical architectural space of the museum. In these moments, a sense of self-reflexive play or recursive presence occurs within the game and within the game within the game. The double-coded placement, being simultaneously within the physical and virtual museums that had invited these artists to virtually destroy them, contributed to Bernstrup and Torsson's loss of interest in continuing the project. Rather than simply modeling every museum that invited them, they discontinued *Museum Meltdown* but continue to work on projects, both individually and (more recently) together, that explore the mediated intersections of analog/physical and digital / game engine environments and architectures.

Chris Reilly's series *Everything I Do is Art, But Nothing I Do Makes Any Difference* from 2005 and 2006 directly connects and converses with these previous projects (fig. 62). Like *Museum Meltdown, Everything I Do is Art* also exists in three updated versions. In 2005, Reilly created an art mod that responded to an installation by his friend and fellow artist Patrick Rios using the *Half-Life 2* game engine. Rios's installation was a room in the School of the Art Institute of Chicago's exhibition galleries, which was ambiguously but industriously filled with materials, and in which Rios took up occasional residence as the "featured artist" of a fictional organization called the Chicago Institute for Advanced Research and Discussion. Rios's installation was based on the implicit assumption that all of his undifferentiated activities constituted his art. Reilly responded by modeling the installation and then personally performing the destruction (via his art mod) of Rios's work in an adjacent room. Standing in the gallery, observers witnessed Reilly's performative art mod during the closing reception for Rios's exhibition. One could watch Reilly destroy the simulated installation while keeping the real installation in view. This split vision presented another level of self-reflexivity to this performative art mod.

In 2006, Reilly upgraded his art mod to not simply include one room of the three-level warehouse-style exhibition space, but rather to model the entire building as well as the streets and surfaces of adjacent buildings visible through the windows of the gallery. This version was exhibited as multiple playable levels as Reilly's thesis work for the 2006 undergraduate exhibition. His art mod was installed in one of the last rooms on the top, third floor of the gallery so that visitors / players would have traversed the entire exhibition before coming to his work. Reilly modeled various pieces of art made by his fellow students and provided visitors / players the opportunities to create what he referred to as "abstract expressionist" works using the simulated walls as canvases and saw blades, bullets, harpoons, and buckets of red, green, and blue paint as the "painting" materials. As with *Museum Meltdown,* Reilly included the game-play inherited from *Half-Life 2,* filling the gallery with murderous monsters, robots, and zombies that have to be killed or destroyed in order to survive in the mazelike structure of the exhibition. Extending the form further, Reilly forced visitors / players to destroy works by the other artists / art students by hiding health points and extra ammo inside the artworks. Whereas *Arsdoom* and *Museum Meltdown* made the game within the game optional, *Everything I Do is Art* foregrounds this destruction as a necessary part of survival in order to experience the work. Additionally, the ability to create abstract expressionist works by mutilating the gallery interiors underscores Reilly's insistence on engaging with questions of "realism" through simulated violence in order to play with and critique the institutional context of the exhibition of these art mods.

Although others have made the connections before between *Everything I Do is Art* and *Museum Meltdown,* Reilly did not take direct inspiration from *Museum Meltdown.*[14] As a student of mine during the time of his art-mod production, Reilly was absent during a critical discussion of *Museum Meltdown.* Later I introduced him to the project, but not until he had begun work on *Everything I Do is Art.* Similarly, in my interview with Bernstrup and Torsson in 2007, they do not identify *Arsdoom* as an influence or even acknowledge an awareness of the project. Instead, they cite the first-person shooter games they were playing in the mid-1990s. And if Baumgaertel's desire to position *Arsdoom* as unprecedented is accurate, then these works cannot be considered in a fixed, chronologically arranged genealogy of recent media art histories. Rather, these art mods coexist in conversation, as points of articulation, amid the game cultures they come from and feed back into, in the ongoing discourse of art games and the development of art mods.

CODA: DISTINGUISHING ART FROM PLAY

13

ZIGZAGGING WITH FULL STOPS FROM PLAY TO ART

ELLEN HANDLER SPITZ

"Who are you today?" I ask, mock-seriously, looking down at the tousled blond three-year-old who greets me at the door in answer to my ring. "And who am I?"

This chapter, like the bemused question I posed to the little fellow above, comes to its first full stop right away. This is because, although my purpose here is to argue that childhood, play, games, and art ought *not* to be unproblematically joined, I have found that the best I can do is to offer questions rather than assertions. Direct links between children's play and art have been praised by poets, presumed by philosophers, and promulgated by psychologists, and all of this activity has occurred in such profusion that an exhaustive compendium of those involved would consume the entire space allotted me for this chapter. A very short list of authors from a variety of disciplines who have proffered such links either implicitly or explicitly would feature Locke, Rousseau, Blake, Wordsworth, Coleridge, Baudelaire, Huizinga, Rilke, Walter Benjamin, Freud, and Gombrich, a list that fails, of course, to include a single one of the myriad visual artists who have made similar claims, to wit, that children's play leads to art; that play is an early form of art; that art itself—in reverse—is a form of play; that art-making is to adults what play is to children; and that art, devoid of play, cannot be deemed of the highest caliber.

Rightly, such claims deserve to be examined individually rather than *conflated;* yet my own questions—which have grown out of work that has put me in close touch with young children—remain not only unanswered but unasked. For example, granted that we can and do find connections between child's play and art, why is it that we fail to notice that whereas *all* children play, very *few* grow up to become artists? If the links are so strong and so obvious, why should this be the case? What are the significant *differences* between play and art? What can and does an artist do that a child cannot do? What is it, for example, that gives a work of art the spin that takes it sailing over the picket fence and out into the world so that strangers want to contemplate it, enjoy it, learn from it? Whereas, on the contrary, child's play normally takes place within the confines of the so-called picket fence, does not sail over, normally remains entirely within the

---

Some material in this chapter is drawn from my book *The Brightening Glance: Imagination and Childhood* (New York: Pantheon, 2006) and my quarterly column, "Apropos the Arts: Art as Play? The Digital and the Surreal" in *American Imago* 66, no. 1 (2009): 111–18.
I wish to thank David Getsy for convening the symposium for which this chapter was first framed and for his unflagging confidence in the value of our theme.

FIG. 63

René Magritte, *Key of Dreams,* 1930, oil on canvas, 81 × 60 cm. Private collection.

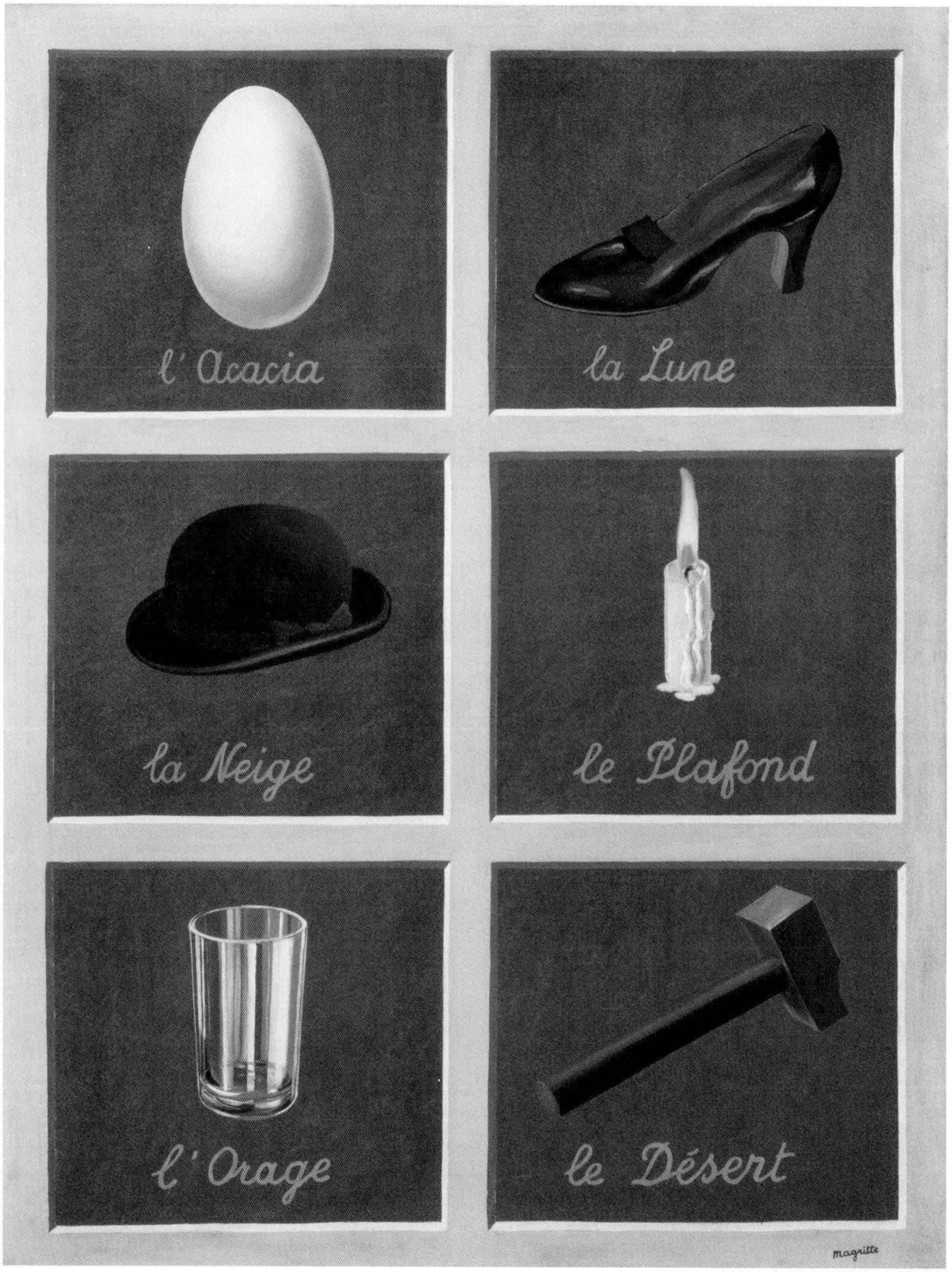

child's own purview, and is rarely of interest to anyone else (with the exception perhaps of the child's own parents, grandparents, and certain researchers). Works of art, on the other hand, when they attain public significance, do so because they extend beyond the immediate range of their makers; they transcend their original contexts. They possess an interest that goes beyond any personal relation with their maker. Yet theorists (and others) who draw straight lines from children's games, drawings, jokes, and imaginary worlds to art are prone to gloss over this distinction.

In this chapter, I had initially sought not only to raise doubts of this sort but to offer scholarly, well-formulated *conclusions* apropos. Instead, the questions must continue to hover and to circulate, while I trace, in the pages to follow, a few zigzagging lines of connection and rupture.

In her beautifully written catalogue essay for a Compton Verney exhibition, *Only Make Believe: Ways of Playing,* Marina Warner foregrounds the ambiguity and kaleidoscopic nature of the English word "play." She includes in her list of its meanings "mimicry and laughter, feigning and struggle, illusion and display, performance, masquerade, ritual and ceremony,... [and, she also cites] a myriad of dolls and toys...games, sports, and races, tumbling and juggling, guising and miming, flyting and flirting—even gambling."[1] The cluster of signification is manifold. Following her discussion for a moment, we note her argument that "ways of making art, and the forms and media of artefacts, have effloresced dramatically over the last twenty years, and they now entangle aesthetics ever more deeply into ways of playing." I actually think we can see this most clearly in much of the art that is being created through the manipulations of technology in our apparently advanced age of mechanical and electronic reproduction where, say, a landmark art-and-technology show like *010101: Art in Technological Times,* at the San Francisco Museum of Modern Art in 2001, displayed works redolent of the artists' wonder and joy at the playful possibilities of emergent media. Indeed, the interactive digital works on display at that show and at many others since then invite their visitors into universes of co-manipulation, improvisation, drama, and virtual reality. Has then, in that sense, art become play? Have we entered into a twenty-first-century world in which art—more and more—resembles play? Play, that is, in the sense of bemused experimentation, illusion, virtuality, juxtaposed imagery, curiously conjoined objects and ideas moving about and being displayed "as if"? After all, as Freud speculates in his essay "Creative Writers and Day-Dreaming," "Perhaps we may say that every child at play behaves like an imaginative writer [we may read: artist], in that he creates a world of his own or, more truly, he rearranges the things of his world and orders it in a new way that pleases him better."[2]

An example of this notion of play-as-art might be found in some of the media-based work of John Maeda, whose *Tap Type Write* (1998) can be seen as a joyful piece made by the artist initially for his own young children, who kept asking him for permission to play at his computer keyboard. The work invites you to sit down and to type a message. Then as soon as you touch the keys, you have a surprise: letters of different fonts suddenly begin to prance and cavort in a whimsical wild-style choreography. Circles, zigzags, and diagonals appear on the screen before your eyes. It's like a kaleidoscope taken to a higher power, utterly playful and delightful unless, that is, you are in the mood to look for deep meaning, in which case you might be frustrated and disappointed. I do think, however, that Maeda goes beyond pure fun in this work to suggest important and often overlooked connections between the body and language and between gesture and writing and between art forms that are often kept separate, such as dance and words (although several contemporary choreographers, notably Maguy Marin of France, have recently been exploring this realm of interdisciplinarity). Maeda's work brings to mind as well some of the particularly jazzy and dynamic New York City subway-car graffiti of the early 1980s.[3] It also might be linked to works by the Belgian surrealist René Magritte, who, in his 1930 painting *Key of Dreams* (fig. 63), divides a small canvas into six identical squares. In each, the artist paints a deliberately recognizable object and then, just as deliberately, misnames it. Of course, he is teasing us, and, once again, if we are in a mood for meaning, we will be disappointed because the connections are not meaningful. Magritte, like the computer artist, returns us to our childhood in this work by evoking alphabet primers and our earliest picture books and by disrupting the connections we assume to be in place between words and objects. He shows us (like my little blond friend, cited earlier) just how arbitrary those assumptions are and, by implication, how silly we are to place faith in them. Magritte's play, unlike Maeda's, is not with letters but with words and images, and his project seems somehow more aggressive. Magritte's fun feels less innocent and friendly than Maeda's; it is as though he wants to play a practical joke on us and induce not merely pleasure but a measure of anxiety as well. Later I will return to this matter of anxiety.

Seven-year-old Adam is hard at work in the playroom. After an hour, I come to have a look, and a wonderful sight greets my eyes: a wildly fanciful architectural contraption has arisen and transformed the space of the room. It consists of two mahogany leather-topped stools with a folding chair upended between them, all three pieces of furniture having been connected by a red-and-white-striped jump rope that is suspended and held in place by a stack of picture books. Adam's construction includes an overturned wicker basket surmounted by a strategically placed rattan bull in fuschia, aqua, and gold—a kind of miniature piñata—as well as tiny figurines of bears in clothes, a rubber wide-mouthed hippo, and an alphabet block that reads "S." Lincoln Logs lean like buttresses against the structure at various points. The entire construct abuts a table covered with woven Bedouin cloths from the Old City of Jerusalem. Three armored knights on horseback, a fuzzy toy armadillo from Texas, and an elephant form a posse at right angles to which Adam has positioned a jaunty Air France teddy bear. Propped at the other end on a platform consisting of two Babar books, a tiny giraffe surveys the scene. Suddenly, a paternal voice is heard:

"It's time to leave."

The little boy ruefully extricates himself from his immersion in the creative flow, but before leaving he looks at me and commands in a tone of artistic authority:

"Don't move anything! It isn't finished."

How do we relate Adam's play to art? Is Freud right?

In Germany, in Hannover and Kassel, I have observed several children's rooms and play spaces. What strikes me is how one six-and-a-half-year-old girl knows exactly where her possessions are located but has used them to construct the most complex scenarios, bricolages, and displays involving a wide assortment of objects that reflect her most passionate interests.

A highly imaginative child, Klara inhabits a visually exciting space dominated by primary colors. Her double-decker bed, equipped with a raised canopy covered with blue, yellow, and red curtains, sports peep holes so that her sleeping quarters resemble a fanciful two-tiered tent. Stuck into its slats are dozens of postcards of horses (her favorite animal); the floor is populated by hordes of stuffed animals of many other species and sizes, including a plush horse large enough for her to mount and a seemingly infinite number of dinosaurs. On the day of my visit, the blue-carpeted floor is so crowded with objects that I cannot figure out how to get in without tripping or rearranging something. Today Klara is staging a race

between the toy horses and dinosaurs. She has designed a complex farm with a fenced-in area, so that farm and race are contiguous, filling all the available space on the floor. I note her easel in a corner, her wealth of picture books, her boxes of small toy figurines of people as well as a host of other colorful objects that overflow the shelves. Her room teems with life, energy, and expressive potency. It reminds me, I suddenly realize, as I stand there contemplating it, of some of the more interesting and compelling artists' installations at Documenta 11, the international contemporary art show in Kassel that I had come to Germany to see. In fact, I muse with a secret smile, it is perhaps even, in some ways, more interesting.

Contemporary artists whose installations might bear comparison with Klara's room would include Pascale Tayou, George Adeagbo, and Thomas Hirschhorn. And yet, surely, the child's room is not art. But the question is, just as surely: Why not?

That iconoclastic thought brings to mind the work of a contemporary New York artist, Ellen Brooks, who has, for a number of years, pondered the way children seek spaces of "comfort and security, but also of concealment and separation," as she put it to me. To explore this theme, Brooks makes sculptural works derived from the secret spaces of her own childhood. Her art evokes the blanket houses, forts, and hideaways children build for themselves out of whatever they are able to find and conscript (figs. 64 and 65). Brooks uses armchairs, sheets, blankets, and colorful quilts as well as sticks and stones to construct—both indoors and outdoors—her tents, huts, and cavelike structures. In addition to making these cozy but also eerie and uncanny enclosures, she photographs them and exhibits her photographs. Sometimes, she says, she climbs inside the structures and spends time there just to sense the changes they induce in her sense of her own body and her consciousness. Anxiety, she believes, plays a key role in her work—stemming from memories of visceral feelings of embarrassment, shame, and curiosity about the forbidden, and fears of being discovered by grown-ups.

Brooks's term for what children do is *primary architecture.* Conjure a make-believe fort, a raft, an igloo of snow, a tree house, or a tabernacle of old sheets thrown over a card table. Two small friends sequestered in a hideaway whispering furtively. Or one child alone with an imaginary companion. Or with a pet or a favorite toy. Maybe, even, a secret language that is being spoken, because, as Bachelard writes in *The Poetics of Space,* "Words—I often imagine this—are little houses, each with its cellar and garret."[4] Oliver Sacks, the neurologist, writes apropos in his memoir, *Uncle Tungsten,* of crawling happily into a triangular space under the stairs of his parents' London home, where the Passover dishes were kept hidden all year: "I felt snug there, in my secret hideaway—no one besides me was small enough to fit in."[5]

But how shall we connect all this imaginative play with art? One way, as per Brooks, is to make art out of it as such, to recapitulate it, to imitate it. But has it per se the force of an *Anlage,* an origin, a source? Perhaps so, at least in many instances. Howsoever that may be, I would like to link its element of anxiety and its concomitant search for security to the oeuvre, once again, of René Magritte, whose pictorial constructions, especially when seen as critiques of perspective (as argued, for example, both by Jean Clair and more recently by Eric Wargo in a mesmerizing article on *La Condition humaine*)[6] induce a nostalgia for childhood experience—for that time, in particular, when contradictions could be simultaneously held and when the aggressively occupying armies of compartmentalization had not yet fully colonized our mental landscapes. The mental state evoked is known in certain psychoanalytic circles as "transitional," as the realm of "potential space," or as the so-called third area, thusly designated by D. W. Winnicott in his writings on play and on the location of cultural experience.[7] It is worthwhile to add in this context that, whereas Magritte had ample personal reasons, stemming from his own troubled childhood, for expressing such anxiety, those reasons are transformed in his paintings such that viewers need know nothing of his biography to shudder (or to laugh) at their nervous flirtations with the uncanny, the grotesque, and the bizarre.[8]

To play by elaborating with objects can often mean using them in ways for which they were not intended. A three-year-old takes an egg slicer out of the kitchen drawer and by twanging its wires transforms it into a musical instrument. A little girl's wooden and cardboard puzzle pictures cannot be completed by visiting children because they are always missing parts. The reason for this is that she, having no interest whatever in solving puzzles, takes their brightest and most intriguingly shaped pieces and turns them into morsels of food for her dolls and stuffed animals.

Magritte also loved transposition. An eye filled with sky. A goblet resting on an unfurled umbrella. A violin wearing a bowtie. And we cannot necessarily separate the art from the play here by invoking superior knowledge on the part of the painter, since children too know the proper use of things even as they

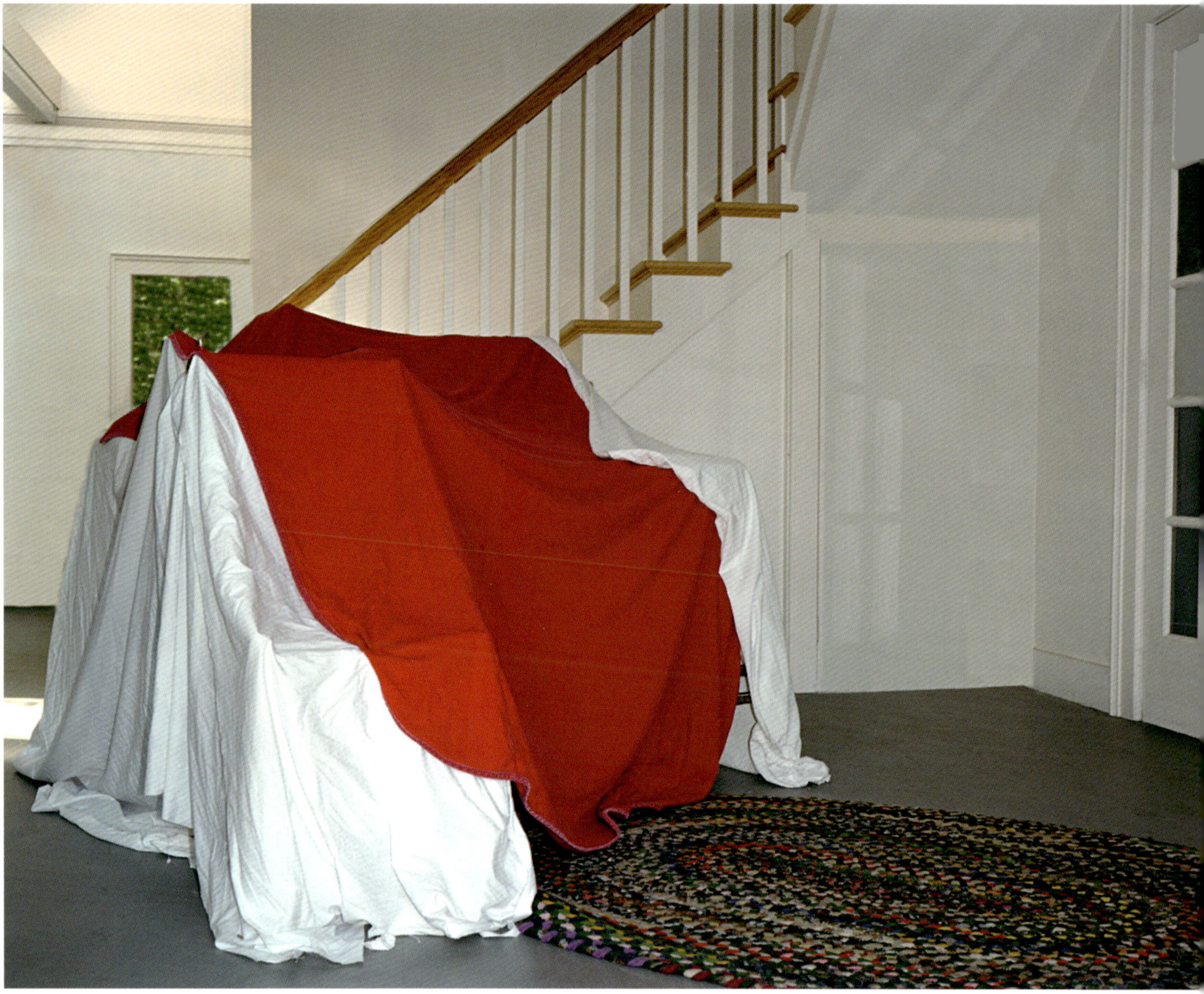

FIG. 64

Ellen Brooks, *Untitled (Red Stairs),* 1998, mixed media.

FIG. 65

Ellen Brooks, *Untitled (Outside / Cardboard),* 1999, mixed media.

transgress them. (I investigated this phenomenon in my research for a book I was writing on children's literature and found that three- and four-year-olds could interpret the images in their picture books both according to the canonical answers expected of them by adults and simultaneously in terms of their own private understanding.)[9] In his "Seven Prolegomenae to a Brief Treatise on Magrittian Tropes," Jean Clair connects Magritte's analogous staging of these various kinds of "visual games," as he puts it, with scenography.[10] By invoking another of Marina Warner's meanings of "play," to wit, play as theater, Clair draws ingenious parallels between the painterly conundra of this twentieth-century surrealist and the efforts of a seventeenth-century stage designer, Nicolà Sabbatini, who was known to have caused a whole stage to burst into flames, to have made mountains rise from beneath a stage floor, rocks transform into men, and clouds crash the stage. Can we, should we, connect all this with children's worlds of metamorphosis: with a chair that changes magically into a ship

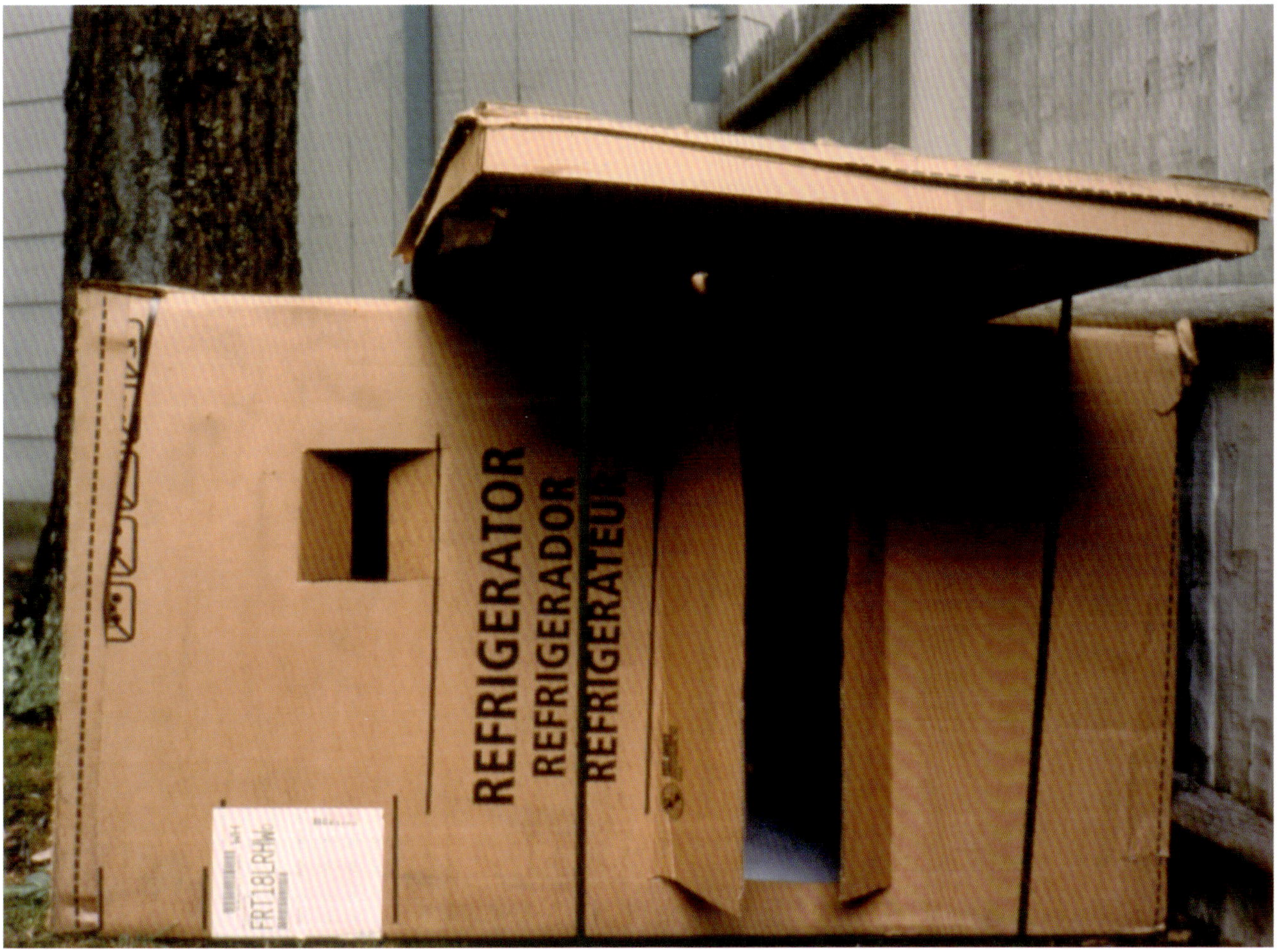

or a castle, for instance, or with a riveting race on a windowpane, as in A. A. Milne's poetry, between two raindrops endowed with names?[11]

E. H. Gombrich, in his *Meditations on a Hobby Horse,* develops his own provocative theory, taking impulse and intention rather than visual similarity as the fount of symbolic elaboration in play.[12] Objects, he thinks, matter to small children just because of what can be done with them and to them. The hobbyhorse, he points out, need not look at all like a real horse. Likewise, a kitten chases a ball of yarn—not because the ball resembles a mouse but because the kitten can do to the ball what it might do to a mouse. Any stick or pole that a child can ride becomes *ipso facto* a hobbyhorse, and it is the riding, not the appearance, that proves the decisive factor. By analogy, manipulation of media has become after all the quintessence of much of today's artistic expression. Especially, I would aver, in the emerging artistic field of interactivity.

Five-year-old Peter's dad is a doctor who works long hours. One Sunday, while Peter is playing in his parents' bedroom, his dad excuses himself, but Peter objects: "You can't leave, Daddy, or I'll get a 'somebody's-going-away pain!'" Rather than ridiculing his son by laughing or ignoring the protest, Peter's dad asks Peter to explain what that would be like. (Note that a doctor's child has spontaneously invented the notion of a "pain" to get his father's attention.) Becoming very excited, Peter says he has an idea and marches down two flights of stairs where he finds and fetches paper, crayons, and a pen. While his father goes off to the bathroom, he draws a picture of the "somebody's-going-away pain."

It turns out to be a whirlwind or dust storm with a stick figure (Peter himself?) in the middle, caught up, as it were, in a tornado of colored lines. After drawing this picture and realizing his father has not yet returned, Peter pierces the paper all over with pen pricks, thus perforating the image with holes that give it a more aggressive and sinister look. We have, then, a child who responds to a sudden sense of impending albeit momentary loss with an artistic solution that is remarkable principally because it has come into being so naturally. It is he who has initiated this solution to his dilemma, a solution we should note that was fostered by his dad's interest in his feelings. The pen pricks are especially remarkable. They denote an emotional shift not only from passive to active but from loss to aggression. Such a shift is familiar and widespread because, of course, most people find it easier and more of a relief to get angry than to bear sorrow. Peter's mild aggression, however, occurs in a creative and proto-artistic rather than a harmful way.

Peter's choice of drawing as a means of coping with the threat of momentary loss and of trying to express his feelings to another person by means of colors, lines, and shapes on paper may be seen as an artistic act. Perhaps if he were to continue, Peter might, over time, develop an artistic bent or be better able to grasp intuitively how, like his own, others' needs and inner states can be projected into graphic forms. Thus, the beginnings of aesthetic expression and arts education may occur—springing from a child's own impulse, act, and a parent's sensitive response.

What Peter made, however, is debatable as a work of art, and I myself would hardly be willing to call it such. Without the story I have just told to go with it, it is devoid of interest. It has no intrinsic aesthetic merit. Minus its context, it is tantamount to the daydream of the ordinary untalented daydreamer Freud writes about, whose tales leave us indifferent.

And so I wonder once again whether any direct line in fact travels between children's nursery games and fully realized works of art that achieve public recognition and acclaim.

I started these remarks by reporting on my greeting to a little boy who habitually wants to be called something different each time I see him and who, in turn, gives me different names as well and who in fact gets quite upset if I fail to remember and refer to him by last time's appellation! In the Israel Museum in Jerusalem, by analogy, there was an exhibition by the Paris-based expatriate Japanese artist Kimiko Yoshida titled "All That Is Not Me" (solo show, Israel Museum, February 2–May 15, 2006). Here the artist, a photographer, using masks and costumes and a variety of other disguises in an arresting set of life-size self-portraits, was, as she put it to me, "fighting out" a battle between subtraction and saturation, that is, between the minimalist aesthetic canon of her own native Japan and what she takes as the seductive Baroque aesthetic of European art. Both she and my little chameleon friend, with their implicit questionings of identity, return me to Yeats's suggestive lines in his poem "Ego Dominus Tuus":

By the help of an image
I call to my own opposite, summon all
That I have handled least, least looked upon.[13]

With this invocation resonating in mind, and with a plethora of images hovering in memory, images made by both artists and children, I continue to ponder whether play morphs uncomplicatedly into valued art, whether art emerges smoothly out of play, and whether, indeed, the differences between these two apparently separable realms have gradually now, in this new century, more than they have in the past, been actually eliding.

A final example of such elision might be found in *SCUMAK (Auto Sculpture Maker)* by Roxy Paine (2001), which drew continuous crowds at the 010101 exhibition at SFMOMA, referred to above. This work consists of a machine that uninterruptedly mass-produces mounds of oozelike sculptural forms. No human hand intervenes. Each sculptural mass of viscous white or tinted plastic that emerges varies slightly and unpredictably in shape from the previous mass. Visitors seem to find this hypnotizing; lost in rapt fascination once they discover it, they gaze at it, and only reluctantly tear themselves away to move on to view the rest of the exhibition. To me, it brings back memories of the beloved children's classic by Dr. Seuss, *Bartholomew and the Oobleck,* with its greenish blobs concocted by tall-hatted magicians who hail from the "mystic mountain Neekatave."[14] And it can also, if one wishes, be seen as a bewitching meditation on one of the core ontological problems of aesthetics proper, namely, *What is a work of art?* Of course, this too links it directly with childhood, since it is children who are prone to ask what philosophers call "primitive questions": Why is the sky blue? What makes people bad? Why did my fish die?[15] Such questions, as well as questions as to what an artist can and cannot do, are of course forever present and the answers forever changing.

Still, when all is said and done, it seems to me that, without trivializing art or aggrandizing children's play and vice versa, these realms will never really be commensurable. They may, in our present age of globalization and technological expansion, draw increasingly on one another, however, to produce works that should, at best, prove astonishing, merry, and even occasionally—in a Wordsworthian sense—wise.

NOTES

INTRODUCTION

1. Pablo Picasso, "Picasso Speaks" (1923), in Alfred Barr, *Picasso: Fifty Years of His Art* (New York: Museum of Modern Art, 1946), 270.
2. Three significant exceptions are Griselda Pollock, *Avant-garde Gambits, 1888–1893: Gender and the Color of Art History* (New York: Thames and Hudson, 1993); Hubert Damisch, *Moves: Playing Chess and Cards with the Museum* (Rotterdam: Museum Boijmans Van Beuningen, 1997); and, more recently, Nike Bätzner, *Faites Vos Jeux! Kunst Und Spiel Seit Dada,* exh. cat. (Vaduz: Kunstmuseum Liechtenstein, 2005).
3. Game Studies is not to be confused with the branch of applied mathematics known as Game Theory, though there are points of intersection. The foundational text of Game Theory is John von Neumann and Oskar Morgenstern, *Theory of Games and Economic Behavior* (Princeton: Princeton University Press, 1953). For a useful historiographical assessment of Game Studies that discusses its relation to Game Theory, see Jan Simons, "Narrative, Games, and Theory," no. 1 (2006).
4. The rapid coalescence of Game Studies as a field is evidenced in the number of *Game Studies* 7, recent titles. The majority of the new work tends to be focused exclusively on video and online gaming. See, for instance, Mark J. P. Wolf, *The Medium of the Video Game* (Austin: University of Texas Press, 2002); Katie Salen and Eric Zimmerman, *Rules of Play: Game Design Fundamentals* (Cambridge: MIT Press, 2004); Noah Wardrip-Fruin and Pat Harrigan, eds., *First Person: New Media as Story, Performance, and Game* (Cambridge: MIT Press, 2004); Jesper Juul, *Half-Real: Video Games Between Real Rules and Fictional Worlds* (Cambridge: MIT Press, 2005); Joost Raessens and Jeffrey H. Goldstein, *Handbook of Computer Game Studies* (Cambridge: MIT Press, 2005); Ian Bogost, *Unit Operations: An Approach to Videogame Criticism* (Cambridge: MIT Press, 2006); Katie Salen and Eric Zimmerman, *The Game Design Reader: A Rules of Play Anthology* (Cambridge: MIT Press, 2006); Ian Bogost, *Persuasive Games: The Expressive Power of Videogames* (Cambridge: MIT Press, 2007); McKenzie Wark, *Gamer Theory* (Cambridge: Harvard University Press, 2007); Steven E. Jones, *The Meaning of Video Games: Gaming and Textual Studies* (New York: Routledge, 2008); Melanie Swalwell and Jason Wilson, *The Pleasures of Computer Gaming: Essays on Cultural History, Theory, and Aesthetics* (Jefferson, N.C.: McFarland and Co., 2008); Zach Whalen and Laurie N. Taylor, *Playing the Past: History and Nostalgia in Video Games* (Nashville: Vanderbilt University Press, 2008); Mark J. P. Wolf, *The Video Game Explosion: A History from PONG to Playstation and Beyond* (Westport, Conn.: Greenwood Press, 2008); and the special issue of *Reconstruction* 6, no. 1 (2006). In addition, I have found particularly useful the position on the specificity of video games developed in Alexander Galloway, *Gaming: Essays on Algorithmic Culture* (Minneapolis: University of Minnesota Press, 2006).
5. Jesper Juul provides a concise summary of the major taxonomic frameworks in the study of games and proposes his own in Juul, *Half-Real,* 29–43.
6. Johan Huizinga, *Homo Ludens: A Study of the Play-Element in Culture* (London: Routledge and Kegan Paul, 1949); Roger Caillois, *Man, Play, and Games,* trans. Meyer Barash (Urbana: University of Illinois Press, 1961).

7. This is also Galloway's position as he attempts to deal with the very different ways in which games and play are manifested in the medium of video games, arguing that Huizinga and Caillois are of limited (and limiting) use. While not discarding these canonical authors altogether, he makes them subordinate to his account of video games as actions. Huizinga's book, he states, "is so far removed from the medium that it can merely gesture a way forward, not provide a core approach." I would argue that the same holds true for the study of games in modern and contemporary art history. See Galloway, *Gaming: Essays on Algorithmic Culture,* 20.
8. Ludwig Wittgenstein, *Philosophical Investigations: The English Text of the Third Edition* (New York: Macmillan, 1973), §§66–67.
9. Huizinga, *Homo Ludens,* 10. Huizinga's phrase, the "magic circle" of play has recently been taken up as the place-holder for this concept. See Salen and Zimmerman, *Rules of Play,* 95.
10. On the expanded sense of the term "virtual," see Richard Norton, "What Is Virtuality?" *Journal of Aesthetics and Art Criticism* 30, no. 4 (1972): 499–505, and, from a very different perspective, Brian Massumi, *Parables for the Virtual: Movement, Affect, Sensation* (Durham: Duke University Press, 2002).
11. For a differentiation of play and game-play, see Bo Kampmann Walther, "Playing and Gaming: Reflections and Classifications," *Game Studies* 3, no. 1 (2003).
12. See, for instance, the discussion in Clifford Geertz, "Deep Play: Notes on the Balinese Cockfight" (1972), *Daedalus* 134, no. 4 (2005): 56–86, in which Geertz argued that the cockfight served an "interpretive" function as "metasocial commentary" on status hierarchies within Balinese culture (82).
13. For an overview of the postwar use of games (the list of topics of which parallels the in-depth investigations in this volume), see Claudia Mesch, "Cold War Games and Postwar Art," *Reconstruction* 6, no. 1 (2006).
14. See Brian Sutton-Smith, *The Ambiguity of Play* (Cambridge: Harvard University Press, 1997); Elliott M. Avedon and Brian Sutton-Smith, eds., *The Study of Games* (New York: John Wiley and Sons, 1971); Brian Sutton-Smith, ed., *The Psychology of Play: Studies in Play and Games* (New York: Arno Press, 1976); Anthony Pellegrini, ed., *The Future of Play Theory: A Multidisciplinary Inquiry into the Contributions of Brian Sutton-Smith* (Albany: State University of New York Press, 1995).
15. For example, see Mihai Spariosu, *Dionysus Reborn: Play and the Aesthetic Dimension in Modern Philosophical and Scientific Discourse* (Ithaca: Cornell University Press, 1989); Michael Apter, *Reversal Theory: Motivation, Emotion, and Personality* (New York: Routledge, 1989); Tilman Küchler, *Postmodern Gaming: Heidegger, Duchamp, Derrida* (New York: Peter Lang, 1994); Jacques Derrida, "Structure, Sign, and Play in the Discourse of the Human Sciences" (1966), in *Writing and Difference,* trans. Alan Bass (London: Routledge, 1978), 278–94; Michael Apter, "A Structural-Phenomenology of Play," in *Adult Play,* ed. J. H. Kerr and M. J. Apter (Amsterdam: Swets and Zeitlinger, 1991).
16. See D. W. Winnicott, *Playing and Reality* (New York: Routledge, 1971); D. W. Winnicott, *Through Paediatrics to Psycho-Analysis: Collected Papers* (New York: Bruner/Mazel, 1958; reprint, 1992); D. W. Winnicott, *The Maturational Processes and the Facilitating Environment: Studies in the Theory of Emotional Development* (New York: International Universities Press, 1965); D. W. Winnicott et al., *Psycho-Analytic Explorations* (Cambridge: Harvard University Press, 1989). On Klein's technique, see Melanie Klein, "The Psycho-Analytic Play Technique: Its History and Significance" (1955), in *The Selected Melanie Klein,* ed. Juliet Mitchell (New York: The Free Press, 1987), 35–54.
17. In this focus, Winnicott has similar aims to his contemporary Jacques Lacan and his discussion of the "mirror stage." See Jacques Lacan, "The Mirror Stage as Formative of the Function of the I as Revealed in Psychoanalytic Experience" (1949), in *Écrits* (New York: W. W. Norton, 1977), 1–7, and Winnicott's response to Lacan in D. W. Winnicott, "Mirror-role of Mother and Family in Child Development," in *Playing and Reality* (London: Routledge, 1969), 111–18.
18. See "Playing: A Theoretical Statement," "Playing: Creative Activity and the Search for Self," and "Creativity and Its Origins," in Winnicott, *Playing and Reality,* 38–85.
19. D. W. Winnicott, "The Location of Cultural Experience," in *Playing and Reality,* 95–103. For a discussion of the emotional engagement with painting, see James Elkins, *Pictures and Tears: A History of People Who Have Cried in Front of Paintings* (New York: Routledge, 2001).
20. For a related case for the usefulness of a Game Studies perspective in art history, see David Getsy, "Pedagogy, Art, and the Rules of the Game," in *Learning Mind: Experience into Art,* ed. Mary Jane Jacob and Jacquelynn Baas (Berkeley and Los Angeles: University of California Press, 2009), 125–35.

CHAPTER 1

1. See Peter Bürger, *Theory of the Avant-Garde,* trans. Michael Shaw (Minneapolis: University of Minnesota Press, 1984); G. H. Bell-Villada, *Art for Art's Sake and Literary Life: How Politics and Markets Helped Shape the Ideology and Culture of Aestheticism, 1790–1990* (Lincoln: University of Nebraska Press, 1996).
2. Rodolphe Gasché, *The Idea of Form: Rethinking Kant's Aesthetics* (Stanford: Stanford University Press, 2003), 7.
3. Allan Megill, *Prophets of Extremity: Nietzsche, Heidegger, Foucault, Derrida* (Berkeley and Los Angeles: University of California Press, 1985), 2.
4. In the visual arts, one need only consider the reception of the readymade to understand both the inadequacy of this schematic and ahistorical definition of play and its effectiveness in neutralizing the impact of avant-garde movements. The readymade's attempt to shift critical focus away from beauty and taste toward the question of what makes the work of art distinct from ordinary objects, as well as its assertion that art is determined not by essences but solely by its field of inscription, is routinely neutralized when the objects are described as "playful" assemblages, much as Duchamp's visual puns are effectively dismissed as "whimsical."
5. Bürger, *Theory of the Avant-Garde,* 42. Bürger thus makes obvious the parallel between enlightenment rationality and its modern outcome, instrumental reason.
6. Immanuel Kant, *The Critique of Judgment,* trans. Werner S. Pluhar (Indianapolis: Hackett, 1987), §2, 45–46. In the citations that follow, the section numbers are indicated by the symbol § followed by the page numbers of the Pluhar translation.

7. Kant, *The Critique of Judgment,* §9, 62.
8. Ibid., §45, 174.
9. Ibid., §16, 76–77.
10. See Mihai Spariosu, *Literature, Mimesis, and Play: Essays in Literary Theory* (Tübingen: Narr, 1989); Kendall L. Walton, *Mimesis as Make-Believe: On the Foundations of the Representational Arts* (Cambridge: Harvard University Press, 1990); Jacques Derrida, "Economimesis," trans. R. Klein, *Diacritics* 11, no. 2 (Summer 1981): 2–25; and René Girard, *To Double Business Bound: Essays on Literature, Mimesis, and Anthropology* (Baltimore: Johns Hopkins University Press, 1978).
11. Kant, *The Critique of Judgment,* §58, 221; §62, 241.
12. Derrida, *The Truth in Painting,* trans. Geoff Bennington and Ian McLeod (Chicago: University of Chicago Press, 1987), 48, 87.
13. Bürger, *Theory of the Avant-Garde,* 42.
14. Work for Kant entails coercion and is therefore the opposite of freedom. See *The Critique of Judgment,* §43, 171.
15. Even the Soviet model can be understood as engaging play in its utopian dimension—the desire for a collapse of work and play in a society in which labor is pleasure. For the repercussions of the Duchampian substitution of "art" for "beauty" in the Kantian formula, see Thierry De Duve, *Kant After Duchamp* (Cambridge: MIT Press, 1996).
16. Derrida argued most compellingly for this contradiction, exposing unstable play within in the very device meant to close off the Kantian gestalt: the frame of disinterest. Derrida, *The Truth in Painting.*
17. Ibid., 48.
18. Mihai Spariosu, *Dionysus Reborn: Play and the Aesthetic Dimension in Modern Philosophical and Scientific Discourse* (Ithaca: Cornell University Press, 1989), 52.
19. Friedrich Schiller, *On the Aesthetic Education of Man in a Series of Letters* (1795), trans. Elizabeth M. Wilkinson and L. A. Willoughby (Oxford: Clarendon Press, 1967). Hereafter all references will be from this edition, abbreviated as *Aesthetic Education;* citations will be identified in roman numerals corresponding to the specific letters in which they are found, followed by the numbered section of the letter, and last by the page number of the Wilkinson/Willoughby translation.
20. Schiller, *Aesthetic Education,* XV, 9, 107.
21. M. H. Abrams, *Natural Supernaturalism: Tradition and Revolution in Romantic Literature* (New York: W. W. Norton, 1973), 212, cited in Constantin Behler, *Nostalgic Teleology: Friedrich Schiller and the Schemata of Aesthetic Humanism* (New York: Peter Lang, 1995), 50.
22. Schiller, *Aesthetic Education,* II, 3, 7.
23. Ibid., VI, 6, 33; VI, 7, 35.
24. Ibid., XII, 1, 79; XV, 2, 103.
25. Ibid., XI, 9, 77; XII, 4, 81; XV, 2, 103.
26. Ibid., XIII, 2, 85; XIII, 6, 93.
27. Ibid., XI, 8, 77; VI, 12, 41; XV, 2, 103.
28. Ibid., XVI, 1, 111.
29. Ibid., XV, 9, 107.
30. Ibid., XV, 4, 103. See also Spariosu, *Dionysus Reborn,* 53–65.
31. See Marjorie Perloff, *The Poetics of Indeterminacy: Rimbaud to Cage* (Evanston, Ill.: Northwestern University Press, 1983).
32. Kant, *The Critique of Judgment,* §9, 62.

33. Behler sees this ascribing of a function for art as Schiller's legacy: "as a major source of inspiration for a left-humanist critique of bourgeois society," his "aesthetic utopia" was a "point of orientation" for Hegel, Marx, Lukács, and Marcuse. Behler, *Nostalgic Teleology,* 1, 2.
34. Spariosu, *Dionysus Reborn,* 60.
35. Schiller, *Aesthetic Education,* XXVII, 4, 209.
36. Ibid., XXVII, 2, 207.
37. Ibid., 6, 51.
38. Ibid., II, 3, 7.
39. Ibid., II, 5, 9. For a fuller examination of those political implications in Schiller that work against autonomy, see Behler, *Nostalgic Teleology,* 25.
40. Schiller, *Aesthetic Education,* IX, 1, 55.
41. Ibid., XXIII, 2, 161.
42. Ibid., XXIII, 4, 161; Specifically, a "melting beauty" acts on the tensed subject and "energizing beauty" acts on the relaxed subject. Ibid., XVI, 5, 115.
43. Ibid., XXIII, 5 163; XVII, 2, 117.
44. Ibid., XXVII, 12, 219; X, 1, 63.
45. Bürger, *Theory of the Avant-Garde,* 98; Behler, *Nostalgic Teleology,* 47.
46. Nietzsche's references to aesthetic theory in his first book, *The Birth of Tragedy* (1872), are to Schiller and not Kant, attesting to the dominance of Schiller's philosophy in Western European aesthetics at the time. See Friedrich Nietzsche, *The Birth of Tragedy* (New York: Random House, 1967), §3, 19 and 43; §7, 58; §8, 61; §19, 117. The following citations will refer to this edition of *The Birth of Tragedy,* with the sections and page numbers indicated for ease of location in other editions.
47. For a fuller characterization of Nietzsche's "break with Schillerian tradition," see Spariosu, *Dionysus Reborn,* 31, 88–89.
48. Friedrich Nietzsche, *Thus Spoke Zarathustra,* trans. Walter Kaufmann (New York: Modern Library, 1995). Regarding the contradictions in his work, see Lawrence Hinman, "Nietzsche's Philosophy of Play," *Philosophy Today* 18, nos. 2–4 (1974): 106–24; and Peter Heller, "Multiplicity and Unity in Nietzsche's Works and Thoughts on Thought," *German Quarterly* 52, no. 3 (1979): 319–38.
49. Hinman, "Nietzsche's Philosophy of Play," 111. Hinman identifies five instances of play in *The Birth of Tragedy* alone, all concerned with the subject/object interface through art, on page 108.
50. Friedrich Nietzsche, *Ecce Homo,* trans. Walter Kaufmann (New York: Vintage Books, 1967), 853, cited in Spariosu, *Dionysus Reborn,* 69 n. 27.
51. See Martin Heidegger, *Hegel's Phenomenology of the Spirit,* trans. Parvis Emad and Kenneth Maly (Bloomington: Indiana University Press, 1988).
52. See Spariosu, *Dionysus Reborn,* 75.
53. Nietzsche, *The Birth of Tragedy,* §24, 141; §25, 143; §25, 144; §12, 81, and §2, 38.
54. Ibid., §1, 33; §4, 45.
55. Ibid., §4, 45; §7, 59; §1, 36.
56. Ibid., §1, 37.
57. Heller, "Multiplicity and Unity in Nietzsche's Works and Thoughts on Thought," 320.
58. Nietzsche, *The Birth of Tragedy,* §24, 139.
59. Ibid., §21, 129; 25, 143.
60. Roger Caillois, *Man, Play, and Games,* trans. Meyer Barash (New York: The Free Press, 1961), 19.
61. Hinman, "Nietzsche's Philosophy of Play," 108. See also Richard Detsch, "A Non-Subjectivist Concept of Play: Gadamer and Heidegger versus Rilke and Nietzsche," *Philosophy Today* 29, no. 2–4 (1985): 156–72.
62. Nietzsche, *The Birth of Tragedy,* §4, 45.
63. Ibid., §1, 38.
64. Heller, "Multiplicity and Unity in Nietzsche's Works and Thoughts on Thought," 328.
65. Nietzsche, *The Birth of Tragedy,* §5, 52.
66. Ibid., §5, 51.
67. Ibid., §24, 142.
68. Ibid., §25, 143.
69. Ibid., §24, 141.
70. See Paul Roazen, "Nietzsche, Freud, and the History of Psychoanalysis," in *Returns of the "French Freud": Freud, Lacan, and Beyond,* ed. Todd Dufresne (New York: Routledge, 1997), 11–23.
71. Nietzsche, *The Will to Power,* trans. Walter Kaufmann and R. J. Hollingdale (New York: Random House, 1967), §1067, 550.
72. Georges Bataille, *On Nietzsche,* trans. Bruce Boone (New York: Paragon House, 1992), 87, 93.
73. Ibid., 115.
74. Nietzsche, *Thus Spoke Zarathustra,* 183–84, cited in Spariosu, *Dionysus Reborn,* 85.
75. Bataille, *On Nietzsche,* 184, 95.
76. Nietzsche, *The Will to Power,* §1067, 549; Hinman,"Nietzsche's Philosophy of Play," 116. See also Gilles Deleuze, *Nietzsche and Philosophy,* trans. Hugh Tomlinson (New York: Columbia University Press, 1983), 25–27.
77. Sigmund Freud, "Beyond the Pleasure Principle" (1920), in *On Metapsychology: The Theory of Psychoanalysis,* Penguin Freud Library, vol. 11, trans. James Strachey (New York: Penguin Books, 1991).
78. See Spariosu, *Dionysus Reborn,* 176, and Heller, "Multiplicity and Unity in Nietzsche's Works and Thoughts on Thought," 319.
79. Sigmund Freud, "Creative Writers and Day-Dreaming" (1907), in *Art and Literature,* Penguin Freud Library, vol. 14, trans. James Strachey (New York: Penguin Books, 1991); and Freud, *Jokes and Their Relation to the Unconscious* (1905), trans. James Strachey, Penguin Freud Library, vol. 6 (New York: Penguin Books, 1991).
80. Freud, "Creative Writers and Day-Dreaming," 132.
81. Ibid., 140.
82. Freud, *Jokes and Their Relation to the Unconscious,* 39.
83. Ibid., 175. See also Spariosu, *Dionysus Reborn,* 179. For evidence that Freud meant *Jokes and Their Relation to the Unconscious* as "the first example of an application of the analytic mode of thought to the problems of aesthetics," see Sigmund Freud, *The History of the Psychoanalytic Movement,* cited in Richard Wollheim, "Freud and the Understanding of Art," in *Modern Critical Views: Sigmund Freud,* ed. Harold Bloom (New York: Chelsea House, 1985), 92.
84. Freud, *Jokes and Their Relation to the Unconscious,* 270.
85. Ibid., 189 n.
86. Samuel Weber, *The Legend of Freud* (Minneapolis: University of Minnesota Press, 1982), 112, 106; Freud, *Jokes and Their Relation to the Unconscious,* 189 n.

87. Freud, *Jokes and Their Relation to the Unconscious,* 215, 130, 265, 74, 225.

88. Ibid., 154. In the economic scheme Freud lays out for the joke, laughter is a sign of repression—the saving up of libidinal energy. That is, we laugh instead of having the sexual discharge we desire. It would seem that play as expenditure makes a first appearance here, anticipating Roger Caillois's attribution (by way of Bataille) of play to expenditure. But counterintuitively, Freud maintains that jokes are instances of *saving,* not expenditure, as they economize on the energy that would have otherwise been expended in inhibition. This permits him to primly describe jokes as efficient and not transgressive. Laughter, then, is a paradoxical sign of repression (of energy) and release (from conscious reason); a sign for the primary processes at its root, but also the sign for a fundamentally unsatisfied desire.

89. Jeffrey Mehlman, "How to Read Freud on Jokes: The Critic as *Schadchen,*" *New Literary History* 6, no. 2 (Winter 1975): 439–61; 448.

90. Freud, *Jokes and Their Relation to the Unconscious,* 133; 138–39.

91. Ibid., 153.

92. Ibid., 140–46.

93. Ibid., chap. 5, 191–211; Weber, *The Legend of Freud,* 110.

94. Freud, *Jokes and Their Relation to the Unconscious,* 155. Freud's startlingly Marxian assertion is not footnoted in the Penguin Freud Library edition, but Joyce Crick, translator of the recent Penguin Classics edition, speculates that this is a reference to Nietzsche. Sigmund Freud, *The Joke and Its Relation to the Unconscious,* trans. Joyce Crick (New York: Penguin Books, 2003), 112 n. 16.

95. Weber, *The Legend of Freud,* 93

96. Freud, *Jokes and Their Relation to the Unconscious,* 69–70.

97. Weber, *The Legend of Freud,* 113–14.

98. Freud, *Beyond the Pleasure Principle,* 299; and "Civilization and Its Discontents," in *Civilization, Society, and Religion,* Penguin Freud Library, vol. 12, trans. James Strachey (New York: Penguin Books, 1991), 308.

99. Freud, "The Economic Problem of Masochism" (1924), cited in J. Laplanche and J.-B. Pontalis, *The Language of Psychoanalysis,* trans. Donald Nicholson-Smith (New York: W. W. Norton, 1973), 98.

100. Freud, *Beyond the Pleasure Principle,* 307–8, 311.

101. Ibid., 284–85. This is of course the famous passage footnoted with the mirror image that Lacan will develop further. The link from Lacan's Imaginary and Symbolic stages to Freudian play is made explicit in Weber, *The Legend of Freud,* 96–97.

102. Freud, *Beyond the Pleasure Principle,* 314, 334 n. 1.

103. Ibid., 330.

104. Ibid., 308.

105. See Hal Foster, *Compulsive Beauty* (Cambridge: MIT Press, 1993), 124–54.

106. Georges Bataille, "The Notion of Expenditure," in *Visions of Excess: Selected Writings,* ed. Allan Stoekl (Minneapolis: University of Minnesota Press, 1985), 117.

107. For Freud's unintentional critique of conventional narratives of harmony and unity, see Leo Bersani, *The Freudian Body* (New York: Columbia University Press, 1986), 63, 66–67.

108. David Frisby considers Simmel's Kantian roots in *Simmel and Since: Essays on Georg Simmel's Social Theory* (New York: Routledge, 1992), 14–15.

109. Georg Simmel, "The Metropolis and Mental Life" (1903) and "The Conflict in Modern Culture" (1918), in Donald Levine, ed., *Georg Simmel: On Individuality and Social Forms* (Chicago: University of Chicago Press, 1971), 324–39, 375–98.
110. Georg Simmel, "Sociability" (1910), in Levine, ed., *Georg Simmel: On Individuality and Social Forms,* 130.
111. Simmel, "Sociability" (1910), 130, 133. See also Simmel, "Sociological Aesthetics," in *The Conflict in Modern Culture and Other Essays,* ed. K. Peter Etzkorn (New York: Teachers College Press, Columbia University, 1968).
112. Simmel, "Sociability" (1910), 129. Sociability is the play-form of social relations: "Its relation to content-determined, concrete sociation is similar to that of the work of art to reality," 128.
113. Simmel, "Sociability" (1910), 130, 133, 138.
114. Georg Simmel, "Sociability" (1917), in *The Sociology of Georg Simmel,* trans. and ed. Kurt H. Wolff (New York: The Free Press, 1950), 42.
115. Simmel, *Schopenhauer and Nietzsche,* trans. Helmut Loiskandl, Deena Weinstein, and Michael Weinstein (Urbana: University of Illinois Press, 1991), xxxix.
116. Simmel, "Sociability" (1917), 42–43.
117. Georg Simmel, "The Dramatic Actor and Reality," in *The Conflict in Modern Culture and Other Essays,* 96, 97. As in Nietzsche and Freud, drama is here considered the art form closest to "life."
118. Simmel, "Sociability" (1917), 55.
119. See Frisby, *Simmel and Since,* 136.
120. Georg Simmel, "Sociological Aesthetics," in *The Conflict in Modern Culture and Other Essays,* 72. Note the commensurability with William Worringer's *Abstraction and Empathy,* trans. Michael Bullock (Chicago: Ivan R. Dee, 1997).
121. Simmel, "Sociability" (1917), 49.
122. Simmel, "Sociological Aesthetics," 73, 74, 80.
123. Simmel, "Sociability" (1917), 57.
124. Georg Simmel, "The Adventure," in *Simmel on Culture,* ed. David Frisby and Mike Featherstone (Thousand Oaks, Calif.: Sage, 1997), 223.
125. Simmel, "The Adventure," 222.
126. Simmel anticipated Benjamin's extended examination of exchange value and use value, and his views also resonate with Benjamin's regarding the role of distance in relation to aura in the work of art, as well as ahistoricity in play forms directly associated with economic exchange—specifically gambling. Simmel was the only sociologist cited in Benjamin's *Passagen-Werk,* most extensively with reference to *The Philosophy of Money.* Walter Benjamin, *The Arcades Project,* trans. Howard Eiland and Kevin McLaughlin (Cambridge: Harvard University Press, 1999), 660–62.
127. Simmel, "Sociability" (1917), 42.
128. Benjamin is citing Alain Emile-Auguste Chartier, *Les Idées et les ages* (Paris, 1927), 1:183–84, in Walter Benjamin, Convolut O, "Le Jeu," *The Arcades Project,* 512 [O 12, 3].
129. Simmel, "Sociability" (1910), 134–35.
130. Simmel, "On Art Exhibitions," cited in Frisby, "The Aesthetics of Modern Life," *Theory, Culture & Society: A Special Issue on Georg Simmel,* no. 3 (1991): 146.

CHAPTER 2

1. Michel de Certeau, "The Scriptural Economy," in *The Practice of Everyday Life,* trans. Steven Rendall (Berkeley and Los Angeles: University of California Press, 1984), 131–53; 136. Although de Certeau believes Duchamp's *Large Glass* figures "the lure of communication," he regards its theme as a "laughable tragedy of language: being mixed together by an optical effect, these elements are neither coherent nor conjoined . . . the bride is never married to a reality of a meaning." De Certeau, *Practice of Everyday Life,* 151. His sources are a book Duchamp did not care for by Michel Carrouges, *Les Machines célibataires* (1954) (Paris: Chêne, 1976), and Jean Clair and Harald Szeemann, *Junggesellenmaschinen/Les Machines célibataires* (Venice: Alfieri, 1976) (to which de Certeau contributed). See Michel de Certeau, "The Arts of Dying: Celibatory Machines," *Heterologies: Discourse on the Other,* trans. Brian Massumi (Manchester: Manchester University Press, 1986), 156–67.
2. One commentator imputes this to artistic intention, describing Duchamp's work as "a free-floating, ceaselessly interactive semiotic field rather than a set of discrete, determinate units of meaning," Sheldon Nodelman, "The Once and Future Duchamp" [book review], *Art in America* 88, no. 1 (January 2000): 37–43; 37.
3. With the death of Walter Hopps in March 2005, followed by that of Anne d'Harnoncourt in June 2008, the secret fragment of *With Hidden Noise* once again passed into total obscurity.
4. Duchamp's friend Charles Demuth said in 1926, "dear Marcel, having used glass so often seems to have added difficulties for the Future—he would, of course," in Pontus Hultén, ed., *Marcel Duchamp: Work and Life* (Cambridge: MIT Press, 1993), see 20 October 1926.
5. Dalia Judovitz, *Unpacking Duchamp: Art in Transit* (Berkeley and Los Angeles: University of California Press, 1995), 106.
6. Hubert Damisch, "The Duchamp Defense," *October* 10 (Autumn 1979): 5–28; Jon Wood, "Brancusi's 'White Studio,'" *Sculpture Journal* 7 (2002): 108–20. Both of these essays are richer than my shorthand can do justice to here.
7. John Cage, "26 Statements *re* Duchamp," in *Marcel Duchamp in Perspective,* ed. Joseph Mashek (Englewood Cliffs, N.J.: Spectrum, 1975), 67–69; 68.
8. Arturo Schwarz, ed., *The Complete Works of Marcel Duchamp,* 2 vols., revised and expanded (London: Thames and Hudson, 1997), 2:197.
9. Ulf Linde in Schwarz, ed., *Complete Works of Marcel Duchamp,* 1:189.
10. Juan Antonio Ramírez, *Duchamp: Love and Death, Even,* trans. Alexander R. Tulloch (London: Reaktion Books, 1998), 34, 38, 42.
11. Thierry de Duve, "The Readymade and the Tube of Paint," *Artforum* 24, no. 9 (May 1986): 110–21. For reasons that will become clear, I do not intend a point-for-point response to de Duve's theory. I am treating his essay as an exemplary object here and do not mean this as a dismissal of de Duve's contributions to the Duchamp scholarship: *Pictorial Nominalism: On Marcel Duchamp's Passage from Painting to the Readymade,* trans. Thierry de Duve and Dana Polan (Minneapolis: University of Minnesota Press, 1991); *Kant After Duchamp* (Cambridge: MIT Press, 1996). I am, however, remarking similarities between "respectable" theory and the more hallucinatory uses of alchemy and psychoanalysis, which are extensive in the Duchamp literature. For an excellent, concise historiography of the scholarship on

Duchamp and alchemy, see Linda Dalrymple Henderson, *Duchamp in Context: Science and Technology in the "Large Glass" and Related Works* (Princeton: Princeton University Press, 1998), 231–32. I discuss and relate psychoanalytic approaches in Gavin Parkinson, *The Duchamp Book* (London: Tate Publishing, 2008).

12. De Duve, "The Readymade and the Tube of Paint," 111.
13. Ibid., 112.
14. See, for instance, Marcel Duchamp, "A Propos of 'Readymades'" (1961), in *Salt Seller: The Essential Writings of Marcel Duchamp,* ed. Michel Sanouillet and Elmer Peterson (London: Thames and Hudson, 1975), 141–42; 142.
15. De Duve, "The Readymade and the Tube of Paint," 113.
16. Ibid., 114.
17. Ibid., 115.
18. Ibid.
19. Ibid.
20. Paul Matisse, ed., *Marcel Duchamp, Notes* (Paris: Centre National d'Art et de Culture Georges Pompidou, 1980), n.p.
21. Philippe Duboy, *Lequeu: An Architectural Enigma* (London: Thames and Hudson, 1986), 352.
22. Umberto Eco, *Interpretation and Overinterpretation* (Cambridge: Cambridge University Press, 1992). Eco's main target was freewheeling interpretation in mainly U.S. literary theory influenced by Jacques Derrida's deconstruction, though he did not necessarily blame Derrida for this, and holds a complex relation to his work. For a fuller context for this phase of Eco's writings, see Michael Caesar, "Secrets, Paranoia, and Critical Reading," *Umberto Eco: Philosophy, Semiotics, and the Work of Fiction* (Cambridge: Polity Press, 1999), 145–61. My own approach toward interpretation in the Duchamp business and art history generally does not really entail a negative appraisal of deconstruction. The literary criticism that most resembles the interpretation I am commenting upon here can be found in the amazing over-reading offered by Ted Hughes, *Shakespeare and the Goddess of Complete Being* (London: Faber and Faber, 1992), and in a book in which the author claims bewildering access to his subject's unconscious through his work, Christopher Ricks, *Dylan's Visions of Sin* (London: Viking, 2003).
23. Eco, *Interpretation and Overinterpretation,* 30.
24. Ibid.
25. Caesar, *Umberto Eco,* 147.
26. Eco, *Interpretation and Overinterpretation,* 30.
27. Simmel quoted in Eco, *Interpretation and Overinterpretation,* 38. See Georg Simmel, "Secrecy," in *The Sociology of Georg Simmel,* trans. and ed. Kurt H. Wolff (London: The Free Press of Glencoe, 1964), 333.
28. Umberto Eco, *Foucault's Pendulum,* trans. William Weaver (New York: Ballantine Books, 1989), 377–78.
29. Umberto Eco, *The Limits of Interpretation* (Bloomington: Indiana University Press, 1994), 27.
30. Peter Bondanella, *Umberto Eco and the Open Text: Semiotics, Fiction, Popular Culture* (Cambridge: Cambridge University Press, 1997), 132–33.
31. "I shall call Hermetic drift the interpretive habit which dominated Renaissance Hermetism and which is based on the principles of universal analogy and sympathy, according to which every item of the furniture of the world is linked to every other element (or to many) of this sublunar world and to every element (or to many) of the superior world by means of similitudes or resemblances." Eco, *Limits of Interpretation,* 24.

32. Interviewed in 1962, Duchamp said that words "such as truth, art, veracity, or anything else are stupid in themselves, so I insist *every word I am telling you now is stupid and wrong,*" quoted in Calvin Tomkins, *Duchamp: A Biography* (London: Pimlico, 1998), 419. Duchamp's position is eloquently expressed by Pierre de Massot, *The Wonderful Book: Réflections on Rrose Sélavy* (Paris: Pierre de Massot, 1924), while the spirit of negation some have seen in his acts and behavior is contextualized in the "history of the art of the No" by Enrique Vila-Matas, *Bartleby & Co.,* trans. Jonathan Dunne (London: Vintage, 2005).
33. I refer of course to Poe's tale here, in which the queen's incriminating letter is stolen by the minister and "hidden" by being left on show, debated extensively and collected in John P. Muller and William J. Richardson, eds., *The Purloined Poe: Lacan, Derrida, and Psychoanalytic Reading* (Baltimore: Johns Hopkins University Press, 1988).
34. Susan Sontag, "Against Interpretation," in *Against Interpretation* (London: Vintage, 2001), 6–7.
35. Ibid., 8.
36. For what follows, I draw mainly upon Martin Parker, "Human Science as Conspiracy Theory," in *The Age of Anxiety: Conspiracy Theory and the Human Sciences,* ed. Jane Parish and Martin Parker (Oxford: Blackwell Publishers/The Sociological Review, 2001), 191–207. Another symptom of the "age of anxiety" is the genre of the conspiracy novel, which includes the ubiquitous works of Dan Brown, but is at its best in the novels of Eco, Thomas Pynchon, and Don DeLillo. For a brilliant reading of paranoia in Pynchon, see Leo Bersani, "Pynchon, Paranoia, and Literature," *Representations* 25 (Winter 1989): 99–118.
37. Parish and Parker, eds., *The Age of Anxiety,* 192.
38. Ibid., 194.
39. Ibid., 192.
40. Ibid., 194.
41. Ibid.
42. Ibid., 196.
43. Ibid., 192.
44. Ibid., 202.
45. Ibid., 198. Parker's target here is Fredric Jameson's view that conspiracy is "the poor person's cognitive mapping in the postmodern age," and that real truths are to be gained from Marxism. See Jameson, "Cognitive Mapping," in *Marxism and the Interpretation of Culture,* ed. Cary Nelson and Lawrence Grossberg (Basingstoke: Macmillan Education, 1988), 356.
46. Parish and Parker, eds., *The Age of Anxiety,* 193.
47. In a longer essay, I would argue that their Hegelianism gives history and art history a particular place in debate on interpretation in the humanities and social sciences. Ernst Gombrich wrote of his reluctance to spin a historical yarn with the aid of Hegel's metaphysics in terms close to those I use here to discuss the Duchamp literature and conspiracy theory: "What gave me pause was not the belief that it is hard to establish such relationships but, paradoxically, that it often seems all too easy." Ernst Gombrich, "'The Father of Art History': A Reading of the *Lectures on Aesthetics* of G.W.F. Hegel (1770–1831)," in *Tributes: Interpreters of Our Cultural Tradition* (Oxford: Phaidon Press, 1984), 62. He goes on to say that "the danger of the Hegelian heritage lies precisely in its temptingly easy applicability. After all, the dialectic makes it all too easy for us to find a way out of every contradiction. Because it seems to us as though everything in life is really interconnected, every method of interpretation can claim success" (63).
48. The Italian word *dietrologia* is used by Don DeLillo, *Underworld* (London: Picador, 1998), 280. See the discussion in Peter Knight, "Dietrology," *Conspiracy Culture: From Kennedy to "The X Files"* (New York: Routledge, 2000), 230–33.
49. I believe the first public airing for Duchamp's well-known Wittgensteinian statement was in an article published in the special "Duchamp" issue of *View* magazine in 1945, reprinted as Harriet and Sidney Janis, "Marcel Duchamp: Anti-Artist," in *The Dada Painters and Poets* (1951), ed. Robert Motherwell, 2nd ed. (Cambridge: Belknap Press of Harvard University Press, 1981), 313. When Duchamp was asked in an important *Life* article about a deeper meaning behind the *Box in a Suitcase,* he responded, "What would you consider the proper solution?" He then continued, "Obviously there can be no solution when there is no problem. Problems are inventions of the mind. They are nonsensical." Winthrop Sargeant, "Dada's Daddy," *Life* 32, no. 17 (28 April 1952): 108. "The solution of the problem of life is seen in the vanishing of the problem." Ludwig Wittgenstein, *Tractatus Logico-Philosophicus,* trans. D. F. Pears and B. F. McGuinness (London: Routledge and Kegan Paul, 1972), 149, prop. 6.521.
50. Examples are Thomas Mann, *Lotte in Weimar* (1939), trans. H. T. Lowe-Porter (Harmondsworth, Middlesex: Penguin Books, 1982), and Simon Schama, *Dead Certainties (Unwarranted Speculations)* (London: Granta, 1991). See Hayden White, "The Burden of History," in *Tropics of Discourse: Essays in Cultural Criticism* (Baltimore: Johns Hopkins University Press, 1978), 27–50; and the discussion by F. R. Ankersmit, "Hayden White's Appeal to the Historians," *History and Theory* 37, no. 2 (May 1998): 182–93.
51. Duchamp quoted in Schwarz, *Complete Works of Marcel Duchamp,* 1:256.
52. Duchamp quoted in Katharine Kuh, "Marcel Duchamp" (1961), in *The Artist's Voice: Talks with Seventeen Modern Artists* (New York: Da Capo Press, 2000), 90.
53. Duchamp, "The Green Box," *Salt Seller,* 30.
54. See, for instance, Alice Goldfarb Marquis, *Marcel Duchamp: The Bachelor Stripped Bare* (New York: MFA Publications, 2002), 292–94.
55. Duchamp quoted in 1961 in Alain Jouffroy, "Conversations avec Marcel Duchamp," *Une Révolution du regard: A propos de quelques peintres et sculpteurs contemporains* (Paris: Gallimard, 1964), 118. Duchamp continues, "To avoid seriousness, one must bring in humour. The only subject I would consider serious is eroticism . . . that's serious!" Jouffroy, *Une Révolution du regard,* 118.
56. Duchamp quoted in 1963, Francis M. Naumann, *Marcel Duchamp: The Art of Making Art in the Age of Mechanical Reproduction* (New York: Harry N. Abrams, 1999), 233.
57. Jeffrey Weiss, *The Popular Culture of Modern Art: Picasso, Duchamp, and Avant-Gardism* (New Haven: Yale University Press, 1994), 107–63.
58. Robert Motherwell, ed., *Dada Painters and Poets,* 110.
59. Ibid., 112.
60. Ibid., 116.
61. Ibid., 119.

62. See the discussion in E. H. Carr, *What Is History?* (1961), 2nd ed. (Harmondsworth, Middlesex: Pelican Books, 1987), 91–99.
63. Weiss, *The Popular Culture of Modern Art,* 125.
64. Ibid., 136.
65. Ibid., 129.
66. For a neighboring interpretation privileging the U.S. context, seemingly unaware of Weiss's, see Michael Leja, "Humbugs for Highbrows: Duchamp's Readymades in New York," *Looking Askance: Skepticism and American Art from Eakins to Duchamp* (Berkeley and Los Angeles: University of California Press, 2004), 221–47.
67. Although Duchamp declared himself satisfied with the content of the 1966 interviews with Pierre Cabanne, Robert Lebel and others were bothered by their tone, which recalled for Lebel that of the "blagueur." Lebel, "Marcel Duchamp maintenant et ici," *L'Oeil* 149 (May 1967): 19.
68. Weiss, *The Popular Culture of Modern Art,* 141.
69. ∞ſ+∞%≠@ >˚@ΔΔ§@<@ ≠@§∞ §ſ∞≠∞§@%Δ%@§>§≠ſ %∞ſ>?>≠!§ >@ ?@>>%>%>< @∞>?@§≠<§@ √ ^√∂=
70. Jacques Derrida, "Structure, Sign, and Play in the Discourse of the Human Sciences" (1966), in *Writing and Difference,* trans. Alan Bass (Chicago: University of Chicago Press, 1978), 278–93.
71. Eco, *Interpretation and Overinterpretation,* 67.
72. Jacques Derrida, "Plato's Pharmacy," in *Dissemination,* trans. Barbara Johnson (London: Athlone Press, 1981), 156.
73. Tilman Küchler, *Postmodern Gaming: Heidegger, Duchamp, Derrida* (New York: Peter Lang, 1994), 15.
74. Ibid., 16.
75. Derrida, *Writing and Difference,* 279.
76. Ibid., 292.
77. Ibid.
78. Susan Rubin Suleiman, "Pornography, Transgression, and the Avant-Garde: Bataille's *Story of the Eye,*" in *The Poetics of Gender,* ed. Nancy K. Miller (New York: Columbia University Press, 1986), 121. Suleiman refers to the indispensable text on Bataille by Derrida, "From Restricted to General Economy: A Hegelianism Without Reserve" (1967), in *Writing and Difference,* 251–77. For more on Duchamp's odd economy and its relation with Bataille's writings, see my parody, "The Laughter and Tears of Eros," in *Marcel Duchamp and Eroticism,* ed. Marc Decimo (Newcastle upon Tyne: Cambridge Scholars Press, 2007).
79. Quoted in Kuh, *The Artist's Voice,* 90.
80. Frank Kermode, *The Genesis of Secrecy: On the Interpretation of Narrative* (Cambridge: Harvard University Press, 1979), 1.
81. Derrida, *Dissemination,* 93. For a relevant approach to Pop Art, Duchamp, and Derrida, see Sarat Maharaj, "Pop Art's Pharmacies: Kitsch, Consumerist Objects and Signs, the 'Unmentionable,'" *Art History* 15, no. 3 (September 1992): 334–50. Maharaj progressed to a strategy of play, relevant to the argument presented in this essay, stating that "monkeydoodle is a way of looking and thinking that apes the straight essay only to muck up its system by letting loose the baboonery of counterforce." Sarat Maharaj, "Monkeydoodle: Annotating the Anti-essay 'after History,'" *Art Journal* 56, no. 1 (Spring 1997): 65. One of the few essays on Duchamp to perform the kind of writing I am advocating here, insofar as it does not impute the connections it feverishly creates within Duchamp's oeuvre to Duchamp's

own intention, is by George H. Bauer, "Duchamp's Ubiquitous Puns," in *Marcel Duchamp: Artist of the Century,* ed. Rudolph E. Kuenzli and Francis M. Naumann (Cambridge: MIT Press, 1990), 127–48. In freely creating an unbelievable number of links within Duchamp's work, Bauer's anti-essay parodies interpretation, corresponding with Martin Parker's attempt to thwart *dietrologia* by an "ironic hyper-conspiracism." Parish and Parker, eds., *The Age of Anxiety,* 205. See also Ulmer's claim, in his review of Derrida's *The Post Card,* that Derrida's "running commentary on the postcard is a deliberately wild hermeneutic." Gregory L. Ulmer, "The Post-Age," *Diacritics* 11, no. 3 (Autumn 1981): 52.

82. Derrida, *Dissemination,* 117.
83. Notably in an article I read only after writing these words, by Seymour Howard, "Hidden Naos: Duchamp Labyrinths," *Artibus et Historiæ* 15, no. 29 (1994): 168–69. To be fair, Howard introduces this piece by saying that his analysis of *With Hidden Noise* and "related" works will be made "sometimes with tongue in cheek" (which is just as well, as he goes on to claim that Duchamp's 1936 *Fluttering Hearts* cover for the journal *Cahiers d'Art* has some connection with the heart condition that kept him out of World War I). Howard, "Hidden Naos," 153, 168. See also Schwarz, ed., *Complete Works of Marcel Duchamp,* 1:128, 1:219. For an interpretation of the Duchamp of *Monte Carlo Bond* as Medusa, facilitated by a selection of puns and the congenial apparatus of psychoanalysis, see Dawn Ades, "Duchamp's Masquerades," in *The Portrait in Photography,* ed. Graham Clarke (London: Reaktion Books, 1992), 94–114; as a castrated John the Baptist, see Mason Klein, "Embodying Sexuality: Marcel Duchamp in the Realm of Surrealism," in *Modern Art and Society: An Anthology of Social and Multicultural Readings,* ed. Maurice Berger (New York: HarperCollins, 1994), 151; as an (anti-) Oedipus, see David Joselit, "Marcel Duchamp's *Monte Carlo Bond* Machine," *October* 59 (Winter 1992): 25; and as the prophet Moses, see Dawn Ades, Neil Cox, and David Hopkins, *Marcel Duchamp* (London: Thames and Hudson, 1999), 139. To spell it out again, I am arguing that rather than throwing further interpretations on the pile, we might now reflect on the existence of the pile itself; we might take the top-heaviness of the Duchamp business as a cue to interpret interpretation in our discipline.
84. The atmosphere of intrigue and connectivity generated around Duchamp's gestures has made it difficult to find a place for simple coincidence. For a brief but illuminating discussion of Duchamp, coincidence, and the pleasures and pitfalls of "tampering with the relation between the disciplinary expectations about meaning and the disruptive possibilities latent in those same expectations" (which is too conservative about the potential for such strategies in art history for my liking), see James Elkins, *Why Are Our Pictures Puzzles? On the Modern Origins of Pictorial Complexity* (New York: Routledge, 1999), 83.
85. Jacques Derrida, *Spurs/Nietzsche's Styles,* trans. Barbara Harlow (Chicago: University of Chicago Press, 1979), 131.
86. Derrida, *Spurs/Nietzsche's Styles,* 133.
87. Richard Rorty, "From Logic to Language to Play: A Plenary Address to the InterAmerican Congress," *Proceedings and Addresses of the American Philosophical Association* 59, no. 6 (June 1986): 748.
88. Gregory L. Ulmer, "The Object of Post-Criticism," in *The Anti-Aesthetic: Essays on Postmodern Culture,* ed. Graham Clarke (Seattle: Bay Press, 1983), 83–110.

CHAPTER 3

1. See "1923," in Hal Foster et al., eds., *Art Since 1900: Modernism, Antimodernism, Postmodernism* (New York: Thames and Hudson, 2004), 188.
2. Jeanine Fiedler has written, "Exploring the possibilities of photography somewhat playfully, the Bauhäuslers overcame a crucial barrier without any conscious intention or theory. They freed photography from its former status as a document merely reproducing reality." Jeanine Fiedler, *Photography at the Bauhaus* (Cambridge: MIT Press, 1990), 9–10.
3. László Moholy-Nagy, *The New Vision: Fundamentals of Design, Painting, Sculpture, Architecture* (New York: W. W. Norton, 1938), 15.
4. Gropius, it should be noted, was in some ways ambivalent about this direction for the school, but he was also a pragmatist, believing that the best hope for the school's survival lay in its allegiance with industry. Gropius quoted in Hans Wingler, ed., *The Bauhaus: Weimar, Dessau, Berlin, Chicago* (Cambridge: MIT Press, 1969), 51–52.
5. Of course, such simple historical dichotomies have been questioned and reworked in recent years. See the essays by various authors in *Albers and Moholy-Nagy: From the Bauhaus to the New World,* ed. Achim Borchardt-Hume (New Haven: Yale University Press, 2006).
6. Georg Simmel, *On Individuality and Social Forms: Selected Writings,* ed. Donald N. Levine (Chicago: University of Chicago Press, 1971), 326.
7. Quoted in Hilton Kramer, "At the Bauhaus: The Fate of Art in 'The Cathedral of Socialism,'" *New Criterion* 12 (March 1994): 8.
8. Ibid.
9. Eleanor Hight, *Picturing Modernism: Moholy-Nagy and Photography in Weimar Germany* (Cambridge: MIT Press, 1995), 194.
10. See Ralph Sachsse, "Notes on Lucia Moholy," and Jeanine Fiedler, "Walter Peterhans: A Tabularian Approach," in Fiedler, *Photography at the Bauhaus.*
11. Foster et al., *Art Since 1900,* 185–86.
12. Moholy-Nagy, *The New Vision,* 20–21.
13. Ernst Bloch, "The Wish-Landscape Perspective in Aesthetics: The Order of Materials According to the Dimension of Their Profundity and Hope," in Ernst Bloch, *The Utopian Function of Art and Literature: Selected Essays,* trans. Jack Zipes and Frank Mecklenburg (Cambridge: MIT Press, 1988), xxxv.
14. Other approaches to play of course exist, including developmental, psychological, and social approaches. For an inventory, see Susanna Millar, *The Psychology of Play* (Harmondsworth, Middlesex: Penguin Books, 1968).
15. Michael Apter, "A Structural-Phenomenology of Play," in *Adult Play: A Reversal Theory Approach,* ed. John Kerr and Michael Apter (Amsterdam: Swets and Zeitlinger, 1991), 13.
16. Hans includes art production as one component of play activity, but, writing in the early 1980s before the art-market boom, naturally does not address the art market, which would complicate and enliven his arguments considerably. James S. Hans, *The Play of the World* (Amherst: University of Massachusetts Press, 1981), 5.
17. Quoted in Hight, *Picturing Modernism,* 7.

18. Beaumont Newhall, "Review of Moholy's Achievement," in *Bauhaus, 1919–1928,* ed. Herbert Bayer et al. (New York: Museum of Modern Art, 1938), 71.
19. László Moholy-Nagy, *Painting, Photography, Film* (Cambridge: MIT Press, 1969), 28.
20. Interestingly, photographers exhibiting a broad range of styles associated themselves with the New Vision, or New Objectivity, movement. While August Sander and Albert Renger-Patzsch claimed that photography's most important inherent property was its ability to render reality in exact detail, Moholy argued that it was photography's sensitivity to light that made it unique as a medium. See Christopher Phillips's essay, "Resurrecting Vision: The New Photography in Europe Between the Wars," in *The New Vision: Photography Between the World Wars,* ed. Maria Morris Hambourg and Christopher Phillips (New York: Metropolitan Museum of Art, 1989).
21. For example, in "A New Instrument of Vision," Moholy enumerates "The Eight Varieties of Photographic Vision," comprising "abstract seeing," "exact seeing," "rapid seeing," "slow seeing," "intensified seeing," "penetrative seeing," "simultaneous seeing," and "distorted seeing." László Moholy-Nagy, "A New Instrument of Vision," reproduced in Liz Wells, *The Photography Reader* (New York: Routledge, 2003), 93–94.
22. Franz Roh's book *Foto-Auge: 76 Fotos der Zeit* (Stuttgart: Akademischer Verlag F. Wedekind, 1929) crystallized this association.
23. Moholy-Nagy, *The New Vision,* 14.
24. Quoted in Hight, *Picturing Modernism,* 194.
25. Moholy-Nagy, "The Concept of Space," in Bayer et al., *Bauhaus, 1919–1928,* 122.
26. Gropius quoted in Andreas Haus, "László Moholy-Nagy," in Fiedler, *Photography at the Bauhaus,* 15.
27. In Schiller's words: "For so long as he only feels, his personality or his absolute existence remains a mystery to him, and so long as he only thinks, his existence in time or his condition does the same." Friedrich von Schiller, *On the Aesthetic Education of Man,* trans. Reginald Snell (New York: Frederick Ungar, 1965), 73–75.
28. Quoted in Haus, "László Moholy-Nagy," 18.
29. In Fiedler, *Photography at the Bauhaus,* 140.
30. Piaget discussed in Millar, *The Psychology of Play,* 49–58.
31. Walter Benjamin, "Spielzeug und Spielen: Randbemerkungen zu einem Monumentalwerk," in *Walter Benjamin: Gesammelte Schriften III,* ed. Hella Tiedemann-Bartels (Frankfurt: Suhrkamp Verlag, 1972), 131.
32. On the undeniable charm of failed attempts, see Howard Gardner, *Artful Scribbles: The Significance of Children's Drawings* (New York: Basic Books, 1980), 140–41.
33. Johan Huizinga, *Homo Ludens: A Study of the Play-Element in Culture* (London: Routledge and Kegan Paul, 1949).
34. Walter Gropius, "Programme of the Staatliches Bauhaus in Weimar," in *Programmes and Manifestations of Twentieth-Century Architecture,* ed. Ulrich Conrads (Cambridge: MIT Press, 1970), 53.
35. See Walter Gropius, *The Theater of the Bauhaus,* trans. Arthur S. Wensinger (Middletown, Conn.: Wesleyan University Press, 1961).
36. Feininger discusses his work with Schlemmer in Fiedler, *Photography at the Bauhaus,* 45–47.

CHAPTER 4

1. Jennifer Milam, "Rococo Games and the Origins of Visual Modernism," paper delivered at the CAA conference in Philadelphia in February 2002. See also Milam, *Fragonard's Playful Paintings: Visual Games in Rococo Art* (Manchester: University of Manchester Press, 2007).
2. See Clement Greenberg, "Avant-Garde and Kitsch" (1939), reprinted in *Pollock and After,* ed. Francis Frascina (New York: Harper and Row, 1985), 21–34.
3. Johan Huizinga, *Homo Ludens: A Study of the Play-Element in Culture* (Boston: Beacon Press, 1955), 26.
4. Ibid., 202.
5. Here the early cultural theories of games trace the footsteps of Walter Benjamin, who addressed Schmitt far more positively in his essay "Critique of Violence" (1921), reprinted in *Reflections,* ed. Peter Demetz (New York: Schocken Books, 1986), 277–300.
6. Huizinga, *Homo Ludens,* 209.
7. Ibid., 205–6.
8. Ibid., 213.
9. Although Huizinga does not discuss it, the National Socialists were keen on *agonistic* play, games, and sport, as their fanatical orchestration of the 1936 Olympic Games would indicate. Furthermore, during the Nazi period, several major and minor chess players aligned themselves with the party, most famously the Russian world champion Alexander A. Alekhine. A collaborator in France, Alekhine began playing in Nazi chess tournaments after the occupation and published several inflammatory essays about Jewish chess players. Efim Bogoljubow, a Russian who became a naturalized German, was a trainer for the NS Greater Germany Chess Federation and challenged Alekhine for the world championship. Other, less accomplished Nazi chess players included Willi Schlage and Emil Joseph Diemer (also a "chess reporter of the Great German Reich"). Agonistic struggle within chess or sport clearly served as a useful militaristic metaphor for the National Socialists.
10. Roger Caillois, *Man, Play, and Games,* trans. Meyer Barash (New York: The Free Press, 1961), 100.
11. Ibid., 105–7.
12. Emmanuel Garrigues, ed., *Archives du surréalisme. Les Jeux surréalistes: mars 1921–septembre 1962* (Paris: Gallimard, 1995), 114ff. The results of the "Recherches Expérimentales" were also published in *Le Surréalisme au service de la Révolution* 6 (May 15, 1933). By the fifth "Recherche" session of 1933, Caillois's name disappears from the roster of surrealist game players as they are catalogued by Garrigues. Of the sessions that Caillois participated in, the topics were: sessions A and B, "Sur la connaissance irrationnelle de l'objet"; for session C, "Sur les possibilités irrationelles de penetration et d'orientation dans un tableau"; and for session D, "Sur les possibilités irrationelles de vie à une date quelconque."
13. In keeping with his general interest in play and creativity in these years, Caillois published "De la Féerie à la science fiction," an essay on fairy tales and fantastic literature, in the same year as *Man, Play, and Games* (1958). On Caillois's postwar works and his critical turn against not only Bataille but also Claude Lévi-Strauss, see Claudine Frank, "Introduction," in *The Edge of Surrealism: A Roger Caillois Reader,* ed. Claudine Frank, trans. Claudine Frank and Camille Naish (Durham: Duke University Press, 2003), 46ff.
14. Frank, "Introduction," 28–31.
15. Frank relates that sources disagree on the level of Caillois's involvement in Acéphale.
16. Caillois comments on Duchamp in "L'Imagination rigoureuse," in *Cases d'un échiquier* (Paris: Gallimard, 1970), especially 38–46; and on Breton's postwar games in "Actualité des Kenningar," *Nouvelle nouvelle revue française* 30 (June 1955).
17. On Caillois's notion of "diagonal science," see Frank, "Introduction," 49–50.
18. Quoted in Mel Gooding, ed., *Surrealist Games* (Boston: Shambhala Redstone Editions, 1993), 137–38.
19. This list of games follows the titles attributed by Audouin and Breton. The dates given correspond to the first publication of the results of the game in question, or the first published description of the game, as listed in ibid., 143–55. The games were mostly published in *La Révolution surréaliste* and *Médium,* though some also appeared in *Documents* and *Littérature.* In his essay, Breton does not mention the *jeu de la vérité,* the results of which were only first published in 1990 (French) and 1992 (English), perhaps because of their explicit nature. See José Pierre, ed., *Investigating Sex: Surrealist Research, 1928–1932* (London: Verso Books, 1992).
20. It is this game, *l'un dans l'autre*—where any one object can be derived from any other—that invoked Caillois's condemnation of Breton's totalizing artistic framework; see his essay "The Image."
21. This latter game, whose format is akin to that of a survey, proceeds as follows: if one were told that a particular individual had returned from the dead, would you receive her or him in your home? Breton published the statistical results, and his own elaborated responses, in order of approval. Breton's comments are noted in parentheses: Baudelaire, yes, 100 percent; Gustave Moreau, yes, 100 percent ("Oui grand serrurier"); Charles Fourier, yes, 94 percent; Freud, yes, 94 percent; Gauguin, yes, 88 percent ("Oui avec grands honneurs"); Lenin, yes, 88 percent; Goya, yes, 87 percent; Juliette Droucet, yes, 87 percent; Hegel, yes, 82 percent; Huysmans, yes, 82 percent; van Gogh, yes, 76 percent ("Oui par égards mais avec mais, le souci d'abréger"); Seurat, yes, 71 percent ("Oui calmement en harmonie"); Marx, yes, 65 percent; Nietzsche, yes, 60 percent; Mallarmé, yes, 59 percent; Balzac, yes, 56 percent; Goethe, yes, 50 percent, no 50 percent; Poe, no, 56 percent; Chateaubriand, no, 59 percent; Verlaine, no, 87 percent; and finally Cézanne, no, 88 percent ("Non rien à se dire"). See Gooding, ed., *Surrealist Games,* 154; Philippe Audouin, "1964," in *Dictionnaire des Jeux,* ed. René Alleau (Paris: Réalités de L'Imaginaire Tchou, 1964), 481–82; and Breton in *Médium, nouvelle série communication surréaliste,* no. 1, as cited in *André Breton: La Beauté convulsive* (Paris: Editions du Centre Pompidou, 1991), 411.
22. André Breton, "Second Manifesto of Surrealism" (1930), reprinted in *Manifestoes of Surrealism* (Ann Arbor: University of Michigan Press, 1969), 117–94.
23. Gooding, ed., *Surrealist Games,* 124–25, 160; Audouin, "1964," 485.298.
24. On the importance of alchemy and the tarot to the Surrealists, see Ralf Covents, *Surrealistische Spiele: Vom "Cadavre exquis" zum "Jeu de Marseille"* (Frankfurt: Peter Lang, 1996), 104–8. Breton spoke specifically about the resonances between alchemy and Surrealism's investigations of language. Salvador Dalí also produced a tarot game, the "Tarot Universal Dalí," in 1984.

25. Caillois, *Man, Play, and Games,* 18.
26. Duchamp's agonistic art challenges the view that a coherent shift can be traced between a purely ludic-focused Dada to the agonistic investigations of the Surrealists.
27. Caillois, *Man, Play, and Games,* 15.
28. As cited by Dickran Tashjian, "Nothing Left to Chance: Duchamp's First Retrospective," in *West Coast Duchamp,* ed. Bonnie Clearwater (Miami Beach: Grassfield Press, 1991), 82 n. 30. In this essay, Tashjian describes the events surrounding the Duchamp retrospective staged by Hopps in Pasadena in 1963. Hopps's heroicizing Las Vegas story can be found in "Duchamp in Vegas," in *Marcel Duchamp joue et gagne,* ed. Yves Arman (Paris: Marval, 1984), 43–44. His statement is dated 1983, twenty years after the event took place.
29. See, for example, Jean-François Lyotard with Jean-Loup Thébaud, *Just Gaming* (Minneapolis: University of Minnesota Press, 1985); Jacques Derrida, "Structure, Sign, and Play in the Discourse of the Human Sciences," in *Writing and Difference* (Chicago: University of Chicago Press, 1978), 278–94; and Tilman Küchler, *Postmodern Gaming: Heidegger, Duchamp, Derrida* (New York: Peter Lang, 1994).
30. Arturo Schwarz cites several sources, including Truman Capote, who recalls Duchamp discussing chess as an "art activity," and, via Calvin Tomkins, Edward Lasker, who reminisced about Duchamp's chess-playing style: "He would always take risks in order to play a beautiful game, rather than be cautious and brutal to win." See Arturo Schwarz, "Game of Precision: An Aspect of the Beauty of Precision," in *The Complete Works of Marcel Duchamp* (New York: Harry N. Abrams, 1969), 57ff. At the New York State Chess Association banquet of 1952, Duchamp also commented that chess interested him most as a realm that could realize the beautiful. This address is reprinted in "Ephemerides," in *Marcel Duchamp,* ed. Pontus Hulten (Cambridge: MIT Press, 1993), entry for August 30, 1952. Finally, the entire installation behind the wooden door of the *Etant donnés* (1946–66) is built upon a black-and-white tiled floor, which recalls the horizontal playing field of the chessboard. *Agôn* therefore seems to have remained central to Duchamp's oeuvre.
31. For a basic introduction to *The Large Glass,* see Richard Hamilton, "The Large Glass," in *Marcel Duchamp,* ed. Anne d'Harnoncourt and Kynaston McShine (New York: Museum of Modern Art, 1973), 57–68; and Dawn Ades, *Marcel Duchamp* (New York: Thames and Hudson, 1999), 66–121.
32. For a detailed summary of Duchamp's chess activity, see Schwarz, "Game of Precision," 57ff.
33. Bradley Bailey traced Duchamp's engagement with French mathematics in his chess- and roulette-related artworks and activities in his paper, "The Dukes of Hasard: Marcel Duchamp and the French Probabilists," presented at the CAA conference in Philadelphia in February 2002. See also Bradley Bailey and Francis Naumann, *Marcel Duchamp: The Art of Chess* (New York: Readymade Press, 2009).
34. Caillois wrote on Duchamp's treatise in *La Nouvelle Revue Française* (September 1937), as cited in his later essay, "L'imagination rigoureuse."
35. It should be noted that as early as 1936, Duchamp posed for publicity photographs playing chess; the *Los Angeles Times* of August 16, 1936, published a photo of Duchamp at the Arensbergs', absorbed at the chessboard, with his *Nude Descending a Staircase* forming a backdrop. Ironically, the caption, read "Artist Views Masterpiece."

36. For example, *The Large Glass, 3 Standard Stoppages* (1913–14), and the *Nine Malic Moulds* (1914–15) were all replicas of originals produced or acquired for the Pasadena exhibition. A thoroughgoing critique of the notion of originality, and of the singular and original artwork, is certainly advanced by these works as well. The important subject of the Duchampian multiple is addressed in "Marcel Duchamp and the Multiple," in Arman, ed., *Marcel Duchamp,* 31–36; Tashjian, "Nothing Left to Chance," 68–69; and by Jones in her chapter "Duchamp's Self-Reflexivity: Art and Object Making After 1959," in *Postmodernism and the En-gendering of Marcel Duchamp* (Cambridge: Cambridge University Press, 1994), 94–99.
37. Wasser in fact photographed the entire match between the two. The proof sheet has also been published in the *West Coast Duchamp* exhibition catalogue. See Tashjian, "Nothing Left to Chance," 71–74.
38. On the relation of Duchamp's art to the history of chess, see Bradley Bailey, "*The Bachelors:* Pawns in Duchamp's Great Game," *Tout-Fait: The Marcel Duchamp Studies Online Journal* 1, no. 3 (December 2000), http://www.tout-fait.com/issues/issue_3/Articles/bailey.bailey.html.
39. Hulten, "Ephemerides," entry for August 30, 1952.
40. Ibid.
41. Schwarz, *Complete Works,* 88. Schwarz offers no further details about the Babitz/Duchamp game.
42. Babitz, who became a Southern California journalist, did break her silence regarding the match with Duchamp in a 1991 essay; see Eve Babitz, "I Was a Pawn for Art," *Esquire,* September 1991, 164–74. She maintains that Wasser set up the game and photo session without Hopps's knowledge, and that Duchamp made a special appearance at the Pasadena Museum to play the staged match with her. This photograph and Duchamp's complicity in its staging is a blind spot in Jones's *Postmodernism and the En-gendering of Marcel Duchamp.* Jones calls the Babitz/Duchamp photo "notorious" and claims that Duchamp passively acquiesced to participation. She therefore refuses to acknowledge Duchamp's role in the construction of this image.
43. On Man Ray's photos of Duchamp/Sélavy, see Amelia Jones, "The Ambivalence of Male Masquerade: Duchamp as Rrose Sélavy," in *The Body Imaged,* ed. Kathleen Adler and Marcia Pointon (Cambridge: Cambridge University Press, 1993), 21–32.
44. Tashjian, "Nothing Left to Chance," 71.
45. Schwarz, *Complete Works,* 88.
46. Arman's contribution to the Duchamp retrospective catalogue of the 1973 exhibition at the Philadelphia Museum of Art, in which he inserted notation of a fictional game between Duchamp and Rrose Sélavy into the actual chess score of one of the games of the 1972 world championship match between Boris Spassky and Bobby Fischer, cleverly underscores the Freudian dynamics of this final point. See Arman, *Marcel Duchamp,* 182–84. Arman's fictional notation is also a shorthand catalogue raisonné of Duchamp's major works.
47. Games seem to have also served this purpose amid the most horrific circumstances of World War II. Holocaust survivors have told of how they continued to play board games and chess as a means to preserve their sanity in the camps.

CHAPTER 5

1. Kirsten Hoving, *Joseph Cornell and Astronomy: A Case for the Stars* (Princeton: Princeton University Press, 2008).
2. Louis Marin, "Toward a Theory of Reading in Visual Art: Poussin's *The Arcadian Shepherds,*" in *The Reader in the Text,* ed. Susan Suleiman and Inge Crosman (Princeton: Princeton University Press, 1980), 293–324.
3. Jane Philbrick, ed., *The Return of the Cadavre Exquis* (New York: The Drawing Center, 1993).
4. Georges Perec, *La Disparition* (Paris: Gallimard, 1969).
5. Quoted in Mary Ann Caws, ed., *Surrealism* (London: Phaidon Press, 2004), 261.
6. "On the irrational possibilities of penetration and orientation in Giorgio de Chirico's Painting *The Enigma of a Day*" (1933), in Caws, ed., *Surrealism,* 261.
7. "Reponses to the Enquiry on Love" (1929), in Caws, ed., *Surrealism,* 227.

CHAPTER 6

1. See André Breton, "Surrealism and Painting" (1928), in Herschel Chipp, *Theories of Modern Art* (Berkeley and Los Angeles: University of California Press, 1968), 408.
2. The primary exception to this is Werner Spies, *Picasso: The Sculptures* (Ostfildern: Hatje Cantz, 2000), 150–57. Spies notes the relation of these works to the context of Surrealism's interest in found and ethnographic objects and remarks on their compositional reliance on Picasso's earlier drawings. Yve-Alain Bois and Rosalind Krauss have also connected these works with the *informe* in Yve-Alain Bois and Rosalind Krauss, *Formless: A User's Guide* (New York: Zone Books, 1997), 24, 31. Further, Kenneth Silver briefly discussed these works in the context of the Mediterranean and of André Masson's use of sand in his paintings in Kenneth Silver, *Making Paradise: Art, Modernity, and the Myth of the French Riviera* (Cambridge: MIT Press, 2001), 66–68.
3. Johan Huizinga, *Homo Ludens: A Study of the Play-Element in Culture* (London: Routledge and K. Paul, 1949), 10.
4. Two significant exceptions are Roland Bothner, *Grund und Figur: Die Geschichte des Reliefs und August Rodins Höllentor* (Munich: Wilhelm Fink, 1993); Ernst-Gerhard Güse, *Reliefs: Formprobleme zwischen Malerei und Skulptur im 20. Jahrhundert* (Münster: Westfälisches Landesmuseum für Kunst und Kulturgeschichte Münster, 1980).
5. Yve-Alain Bois, *Matisse and Picasso* (Paris: Flammarion, 1999), 57.
6. A related work from 1932 is often grouped with the sand reliefs. This later work does bear a similarity in overall technique, but it uses paint as a unifying ground rather than sand. See Spies, *Picasso: The Sculptures,* 156.
7. Françoise Gilot, *Life with Picasso* (New York: McGraw-Hill, 1964), 23–24. It is unclear if the sand reliefs were kept in the vitrine. While Gilot's account claims this, she may have been confusing them with the slightly later slender wooden carvings from 1930–31 that she also discusses. Brassaï's photograph and account of the vitrine, both roughly contemporary with Gilot's experience, do not show any of the reliefs. Given the size of the vitrine, it is unlikely that even these small sand reliefs would be included, as a group, in it. It is more likely, however, that they had a place on the wall in

the room or in another easily accessible place because of the prominence they have in Gilot's anecdote.

8. Spies, *Picasso: The Sculptures,* 156.
9. Some of his constructed and welded metal sculptures, such as *Woman in the Garden* (1929), did use a unifying layer of paint.
10. For a general discussion of the shadow with a view toward its pictorial depiction, see Michael Baxandall, *Shadows and Enlightenment* (New Haven: Yale University Press, 1995), 1–15. Shadows also played a pivotal role in Surrealism in the 1930s. For a discussion, see Denis Hollier and Rosalind Krauss, "Surrealist Precipitates: Shadows Don't Cast Shadows," *October* 69 (1994): 110–32.
11. For art-historical discussions of this myth, see Robert Rosenblum, "The Origin of Painting: A Problem in the Iconography of Romantic Classicism," *Art Bulletin* 39, no. 4 (1957): 279–90; George Levitine, "Addendum to Robert Rosenblum's 'The Origin of Painting: A Problem in the Iconography of Romantic Classicism,'" *Art Bulletin* 40, no. 4 (1958): 329–31; Frances Muecke, "'Taught by Love': The Origin of Painting Again," *Art Bulletin* 81, no. 2 (1999): 297–302. Pliny the Elder, *Natural History,* book 35, chapter 43: "Butades, a potter of Sicyon, was the first who invented, at Corinth, the art of modeling portraits in the earth, which he used in his trade. It was through his daughter that he made the discovery; who, being deeply in love with a young man about to depart on a long journey, traced the profile of his face, as thrown upon the wall by the light of the lamp. Upon seeing this, her father filled in the outline, by compressing clay upon the surface, and so made a face in relief, which he then hardened by fire along with other articles of pottery. This model, it is said, was preserved in the Nymphæum at Corinth, until the destruction of that city by Mummius." Pliny the Elder, *The Natural History,* ed. John Bostock (London: Taylor and Francis, 1855).
12. For a brief discussion Picasso's use of the silhouette and the shadow puppet, see Anne Baldassari, "'Heads Faces and Bodies': Picasso's Use of Portrait Photographs," in *Picasso and Portraiture: Representation and Transformation,* ed. William Rubin (New York: Museum of Modern Art, 1996), 204–9. See also the brief discussions in Kirk Varnedoe, "Picasso's Self-Portraits," in *Picasso and Portraiture,* ed. Rubin, 150. Also of note is a 1928 portrait of Max Jacob as Roman Senator, drawn to emulate the cameo format (PP 28-237).
13. Strictly speaking, the story of Dibutade involved her father, Butade, later taking her tracing one step further, filling in the outline with clay, and firing it with his other pottery (he was a potter). Nevertheless, this myth has been understood as the origin of painting, and its sculptural equivalent has been frequently overlooked in the subsequent visualizations of the myth. For examples, see references in note 11 above. As Rosenblum illustrates in "The Origin of Painting," there were sculptural images of this myth. It should be noted, however, that the shadow itself could only be approximated with an incised line or through the use of real projected shadow (made more visible through the photography of the relief).
14. The standard account has it that they met on January 8, 1927, as relayed in Gilot, *Life with Picasso,* 235. A hypothesis that they met much earlier, in January or February 1925, was put forth in Herbert Schwartz, *Picasso and*

Marie-Thérèse Walter, 1925–1927 (Inuvik, Canada: Éditions Isabeau, 1988), and is taken up in Robert Rosenblum, "Picasso's Blond Muse: The Reign of Marie-Thérèse Walter," in *Picasso and Portraiture,* ed. Rubin, 336–83, esp. 39–40 and 82 nn. 13–16. For a response, see Rosalind Krauss, *The Picasso Papers* (New York: Farrar, Straus and Giroux, 1998), 233–34 and 65–68 nn. 20–26. Some of the earlier literature assumed an even later meeting date of 1930 or 1931, owing to some inaccurate autobiographical information introduced by Picasso. Lydia Gasman confirmed a meeting year of at least 1927 and, based on interviews with Walter, discussed Picasso's initiation of Walter into sexual activity. See Lydia Gasman, "Mystery, Magic, and Love in Picasso, 1925–1938," 2 vols. (Ph.D. diss., Columbia University, 1981), esp. 1:64–65 and 1:267.

15. The many beach scenes of these years relate closely to the excitement and difficulties of the affair with Walter. Biographical studies of Picasso's work have noted the tensions in the beach scenes that often depict figures entering locked cabanas, much as Picasso himself did in order to meet secretly with Walter. For an extensive discussion of the so-called cabana series, see Gasman, "Mystery, Magic, and Love in Picasso, 1925–1938," vol. 1, "The Cabana Series." Gasman argues that Picasso chose the relatively rare and outdated wooden cabana as "a disguised symbol for himself" in a series of works from 1927 to 1938 (1:8). Gasman also notes that a "minuscule Cabana with an arcaded entrance" appears in sand relief 7 (1:375).
16. "On the evidence of his paintings, his sculpture, and hundreds of drawings in sketchbooks, the sexually most important affair of his life was with Marie-Thérèse Walter whom he first met in 1931 [*sic*]. He has painted and drawn no other woman in the same way, and no other woman half as many times. It may be that she became a kind of symbol for him, and that in time the idea of her meant more to him than she herself." John Berger, *The Success and Failure of Picasso* (New York: Pantheon Books, 1965; reprint, 1980), 154–55. See also John Richardson, "Picasso and Marie-Thérèse Walter," in *Through the Eye of Picasso, 1928–1934: The Dinard Sketchbook and Related Paintings and Sculpture* (New York: W. Beadleston, 1985).
17. See Adam Gopnik, "P Loves MT: A Note on the First Appearance of Marie-Thérèse Walter in the Picasso Theater," *Marsyas* 21 (1981–82): 57–60. For an analysis of polyvalence in Picasso's deployment of the cryptogram of his and Walter's initials, see Louis Marin, "Picasso: Image Writing in Process," *October* 65 (1993): 94–96.
18. Her flat was at no. 44. Rosenblum, "Picasso's Blond Muse," 342.
19. I do this cautiously, however, as the Picasso literature has been characterized by an excess of biographical interpretation that reduces each work merely to an illustration of his given autobiographical moment. Nevertheless, it cannot be ignored that Picasso regularly made his personal life a catalyst for his artistic developments—as with Walter. For an analysis that takes its starting point from a critique of the dominance of biographical interpretations of Picasso, see Rosalind Krauss, "In the Name of Picasso," *October* 16 (1981): 5–22. A related claim is later taken up in Krauss, *The Picasso Papers.*
20. The terms "telic" and "paratelic" derive their most common usage from Reversal Theory, a structural account of human activity and motivation in the field of psychology. See Michael Apter, *Reversal Theory: Motivation, Emotion, and Personality* (New York: Routledge, 1989), 30–38.
21. Diana Widmaier Picasso, "Marie-Thérèse Walter and Pablo Picasso: New Insights into a Secret Love," in *Pablo Picasso and Marie-Thérèse Walter: Between Classicism and Surrealism,* ed. Markus Müller (Bielefeld: Kerber Verlag, 2004), 31. Emphasis added. The source of this statement by Picasso is not indicated in her text.

CHAPTER 7

1. An illustration of this work can be found in *Joseph Cornell/Marcel Duchamp... In Resonance* (Philadelphia: Philadelphia Museum of Art, 1998), 175.
2. For a more complete discussion of this classic ballet and its relationship to Cornell, see Hugh Stevens, "Joseph Cornell's 'Dance to the Music of Time': History and Giving in the Ballet Constructions," in *Joseph Cornell: Opening the Box,* ed. Jason Edwards and Stephanie L. Taylor (Oxfordshire: Peter Lang, 2007), 87–109.
3. Lemony Snicket is a pseudonym for the author Daniel Handler. The first book in the series, *The Bad Beginning,* was released in 1999; the last, *The End,* was released in 2006.
4. Robert Cornell was born in 1910 and died in 1965.
5. Lynda Roscoe Hartigan, "Joseph Cornell: A Biography," in *Joseph Cornell,* ed. Kynaston McShine (New York: Museum of Modern Art, 1980), 94.
6. Diane Waldman, *Joseph Cornell: Master of Dreams* (New York: Harry N. Abrams, 2002), 15–16.
7. Hartigan, "Joseph Cornell: A Biography," 95.
8. Pepe Karmel, "Art Review: Seeming So Sweet the Bite Goes Unnoticed," *New York Times,* January 19, 1996, C26.
9. This work is reproduced in *Joseph Cornell: Shadowplay, Eterniday,* ed. Lynda Roscoe Hartigan (Washington, D.C.: The Voyager Foundation, 2003), 66.
10. Charles Simic, "Untitled (Bébé Marie) early 1940s," in *Dime-Store Alchemy: The Art of Joseph Cornell* (Hopewell, N.J.: Ecco Press, 1992), 45.
11. Dickran Tashjian, "Joseph Cornell: The Art of Play," in *Joseph Cornell Jiøí Koláø* (New York: Pavel Zoubok Gallery, 2007), 6.
12. In July 1946, Cornell noted the memories of childhood he had experienced that day, inspired by smells he had encountered: "Sprig of growing mint plucked its pungency bringing back Adirondacks with the usual magical experience and unexpected vividness. Smell of gasoline brings back days of childhood father's boat." Mary Ann Caws, *Joseph Cornell's Theater of the Mind: Selected Diaries, Letters, and Files* (New York: Thames and Hudson, 1993), 245. Years later, while working on an assemblage that had been "long dormant" in his studio, he noted a "correspondence in the realization of relationship to Adirondack mountains 1921 vacation—discovery of music—Russian overture 'Barber of Seville' in Richard Jessup lodge house." Ibid., 130.
13. For reproductions of this dossier, see Lynda Roscoe Hartigan, *Joseph Cornell: Navigating the Imagination* (Salem, Mass.: Peabody Essex Museum, 2007), 310–11. Cornell also created a print homage to the young Berenice that was published in *View* in January 1943. Hartigan's catalogue reproduces many pages from that magazine on pages 312–15. Kirsten

Hoving has unpacked the meaning of this work in a compelling articulation of Cornell's fascination with the night skies in her *Joseph Cornell and Astronomy: A Case for the Stars* (Princeton: Princeton University Press, 2008), 89–119.

14. Caws, *Joseph Cornell's Theater of the Mind,* 86, 87.
15. Cornell's English teacher was probably mystified by this comment, and only gave him a grade of C- on the report. The entire handwritten document, dated October 29, 1918, and entitled "The Greatest Magician in the World," is included in the online Cornell papers of the Archives of American Art. Joseph Cornell Papers, Archives of American Art, Smithsonian Institution (Series 1, Biographical Material: Student Papers, 1918, 1921 [Box 1, Folder 32], frames 1–4). http://www.aaa.si.edu/collectionsonline/cornjose/.
16. An example is reproduced in Waldman, *Joseph Cornell: Master of Dreams,* 63.
17. Dawn Ades, *Surrealist Art: The Lindy and Edwin Bergman Collection at the Art Institute of Chicago* (Chicago: Art Institute of Chicago, 1997), 58.
18. Lynda Roscoe Hartigan, "Medici Slot Machines," in *Joseph Cornell: Shadowplay, Eterniday*, 106. The quote continues: "However, in Cornell's translation that reference takes on a subtle, sobering inflection, especially since he initiated the series during the Second World War. Concerned about the destruction of life, property and European culture (much of it owing a debt to the Medici), Cornell used the shooting gallery motif to symbolize the indiscriminate damage that chance can cause."
19. Frank O'Hara, "Ave Maria," from *Lunch Poems* (1964) (San Francisco: City Lights, 2001), 51–52.
20 Simic, "Medici Slot Machine," in *Dime-Store Alchemy,* 26–27.
21. Walter Hopps has likened this work to a "great Northern Renaissance altarpiece." See *Joseph Cornell: Shadowplay, Eterniday,* ed. Hartigan, 70.
22. Joseph Cornell Papers, Archives of American Art, April 1945 (typed August 19, 1945).
23. Lauren Bacall, *By Myself* (New York: Ballantine Books, 1978), 136, 145.
24. See chapter 2, "A Cinematic Imagination: *The Penny Arcade Portrait of Lauren Bacall,*" in Jodi Hauptman, *Stargazing in the Cinema* (New Haven: Yale University Press, 1999), 55–83.
25. Richard Vine, "'Eterniday': Cornell's Christian Science 'Metaphysique,'" in *Joseph Cornell: Shadowplay, Eterniday,* ed. Hartigan, 35–49.
26. Several of these photographs are reproduced throughout Dore Ashton's *Joseph Cornell Album* (New York: Da Capo Press, 1974).

CHAPTER 8

1. Amelia Jones has analyzed the ways in which U.S. artists and art historians, since midcentury, have habitually located Duchamp as the paternal origin of postmodernism in her book *Postmodernism and the En-gendering of Marcel Duchamp* (New York: Cambridge University Press, 1994).
2. Wilke first used the term "performalist self-portrait" in 1979 and retroactively applied it to her earlier images. The neologism combines two seemingly antithetical art concepts: performance and formalism. These photographic self-portraits were taken with another's technical help, but Wilke always claimed creative authorship over them.

3. See Laura Mulvey, "Visual Pleasure and Narrative Cinema" (1975), reprinted in *Art After Modernism: Rethinking Representation,* ed. Brian Wallis (Boston: New Museum of Contemporary Art, New York, in association with David R. Godine, Publisher, 1984), 363.
4. Linda Hutcheon, *A Theory of Parody: Teachings of Twentieth-Century Art Forms* (New York: Methuen, 1985), 6.
5. Luce Irigaray, "Pouvoir du discours/subordination du féminin," in *Dialectiques* 8 (1975), which is translated as "The Power of Discourse and the Subordination of the Feminine," in Luce Irigaray, *This Sex Which Is Not One,* trans. Catherine Porter (Ithaca: Cornell University Press, 1985), 68–85.
6. Irigaray, "The Power of Discourse and the Subordination of the Feminine," 76. Although there are no direct ties between Wilke and Irigaray, both were working in the 1970s and a parallel methodology is noticeable. Unlike Irigaray, however, Wilke does not have to suggest or evoke the body. She performs her/the body in all its materiality to be dealt with both theoretically and physically.
7. Hutcheon notes that parody and mimesis ("in all its seriousness") are related, *Theory of Parody* 28. Whether applying a feminist understanding of mimesis or a broad definition of parody, both terms require repetition and difference to succeed as "active subversion[s] of established modes of representation and expression of women's experience," as Rosi Braidotti describes Irigaray's concept of mimesis in her "Of Bugs and Women," in *Engaging with Irigaray,* ed. Carolyn Burke, Naomi Schor, and Margaret Whitford (New York: Columbia University Press, 1994), 121.
8. Susan Rubin Suleiman, *Subversive Intent: Gender, Politics, and the Avant-Garde* (Cambridge: Harvard University Press, 1990), 179. Suleiman is influenced by the ideas of D. W. Winnicott, which are found in his book *Playing and Reality* (New York: Basic Books, 1971).
9. Suleiman, *Subversive Intent,* 180.
10. Suleiman encourages women to play in their artistic production and offers her ideal rendition of a "modern chorus:" "Revise, re-view / To see things anew / Teach the daughter to play / Imagine the mother playing." Ibid., 10.
11. *Mastication Box* was created for the 1975 exhibit "Artists Make Toys," held at The Clocktower, Institute of Art and Urban Resources in New York (January 1–February 15). There is only one *Mastication Box,* which was originally intended to be rented out on a nightly basis.
12. In the United States, women embracing their sexuality and the right to its related pleasures dovetailed with feminist political action in the 1970s and beyond. In 1974, Betty Dodson wrote, illustrated, and self-published her successful book *Liberating Masturbation: A Meditation on Self Love.* See also Erica Jong, *Fear of Flying* (New York: Signet, 1973), and "Organs and Orgasms," in Alix Shulman, *Woman in Sexist Society: Studies in Power and Powerlessness,* ed. Vivian Gornick and Barbara K. Moran (New York: New American Library, 1972).
13. Frederick Ahl, "Art in Puns and Anagrams Engrave (Ars Est Caelare Artem)," in *On Puns: The Foundation of Letters,* ed. Jonathan Culler (Oxford: Basil Blackwell, 1988), 21. The full sentence reads: "Puns add an alien set of referends which multiply meaning and totally undermine the explicit." Moreover, in contrast to what Irigaray deems "phallogocentric" language, she advocates an alternative use of language that jams the "theoretical machinery" and suspends its "pretension to the production of a truth and of a meaning that are excessively univocal," Irigaray, *This Sex Which Is Not One,* 78. And Mikhail Bakhtin cites such linguistic ambiguities or "hybrid constructions" (a pun that "contains mixed within it two utterances, two speech manners, two styles, two 'languages'") as key to the interactive, always changing nature of antiauthoritative (carnivalesque) "dialogical" language. See M. M. Bakhtin, *The Dialogic Imagination,* trans. Caryl Emerson and Michael Holquist (Austin: University of Texas Press, 1981), 304–5. Interestingly, Gail M. Schwab reads Irigaray as dialogic in her essay, "Irigarayan Dialogism: Play and Powerplay," in *Feminism, Bakhtin, and the Dialogic,* ed. Dale M. Bauer and S. Jaret McKinstry (Albany: State University of New York Press, 1991).
14. Fixity and/or clarity can be seen as part of hegemonic ideology, as R. A. Shoaf writes: "The juxtologist critic is not afraid of coincidence, does not seek (Cartesian) certitude, is always suspicious of 'clarity' (whose ideology, he asks, is served by this 'clarity'?)." R. A. Shoaf, "The Play of Puns in Late Middle English Poetry: Concerning Juxtology," in *On Puns: The Foundation of Letters,* ed. Jonathan Culler (Oxford: Basil Blackwell, 1988), 61.
15. Joanna Frueh, "Hannah Wilke," in *Hannah Wilke: A Retrospective,* ed. Thomas H. Kochheiser (Columbia: University of Missouri Press, 1989), 33. Frueh takes this quote from Duchamp, who writes: "My irony is that of indifference." In Elmer Peterson and Michel Sanouillet, eds., *The Essential Writings of Marcel Duchamp: Salt Seller = Marchand du Sel,* trans. Elmer Peterson (London: Thames and Hudson, 1975), 6. See also George H. Bauer, "Duchamp's Ubiquitous Puns," in *Marcel Duchamp: Artist of the Century,* ed. Rudolf E. Kuenzli and Francis M. Nauman (Cambridge: MIT Press, 1990).
16. When I refer to the "women's movement," I generally mean the movement led by the National Organization for Women in the United States. Of course, however, there were and are many different forms of feminism active simultaneously in the United States and around the world.
17. See Mikhail Bakhtin, *Rabelais and His World,* trans. Hélène Iswolsky, with a prologue by Michael Holquist (Bloomington: Indiana University Press, 1984). Here Bakhtin writes: "Carnival celebrated temporary liberation from the prevailing truth and from the established order; it marked the suspension of all hierarchical rank, privileges, norms, and prohibitions. Carnival was the true feast of time, the feast of becoming, change, and renewal. It was hostile to all that was immortalized and completed" (10).
18. Indeed, the sociopolitical transformations at the end of the twentieth century regarding many women's lives in the United States are understood here to be a result of the carnivalesque spirit of renewal and rebellion linked to the women's movement. As Bakhtin remarks: "Great changes, even in the field of science, are always preceded by a certain carnival consciousness that prepares the way." Bakhtin, *Rabelais and His World,* 49. See also Michael Holquist's prologue to Bakhtin, *Rabelais and His World,* in which he writes: "Bakhtin's carnival… is not only not an impediment to revolutionary change, it is revolution itself. Carnival must not be confused with mere holiday or, least of all, with self-serving festivals fostered by governments, secular or theocratic" (xviii). For a more thorough discussion of the relationships between feminism, humor, art, and the carnivalesque spirit, see Debra Wacks, "Subversive Humor: The Performance Art of Hannah Wilke, Eleanor Antin, and Adrian Piper" (Ph.D. diss., City University of New York, 2003).

19. Montano explored various personalities in her ongoing project, *Art in Everyday Life* (1969–81), which included the persona "Chicken Woman." See Linda Montano, *Art in Everyday Life* (Los Angeles: Astro Artz, 1981).
20. For this chapter, "spectacle" is understood as excessive visibility, not necessarily as a function of commodity culture, as Guy Debord defines it in *The Society of the Spectacle* (Detroit: Black and Red, 1970).
21. In 1934, Duchamp published the *Green Box,* which contains notes for *The Large Glass.* More instructions were discovered after his death. For details, see Arturo Schwarz, *The Complete Works of Marcel Duchamp,* 2 vols. (New York: Delano Greenidge Editions, 1997). See also Richard Hamilton, "The Large Glass," in *Marcel Duchamp,* ed. Anne d'Harnoncourt and Kynaston McShine (New York: Museum of Modern Art and Philadelphia Museum of Art, 1973). It is interesting to remember that Wilke and Hamilton were lovers in the mid-1970s.
22. Eleanor Heartney notes: "During the '70s a surprising number of women artists and writers adopted a quasi-pornographic content or form in order to assert the claims of female desire and sexuality as part of the women's movement's general challenge to patriarchy." Eleanor Heartney, "A Necessary Transgression," *New Art Examiner,* November 1988, 22.
23. In her 1976 video, *Philly,* Wilke walks into a bathroom holding her white suit and says: "I want to really change from this dirty mess to this male character." According to Wilke's widower, Donald Goddard, Wilke sometimes saw her white outfit as a type of "rabbinical costume." Donald Goddard, conversation with Debra Wacks, July 15, 1998. This suit is immortalized in a series of eight black-and-white photographs by Wilke entitled *Suit Suite* (1976–78), which visually respond to Duchamp's drawing *Jaquette (Jacket,* 1956), as well as to his readymade *Waistcoat* (1958).
24. Octavio Paz, *Marcel Duchamp: Appearance Stripped Bare,* trans. Rachel Phillips and Donald Gardner (New York: Viking, 1978), 50. Cited in Frueh, "Hannah Wilke," 38.
25. Mary Russo, *The Female Grotesque: Risk, Excess, and Modernity* (New York: Routledge, 1994), 53.
26. Kathleen Rowe, *The Unruly Woman: Gender and the Genres of Laughter* (Austin: University of Texas, 1995), 12.
27. Rowe writes: "Because public power is predicated largely on visibility, men have long understood the need to secure their power not only by looking but by being seen, or rather, by fashioning—as subject, as author, as artist—a spectacle of themselves. How might women use spectacle to disrupt that power and lay claim to their own?" (11). Rowe answers this question: "I want to suggest that women might begin to reweave the web of visual power that already binds them by taking the unruly woman as a model—woman as rule-breaker, joke-maker, and public, bodily spectacle" (12 and 31). Rowe builds on both Russo's ideas regarding the grotesque and Natalie Zemon Davis's *Society and Culture in Early Modern France* (Stanford: Stanford University Press, 1975).
28. Hans-Christof Stenzel, director, *C'est la Vie Rrose,* film, 83 minutes, Technicolor, 1977. With camera work by Lothar E. Stickelbrucks.
29. Later in *Philly,* Wilke created another gum sculpture and gave it to curator Anne d'Harnoncourt to preserve.

30. Such loosening of strict museum rules is almost unthinkable now, only demonstrating the extent of carnivalesque seepage that occurred during the 1970s.
31. The photograph was taken by Julian Wasser at Duchamp's first major retrospective in 1963 at the Pasadena Art Museum, now the Norton Simon Museum of Art. Interestingly, Eleanor Antin also parodied this image in her photograph "War Games," from the series *The Angel of Mercy: My Tour of Duty in the Crimea* (1977).
32. We now know that the woman photographed is Eve Babitz.
33. Suleiman, *Subversive Intent,* xvii. Suleiman locates this "double allegiance," for instance, in the work of Cindy Sherman in relation to Hans Bellmer's photographs.
34. Frueh briefly conducts a psychoanalytic reading of Wilke as rebellious daughter and Duchamp as heroic father, in Frueh, "Hannah Wilke," 35.
35. Roland Barthes, *The Pleasure of the Text,* trans. Richard Miller (New York: Hill and Wang), 37.
36. There are many conflicting interpretations and discussions surrounding *Etant donnés*...on which Duchamp worked from 1946 until his death in 1966.
37. In 1988, Wilke created a "text" for her "memoirs," which she also entitled *I Object: Memoirs of a Sugar Giver.* It is a compilation of various correspondences she had received along with some of her own writings. The text is reprinted in Alfred M. Fischer, "Die wirkliche Braut, entkleidet," in *Ubrigens sterben immer die anderen: Marcel Duchamp und die Avantgarde seit 1950* (Cologne: Museum Ludwig Köln, 1988), 263–71.
38. Wilke, "Visual Prejudice" (1980), reprinted in *Hannah Wilke: A Retrospective,* ed. Thomas H. Kochheiser, 141.
39. In her article on women's body art, Lucy Lippard explains that "when women use their own bodies in their art work, they are using their *selves;* a significant psychological factor converts these bodies or faces from object to subject." Lucy Lippard, "The Pains and Pleasures of Rebirth: European and American Women's Body Art," in *From the Center: Feminist Essays on Women's Art* (New York: E. P. Dutton, 1976), 124.
40. Richard Hamilton took the photograph under Wilke's directiåon.
41. Peterson and Sanouillet, *The Essential Writings of Marcel Duchamp.*
42. For an image of *Wedge of Chastity,* along with the other wedge works by Duchamp that visually anticipate Wilke's *Wedges of*...(e.g., *Not a Shoe,* 1950, *Female Fig Leaf,* 1950, and *Objet-Dard,* 1951), see *Marcel Duchamp,* ed. Anne d'Harnoncourt and Kynaston McShine, 308–9.
43. Here Wilke parodies both herself and an early performance piece, *My Count-ry 'Tis of Thee* (1976), where she mimicked the caryatid figures standing at the Albright-Knox Art Gallery in Buffalo, New York.

CHAPTER 9

1. Friedrich Nietzsche, *The Will to Power,* trans. Walter Kaufmann and R. J. Hollingdale (New York: Vintage, 1968), §845 (1885–86), 445.
2. George Brecht, *Chance Imagery* (New York: A Great Bear Pamphlet/ Something Else Press, 1966; reprint, Ubu Classics, 2004), 8–9.
3. Ibid., 23.
4. Jackson Mac Low, "The Poetics of Chance and the Politics of Simultaneous Spontaneity," in *Talking Poetics from the Naropa Institute: Annals of the Jack Kerouac School of Disembodied Poetics,* ed. Anne Waldman and Marilyn Webb (New York: Random House, 1979), 175.
5. John Cage, "Juilliard Lecture" (1952), in *A Year from Monday: New Lectures and Writings* (Middletown, Conn.: Wesleyan University Press, 1967), 105.
6. John Cage, "Experimental Music" (1955), in *Silence: Lectures and Writings* (Middletown, Conn.: Wesleyan University Press, 1973), 12.
7. George Maciunas to Tomas Schmit, November 8, 1963, reprinted in *Fluxus etc. Addenda II: The Gilbert and Lila Silverman Collection,* ed. Jon Hendricks (Purchase, N.Y.: Neuberger Museum, 1983), 165–66.
8. See Dick Higgins, *A Dialectic of Centuries: Notes Towards a Theory of the New Arts,* 2nd ed. (New York: Printed Editions, 1978), and *Horizons: The Poetics and Theory of the Intermedia* (Carbondale: Southern Illinois University Press, 1984).
9. Higgins, "An Exemplativist Manifesto," in *A Dialectic of Centuries,* 162.
10. Higgins, "Boredom and Danger," in *A Dialectic of Centuries,* 45.
11. Dick Higgins, *foew&ombwhnw* (New York: Something Else Press, 1969); "Games of Art" (1966), 31–45; "Intending" (1966), 47–69; "Boredom and Danger" (1966), 95–125; and "Structural Researches" (1967), 127–65.
12. Higgins, "Exemplativist Works of Art," in *A Dialectic of Centuries,* 23–27.
13. Higgins, "Intending," in *A Dialectic of Centuries,* 30.
14. Higgins, "An Exemplativist Manifesto," 159.
15. Higgins, "Intending," 32.
16. Higgins, "Exemplativist Works of Art," 26.
17. Marcel Duchamp, "The Creative Act" (1957), reprinted in *Marcel Duchamp,* ed. Robert Lebel, trans. George Heard Hamilton (New York: Grove Press, 1959), 77–78.
18. Higgins, "Exemplativist Works of Art," 24.
19. Higgins, "Intending," 28.
20. Peter Carse, *Finite and Infinite Games* (New York: Ballantine Books, 1987).
21. Higgins, "Boredom and Danger," in *A Dialectic of Centuries,* 43.
22. Ibid., 49.
23. Ibid., 45.
24. Higgins, "Structural Researches," in *foew&ombwhnw,* 149.
25. Higgins, "Horizons," in *Horizons,* 4.
26. Higgins, "Intending," 59.
27. Dick Higgins to George Maciunas, letter, November 19, 1974, Collection Archiv Sohm, Staatsgalerie, Stuttgart, Germany.

CHAPTER 10

1. This change took place as part of her membership in the New York Graphic Workshop, which included the Uruguayan Luis Camnitzer and the Venezuelan José Guillermo Castillo. For an in-depth analysis of the activities of Liliana Porter in New York, see Shifra Goldman, "Presencias y ausencias: Liliana Porter en Nueva York, 1964–1974," in *Liliana Porter: Obra gráfica, 1964–1990,* ed. Mari Carmen Ramírez (San Juan: IX Bienal de San Juan del Grabado Latinoamericano y del Caribe, 1991), 1–26.
2. Inés Katzenstein, "Liliana Porter: Fotografía y ficción," in *Liliana Porter: Fotografía y ficción* (Buenos Aires: Centro Cultural Recoleta, 2004), 19–37.

3. I have addressed Porter's interest in the interplay between reality, illusion, and simulacra in my book *Liliana Porter and the Art of Simulation* (Aldershot: Ashgate, 2008).
4. Ana Tiscornia, "El vago azar o las precisas leyes: Entrevista a Liliana Porter," *Offset 2* [Guatemala] (May 2001): 3; Ana Tiscornia, "A Rabbit That Escapes: Interview with Liliana Porter," trans. Jane Brodie, in *Liliana Porter: Fotografía y ficción,* 210.
5. Luis Camnitzer, "The Poetry of Communication," *Art Nexus* (February–April 2000): 70.
6. Gerardo Mosquera, "Liliana Porter: Shaking Hands with Mickey," *Third Text* 42 (Spring 1998): 75.
7. Eva Forgacs, "Toys Are Us: Toys and the Childlike in Recent Art," *Art Criticism* 16, no. 2 (2001): 6, 12–13. Forgacs discussed the works of Christian Boltanski, Jörg Immendorff, Mike Kelley, Annette Messager, Ellen Phelan, Nayland Blake, Yoshimoto Nara, Zbigniew Libera, David Levinthal, A. R. Penk, Jean-Michel Basquiat, Keith Haring, and Kim Dingle. Additional artists working with comparable imagery, including Shonagh Adelman, Gottfried Helnwein, Takashi Murakami, Joyce Pensato, Laurie Simmons, and Heidi Zumbrun, were featured in the exhibition and catalogue *The Darker Side of Playland: Childhood Imagery from the Logan Collection,* ed. Heather Whitmore Jain (San Francisco: San Francisco Museum of Modern Art, 2000).
8. Heather Whitmore Jain, "The Darker Side of Playland: Childhood Imagery from the Logan Collection," in *The Darker Side of Playland.*
9. Interestingly enough, no children are specifically involved in any part of Porter's creative process—neither as creators nor as the intended audience—although they might certainly enjoy the works just as much. Moreover, she avoids including anything that would seem childish or gratuitously irrational, preferring to tap instead into that part of our inner child that accepts the unusual while still questioning our most cherished assumptions.
10. Porter chose to capitalize only the first words in all the English titles in *For you / Para usted.* She followed the standard rules of capitalization of English titles in her later films.
11. I have discussed these movies in more depth elsewhere. See Florencia Bazzano-Nelson, *Liliana Porter and the Art of Simulation,* and "Malice in Wonderland," *Original-Copia... Original?* Proceedings of III Congreso Internacional de Teoría e Historia del Arte and XI Jornadas del Centro Argentino de Investigadores de Arte (CAIA) (Buenos Aires: CAIA, Universidad de Buenos Aires, 2005), 133–45.
12. Other collaborators in this film included co-director Ana Tiscornia, a well-known Uruguayan-born artist who is very familiar with Porter's work, and Sylvia Meyer, the Uruguayan-born musician who selected, composed, and performed the music in *The Fox in the Mirror* and Porter's previous films.
13. Charles Baudelaire, "A Philosophy of Toys" (1863), in *The Painter of Modern Life and Other Essays,* trans. Jonathan Mayne (New York: Da Capo Press, 1964), 198.
14. Walter Benjamin, "A Glimpse into the World of Children's Books," in *Selected Writings, Vol. 1, 1913–1926,* ed. Marcus Bullock and Michael W. Jennings (Cambridge: Belknap Press of Harvard University Press, 1996), 435.

15. The many different possible play situations and types of games could be divided into age groups and by the degree of complexity of their rules, ranging, for instance, from child's play among small children to highly competitive professional sports, from playground games such as "hide and seek" to sexual games and games of chance, such as roulette. There is also a great variety of games in different disciplines, such as war and strategy games and economic game theory.
16. The scholars whose writings I have consulted in the preparation of this chapter include: Mihaly Csikszentmihalyi, former chair of the psychology department at the University of Chicago; American developmental psychologist Catherine Garvey; Dutch cultural historian Johan Huizinga; neo-Freudian psychiatrist Erik H. Erikson; early-childhood education expert Sally Jenkinson, and British pediatrician and psychoanalyst Donald W. Winnicott.
17. See discussions in Johan Huizinga, *Homo Ludens: A Study of the Play-Element in Culture* (1944; reprint, Boston: Beacon Press, 1960), 7; Catherine Garvey, *Play,* enlarged edition (Cambridge: Harvard University Press, 1990), 3–4; Mihaly Csikszentmihalyi, "Some Paradoxes in the Definition of Play," in *Play as Context,* 1979 Proceedings of the Association for the Anthropological Study of Play, ed. Alyce Taylor Cheska (West Point, N.Y.: Leisure Press, 1979), 20; D. W. Winnicott, *Playing and Reality* (London: Routledge, 1971).
18. Csikszentmihalyi, "Some Paradoxes," 20.
19. Garvey, *Play,* 6.
20. Huizinga, *Homo Ludens,* 12.
21. Ibid., 11.
22. Ibid., 12. According to Huizinga, "The profound affinity between play and order is perhaps the reason why play...seems to lie to such a large extent in the field of aesthetics...Play casts a spell over us; it is 'enchanting,' 'captivating.' It is invested with the noble qualities we are capable of perceiving in things: rhythm and harmony" (10).
23. Donald W. Winnicott, "The Location of Cultural Experience," in *Transitional Objects and Potential Spaces: Literary Uses of D. W. Winnicott,* ed. Peter L. Rudnytsky (New York: Columbia University Press, 1993), 8–9. See also Inés Katzentstein, "Liliana Porter," in *Blanton Museum of Art: Latin American Collection,* ed. Gabriel Pérez-Barreiro (Austin: Jack S. Blanton Museum of Art, University of Texas at Austin, 2006), 323.
24. Liliana Porter, cited in Tiscornia, "El vago azar o las precisas leyes," 5. My translation.
25. Margaret Lowenfeld, "The Nature and Use of the Lowenfeld World Technique in Work with Children and Adults," *Journal of Psychology* 30 (1950): 325–31.
26. The Borgesian notion of the "Chinese encyclopedia" comes originally from Jorge Luis Borges's short essay "El idioma analítico de John Wilkins" (*Otras inquisiciones* [1952], in *Obras completas: 1923–1972* [Buenos Aires: Emecé, 1974], 708), in which he mentioned a fictional Chinese encyclopedia containing an arbitrary list of animals classified according to a taxonomy that appears rather nonsensical to us (and no doubt to the Chinese as well, who may find Borges's choice of their culture problematic). Michel Foucault cited this story at the beginning of his book *The Order of Things: An Archaeology of the Human Sciences* (New York: Pantheon Books, 1970). In Argentina, the Chinese, who live at the antipodes of that South American country, were often used to symbolize the incomprehensible, that is, the limitations of one's own knowledge. Hence, Argentines say, "It's Chinese to me" in the same way that in the United States people say, "It's Greek to me."
27. Lowenfeld, "The Nature and Use of the Lowenfeld World Technique," 327–28.
28. Translated from the Spanish by Pedro Cuperman from Emanuel Swedenborg, *Arquitectura del cielo* (Buenos Aires: Adriana Hidalgo, 2004), 114. I am grateful to Liliana Porter for making me aware of this particular translation of Swedenborg's work.
29. At present, this movie is not available to the general public, so I will describe its contents in some detail.
30. Luis L. Franco, "Los cantares españoles y las coplas autóctonas: El 'Folklorismo' y la musa herrante," *Nuevos Ritos* (June–July 1926): 24–26. http://bdigital.binal.ac.pa/bdp/revistas/nritos/ritosjun-julio1926-2.pdf.
31. "De terciopelo negro tengo cortinas, para enlutar la cama si tu me olvidas."
32. Liliana Porter, e-mail message to the author, May 1, 2008.
33. Liliana Porter, telephone interview with the author, January 19, 2008.
34. Ibid.
35. Ibid.; Porter, e-mail message, May 1, 2008.
36. Porter, e-mail message, May 1, 2008.
37. Among these musicians, we see a nutcracker, whose mouth seems to open wide, delicate porcelain mandolin players sitting altogether, and a poodle and a monkey playing violins.
38. The original intent had been to shatter the figurine into small pieces. The fact that it was so hard surprised everyone when they were filming this part of the movie and created a moment of great hilarity. The filming was allowed to continue as Ana Tiscornia tried to dislodge the impacted figure from the worktable, but she could not (Liliana Porter, personal interview with the author, New York, July 2007). I assume the figure would have looked like the creative destructions Porter used in her series of assemblages entitled "Reconstructions."
39. According to Porter, the "general idea [of *Fox in the Mirror*] is that of a concert. Or more precisely, of 'disconcert' (as a friend told me), a feeling that appears in my oeuvre often enough" (*Bola de Nieve: Espacio Fundación Telefónica,* "Liliana Porter," January 13, 2008). See http://www.boladenieve.org.ar/?q=node/707. My translation.
40. The concert begins again with a close-up of several trumpet players, which is interrupted by an operatic female voice that introduces the figure of a small man carrying newspapers on a red background. This motif seems connected to the other labor-related images from communist China included in the movie. As the music progresses, we hear the choir and drums as the camera focuses on two figurines playing the drum, a ceramic girl in pigtails and a windup rabbit, both rather sinister-looking characters.
41. Judith Savioff, "Me encantaría ser un clásico," *Diario Perfil,* November 18, 2007. http://www.diarioperfil.com.ar/edimp/0209/artículo.php?art=4078&ed=0209. My translation.
42. Walter Benjamin, "Alabanza a la muñeca," cited in Ricardo Forster, "Walter Benjamin en la tierra de la infancia," *W. Benjamin, Th. W. Adorno: El ensayo como filosofía* (Buenos Aires: Ediciones Nueva Visión, 1991), 115.

CHAPTER 11

1. Johan Huizinga, *Homo Ludens: A Study of the Play-Element in Culture* (London: Routledge and Kegan Paul, 1949); Roger Caillois, *Man, Play, and Games,* trans. Meyer Barash (Urbana: University of Illinois Press, 1961).
2. McKenzie Wark, *Gamer Theory* (Cambridge: Harvard University Press, 2007).
3. Jon Dovey and Helen W. Kennedy, *Game Cultures* (London: Open University Press, 2006).
4. Guy Debord, "Report on the Construction of Situations and on the International Situationist Tendency's Conditions of Organization and Action," June 1957. Reprint on Situationist International Online, trans. Ken Knabb. http://www.cddc.vt.edu/sionline/si/report.html.
5. Guy Debord, "Contribution to Situationist Definition of Play," *Internationale Situationniste* 1 (June 1958). Reprint on Situationist International Online, trans. Reuben Keehan. http://www.cddc.vt.edu/sionline/si/play.html.
6. Guy Debord, "Theory of the Dérive," *Les Lèvres Nues* 9 (November 1956), *Internationale Situationniste* 2 (December 1958). Reprint on Situationist International Online, trans. Ken Knabb. http://www.cddc.vt.edu/sionline/si/theory.html.
7. Ibid.
8. Gilles Ivain [Ivain Chtcheglov], "Formulary for a New Urbanism, October 1953," *Internationale Situationniste* 1 (June 1958). Reprint on Situationist International Online, trans. Ken Knabb. http://www.cddc.vt.edu/sionline/si/presitu/formulary.html.
9. Chaim Gingold, "Miniature Gardens and Magic Crayons" (M.A. thesis, Georgia Institute of Technology, 2003); Henry Jenkins, "Game Design as Narrative Architecture," in *First Person: New Media as Story, Performance, and Game,* ed. Noah Wardrip-Fruin and Pat Harrigan (Cambridge: MIT Press, 2004), 117–30.
10. Ivain, "Formulary for a New Urbanism."
11. Guy Debord, "Theory of the Dérive."
12. Blast Theory, Project statement for *Uncle Roy All Around You* (inception 2003). http://www.blasttheory.co.uk/bt/work_uncleroy.html.
13. Guy Debord, "Report on the Construction."
14. Brian Holmes, "The Revenge of the Concept," January 20, 2003. http://www.mail-archive.com/nettime-1@bbs.thing.net/msg00280.html.
15. Katie Salen and Eric Zimmerman, *Rules of Play: Game Design Fundamentals* (Cambridge: MIT Press, 2004).

CHAPTER 12

1. The Web-based *selectparks* project categorizes the intersections of art and game cultures in its "archive" section using the following subcategories: "art mods," "machinima," "sonichima," "art games," "location-based games," "political games," "open-source games," "mobile games," "browser games," "sex games," "performance instruments," "sculpture," "digital imaging," "exhibitions," and "DVDs." selectparks, archive, http://www.selectparks.net, 2007.09.01.

2. Christiane Paul, *Digital Art* (London: Thames and Hudson, 2003).
3. Tilman Baumgaertel, "Modification, Abstraction, Socialization: On Some Aspects of Artistic Computer Games," Media Art Net, 2004, http://www.medienkunstnetz.de/themes/generative-tools/computer_games/scroll/
4. Ibid.
5. Hans-Peter Schwarz, *Media-Art-History,* exh. cat. (Karlsruhe: Center for Art and Media with Prestel Verlag, 1997).
6. Baumgaertel, "Modification, Abstraction, Socialization."
7. Julian Oliver, archive: *Art Decal,* 2006.10.20, selectparks, http://www.selectparks.net/modules.php?name=News&file=article&sid=604.
8. Orhan Kipcak, *Arsdoom—art adventure,* 1995, Ars Electronica Archive, Catalog Archive, http://www.aec.at/en/archives/festival_archive/festival_catalogs/festival_artikel.asp?iProjectID=8643.
9. Ibid.
10. Axel Stockburger, "The Rendered Arena: Modalities of Space in Video and Computer Games" (thesis, University of the Arts, London, 2006).
11. Lev Manovich, *The Language of New Media* (Cambridge: MIT Press, 2001).
12. Ibid.
13. Interview with Tobias Bernstrup and Palle Torsson by the author, August–September 2007. Subsequent quotations from Bernstrup and Torsson also come from this interview.
14. Régine Debatty, *Everything i shoot is art,* 2006.10.20, *We Make Money Not Art,* http://www.we-make-money-not-art.com/archives/009212.php.

CHAPTER 13

1. Marina Warner, "Self-Portrait in a Rear-View Mirror," in *Only Make Believe,* exh. cat. (Warwickshire: Compton Verney House Trust, 2005).
2. Sigmund Freud, "Creative Writers and Day-Dreaming" (1907), *Standard Edition,* 9:142–53.
3. See Ellen Handler Spitz, "An Insubstantial Pageant Faded," in *Image and Insight: Essays in Psychoanalysis and the Arts* (New York: Columbia University Press, 1991), 28–56.
4. Gaston Bachelard, *The Poetics of Space: Childhood, Language, and the Cosmos* (1958), trans. Maria Jolas (Boston: Beacon Press, 1969).
5. Oliver Sacks, *Uncle Tungsten: Memories of a Chemical Boyhood* (New York: Vintage / Random House, 2001).
6. Jean Clair, "Seven Prolegomenae to a Brief Treatise on Magrittian Tropes," *October* 8 (Spring 1979): 89–110; and Eric Wargo, "Infinite Recess: Perspective and Play in Magritte's 'La condition humaine,'" *Art History* 25, no. 1 (February 2002): 47–67.
7. D. W. Winnicott, *Playing and Reality* (London: Routledge, 1971).
8. See Ellen Handler Spitz, *Museums of the Mind: Magritte's Labyrinth and Other Essays* (New Haven: Yale University Press, 1994).
9. Ellen Handler Spitz, *Inside Picture Books* (New Haven: Yale University Press, 1999).
10. Clair, "Seven Prolegomenae."
11. A. A. Milne, *Now We Are Six* (1927; New York: Dell, 1955).
12. Ernst Gombrich, *Meditations on a Hobby Horse: And Other Essays on the Theory of Art* (New York: Phaidon Press, 1963), 1–11.
13. William Butler Yeats, "Ego Dominus Tuus" (1919), in *Collected Poems* (New York: Macmillan, 1957), 157.
14. Dr. Seuss (Theodor Seuss Geisel), *Bartholomew and the Oobleck* (New York: Random House, 1949).
15. See Gareth Matthews, *Philosophy and the Young Child* (Cambridge: Harvard University Press, 1980).

CONTRIBUTORS

FLORENCIA BAZZANO-NELSON is Assistant Professor of Art History in the Department of Film, Video and New Media at the School of the Art Institute of Chicago. Her research has focused on modern and contemporary art and art criticism of Latin America. She is the author of *Liliana Porter and the Art of Simulation* (2008) and *Marta Traba en circulación* (2010).

JON CATES is Assistant Professor of New Media in the Department of Film, Video and New Media at the School of the Art Institute of Chicago. His art projects have been presented internationally in cities such as Berlin, Beijing, Madrid, Mexico City, Chicago, New York, and Boston as well as being widely disseminated online. His research and writings focus on Media Art Histories and related subjects.

MARY ANN CAWS is Distinguished Professor of Comparative Literature, English, and French at the Graduate School of the City University of New York and author of numerous books on Surrealism and its legacies, including *The Surrealist Look: An Erotics of Encounter* (1997), *Salvador Dali* (2008), *Picasso's Weeping Woman: The Life and Art of Dora Maar* (2000), and *Robert Motherwell: What Art Holds* (1995). Her recent edited volumes include *Surrealism* (2004 / 2010), *Surrealist Love Poems* (2002), *Surrealist Painters and Poets* (2001), and *Joseph Cornell's Theater of the Mind* (2000).

DAVID J. GETSY is the Goldabelle McComb Finn Distinguished Chair in Art History and Associate Professor at the School of the Art Institute of Chicago. His research focuses on the history and theory of modern sculpture and its legacies in contemporary art practice. He is the author of *Rodin: Sex and the Making of Modern Sculpture* (2010) and *Body Doubles: Sculpture in Britain, 1877–1905* (2004) and editor of *Sculpture and the Pursuit of a Modern Ideal in Britain, c. 1880–1930* (2004).

SUSAN LAXTON is Assistant Professor of the History of Photography at the University of California, Riverside. Currently a fellow at the Institute for Advanced Study in Princeton, she is finishing a book on the ludic strategies of the interwar avant-gardes. Her work on play and art resulted in the exhibition *Paris as Gameboard* (2002) at the Wallach Gallery, Columbia University, as well as essays in *October, Papers of Surrealism,* and anthologies on chance and the game of *cadavre exquis.*

CLAUDIA MESCH is Associate Professor of Art History at Arizona State University. Her research focuses on postwar modernism's ties to European intellectual history, particularly Surrealism, and to Cold War politics. Her books include *Joseph Beuys: The Reader* (edited with Viola Michely, 2007) and *Modern Art at the Berlin Wall: Demarcating Culture in the Cold War Germanys* (2009). A founding editor of the e-journal *Journal of Surrealism and the Americas* (jsa.asu.edu), she is working on a study of Surrealism's preoccupation with Native American culture.

KEVIN MOORE is an independent scholar and curator whose work focuses on the history of photography and contemporary art. He is the author of *Starburst: Color Photography in America, 1970–1980* (2010) and *Jacques Henri Lartigue: The Invention of an Artist* (2004).

GAVIN PARKINSON is Lecturer in European Modernism at The Courtauld Institute of Art and is the author of *Surrealism, Art, and Modern Science: Relativity, Quantum Mechanics, Epistemology* (2008) and *The Duchamp Book* (2008).

ANNE-MARIE SCHLEINER is engaged in gaming and net culture in a variety of roles as a writer, critic, curator, and gaming artist/designer. Her work investigates avatar gender construction, computer gaming culture, hacker art, and experimental game design. She has curated online exhibits of game mods and add-ons, including the exhibits "Cracking the Maze: Game Patches and Plug-ins as Hacker Art," "Mutation.fem," and "Snow Blossom House." She has designed the games *Anime Noir* and *Heaven711* and was one of the initiators of the antiwar art actions Velvet-Strike and OUT. She has exhibited online and at the New Museum, the Whitney Museum of American Art, and the Centro de la Imagen Museum. She was an assistant professor of digital art at the University of Colorado, Boulder, and now teaches game design at the National University of Singapore. She currently is a doctoral candidate in the ASCA program at the University of Amsterdam.

OWEN F. SMITH is the Director of the Intermedia MFA Program at the University of Maine, where he is also professor of Art History and Digital Art in the Department of Art and the Chair of the Department of New Media. He received his B.A. in Art History and Russian Studies, his M.A. in Anthropology, and his Ph.D. in Art History from the University of Washington. He has lectured widely in the United States and Europe on twentieth-century art, with a research focus on alternative art forms. His book on the history of Fluxus, *Fluxus: The History of an Attitude,* was published by San Diego State University Press in 1998. More recently he was the co-editor of a two-volume special issue of *Visible Language: Fluxus and Legacy* 39, no. 3 (Fall 2005), and *Fluxus After Fluxus* 40, no. 1 (Winter 2006). Smith is also a practicing artist who works in digital art and new media forms and has exhibited his work in more than eighty national and international exhibitions over the last ten years.

ELLEN HANDLER SPITZ currently holds the Honors College Professorship of Visual Arts at the University of Maryland, Baltimore County (UMBC). She is the author of *Art and Psyche* (1985), *Image and Insight* (1991), *Museums of the Mind* (1994), *Inside Picture Books* (1999), *The Brightening Glance* (2006), and *Illuminating Childhood* (2010). She co-edited *Freud and Forbidden Knowledge* (1994) and *Bertolucci's "The Last Emperor": Multiple Takes* (1998).

STEPHANIE L. TAYLOR has published numerous articles on the life and work of American artist Joseph Cornell and was the co-editor of a volume of essays, *Joseph Cornell: Opening the Box* (2007). She is currently working on a manuscript about this artist. She is a tenured professor of modern and contemporary art history at New Mexico State University. She has been the recipient of fellowship awards from the Smithsonian American Art Museum and the Georgia O'Keeffe Research Center.

DEBRA WACKS is an independent scholar who occasionally teaches at Hong Kong Baptist University. She received her Ph.D. in Art History with a certificate in Women's Studies from the City University of New York Graduate Center. In 2001, she curated the exhibition *SMIRK: women, art, and humor* for the Firehouse Art Gallery, New York. Wacks has contributed to *The Drama Review,* to the catalogue for the Berlin Art Academy exhibition *Smile Machines: Humor—Art—Technology,* and to *Art Journal.* Her book, *Subversive Humor: The Performance Art of Hannah Wilke, Eleanor Antin, and Adrian Piper*, is forthcoming.

INDEX

Note numbers in italics refer to illustrations.

R

S

ACKNOWLEDGMENTS

This volume is the result of the diligence of a number of people. I would like to thank the authors for their hard work and commitment to the project. I am also grateful to Eleanor Goodman, Danny Bellet, Laura Reed-Morrisson, Cherene Holland, Patty Mitchell, and the entire staff of the Pennsylvania State University Press for making this project a reality. The authors and I are also very grateful to the following institutions, which provided important support for the overall book: the Newcomb Art Department of Tulane University, the College of Arts and Sciences of New Mexico State University, the Intermedia Program of the University of Maine, and the Goldabelle McComb Finn Chair of School of the Art Institute of Chicago.
—David J. Getsy, editor

Library of Congress Cataloging-in-Publication Data

From diversion to subversion : games, play, and twentieth-century art / edited by David J. Getsy.
p. cm. — (Refiguring modernism)
Includes bibliographical references and index.
Summary: "Examines the wide-ranging influence of games and play on the development of modern art in the twentieth century"— Provided by publisher.
ISBN 978-0-271-03703-5 (pbk. : alk. paper)
1. Play in art.
2. Games in art.
3. Art, Modern—20th century—Themes, motives.
I. Getsy, David.

N8236.P47F76 2011
709.04—dc22
2010018240

Printed in China by Asia Pacific Offset
Published by The Pennsylvania State University Press,
University Park, PA 16802-1003
Design by Diane Jaroch

The Pennsylvania State University Press is a member of the Association of American University Presses.

It is the policy of The Pennsylvania State University Press to use acid-free paper. Publications on uncoated stock satisfy the minimum requirements of American National Standard for Information Sciences—Permanence of Paper for Printed Library Material, ANSI Z39.48–1992.

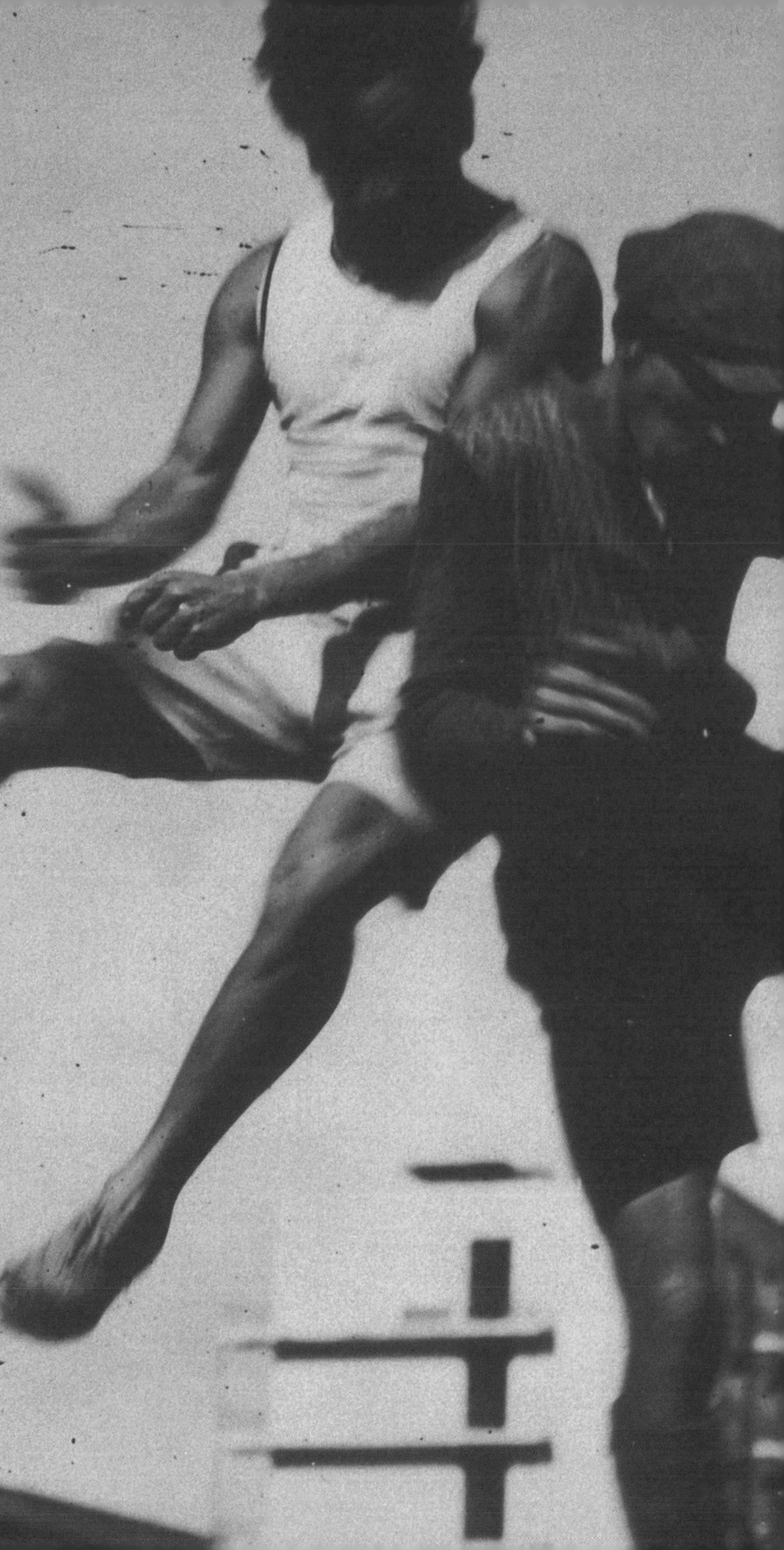

Aside from the editor, the contributors are:
Florencia Bazzano-Nelson
Jon Cates
Mary Ann Caws
Susan Laxton
Claudia Mesch
Kevin Moore
Gavin Parkinson
Anne-Marie Schleiner
Owen F. Smith
Ellen Handler Spitz
Stephanie L. Taylor
Debra Wacks

David J. Getsy is Goldabelle McComb Finn Distinguished Chair in Art History and Associate Professor at the School of the Art Institute of Chicago.

Refiguring Modernism: Arts, Literatures, Sciences, published by Penn State University Press, emphasizes interdisciplinary approaches to the study of modernism. Rather than seeking scholarship that fills in the details of our knowledge of well-established aspects of modernism, the series seeks work that will push the field in new directions, ask fresh questions, challenge long-held orthodoxies, and refigure our understanding of the modernist era.